THE
TERRITORIAL
AIR FORCE

For my mum, Kathleen Wilkinson, I am so glad that you knew I had passed my doctorate. You were always so very proud of me. I love you and miss you every day.

For Che and Lenna, you bring so much joy to my life. I love you both. May you always be happy.

THE TERRITORIAL AIR FORCE

THE RAF'S VOLUNTARY SQUADRONS, 1926–1957

LOUISE WILKINSON

AIR WORLD

AIR WORLD

THE TERRITORIAL AIR FORCE
The RAF's Voluntary Squadrons, 1926–1957

First published in Great Britain in 2020 by
Air World
An imprint of
Pen & Sword Books Ltd
Yorkshire – Philadelphia

ISBN 978 1 52675 104 1

Typeset by Aura Technology and Software Services, India.

Printed and bound in England by TJ International Ltd, Padstow, Cornwall.

Pen & Sword Books Limited incorporates the imprints of Atlas, Archaeology, Aviation, Discovery, Family History, Fiction, History, Maritime, Military, Military Classics, Politics, Select, Transport, True Crime, Air World, Frontline Publishing, Leo Cooper, Remember When, Seaforth Publishing, The Praetorian Press, Wharncliffe Local History, Wharncliffe Transport, Wharncliffe True Crime and White Owl.

For a complete list of Pen & Sword titles please contact

PEN & SWORD BOOKS LIMITED
47 Church Street, Barnsley, South Yorkshire, S70 2AS, England
E-mail: enquiries@pen-and-sword.co.uk
Website: www.pen-and-sword.co.uk

Or
PEN AND SWORD BOOKS
1950 Lawrence Rd, Havertown, PA 19083, USA
E-mail: Uspen-and-sword@casematepublishers.com
Website: www.penandswordbooks.com

MIX
Paper from
responsible sources
FSC
www.fsc.org   FSC® C013056

Contents

Acknowledgements

So many people have contributed to the completion of this book, and each one deserves recognition. Firstly thanks must go to Professor John Buckley of the University of Wolverhampton, who was my Director of Studies and encouraged and supported me throughout my PhD. Thanks also go to the Royal Air Force Historical Society who awarded me the Henry Probert Bursary to help with my research visits to London. Thanks go to veteran John Pollock who had served in the Royal Auxiliary Air Force and provided me with much needed information and photographs. Ernie Cromie and Alan Taylor helped me with information on the University Air Squadrons which I was struggling to find.

Finally, thanks go to Pam, Lyndsey and Kerrianne who have been with me all the way through my research and studies, and have never really complained about it, even though they weren't remotely interested in what I was doing !!!

Acronyms

Air Member for Personnel Development	AMP
Aircraftsman Second Class	AC2
Auxiliary Air Force	AAF
Commanding Officer	CO
Distinguished Flying Cross	DFC
Distinguished Flying Medal	DFM
Elementary and Reserve Flying Training School	ERFTS
Navy Army Air Force Institute	NAAFI
Non Commissioned Officer	NCO
North Atlantic Treaty Organisation	NATO
Operational Record Book	ORB
Royal Aero Club	RAeC
Royal Air Force	RAF
Royal Air Force Volunteer Reserve	RAFVR
Royal Auxiliary Air Force	RAuxAF
Royal Flying Corps	RFC
Royal Naval Air Service	RNAS
Royal Naval Volunteer Reserve	RNVR
Special Reserve	SR
Territorial Air Force	TAF
Territorial Army	TA
Territorial Force Association	TFA
The National Archives	TNA
University Air Squadron	UAS

List of Illustrations

List of Tables

Abstract

Little has been written about the Territorial Air Force (TAF) as a voluntary military organisation and no sustained analysis of its recruitment and social composition undertaken. Made up of three different parts, the Auxiliary Air Force (AAF), the Special Reserve (SR) and the Royal Air Force Volunteer Reserve (RAFVR), these three separate and different groups have not featured significantly in existing literature. Current historiography of the AAF and SR is dominated by the experiences of 600 and 601 Squadrons based in London and presents a popular image of a gentleman's flying club, whilst that of the RAFVR presents an image of a much more egalitarian institution, intended to be a citizens' air force. This book presents new and detailed research into the recruitment and social backgrounds of men serving in both the pre and post-war TAF. It seeks to provide an overview of the social composition of all AAF and SR squadrons. Using primary documents from The National Archives (TNA) and recently digitised press records, it explores the recruitment processes, social backgrounds and social relations of personnel in the TAF. Whilst focusing primarily on officers, it looks too at the experience of non-officer recruits. Its findings indicate that the structures and cultures of the AAF and SR squadrons were indeed similar to the well-publicised London squadrons, whilst those for the RAFVR were much more elite than was expected. Military voluntarism continued to play a key role in the defence of twentieth-century Britain, but the underlying tensions and weaknesses associated with a class-based voluntary culture meant that the TAF had to change in response to new pressures. The book charts how these changes began to manifest themselves in the post-war world. Class ceased to be the key determining factor in the recruitment of officers as the organisations faced new challenges. Within both the AAF and the RAFVR the pre-war impression of a gentlemen's flying club finally gave way to a more meritocratic culture in the post-war world.

Introduction

The original RAF reserve was made up of two different parts, the Auxiliary Air Force (AAF) and the Special Reserve (SR). Separate and deliberately different, they were created to appeal to young men from across the country who could fly, or who wanted to learn to fly, and men who had a trade, or who wanted to learn a trade. Limitations in the recruitment processes for these two organisations resulted in there being a need for a new and different reserve, the Royal Air Force Volunteer Reserve (RAFVR), which came into being in 1936 and began recruiting in 1937. The AAF, which eventually included the SR, (who were merged into them in 1936) became known as a "gentleman's flying club" with distinct exclusivity; in fact, Max Aitken, a former member of 601 (County of London) Squadron, a Conservative MP and Chairman of Express Newspapers remembered that:

> "My companions were a pretty wild and high-spirited group many of whom I already knew from skiing and after skiing parties at St Anton. They were the sort of young men who had not quite been expelled from their schools, whom mothers warned their daughters against – in vain – who stayed up far too late at parties. Does that sort of young man still exist? I do not know, but in those days they were quite common and they clustered in unusual density at the Headquarters of 601 Squadron."[1]

Such were descriptions of the men who volunteered to join the AAF and SR squadrons. In fact: "In all the history of arms, there can seldom have been a body of men more outwardly confident and pleased with themselves than the pilots of the Auxiliary Air Force – amongst them were lawyers and farmers, stockbrokers and journalists, landowners, accountants and playboys. They represented par excellence, that powerful amateur tradition which characterised so much of British life before the war."[2]

Moreover, "these amateurs were kindred spirits, young men who had often been educated together in public schools, and who had learned the importance of duty, and camaraderie."[3] Men who worked in similar environments and who were willing to give up one night a week, each weekend and two weeks in the summer for the annual training camp, to serve their country within the TAF, in either the AAF, in squadrons numbered between 600 and 616, or SR squadrons numbered between 500 and 504. From the start it was apparent that, "to be an auxiliary, it was essential to be the right person from the right background. The expense of the auxiliary lifestyle saw to that if nothing else did." Indeed, "the auxiliary officers were what we would call 'the gentleman type,' hare and hounds and field sports type. Amateur jockeys and that sort of thing. There was an officer class and an airman class and there was a gulf. It was more pronounced there than anywhere else in the service."[4]

Consequently, there is an enduring image of the men who joined the TAF, rich young amateurs who volunteered to serve their country and fly these new machines in peace and in war. However, the Second World War led to the development of faster aircraft and the growth of technology which resulted in the need for a different kind of volunteer, a more technically minded and skilled man. Indeed some believed that: "Before the war most pilots were officers and it didn't matter whether you had brains or not, you would fly the aircraft. The officers weren't the brightest by any means, and often it was your family relationship that got you your position. It wasn't the case after the war, the fittest and the brightest became pilots."[5]

This exclusivity meant that during its entire lifetime the AAF was constantly under-manned in terms of both pilots and aircrew. Consequently, during 1935, discussions took place with a view to the formation of another voluntary organisation, which was to be called the RAFVR. This reserve, it was decided, would end the shortage of volunteers, because it was to be a "citizens' air force", having no social or educational barriers to enlistment. This would make it very different to the AAF who believed that their selectiveness was important and could not be compromised when it came to recruiting. Enlisting began for the new reserve in March 1937, with application forms being sent to the Air Ministry, followed by selection boards taking place across the country. Requirements for the RAFVR were as follows:

"Candidates must be between eighteen and twenty-five, be physically fit and have had an education up to the standard of the School Certificate, or the Leaving Certificate in Scotland. Previous flying experience is not necessary.

Selected candidates will be enlisted as airman pilots with the rank of sergeant; later they will have opportunities of promotion to commissioned rank on merit. The initial period of service will be five years. Training will be given at weekends and other times, including evenings. Flying training will be given at the aerodromes and ground training at town centres centrally situated."[6]

Thus, the recruitment process for young men volunteering for the RAFVR was much more prescribed than that of the AAF.

This book chronicling the history of the TAF will highlight the policy and decision-making process which led to the formation of the TAF and will consider how successful these organisations became, in terms of their ability to recruit young men. Was the Auxiliary Air Force an exclusive "gentleman's flying club" compared to the RAFVR whose volunteers came from lower middle class and working class backgrounds, making it "a citizen's air force?"

The Territorial Air Force (TAF) was a voluntary organisation made up of three separate entities whose job it was to provide a reserve supply of officers and airmen who would be trained and immediately able to provide reinforcements for the Royal Air Force (RAF). The focus will be on the social composition of the TAF, and will not consider technical or institutional areas of the TAF. It is important to note here that the TAF is a blanket term used throughout the book when discussing the Auxiliary Air Force (AAF), Special Reserve (SR) and Royal Air Force Volunteer Reserve (RAFVR). However, there will be times when only the Auxiliaries will be discussed, or only the Volunteer Reserve, so there will be some use of different titles for these part-time volunteers. When a collective term is needed, it will be Territorial Air Force; otherwise it will be individual sections of the reserves by names.

The book will consider the decision taken by the government in the aftermath of the First World War to establish two different forms of voluntary force in 1925, the AAF and the SR. Given the shortcomings of both the AAF and the SR squadrons, the SR was merged into the AAF in 1936. However, the failings of the combined AAF still did not overcome the issues of this kind of reserve, which meant that it was never able to recruit enough young men to take it above the 50 per cent of the required strength. In 1936, the decision was taken to set up a different kind of reserve which would deal with the recruiting problems faced by the Auxiliaries. The new reserve would operate alongside them and would be called the RAFVR. This of course raises several questions which relate to the decisions made in 1920 when the original reserve was developed, and there will be a detailed examination of Government and Air Ministry documents, housed at The National Archives, which discuss the thinking behind the new reserve and why two different organisations rather than one were set up in the first place. Having tried to rationalise the decision making of the government at the end of the First World War, consideration is then given to the reforming of the RAF reserves at the start of 1946. This is important because the Government fell into the same trap by following the same framework for the reserves as it had followed in the 1920s, resulting in an AAF which had similar problems to its predecessor, and again which was not completely fit for purpose. Similarly, the RAFVR was also reformed in 1946 in the image of its 1936 counterpart. Why did the Government take these steps and again end up with two different reserve forces?

Moving on, there will be a focus and evaluation of the process of recruitment within the AAF, the SR and the RAFVR to discover how young men were recruited and the kinds of recruits who were accepted as pilots and officers within each of the organisations. This will allow analysis of the influence that class structures had upon recruitment. For example, were the requirements for commissions the same for all of the three reserves? And furthermore, were the requirements the same for the pre and post-war TAF? This will enable a social analysis of the types of young men to whom the TAF appealed. By identifying all of the officers and presenting their individual biographies, conclusions will be drawn as to whether a specific "type" of young men were sought out who were interested in becoming officers within the TAF. Was this kind of man in the AAF the same as the man in the RAFVR? Existing literature implies that the men were very different in the two organisations, and that this was exactly what the government wanted when it set up the RAFVR in 1936.

Current thinking would imply that class had a major impact on entrants to the Auxiliary and SR squadrons, and less bearing on recruits to the RAFVR. In so much as the AAF and SR squadrons reflected a snapshot of interwar society, so recruitment to the AAF squadrons may well have been down to who you knew and how influential they were and this perhaps suggests why the majority of the very few mentions of the AAF across the current literature tends to liken it to a gentleman's flying club and often this image is based on the flamboyancy and composition of the two London squadrons, 600 (City of London) Squadron and 601 (County of London) Squadron. With the establishment of the RAFVR in 1936, different criteria became important when selecting men to become pilots and officers. There will also be significant analysis of the data relating to social composition of all three forces.

Were there significant differences between northern and southern squadrons, or those squadrons in Scotland, Ireland and Wales? Men have been identified who took up commissions within the three different segments of the TAF. Then, the background information of as many entrants as possible has been sourced and this allows a detailed analysis of individual squadrons and also squadrons in particular areas of the United Kingdom. This enables the research to make comparisons between squadrons in England, Ireland, Scotland and Wales, as well as those squadrons in the north of England and the south of England. Nevertheless, it should be noted that those men applying to join the AAF joined specific squadrons, and each of these squadrons had a particular location within the United Kingdom, whereas those men volunteering to join the RAFVR joined the organisation, and then could be sent to join any of the RAF squadrons across the country. Therefore, the men of the RAFVR do not have squadron numbers and consequently do not figure in the analysis between north and south, or between England, Scotland, Wales and Ireland, and this must be taken into account when the results are analysed. Finally, the data provided by the research, however limited, does shed light upon the differences between those men who volunteered to join squadrons in the different regions of the United Kingdom.

Both Auxiliary and SR squadrons were located in industrial areas or cities and there are several ways in which the various squadrons attempted to integrate, formally and informally. Formal interaction between the squadron and the local community took place through squadron open days which were held each year at local aerodromes, where there would be a flying display and the aerodrome would be open for the local people to observe the auxiliary squadron at work. Informal interaction took place through sporting events such as football matches between a squadron team and a local team, or a tug of war challenge. Moreover, squadron dances also gave the opportunity for informal interaction, as did social contact in local public houses and cinemas. This issue will be considered with the help of local press and individual squadron histories in order to establish their impact and effectiveness. As a reminder, men of the RAFVR were posted to regular RAF squadrons, and this has meant that there is no real way of establishing how these young men integrated with their local communities. However, the relationship between the AAF and their local community was important because, unlike the regular RAF and the RAFVR, the auxiliaries were specifically tied to their local area and as such, were keen to invest in it.

Finally, why were these voluntary organisations wound up in the late 1950s. The main reason for this is given in some of the literature and involves the rapid changes in aircraft technology compared to the part-time nature of the reserves. In other words, the reserve pilots did not have enough time to train in order to become efficient in these new jet aircraft. Also it is suggested, many of the RAF stations around the country which were run in the main by reserves did not have runways which were of a sufficient length to receive these jets. But, was it the socio-cultural changes taking place in post-war society which made class become less important than it was in the inter-war years, or was it the fact that the new technology meant that qualified and professionally trained men were necessary to both fly and maintain the more modern jet aircraft?

To address all of these questions the book will adopt the following structure. Chapter 1 will put forward the reasons why the government chose to set up three different types of reserve force, the AAF, the SR and the RAFVR. It will explore in detail the planning of the reserves from the early 1920s through to the impact of the Second World War, considering existing examples of reserve forces, the Territorial Army (TA) and the Royal Naval Volunteer Reserve (RNVR).

Chapter 2 will discuss the recruitment process of the AAF, the SR and the RAFVR. It will focus on the requirements necessary for entrance as pilots of these reserve squadrons and will discuss the merger of the SR squadrons into the AAF in 1936, presenting the arguments for and against the merger. It will also discuss the role of the University Air Squadrons (UAS) in the RAF reserves and will then move on to discuss the formation and recruitment process of the RAFVR in 1936.

Chapter 3 will focus on the social composition of the TAF from the mid-1920s until the onset of war in 1939. It will present data and analysis in the form of tables. It will consider the differences between northern and southern squadrons and will also look at the data for England, Ireland, Scotland and Wales. To provide a more detailed analysis of whether or not more localised AAF squadrons were made up of young men from similar backgrounds as those from the more well-known London based squadrons, 600 (City of London) Squadron and 601 (County of London) Squadron. The key focus of this chapter will be the social backgrounds of the young men recruited to join the AAF and RAFVR prior to the Second World War, specifically the role of class and its importance in officer recruitment for the RAF reserves.

Chapter 4 will focus on the Second World War between 1939 and 1945. During this period all of the AAF squadrons and all of the volunteers in the RAFVR were embodied into the RAF for the duration of hostilities. Moreover, the RAFVR became the route through which all new personnel for the RAF were trained. The chapter will discuss each of the Auxiliary squadrons and their role during the war, and will identify individual members of each squadron who actually served during the war. It will also identify the location of each of the squadrons throughout the war, thus giving squadron postings across the globe. With regard to the RAFVR, again individuals who served during the war who could be identified have been mentioned with any relevant information that could be found.

The emphasis of Chapter 5 is on the reconstitution of the TAF which began following the conclusion of the war in 1945. It will look at the decisions made supported by primary source material, such as documents and letters from the Air Ministry, from the National Archive. It will also discuss National Service which ran throughout a significant part of the post-war period and had a major impact on recruitment for both the RAuxAF and the RAFVR. Examples of recruitment posters from the 1950s are included to reinforce one of the ways in which the government and Air Ministry attempted to increase recruiting to both the RAuxAF and the RAFVR. Finally this chapter will consider the reasons for the disbandment of the Royal Auxiliary Air Force (RAuxAF) squadrons in 1957.

Chapter 6 will concentrate on the social composition of the TAF in the years after the end of the Second World War. In a similar way to Chapter 3, data will be presented which will be used to identify whether or not there was a significant change in the types of men who volunteered and were successfully recruited into the TAF. The chapter will try to identify differences between those men in the pre-war squadron and those in the post-war squadrons. Finally, conclusions will be drawn which will bring together common threads enabling deductions to be made about the social composition of the TAF as a whole in the period 1930-1957.

Methodology

Several different sources have been examined to undertake the research. In the first instance, The National Archives (TNA) hold most of the surviving Air Ministry records covering the pre-war and wartime period which can be found in Air Historical Branch Records: Series 1. This consists of: "papers mostly dated 1914-1918 received by the Air Historical branch from Air Ministry Departments from formations of the Royal Flying Corps (RFC) and Royal Air Force (RAF) and various other sources for use in the official history of the Air Ministry, squadron histories and operation narratives."[7] Other documents held at The National Archives are government papers relating to the creation and establishment of the Auxiliary Air Force (AAF), Special Reserve (SR) and Royal Air Force Volunteer Reserve (RAFVR), the procedures followed, the rules that were put in place and the funding that was decided upon. These can be found in the Correspondence of the Air Ministry relating to aviation and aeronautics.

There are also Operational Record Books (ORB) for each of the individual AAF and SR squadrons. These books list in chronological order the activities of both the squadron and the RAF station - on a daily basis in many cases - showing the personnel in each squadron or station at any given time. They note other activities that took place on each day including some social events, records of illness and flying incidents. Record books in this series, The National Archives guide points out, "provide a daily record of events in each squadron entered on Form 540 with appendices. The object of the operational record book (ORB) was to furnish a complete historical record of a unit from the time of its formation, including an accurate record of operations carried out."[8] The ORBs provide some of the basic factual bricks upon which the research is built. These documents are largely factual, presenting the government policies of the time, although they are open to interpretation when cross-referenced with the established historiography relating to the formation of the Air Services from 1912-1918. The debates around the construction of the Air Force Reserves can also be found within these documents.

There are also a number of documents held in the archives of the Imperial War Museum. These consist of private papers donated to the museum by members of the armed forces, including flight log books and diaries. Many of these relate to the period of the Second World War. The archive also holds some duplicate ORBs in the collection. Other documents such as letters and diaries can be found at the RAF Museum at Hendon which also holds private papers from individual members of some AAF squadrons. Initial research in these archives however suggested that they would be of little use to this study as they are in the main, related to the RAF rather than the TAF.

The local press have played a significant role in contextualising the growth and development of the TAF in relation to regional events; one of the key factors in choosing the location of Auxiliary squadrons was that recruitment was to focus on local personnel; their purpose was to build strong links and bonds with the local community. Newspapers from each local area have recorded events that took place including open days, squadron dances and sporting events.

Press records across the country have been used to identify the social backgrounds of UK volunteers to the TAF. Contacts have been made with AAF and SR squadron associations and this has provided additional information about individuals and squadron activities. The recent digitisation of several major press records, most notably *The Times* Digital Archive, offering a complete two hundred year run of the paper from its inception in 1785 to 1985, has enabled thorough searches of local squadrons and their volunteers. Digitisation of the *London Gazette* has also enabled the identification of men commissioned into the AAF and SR squadrons and also any promotions and bravery awards which were made across the United Kingdom. As part of this section, details of the names of each AAF and SR squadron across the whole of the United Kingdom have been taken down, including the name of each officer, the date he was commissioned and then any extra background information that can be found. These details can be found in Appendix 2. This information was located by searching through the *London Gazette* Archive squadron by squadron to identify each new officer. *The Times* Digital Archive was then used to piece together any background information that was found which would help to make a pen portrait of each individual officer and which would then enable the research to draw conclusions about the backgrounds of the officers across the UK overall between 1924 and 1945.

INTRODUCTION

Ten general categories were selected by the author as representing the activities of a young man from a specifically high or middle class group. The first category was that of public school. Was the young man educated in one of the countries public schools? For example: Eton, Westminster, or Harrow. Attending one of these schools reflects the financial background from which a young man comes, since the termly fees were beyond the reach of ordinary working class families.

The second category was attending Oxford or Cambridge University. Again this category highlights the names of young men whose parents could afford to pay for them to study, rather than immediately taking up a job or an apprenticeship. Indeed, Dyhouse points out in 2006 that: "Studies of Oxbridge make it clear that these institutions catered for a social elite. Students from working class homes were very much outnumbered by those who might be seen as having regarded college life as something in the nature of a 'finishing school for young gentlemen.'"[9] The third category was attending any other university. This too reflects the financial background of the young man's family, as this was a time when education cost money, although scholarships were available to those who excelled in particular subjects. "In the mid to late 1930s university tuition fees averaged around £40 per annum. This was considerably less than the cost of studying at a college in Oxford or Cambridge, where the fees were estimated at between £200 and £275 for a man."[10] These figures need to be put into context by considering that the average annual income for a working class man was around £208, therefore attendance at an Oxbridge University, and even a university in general, was beyond the reach of most working class families.

The next category chosen was elite sport. By this the research identified any young men who took part in sports which were specifically linked to those of a high social class or those with money. For example, rowing, shooting, hunting, fencing, cricket and yachting. Taking part in these activities reflected a man's social status. The next three categories were chosen because they record significant events in a person's life, and to have these events marked by an announcement in *The Times* again shows status. The events chosen were birth announcements, that is for a young man to mark the birth of one or all of his children with an announcement in the paper; marriage, that is for the young man or a member of his family to mark his engagement or marriage through an announcement in the newspaper and finally a death announcement or obituary, which involved another person in the family using the paper to announce the death of the named man and then reflected upon his life. The next two categories chosen represented the chosen career of the young man. Options given were either the profession that the young man worked in, such as law, medicine or accountancy. Business, for example, insurance, banking and finance in the City of London, or Industry, such as engineering, or, did the young man work for his family's business. This shows that the business was prepared to support the young man in the time off he needed to be a member of a part-time squadron. Finally, the last category was whether or not the young man had been a member of a University Air Squadron (UAS).

These ten categories were measured and used to suggest the social status of a young officer recruit, based largely on the cost and the status of *The Times* newspaper. Moreover, these categories could in fact be used to measure status across the civilian population during this period too. A Google search of the man's full name was also undertaken which threw up individual squadron web pages as well as the Commonwealth Graves Commission and the research of other individuals. Finally, squadron histories were also used to try to find out biographical information about all of the men who had been identified. This method of identifying men and then discovering their background was used across the AAF and the RAFVR. In this way, the research findings were measurable and were also accurate. This can be shown when the tables which appear in Chapter 3 and Chapter 5 are studied. Post 1946, the AAF was reformed and went on to be on operational duties until it was disbanded in 1957. Here too the *London Gazette* and *The Times* Digital Archive have been used to assess those officers who re-joined after the war was over, and to help ascertain the backgrounds of the officers who signed up for the reserves during that time.

It was much more difficult to build up pictures of individual officers for the RAFVR. With the AAF, all newly commissioned men were allocated to their local squadron, and all squadrons were numbered between 600 and 616, with the SR all newly commissioned men were allocated to their local squadron and all squadrons were numbered between 500 and 504. These individual squadrons have proved to be much simpler to research, whereas the RAFVR officers were commissioned and then sent to any of the RAF squadrons. To identify RAFVR officers, the search engine of the *London Gazette* was used focusing on the term "RAFVR." This produced a massive number of names and these names were listed in the first instance, then put into alphabetical order and then cross-referenced against *The Times* Digital Archive. The final piece therefore, provides a comprehensive list of all officers across the TAF.

INTRODUCTION

It should be noted that whilst it has proved difficult to research the backgrounds of the AAF and SR officers, it has been virtually impossible to trace the backgrounds of the airmen and ground crews. Digital archives tend to present biographical information of those from more privileged backgrounds, thus officers have been easier to trace. Since the officers were primarily pilots, their activities were also recorded in squadron ORBs. The airmen and ground crew do not focus in either of these sources and therefore the focus has been primarily on the backgrounds of AAF, SR and RAFVR officers across the United Kingdom.

In conclusion, the focus on recruitment and class is an innovative angle upon which to draw conclusions about the way in which the TAF was brought into being, and the way in which recruitment relied so heavily upon social class in the pre-war world, whilst relying upon technical skills and knowledge in the post-war world. The research provides a mirror to reflect upon the changes taking place in society in the United Kingdom during the period 1925-1957 and will provide an important contribution to knowledge with regard to the role played by both recruitment and social class within a military institution.

Chapter 1

The Creation of the Reserve Forces

This first chapter will provide an analysis of the decisions made by the government to follow the ideas of Hugh Trenchard and form a Territorial Air Force (TAF). It will discuss the models of the Territorial Army (TA) and the Royal Naval Volunteer Reserve (RNVR), and using primary source documents from The National Archives it will analyse the reasoning as to why those at the Air Ministry did not do what the other two branches of the armed forces did, which was to set up one single reserve, and instead chose to set up two initial types of reserve, the Auxiliary Air Force (AAF) and the Special Reserve (SR). It will then move on to consider why, in 1936, a second type of reserve, the Royal Air Force Volunteer Reserve (RAFVR), was set up. Existing literature says that the AAF was in direct competition with the SR squadrons hoping that each would appeal to different recruits and as such, there would be similar numbers of recruits in both, based almost entirely upon whether a man could fly or not. This would be the determining factor for officer recruits within the separate organisations. With the introduction of the RAFVR in 1936, it is currently claimed that the volunteers for this organisation were from somewhat different backgrounds from those for the AAF and SR and in this respect, the government of the day had actually formed a more trans-class reserve which would appeal to many more young men.

The future defence policy of Britain was influenced by the first flight across the English Channel on 25 July 1909 by the Frenchman, Louis Bleriot. For centuries Britain had considered itself to have been safe from a land attack because of its island status. For protection, it had only needed a small standing army and a navy.[1] Therefore, the implications of Bleriot's flight were enormous both for aviation and for Britain. Britain's island status was no longer such a factor in itself to prevent it from attack.[2]

The Government's, military and naval chiefs' suspicion and concern about the development of aviation[3] meant that Britain fell behind other

1

countries in terms of expenditure on aeronautical development. In April 1909, Britain had spent a mere £5000, compared to France's £47,000 and Germany's £400,000.[4] This lack of financial commitment to the research and development of aviation was a reflection of the views of the majority of the British Government and military at the time.

The first major move towards the recognition of the possible role of aviation in future defence policy came from the army in February 1911 when it organised an Air Battalion of the Royal Engineers. In the same year, the navy allowed four naval officers to learn to fly. The Admiralty bought two aeroplanes and set up a small naval flying school at Eastchurch.[5] At the end of the year, the Prime Minister, Herbert Henry Asquith, appointed a Sub-Committee of Imperial Defence, chaired by Lord Haldane, whose role it was to decide what measures would be needed to ensure that Britain developed "an efficient aerial service."[6] The sub-committee's membership included proponents of an aviation corps, Colonel David Henderson and Captain Frederick H Sykes, men with army careers and backgrounds, who could both fly.[7] The sub-committee recommended an aeronautical service comprising the Royal Flying Corps (RFC), with a naval wing and a Central Flying School. The RFC was constituted by Royal Warrant on 13 April 1912 and was controlled by the Army Council and commanded by Captain Sykes.[8] Given the Admiralty's resistance to inter-service links, the RFC was forced to cede the naval wing, which was renamed the Royal Naval Air Service (RNAS) on 1 July 1914.[9]

Candidates for the RFC had first to qualify for the Royal Aero Club (RAeC) Pilot Certificate by taking a civilian flying course at their own expense. The RAeC had been created in 1901 and was itself very influential in the growth of aviation in Britain. It was responsible for the training of most military pilots up to 1915 when military schools took over the job. The club controlled all private and sporting flying in the United Kingdom and regulated flying records and competitions. By the end of the First World War, more than 6,300 military pilots had taken the RAeC Aviator Certificates, and a new Light Aeroplane Club scheme was formed ensuring that between 1925 and 1939 about sixty Flying Clubs were started, training over 5,000 pilots, supporting the aircraft industry and providing a nucleus of Royal Air Force (RAF), AAF and RAFVR pilots for the Second World War. In many ways the voluntaristic mentality of the RAeC was to influence the government and military thinking between the wars because the club actually prevented the development of a larger professional air service due to its control over civilian flying.[10]

The Royal Navy were quicker to accept the potential of aviation, preparing their pilots for a more offensive role so that by 1913, the RNAS pilots were learning the skill of bomb dropping, whilst the army continued to develop the role of reconnaissance. This acceptance by the Royal Navy of the potential of aviation echoed the technocratic nature of their service and reinforces the view that the navy was more likely to see the possibilities of aircraft than the army since the latter had undergone very little technological change over the centuries.[11] However, Andrew Whitmarsh argues that "neither the British army nor many of its senior officers were really so dismissive of military aviation before 1914. In many cases, aircraft were officially incorporated into manoeuvres and other training exercises, an indication that the army recognised their potential value and wanted to experiment with their use in the field."[12]

The First World War proved to be the testing ground for the creation of the modern RAF. It allowed for the expansion of the RFC and highlighted the crucial role that aircraft could play in future conflicts. As the war progressed, the British Government entered into discussions to decide the future of aviation within the military and in June 1917, a Cabinet Committee was formed, chaired by General Jan Christian Smuts, Minister of Defence of South Africa and a member of the War Cabinet. As he was not British, he was detached from the inter-service rivalry that existed between the army and the Royal Navy and also in many ways, from the influence of government. The first report of the committee was issued on 19 July 1917 and recommended that a single command be established for all fighter aircraft, anti-aircraft and search batteries and all observation posts. The second report, issued on 17 August 1917, was even more far reaching, arguing for the creation of a separate Air Ministry and Air Staff to amalgamate the RFC and the RNAS into a new Air Service that was independent of the army and the navy. Smuts believed that aerial operations would in fact supersede the operations of the navy and army given their potential to devastate enemy territory, centres of industry and cities.[13]

Both the army and the navy opposed the report because each saw this proposed new force as a threat to their funding; however, Parliament passed The Air Force (Constitution) Act on 29 November 1917. The RNAS and The RFC were merged on 1 April 1918 and on that day, a new third service; the Royal Air Force was established. By the end of the war, the RAF possessed more than twenty-two thousand aircraft making it the world's largest air force.[14]

The infant Royal Air Force had to learn to compete for resources with the older military and naval services with their established lobbyists and elite supporters. The new organisation had to battle against historically preconceived and long-established ideas and protocol, and fight many attempts by the army and navy to claim back their own aviation units. All of this was conducted in a climate of severe and continuous financial restraint. In 1919, at the request of the Treasury, the "Ten Year Rule" was introduced, a rolling programme which involved a planning assumption which presupposed that there would be no major war involving Britain for ten years. It allowed the government to reduce spending on armaments in line with post-war public opinion. Indeed, the new Auxiliary Air Force became a function of the Ten-Year Rule as its creation enabled the government to spend less on armaments whilst still hoping to maintain an adequate military presence in both Britain and the Empire through the use of volunteers. The British Government failed to take seriously the growing evidence of German rearmament and militancy during the 1930s and underestimated the threat that Germany posed to Britain and Europe.[15] Therefore the armed air services faced a difficult environment for much of the interwar period which influenced the shape that the service took and in particular its increasing dependence on voluntary support.

In November 1919, Winston Churchill was appointed to the post of Secretary of State for War and Air. He invited Hugh Trenchard to accept the post of Chief of the Air Staff. Aware that war and therefore grandiose plans for air defence in Britain would be unacceptable, Trenchard produced a White Paper called "An Outline of the Scheme for the Permanent Organisation of the Royal Air Force" in December 1919.[16] He saw the potential of the RAF to "police" the British Empire, so reducing the cost of staffing large garrisons overseas and therefore reducing military expenditure as a whole.[17] Furthermore, the suggestion of an air force reserve initially included in the 1917 Act addressed the problem that to fund a full time air force would be a costly exercise and may not fit with the interwar public's desire for disarmament.

The creation and organisation of the RAF reserve forces during the interwar period was based upon the recruitment process and structure of the army.[18] This meant that the initial process of being nominated for a commission was linked to social and political influence rather than intellectual, military or technical ability. Reforms directed by Edward Cardwell, Secretary of State for War on 1 November 1871, removed the purchase of commissions whereby officers were drawn from the aristocracy and landed gentry and sought to streamline the recruitment process. Cardwell's reforms meant that recruiting for regiments took place locally and this model for the army became the framework upon which the AAF was built, linking the locality to the squadron.[19] Furthermore, the AAF came to resemble the entrepreneurial private forces of the pre-Cardwell period. There was a reliance on its pilots holding a pilot's licence, which meant that they had to come from wealthier backgrounds since flying was new and expensive. The AAF was inevitably the product of the time, shaped in part by a pre-war ambiguity about the value of the air services per se, but also shaped by older military traditions such as the yeomanry, pre-Cardwell commissions and regimental systems; it also developed its own distinctive culture. The selection process that operated in the AAF, based as it was on the availability of time, money and connections, was undeniably elitist and can be contrasted with government and public service recruitment which increasingly bore the imprint of a more democratic and accessible culture, or indeed the regular RAF and Territorial Army (TA) which were also more democratic organisations in terms of the men who served in them.

The TA had been in existence for many years before the idea of the TAF came into being and was used as a model for the new voluntary air service. Since 1794, the army had used two groups of volunteers, the Militia, raised from the civilian population and the Yeomanry or cavalry, recruited from men holding small landed estates or freeholds. These volunteers trained on a part-time basis, but could be embodied for full-time service when there was a risk of invasion or indeed in some colonial conflicts like the Boer War.[20] Clearly the army could not retain in peacetime all the soldiers it needed to meet the needs of war, and reservists helped it to make the transition. They also formed part of a bridge linking the army to wider society and, given the traditional ambivalence of British civilians towards soldiers and standing armies, especially as the army's visibility across the nation was diminishing, this role was of pivotal importance.[21]

Richard Burdon Haldane, Secretary for War in 1908, was the founder of the TA, which was seen to be a volunteer force locally organized to provide a reserve of trained and disciplined manpower for use in an emergency, but which were not dependent on local patronage. Peter Dennis notes that the volunteers had originally been established as a "private and exclusive military club, membership of which entailed the payment of entrance and annual fees".[22] Haldane, on the other hand, had a different vision of the TA, seeing it administered locally and hence he decided that funding would be undertaken by the County Territorial Associations, a body whose duty it was to recruit and organise the service.[23] In 1907 the associations were created, and in 1922, the title was changed to Territorial and Auxiliary Forces Associations, made up of TA and AAF members. Though possibly not typical, detailed records are available for Glasgow and they can provide an example of how a County Joint Association might be composed. The Lord Lieutenant was President of the Association which, in this case, had a further fifty-one ordinary members. Twenty-four (slightly less than half) were military members (i.e. the army); three were AAF members; eight were representative members, and sixteen co-opted members with a chairman and vice-chairman elected from the membership. The military members were appointed by the Army Council from amongst the officers of the local TA along with the officers of the former Yeomanry and Volunteer Forces in the locality. Similarly, the Air Force members were drawn from serving and former-serving officers in the AAF or in the regular RAF. The representative members reflected corporate interests of the city with seven recommended by the Corporation of the City of Glasgow and one by the governing body of the University of Glasgow. The co-opted members allowed the Association to draw in a range of other interests including not less than three representatives of the employers and not less than three representatives of the workmen, and "as far as possible person's representative of the interests of the employers and workmen in the aircraft industry in the county".[24] This Association provided a forum for both the local elite and the army elite to wield power and have a say in the military organisation of the county. There was a distribution of interests between the military and local employers and employees and the aim was to provide a framework for representation within the Association. This was reflected in all of the County Associations across the country.

Sir Hugh Trenchard wanted to create an air force reserve that would be raised on a territorial basis and which would allow for the skills and expertise that had been developed within the RFC to be preserved, thus allowing for future expansion when the political climate was more propitious. In July 1920, a confidential document originating from the Air Ministry entitled "Territorial Air Force", proposed a scheme in which a new organisation would be created. The TAF would take over the responsibility for the aerial defence of the United Kingdom; furthermore, should a war begin, the TAF would be able to reinforce the RAF.[25] Consequently, it is clear that Trenchard saw the TAF as an alternative to increased military spending on the RAF, which would enable him to gain support for his air reserves, without challenging the government's position on disarmament and reduction of military spending.[26]

Prospects for the new TAF looked good when in 1924 Winston Churchill noted:

> "We propose this year to begin the formation on a very small scale of a Territorial Air Force, for which £20,000 is taken in the Estimates. Our idea is to have six squadrons stationed near centres where there is a large engineering population, and where aerodromes are available. Each squadron would have a small nucleus of regular air mechanics and it is hoped that the skilled voluntary element in the neighbourhood will form this small nucleus."[27]

Churchill was outlining the basic principles of the TAF but potential problems of a voluntary reserve were noted by the Under Secretary of State who believed that a reserve for the RAF would be "doomed to failure, unless managed by the existing County Associations, who had the necessary administrative machinery and experience".[28] Parallels can be drawn between the nature of the TAF and the First World War Pals battalions, where friendships, working relationships and shared locations were crucial in increasing recruitment to the army. Viscount Templewood noted "the intention was to give the officers and men continuity of service in their local unit with all the advantages that come from knowing each other and working together".[29] Thus schools, businesses, industries and areas sent men to join up, and this maintained the local interest in the battalion throughout the duration of the war. In the same vein, TAF squadrons were to be comprised of local volunteers serving at a local aerodrome and this, it was hoped, would attract support from the local community.

The winter of 1920-21 saw a downturn in the economy brought about by large reductions in government spending, an increase of taxation and the failure to increase British exports. Coupled with overproduction there was a decline in demand for coal and textiles resulting in a rise in unemployment. The government blamed high levels of public expenditure for much of the economic crisis and appointed Sir Edward Geddes to chair the committee on National Expenditure. The final report, published in February 1922, was nicknamed the Geddes Axe, a sweeping round of public service cuts specifically in the army, navy, education and public health. It was in this political climate that Trenchard began to lobby for the new reserve forces to be created. However, concerns were raised about whether "aircrew, and especially pilots, could achieve and retain proficiency in the air as a part-time and mainly weekend activity".[30] Following a meeting on 5 June 1923, notes regarding the formation of Special Reserve and Auxiliary Air Force squadrons located in The National Archives talk about the necessity for two separate organisations:

> "The creation of the second- and third-line squadrons was in the nature of an experiment as the RAF, unlike the army or navy, had never had either a Special Reserve or Territorial force. It was considered necessary to form two separate organisations so that the conditions of service for the reserve provided for enlistment on as broad a basis as possible. Also, as the creation of the reserve forces was experimental, the most efficient and economical method of administration could only be ascertained by experience and two separate forces would provide a wider national appeal. In addition, it might be necessary to expand to a large number of squadrons in either or both forces, whichever proved by experience to be the more efficient and popular form or organisation."[31]

Judging from these preliminary talks regarding the creation of two different types of reserve forces it would appear that the SR squadrons were in direct competition with the AAF squadrons from the start and this is apparent from the way in which they were created, in a way that was deliberately different to ascertain which type of squadron recruited better than the other, and which functioned in a more cost effective and administrative manner. Men like Trenchard, who were pushing forward plans to create a reserve force for the RAF clearly looked at the actions of the army as a baseline upon which to model the reserve forces of the RAF. This becomes clear when we see that "the Special Reserve squadrons were intended to be formed on a militia basis, whilst the Auxiliary Air Force was to be formed more nearly on a territorial basis."[32] Samuel Hoare was Secretary of State for Air and one of the staunch advocates of the AAF. The idea in general was that SR squadrons would attract people to whom a closer connection with the life of the regular air force appealed, while AAF squadrons envisaged the recruitment of officers and men who wished to serve together on a more local and amateur basis.[33] With regard to the SR squadrons, "the idea was following the lines of the militia, to provide a means of bringing skeleton units quickly to full strength with trained reservists ... in consequence it has been considered that Cadre units would be expected to be mobilised and ready appreciably sooner than AAF units."[34]

THE CREATION OF THE RESERVE FORCES

In 1924 the Auxiliary Air Force and Air Forces Reserve Act was passed. This allowed for six Auxiliary squadrons and seven SR squadrons, the eventual aim being twenty Auxiliary squadrons in total. The SR squadrons were to be cadre squadrons with their main role to be providing the defence of the United Kingdom. John James notes that "the Special Reserve squadrons were in some measure the equivalent of the territorial battalions of the County Regiments or even territorial units of the Corps."[35] They were organised as heavy bomber squadrons and all of their squadron numbers were located in the 500s. "All the SR squadrons would be commanded by a regular officer and given a nucleus of regular Senior Non-Commissioned Officers and airmen to support the two-thirds or so of the unit strength drawn from the reservists living nearby."[36] The notes[37] regarding the formation of SR and AAF squadrons highlight the main differences between the two types of squadrons. With regard to the SR squadrons, officers and men were to be recruited direct by the units, officers were taught to fly in the units, airmen had to be skilled tradesmen and were enlisted in their trades and the squadrons were formed near centres of engineering population. The AAF on the other hand recruited both officers and airmen through the local Territorial and AAF associations, officers were not accepted unless they could already fly and on acceptance the cost of training was refunded, airmen need not be skilled tradesmen because they were taught their trades in the units and squadrons were formed near large towns and had town headquarters where training was carried on throughout the year culminating in an annual camp.[38]

In June 1925 Air Ministry Pamphlet No 2 entitled "Notes for the information of candidates for commissions in the General Duties Branch for service in Special Reserve Squadrons" stated:

> "Special Reserve Squadrons will be raised and maintained in certain localities as part of the air defence of Great Britain. In peacetime each of these squadrons will be located at an aerodrome in the vicinity of the town from which the Special Reserve personnel of the squadron are recruited. Each squadron is associated for purposes of Home Defence with a regular air force aerodrome which will form its war station and to which it will proceed when called out to take its place in the air defences of the country ... approximately two thirds of the squadron will be composed of Special Reserve personnel living in the neighbourhood of the aerodrome and

keeping themselves efficient by attendance at the aerodrome and compliance otherwise with the conditions of their service. These conditions are made as elastic as possible to minimise interference with the civil life of officers and airmen."[39]

These conditions of service were different from those of the AAF. Selection of officers to new AAF squadrons was left to the commanding officer of each squadron who "will nominate to the Air Ministry gentlemen to fill the remaining vacancies on the establishment of his unit".[40] The way in which the reserve forces were created highlighted the thinking of those in power in the Air Ministry and the way in which they were influenced by the history of the military at that time. The clear differences between the SR based on the old Militia and the AAF on the other hand "resembling much more closely the old Yeomanry regiments, drawn from the landed and fairly well-to-do gentry of the countryside. The Auxiliary Squadrons with their air of the gentlemen's club or the hunt were day or light bomber units."[41]

In an era when flying was a growing sport and air displays a popular form of entertainment, the reserve units had little difficulty in attracting recruits. Many squadrons ran an active social programme and some took on the characteristics of a club, often clubs with a membership of high social standing. Viscount Templewood, Secretary of State for War, commented:

> "Trenchard envisaged the Auxiliaries as a *corps d'elite* composed of the kind of young men who earlier would have been interested in horses but who now wished to serve their country in machines. He conceived the new mechanical yeomanry with its aeroplanes based on the great centres of industry. *Esprit de corps* was to be the dominating force in the squadrons and each, therefore, was to have a well-equipped headquarters, mess and distinctive life of its own. Social meetings were to be encouraged and on no account was any squadron to be regarded as a reserve for filling up regular units."[42]

Having considered the formation of the two different types of reserve squadrons, as time went on, members of the RAF Establishment Committee began to consider their options with regard to personnel in the future and the idea of merging the SR squadrons into the AAF began to be discussed. Accordingly, "as early as 1926, the then Air Officer Commanding, SR and AAF proposed the merger of the SR squadrons into the AAF". He suggested that the formation of each type was experimental and that experience had now shown that this would be the best course ... in 1930, a Sub-Committee of the RAF Establishment Committee reporting on another matter suggested that an enquiry was desirable as to whether the SR squadrons should not be dropped. In 1933 it was noted that:

> "For some time past I have been watching the comparative progress of the Auxiliary and the Cadre squadrons. I do not think that there is any doubt that in general *espirit de corps* and efficiency in doing the duties assigned to them, the Auxiliary squadrons are far superior. I find that in past discussions of the subject, it has been generally agreed that it would be advantageous to do away with the distinctive features of the SR squadrons in favour of the AAF. Furthermore, a decision to convert SR squadrons into AAF squadrons would be a timely recognition of the progress of the AAF and one which full advantage could be taken in the Estimates Speech."[43]

It was also pointed out that "speaking very broadly the SR squadrons have been more difficult to recruit and somewhat less successful in the result than the AAF squadrons, more especially as regards airmen. This may arise from the fact that the latter have the civic organisation and tradition of a county association behind them, an advantage which the SR squadrons do not enjoy."[44] Other reasons given were that officers were not taught to fly in the AAF units, whilst some SR officers are already pilots on joining. Skilled tradesmen did not desire to work in their spare time at their own trades. They joined the SR units to learn to do something different. The sub-committee claimed that these reasons coupled with the great success in efficiency achieved by AAF squadrons suggested that all units ought to be on AAF lines.[45]

The arguments put forward, in favour of the merger were that there would be a greater economy of personnel. There would also be a greater ease in recruiting men, because choice would be limited to one rather than two organisations. This would mean that those who wanted to become members of the RAF volunteers would know exactly what they were volunteering for and what was required of them, rather than having to look at two different sets of rules, regulations and opportunities. Another reason given for the merger

11

was the possibility of higher professional standards, because recruiting procedures would be adhered to strictly due to the lack of choice available. Also, there was the idea that the unit belonged to the volunteers and there was likely to be a greater *espirit de corps* if the men were largely reserves as opposed to being largely regulars with a small number of volunteers. Another idea put forward was that an AAF unit which was fostered by the town or county would have much more local influence and atmosphere than a regular squadron because the men would all have dual roles in both the local community and as part of the squadron as a whole. Finally, there was at the time, more interest in the AAF than in the SR squadrons.

The appointment of Adolf Hitler to the post of Chancellor in Germany in January 1933 prompted a realisation that a new threat to national security was emerging and led to the first of eight rearmament schemes being drawn up and approved by the Cabinet in July 1934.[46] A major expansion of the RAF was announced with the number of Home Defence squadrons being increased from fifty-two to seventy-five. The total first-line strength of the RAF was to be increased to one hundred and twenty-eight squadrons within five years.[47] On 22 May 1935, the British Government voted to treble the number of frontline military aircraft available to defend British soil. This amounted to an increase of fifteen hundred aircraft of all types.[48] However, by July 1936, the lack of a cohesive and modern strategy for the RAF was starting to cause major concerns. As a result of RAF expansion, the Air Council decided to re-organise the Air Defence of Great Britain into four specialised Commands.[49] Under this system, the individual Air Officers Commanding were responsible for the planning and development of their Command, whilst the Chief of the Air Staff remained in overall control of operational policy. This enabled the RAF to function in a more coordinated way and to plan more effectively for the impending war with Germany.

Viscount Swinton was Secretary of State for Air and was given the challenge in 1935 of expanding the RAF. He has been described as "the architect of the renaissance of the Royal Air Force and the most emphatic (Cabinet) exponent of effective rearmament".[50] As the RAF was expanded under a series of schemes which involved setting up a system of "shadow armament" factories operating side by side with industries still engaged in peacetime production, it was envisaged that there would be no interference with normal industry and trade. Thus, the motor-vehicle industry became the leading participant working alongside the manufacture of both airframes and aero-engines. Swinton also helped to end the bitter conflict between the Royal Navy and the RAF over the control of naval aviation which had hampered inter-service co-operation in the 1920s and 1930s.[51]

Following the merger of the SR squadrons into the AAF in 1936, it became apparent that the AAF nationally was running at around 51 per cent of establishment and the idea of a new reserve began to be discussed with emphasis being on the ease of entry into the new reserve. The AAF was violently opposed to any idea of grafting an enlarged reserve onto its organisation.[52] As a result, the RAFVR was formed as a more democratic organisation, largely for men who were interested in flying as a sport with the military aspect and military discipline in the background.[53] Its purpose was to fill the gaps between the entry requirements of the AAF and the regular RAF, "the intention was to convey a clear message that whilst there was an educational hurdle to be surmounted there were to be no social barriers for reservists to cross."[54]

Planning for the new reserve took place within the Air Member for Personnel Department (AMP) where Air Commodore Arthur Tedder was Director of Training. In February 1936 W.L. Scott, a senior civil servant in S7, the branch of the Air Ministry Secretariat which served AMP, put forward a paper incorporating the radical ideas which were being discussed within the department, together with some of his own ideas. It contained proposals which explicitly took account of social attitudes in the mid-1930s. Scott wrote that the intention was to recruit from the poorer secondary school boys to the boys from the more expensive public schools. Entry was to be in the rank of Aircraftsman Second Class (AC2) with promotion to sergeant on the following day. This decision to enrol men as sergeants rather than officers reflects a clear choice between the public-school man and the secondary school man. In practice the RAFVR came to contain men from the wide range of educational background which had been envisaged in its planning – from the universities and public schools to council elementary schools backed up with night school study. Four possible names for the reserves were put forward, Citizen Air Force, Royal Volunteer Air Force, Civic Division of the Royal Air Force and Royal Air Force Volunteer Reserve. There was no doubt "that the public schools as a whole are, even now, extraordinarily ignorant and misinformed about the Service, despite some valuable individual propaganda work. We have in fact scarcely begun to touch what shall be our main source of supply for pilots, and unless we can take some effective steps at once to enlist the support of the schools there is a grave risk that the greatly increased annual requirements will lead to a general lowering of the standards of entry."[55] Scott noted that "the use of the AAF organisation as an alternative to the present scheme based on the existing RAF Reserve had been fully considered by the Air Ministry but had finally been rejected by the Secretary of State, partly because a separate organisation could be set up with less delay, and partly because the proposed Volunteer Reserve in which officers and men were to be on the same social standing could not be developed satisfactorily within the AAF units in the TA organisation."[56]

The RAFVR was not organised as squadrons. Town centres were used close to aerodromes. Treasury approval was obtained in July 1936, but there were some delays in getting money released for flying training between January and April 1937. Between January and April 1937 men had to spend a full time period at an existing Elementary and Reserve Flying Training School (ERFTS) before returning home to continue training at a local airfield. By October 1937 there were nineteen EFRTS in operation. This method of training was new because it was based on a network of civil aerodromes with each of them linked to a town centre. The latter was provided as a centre for the ground instruction of the volunteers and was also intended to be a focal point for their social activities. Men had to attend aerodrome centres on alternative weekends and went to town centres for ground instruction on weekday evenings. There was a compulsory fifteen-day period of continuous annual training. The aerodrome centres were open every day so men could put in additional attendance. It was certainly in the interests of firms running the centres to encourage as much attendance as possible since their income was related to the number of flying hours they produced. After the Munich Conference where Germany's annexation of the Sudetenland was agreed, some who had reached an appropriate stage of training were required to spend a period of attachment to an RAF squadron. In late 1938 AMP noted with satisfaction that around 50 per cent of employers approached had proved willing to allow such periods of release for their men. Not everyone who joined the RAFVR was able to fly and those who did not make the grade as pilots re-mustered as observers and other categories of aircrew. By November 1938 recruitment for observers, wireless operators, air gunners and ground crew began. For the RAFVR, young men were to be attracted from the middle class in its widest sense with no suggestion of any pre-determined social hierarchy. The sporting aspects of flying were to be stressed in recruitment.

Thus, the RAFVR would have a wider appeal to potential pilot recruits and would ensure that background and status did not become an obstacle for enlistment, as perceived to be the case in the AAF. Air Vice-Marshal Arthur

Tedder intended that the RAFVR should not be connected to the County Associations to whom the AAF was connected and largely controlled. He intended to recruit from a wide range, including poorer secondary school boys as well as boys from the more expensive public schools, since these young men from contrasting social backgrounds would have to be able to work together both in the air and on the ground. Subsequently, Tedder's idea was that the RAFVR would be more accessible to local people because regulations surrounding entry were less rigid. Members of the RAFVR did not need to be officers to fly, and it also allowed men without a trade to become serving members, enabling them to train on entry. The decision to create the RAFVR was significant since:

> "In January 1938 the AAF was running at only 51 per cent of its peacetime establishment of pilots and following a committee of enquiry chaired by Under Secretary of State, Harold Balfour, it was forced to begin – in the face of opposition from amongst its squadrons – to train some of its own non-commissioned ground and aircrew members as pilots to compensate for the shortfall of its officer numbers. Even so, it entered the war still seriously below its established strength."[57]

The original plan for the RAFVR was based on Scheme F requirements and was the recruitment of 800 pilots in each of the years 1936, 1937 and 1938, but the Reserve made a late start with recruiting not beginning until January 1937 and the programme had therefore to be modified.[58] By 1939, there were approximately five thousand RAFVR pilots. It was hoped that by January 1939, thirty-three aerodromes and twenty-six town centres would be providing training for a population of 2500 volunteer reservists. It was contemplated also that an aircrew, as opposed to a pilot's selection, would also be formed in the RAFVR. It was also intended eventually to form a ground section into which civilians would be entered for training as officers in equipment, medical, engineering, signals and other specialist duties if and when the need arose.[59] The progress and development of the RAFVR was slow due to lack of aircraft and equipment. It was not until the lack of reserves became seriously alarming in 1938 that there was any large expansion of the RAFVR. Up to the outbreak of war the RAFVR consisted mainly of pilots who had been trained to fly elementary types of aircraft. Some provision of advanced and service aircraft was made in 1938 and 1939 and the scheme was extended to non-pilot aircrew. Combined with the AAF the two reserve forces made up a large pool of pilots and airmen who would be ready to fight if war broke out. By the outbreak of the Second World War, the RAF had a valuable reservoir of sixty-three thousand men trained as pilots as well as in medical and technical trades.[60]

The strain on national resources, combined with the realisation that the pursuit of parity had failed to halt German rearmament, led during the second half of 1937 to a Treasury Review of Defence Expenditure, which in turn caused a complete reappraisal of British overseas and defence policy. Sir Thomas Inskip, Minister for the Co-ordination of Defence, carried this out and he submitted his report to the Cabinet on 15 December 1937. Inskip's review, entitled "Interim Report on Defence Expenditure" marked the start of a fundamental change in British preparations for any future war in the air. He argued that the role of the RAF should not be to deliver an early knockout blow to the Germans but instead to prevent them from knocking out the British.[61] This was a complete reversal of priorities. The emphasis had moved from long-range bomber production to that of fighter production. As a consequence of German rearmament, the Spanish Civil War and the Munich crisis of 1938, the RAF began an expansion programme which resulted in a further eight AAF squadrons being formed. In 1937, priority was given to bomber production, then a year later fewer bombers and more fighters. After the Munich crisis, by late 1938, the emphasis was on creating modern fighter aircraft. At the start of 1939, RAF strength stood at 135 squadrons, and in addition to this, the AAF comprised nineteen squadrons.[62] In August 1939 members of the AAF and RAFVR were embodied into the RAF. There were twenty-one AAF squadrons at the outbreak of war, fourteen squadrons which were fighter units, four squadrons that operated under the control of Coastal Command and two squadrons whose duties were army co-operation. Shores notes:

> "At this stage, as the AAF was being mobilised, all units were
> undoubtedly at their most 'pure' as 'auxiliary' squadrons.
> Certainly their ground crew personnel were essentially those who
> had faithfully served their chosen units throughout much of the
> 1930s and who were all enlisted under provisions which allowed
> the AAF personnel to refuse a posting to any other unit."[63]

In 1939 the AAF was merged into the RAF for the duration of hostilities, furthermore, a major change in recruitment took place in 1939 when a

Committee under the chairmanship of Sir James Barnes, Under Secretary of State for Air recommended increases in pay and allowances for the AAF and also required them to accept airmen pilots, first by training some of their own ground crew and then by taking in direct-entry men. Many AAF squadrons reacted violently to this order but were forced to comply and this resulted in a handful of AAF Sergeant Pilots in British AAF squadrons. On enlistment, recruits for other ranks were guaranteed that they would never be called upon to serve further than five miles from their home airfield. By the end of the war, the original twenty-one AAF squadrons "became increasingly indistinguishable from all of the other squadrons fielded by the wartime RAF",[64] due to an influx of pilots and aircrew from the RAFVR, the RAF and aircrew from allied forces and original members of the AAF being posted out to different squadrons. Furthermore, all new members to the Royal Air Force during the war were recruited and trained through the RAFVR.

Conclusion

This chapter has used existing literature and documents from the National Archive to analyse the reasons why not one but three different forms of the TAF were formed. Using the TA and the RNVR as a model, the men in the Air Ministry and the government shaped what they believed would be a reserve which could be called upon, should the need arise, to defend the country. As Peter Dennis noted when writing about the TA, "the volunteers had originally been established as a private and exclusive military club, membership of which entailed the payment of entrance and annual fees."[65] This idea is reflected by some of the AAF squadrons who took on the characteristics of a club, and perhaps explains why the AAF wanted to maintain their exclusivity throughout the organisation's existence. Similarly, Lord Haldane wanted the TA to be managed locally, and the AAF was managed by local committees as well. Furthermore, it is very apparent that the creation and organisation of the RAF reserve during the inter-war period was based upon the recruitment process and structure of the army; therefore, being nominated for a commission was linked to social and political influence. It is understandable that the TA would have such an influence on the creation of the RAF reserve, since throughout its history it had been regarded as successful. Also, there had never been an RAF reserve before, so the government was bound in a way to look at what else existed. The setting up of two different organisations, the AAF and the SR, was an experiment so that the conditions of service provided for enlistment on as broad a basis as possible. Moreover, they were looking for the most efficient and economical organisation. Once it was realised that the AAF was the more popular of the two, the SR was merged into the AAF; the experiment had drawn to its conclusion. However, the poor performance of the Auxiliaries in terms of recruitment meant that the idea for a new reserve with the emphasis being on ease of entry came along and was acted upon, bringing the RAFVR into the picture. Consequently, this chapter has provided a detailed examination of the reasoning behind the way in which the TAF was developed, and has focused on the ideas behind the decisions which were made, based upon the existing two reserve forces.

Chapter 2

The Recruitment Process of the Territorial Air Force 1925–1939

Introduction

This chapter examines the way in which men were recruited for the three different organisations – the Auxiliary Air Force (AAF), the Special Reserve (SR) squadrons and the Royal Air Force Volunteer Reserve (RAFVR). It will consider how these men joined, and what kinds of men were accepted into the organisations as both pilots and officers. It will also analyse the influences class and social status had on recruitment in the run up to the Second World War. As Christopher Shores points out:

> "The activities and recruiting policies of some of these units during the 1930s led many to gain the impression that the members of these squadrons were arrogant and snobbish, considering themselves to be a privileged elite – an impression which appears on occasion not to have been undeserved. Had these young men, with their sports cars, hunters and Savile Row uniforms, been a little more liberal in their entry policies, the RAF might have had rather more trained pilots in the AAF and fewer vacant slots to fill from the slim reserves of the regular RAF."[1]

It will be a central aim of this chapter to assess the validity of this idea. The chapter also explores the key differences between the Auxiliary squadrons and the SR squadrons, as well as the main reasons for the idea of merging the SR squadrons into the AAF squadrons. It will briefly discuss the newly formed University Air Squadrons (UAS) which were set up to promote "air mindedness" and to stimulate an interest in and research into matters aeronautical.[2] The chapter then considers recruitment into the RAFVR and finally gives an insight into the key role played by voluntary activity in the inter-war period.

19

Churchill, in 1924, announced a new proposal which would begin the formation of the TAF, allowing £20,000 from the annual estimates. The plan was to set up six squadrons which would be stationed near engineering centres. However, the Under Secretary of State highlighted potential problems if the TAF squadrons were not managed by the existing County Associations, since they had the necessary experience and administration skills to manage the new volunteer squadrons efficiently. In this way, the new TAF would function in a way, as explained in the previous chapter, which was similar to the Pals battalions from the First World War where recruitment was based on both friendships and working relationships and familiarity with a particular area were all important in increasing recruitment to the army. It was hoped therefore, that the TAF squadrons would attract a steady flow of volunteers who would serve on a part-time basis at a local aerodrome in familiar surroundings, and that this close proximity to the local town would mean that each new squadron would be taken to the heart of the local community.

In the initial formation of the AAF, the Commanding Officer of each unit would be appointed by the Air Ministry after consultation with the Territorial Force Association (TFA) concerned. The Commanding Officer, after consultation with the TFA, would nominate to the Air Ministry gentlemen who would be able to fill the remaining vacancies on the establishment of his unit. Officers had to be physically fit and aged upon appointment between twenty-five and thirty-three. Officers would be required to provide service dress uniform only. They would receive an outfit grant of £40 and a full issue of flying kit gratis. The annual training required of an officer of the Territorial Air Force consisted of: instructional parades, periodic flying and annual camp. Officers within the authorized establishment would receive pay and allowances at current RAF rates. For the other ranks, men must be between the ages of eighteen and thirty-eight, and be physically fit.[3]

This information, which sets out the terms and conditions of recruitment and service within the TAF, was also superimposed upon the terms and conditions of the AAF. Furthermore, within the Air Ministry documents there is a noticeable muddling up between the terms for the AAF and the TAF in the early years of the 1920s.

The Secretary of State for Air, Sir Samuel Hoare, announced at Colchester on 18 October 1923 that "changes to the Royal Air Force would involve three kinds of squadrons. In the first place there will be a backbone of highly trained regular squadrons for the work of fighting, and in addition, a number of Special Reserve squadrons, one third of the personnel of which will be composed of regulars and the remainder of reserve men. There will be a third section of auxiliary bombing squadrons, in which there is to be only a small contingent of regular personnel for purpose of administration and instruction."[4] By this means the country would be provided for the first time with a substantial air force for home defence with an increase of less than ten thousand officers and men. In other words, the existing air power would be doubled with an addition of only one third of its present personnel.[5] Furthermore, if this new plan was to be successful, the patriotic co-operation of the youth and able-bodied men of the nation would be important, since in the main, the SR squadrons and the AAF squadrons will be entirely dependent upon volunteers.[6]

Table 1: Principles governing the SR and AAF squadrons[7]

Special Reserve Squadrons	Auxiliary Air Force Squadrons
SR officers and airmen were recruited directly by the units.	Officers and airmen were enlisted through the local Territorial and AAF associations.
Officers were taught to fly in the units.	Officers were not accepted unless they had learned to fly. On acceptance the cost of training was refunded.
Airmen had to be skilled tradesmen and were enlisted in their trades.	Airmen need not be skilled tradesmen. They were taught their trades in the units.
An SR squadron was normally organised in two or three flights, one of which was entirely regular and the others composed of SR personnel. Headquarters consisted entirely of regular personnel.	An AAF organisation was normally organised in three flights of AAF personnel, controlled and trained by a small permanent headquarters staff.
Each squadron was commanded by a regular officer,	Each squadron was commanded by an AAF officer.
The squadron was formed near centres of engineering population.	Squadrons were formed by large towns and had town headquarters where training was carried out throughout the year, culminating in an annual camp.

Following the new Auxiliary Air Force and Air Forces Reserve Act of 1924, there was an allowance for six auxiliary squadrons and seven SR squadrons, the idea being to supplement the RAF personnel with additional volunteers.

The AAF and SR Squadrons were in direct competition with each other to attract as many men as possible. Pilot volunteers to the SR were taught to fly within the squadron. Volunteer airmen had to be skilled tradesmen in civilian life and remained within their trade in the squadron. These SR squadrons were formed near centres of engineering, therefore ensuring that their appeal would be to men who wanted a closer connection with the life of the regular RAF. Consequently, the SR squadrons resembled the militia from the early days of the Territorial Army. The Auxiliary Air Force, on the other hand, recruited both officers and airmen through the local Territorial and Auxiliary Air Force Associations. Officers were not accepted unless they could already fly, and on acceptance, the cost of their flying training was refunded. Airmen did not need to be skilled tradesmen because they were taught their trade within the unit, giving airmen recruits the opportunity to learn something totally different from their civilian occupation. Squadrons were formed near large towns, and town headquarters carried out training throughout the year culminating in a two-week annual camp. In 1925, it was noted that "there has been a notable awakening of interest in all parts of the country in aviation. This enthusiasm is now taking practical form in the support of flying clubs. The RAF is a corps of specialists and only a high degree of skill in individual trades can ensure that the technical equipment can work effectively."[8]

Recruiting within the Special Reserve Squadrons

The Air Ministry appealed through *The Times* and other newspapers for volunteers to be trained as flying officers on the short-term commission basis. Although applications were to be asked for in writing, over 100 men within the age limits of eighteen and twenty-nine called personally at the Air Ministry for official forms. By the late afternoon, numerous postal applications were received.[9] Advertisements made clear that officer candidates must be at the peak of their physical fitness, since in general terms, at least 50 per cent of candidates failed to come up to the required standard. Moreover, those candidates who were living sedentary lives, should begin to prepare themselves physically for their examination. It was hoped that by the end of 1924, there would be more than 800 pilots in the reserve squadrons.[10]

Normal ages for recruitment would be eighteen to twenty-five, but up to thirty-one if candidates have previously served as a member of the

RAF. The initial period of enlistment would be five years, which could be extended with the consent of the Air Council for further periods. Officers were taught to fly at public expense. For the obligatory uniform of breeches and trousers, boots ankle, black, puttees, shirts, white and walking stick (RAF pattern), a grant of £40 was made available for those not previously commissioned in the RAF.[11]

A good example of how SR squadrons were formed and how men were recruited can be seen through the experience of 501 (County of Gloucester) Fighter Squadron. David Watkins, author of the squadron's history mentions that "in July 1929 two RAF officers arrived at Filton with instructions received from No 1 Air Defence Group to form an SR Cadre Squadron (Day Bomber) in accordance with existing establishment."[12] One of the first airmen to be recruited was Len Prater who remembered that "after an initial application by letter to join the squadron, there followed an interview with the Adjutant where we were questioned about our interests and reasons for joining. Following a medical examination we were officially sworn in, but uniforms were not issued on the camp so we had to report to the TA & Auxiliary Headquarters at Whiteladies Road in Bristol."[13] Once a month weekend camps were held which ensured that airmen were proficient in their chosen trade, as all engineering work was thoroughly checked. Consequently all airmen were well trained and recruitment via letter, interview and medical ensured that recruitment followed a specific format.

Getting into an SR squadron as a pilot was largely based on somebody knowing somebody who might make a good member. He would be introduced to the Commanding Officer and if thought suitably compatible, then the wheels were set in motion for the usual Air Ministry interview and medical. Another factor was the provision for taking at least six months off for continuous training. Later, the Air Ministry dropped the six months off work plan for training and agreed that pilots could be trained at weekends.[14] In the case of 501 Squadron, the first few officers joined in June 1932 as "Pilots in Training". "Already a qualified pilot and member of the local flying club, Cautley Naismyth Shaw owned his own aeroplane, a de Havilland Gypsy Moth, and with his other fellow pilots, Ashley Hall, Tubby Bathurst and Bristol stockbroker Thurlow Laws, Shaw made frequent weekend visits to other flying clubs at Le Touquet and Brussels."[15]

Recruiting for 502 (Ulster) Squadron began straight after the squadron had been formed, and took various forms. In July 1925, a 502 Squadron

Recruiting Office was established in rental premises at 9 Town Hall Street, just off Victoria Street in Belfast, and just over a year later larger premises were rented on the top floor of a block of business premises close to Donegall Square. As part of the recruitment drive, representatives of the local press were taken on flights which were then well reported in the local newspapers and in journals such as *Ulster Life*. In addition, groups of workers from local firms were brought to Aldergrove to see the squadron at work. Such visits were often the result of talks given to local organisations, schools and societies by the Commanding Officer. On 29 March 1928 at Belfast Technical College, he gave an illustrated lecture to 140 representatives of the Association of Shipbuilders, Engineers and Draughtsmen which was followed by a visit to Aldergrove by 150 members of the Association. From time to time, the squadron carried out "around Northern Ireland" flights with formations of aircraft, and these were usually well reported by the press. By the mid-1930s, annual air displays at Aldergrove were also proving to be increasingly important in encouraging recruitment. The first of these was held in July 1933, aircraft from 502 Squadron participated as did visiting aircraft from 602 (County of Glasgow) Squadron, Auxiliary Air Force.[16]

Recruiting within the Auxiliary Air Force

Trenchard's 1919 White Paper showed that "he realised that a fighting service must possess a non-regular branch with its roots firmly set in the civil life of the country. He visualised his Auxiliaries as successors of the old mounted yeomanry. Men who were now attracted to flying machines, who had leisure and a thirst for adventure and were prepared to indulge in uniform."[17] The conditions of service were different from those of the RAF, the main difference being that the AAF was to be raised and maintained by the County Territorial Associations and manned by locally recruited non-regular personnel, with only a small core of regulars as permanent staff. Lord Edmond Grosvenor was the first commanding officer of No 601 Squadron, and its distinguished membership included Sir Philip Sassoon who was later to become Under-secretary of State for Air. The Marquis of Clydesdale flew with No 602; Lord Willoughby de Broke with 605 and Viscount Runciman with No 607.

Those in power within society in the 1920s and 1930s, for example, were men from prominent local and national families, so the recruitment of officers within the AAF was often shaped by the values of these social elites and based on suitability and background. Thus, as Ross notes:

> "Would be officers had to face stiff obstacles. If a vacancy occurred, serving officers would be asked for recommendations. As in the case of airmen, candidates were required to be British subjects of pure European decent, and the sons of British parents. They were first interviewed in depth by the Adjutant. If he felt they were suitable he sent them to the CO's house for social assessment by the Commanding Officer and his wife."[18]

Moreover, Shores goes on to argue that "looking at the contacts many of these pilots undoubtedly had, given the social circles in which they moved, they seem to have had many friends in high places, ready and willing to speak well of them."[19] Tom Moulson, author of *601 (County of London) Squadron* points out that "Number 601 Squadron was born in White's Club, St James's, W1. This was the favourite club and invariable haunt of Lord Edward Grosvenor, a veteran pilot of the First World War, who, while politicians struggled with the idea of forming a territorial air force, proceeded to select members of the club to serve under him in the first squadron."[20]

The evidence which has been collected is in part anecdotal and in part objective and will be presented in more detail in the next chapter. However, it suggests that during the 1930s men were recruited into the AAF on the basis of their social backgrounds. These qualities varied considerably across the country and depended in many cases upon the personal preferences of the commanding officer. For example, "Johnnie Johnson, one of the RAF's top fighter aces, remained convinced that he had failed to get into an AAF squadron when the interviewing officer discovered he was not a fox hunting man. On another AAF squadron there was always 'a social test' in which a prospective officer candidate would be given Sunday lunch and 'several glasses of sherry' to discover if his parlance was no longer that of a gentleman."[21]

Whilst some common attributes were shared by everyone, others were more specifically linked to regions of the United Kingdom. Common trends show that many recruits for officer status were educated at public school followed by attendance at either Oxford or Cambridge University. Also, many of them took part in elite sporting activities such as rowing and motorcar racing. Many worked in business, finance, law or had political interests. Lieutenant Colonel Dore, CO of 604 (County of Middlesex) Squadron noted that:

> "The intention was to ensure that 604 got the best material possible for its officer candidates, and this inevitably meant recruitment came from the upper echelons of 1930s society: the public schools, with Malvern being to the fore, the universities, Oxford and Cambridge, the legal profession, the Stock Exchange and the City. I gave each applicant marks for his school record in scholarship and athletics; and if he could ride a horse, or drive a car or a motorcycle, or sail a boat, or ski or play the piano, I gave him extra marks."[22]

Anecdotal evidence suggests that political and aristocratic connections, coupled with a background in financial or legal institutions, were prerequisites to membership. Furthermore, the selection of the upper-middle classes, who had developed networks from either public school or university, meant that in many ways, volunteering for these squadrons was based primarily on family and social connections rather than technical skills. Another practical factor that played a significant part in the early recruitment of officers was the possession of a flying licence. All entrants to the AAF had to possess a flying licence, and flying was a very expensive hobby. In some cases, officers within the AAF owned their own aircraft.

Empire Air Days helped increase recruitment among the airmen, with the general public being able to come onto the aerodrome and see flying displays, watch the training lectures and see the engineers working on the squadron aircraft. Press coverage of these events helped to maintain a healthy interest in each local squadron and strengthen links between the aerodrome and the local community as well as to boost local support. Additionally, terms and conditions of enlistment were also printed in the local press and local buildings were often taken over to act as points of recruitment for the ground crew.

The Merger of the five Special Reserve Squadrons into the Auxiliary Air Force

In 1927, Air Commodore Hearson decided that the SR squadrons should be converted to AAF squadrons, but the Air Ministry felt that it was far too soon to be drawing this conclusion after only a years' experience. The question was raised again in 1930, largely due to the fact that the lines of difference between the two reserve forces had become blurred, resulting in the AAF beginning to train its pilots, and the SR beginning to accept trained pilots. Moreover, it had become apparent that the SR squadrons had struggled to recruit airmen due to the need for them to be skilled tradesmen, and as such, to remain within their trades. Many of the volunteers had been keener to train for new trades so that they were not just doing the same trade in both service and civilian life. Consequently, the SR squadrons appeared to function in the same way as AAF squadrons, but with a higher contingent of expensive regular servicemen.[23]

In 1935, the matter was discussed within the Air Ministry when it was noted by the Deputy Director Plans that "there is a marked tendency in SR squadrons for the regular and special reserve personnel to keep apart. The SR personnel naturally feel that they can run their own show, and are not dependent on the regulars. The result is that the *espirit de corps*, so noticeable in auxiliary squadrons, is less apparent in the special reserve."[24] Furthermore, Air Chief Marshal R Brooke-Popham recommended the merger noting that:

> "Special Reserve personnel are only available at weekends, i.e. for 1½ days in a week, in the case of several squadrons, at the average weekend only about 20% of the Special Reserve personnel attend and owing to this irregular attendance, Special Reserve personnel seldom become sufficiently competent to have maintenance work wholly entrusted to them. Close supervision by regulars is essential if the safety of the flying personnel is to be considered. Moreover, annual cost for personnel in SR squadrons amounts to £16,000 as opposed to £10,000 for Auxiliary personnel. Consequently the merger of the SR squadrons into the AAF is recommended."[25]

A secret document in April 1935 from the Air Council entitled "The Future of the Special Reserve Squadrons", points out that the original decision of 1923 to form two types of units embodying non-regular personnel, the SR and the AAF squadrons, was taken in order that two alternative methods of development may be tried out simultaneously, there being no data then available to enable a judgement to be formed as to which type of unit would be likely to be the more effective and have the greater popular appeal.

So successful, however, were the AAF considered to be after a year, it was decided to limit the number of SR squadrons to five and form eight squadrons of the AAF. Reasons discussed relating to the merger of the SR into the AAF are listed below:[26]

Table 2: To Maintain or Merge the Special Reserve Squadrons

To Maintain The Special Reserve Squadrons	To Merge The Special Reserve Into The Auxiliary Air Force
By virtue of the substantial regular element within the squadron, this type of unit is definitely more efficient for war purposes than a squadron of the AAF. In particular, it is considered that AAF squadrons would need further training in bombing and armament work after the outbreak of war.	There is a greater *espirit de corps* in the AAF.
The success of the AAF squadrons has been mainly a question of their geographical location, which has accounted, in particular, for the great success of the squadrons formed in the neighbourhood of London. It is suggested that, where AAF squadrons have been formed in neighbourhoods less suitable from the recruiting point of view, their progress has been no better than the SR squadrons.	There is no doubt as to the great political popularity of the AAF squadrons. There are not sufficient funds at present to form additional squadrons of the AAF so the conversion of the five SR squadrons into AAF squadrons would be popular and politically advantageous.
	An AAF unit is somewhat cheaper than an SR unit.
	So long as the number of regular squadrons remains small, there is a strong case for retaining the SR squadrons in view of the military value of the regular flights.
	The conversion of the SR squadrons from night bombers into day bombers, removes one of the main difficulties which has in the past been mooted against changing these units into AAF.

	It might be possible to improve the bombing and armament training of the AAF squadrons, therefore removing the argument that they are less efficient for war.
	There is a shortage of regular personnel and converting the SR squadrons into AAF squadrons would release some regular personnel for utilisation in the new regular units to be formed under the government expansion scheme.
	Conversion into AAF squadrons would be of assistance in simplifying personnel administration and accelerating the flow of pilots through squadrons with a view to building up an AAF Reserve.
	The unit "belongs" to the volunteers and has accordingly a much stronger squadron spirit.
	An AAF unit fostered by the town or county has more local influence and atmosphere. In consequence the ground is better prepared for war recruiting on a squadron basis similar to that of the Territorial Army in 1914.
	The scheme is popular and there are now several applications for the formation of more AAF squadrons.

During 1936, the five Special Reserve squadrons, 500, 501, 502, 503 and 504, were merged into the Auxiliary Air Force, and the two reserves became one. The original five SR squadrons did keep their squadron numbers, even though all AAF squadron numbers were located in the 600 series.[27]

Recruiting within the University Air Squadrons

The first UASs were set up at Oxford and Cambridge Universities in 1925. Their aim was "to promote 'air mindedness' and to stimulate an interest in, and research into, matters aeronautical."[28] Each squadron was staffed and funded by the Air Ministry, but membership involved no service obligations

29

and they did not wear uniform. By 1931, a set of formal regulations were published in AP1401. This restricted membership to seventy-five in each squadron based on annual intakes of twenty-five for a three-year degree course. It also specified the content of the Proficiency Certificate, which required attendance at annual camp, the accumulation of at least fifteen flying hours, three of which should be solo, and passing examinations in the theory of flight, rigging, engines, airmanship and air pilotage (navigation). The new aims of the UASs were 'to encourage an interest in flying' and to 'assist those who might wish to join the RAF'.[29]

In Oxford, an aeroplane hangar was located at the headquarters in Manor Road, Holywell. The hanger contained a Bristol Fighter and a workshop hanger containing several aircraft engines, instruments and accessories. Instruction was given in the following categories: aeroplane engines, the construction and rigging of aeroplanes, wireless telegraphy and telephony, air pilotage, aerial photography, armaments and aeroplane navigational instruments.

It was laid down that during term time there would be no flying, but a fortnight was set aside during the "long vacation" during which the squadron would operate as a unit at a Service aerodrome. During this fortnight, a flight of instructional aeroplanes with flying instructors would be allocated to the squadron and additional facilities would be provided for members of the squadron by Service units on the station.[30]

The third UAS was opened at London University in 1935 and by then members were actively being encouraged to join the RAF or the RAFVR after 1936. In May 1939, the Military Training Act was introduced which meant that all young men aged between twenty and twenty-one, including undergraduates, had to register for military service. This meant that there was a liability to be called up for a six-month period of full-time training, although this was never put into practice. Anyone who had signed up as a reservist prior to April was exempt from the period of military training. Recruitment to these UASs was by word of mouth, recruitment posters and fresher's fairs. The three UASs were disbanded once war was declared in 1939.[31]

Recruiting within the Royal Air Force Volunteer Reserve

As the need to recruit more reserve pilots increased, it became clear that the AAF was an unsuitable organisation to handle the vast number of reserve pilots who had to be recruited and trained. The idea of a Volunteer Reserve was developed in 1936. "Broadly the aim was to train 800 pilots a year in an organisation based not on the County Associations but on town centres situated in industrial areas. The necessary sites were acquired, the contracts with civil flying firms concluded, and the RAFVR came into being in April 1937."[32] The educational requirements would be the same as those for a short service commission and applicants should have attended either a public or other secondary school with achievement up to the standard of the School Certificate of the Oxford and Cambridge Examination Board. This was a very broad requirement and meant that both part- and full-time study could be used to raise the applicant to the required level.[33]

Air Chief Marshal Lord Tedder intended that the RAFVR should not be connected to the County Associations to whom the AAF was connected and largely controlled. He intended to recruit from a wide range, including poorer secondary school boys as well as boys from the more expensive public schools, since these young men from contrasting social backgrounds would have to be able to work together both in the air and on the ground. Subsequently the idea was that the RAFVR would be more accessible to local people because regulations surrounding entry were less rigid. Members of the RAFVR did not need to be officers to fly, and it also allowed men without a trade to become serving members, enabling them to train on entry.

By 1939, there were approximately five thousand RAFVR pilots. Combined with the AAF the two reserve forces made up a large pool of pilots and airmen who would be ready to fight if war broke out. By the outbreak of the Second World War, the RAF had a valuable reservoir of sixty-three thousand men trained as pilots as well as in medical and technical trades.[34]

At the start of 1939, RAF strength stood at 135 squadrons, and in addition to this, the AAF comprised nineteen squadrons.[35] In August 1939 members of the AAF and RAFVR were embodied into the RAF, and all new recruitment into the RAF was through the RAFVR. There were twenty-one Auxiliary Air Force squadrons at the outbreak of war, fourteen squadrons who were fighter units, four squadrons who operated under the control of Coastal Command and two squadrons whose duties were army co-operation. At this time the AAF was at its most pure. In other words, it was completely made up of volunteers who were all tied to the squadron's locality. Once the war began, each AAF squadron was merged into the RAF and began to fill up with members of the RAF and RAFVR, as well as their original members being posted on to different squadrons.

Overall, the reserve forces of the RAF began with two types, the auxiliaries and the SRs, and ended with only one, the AAF. The SR squadrons had merged with the AAF prior to the Second World War, and the AAF had been amalgamated into the RAF in 1939 when war broke out. The RAFVR also became part of the RAF proper as the war progressed and the men who served within either branch of the reserves became full time RAF personnel for the duration of the war. In fact, the only interest that their original part time status held was in terms of their local appeal and interest. As the war developed, the local press often commented on the exploits of former AAF members and charted their careers, as the squadrons became diluted by regular RAF personnel and pilots from overseas. Furthermore, the recruitment processes for the AAF changed after the Second World War due largely to the growth of technical skills which were required to fly and maintain aircraft and the knowledge required to fulfil these tasks required greater education.

Voluntary activity

Voluntary activity within the reserve forces is also an area that has been neglected by historians, and one of the themes of this book is the importance of voluntarism within the AAF in a period when the state continued to rely upon private individuals to play a crucial role in the defence of the nation. Many squadrons ran an active social programme and some took on the characteristics of socially exclusive clubs like the Royal Aero Club.[36] Indeed, the AAF needs to be seen in the context of changes in voluntary social activity during the interwar period when a wide range of new clubs were being created for young men, including Toc H, a voluntary organisation with Christian values, formed in Belgium in 1927[37] and the Round Table, a professional voluntary organisation which was set up in Norwich in 1927, for young men between the ages of eighteen and forty-five.[38] Members of these voluntary groups, including the AAF, were drawn in large part from aristocratic, gentry and bourgeois families in the region and can be seen as part of a long tradition in which social, cultural and political links were constantly being forged between traditional landed society and an emerging middle class culture. It has long been recognised, for example, that the younger sons of landed and aristocratic families entered the Law, the Church, the Army and commerce and this meant that the deep divides that often characterised social relations in many European societies rarely characterised the British class system. These familial networks linking land, commerce and the professions were buttressed later in the nineteenth century by public schools and universities which helped forge a new elite culture made up of members from both upper and middle class society.[39] In keeping with Rotary Clubs and other elite voluntary groups, the auxiliary squadrons attracted members from upper and middle-class society who came from this new elite culture and played an important role in maintaining that culture. This is particularly apparent in 600 and 601 Squadrons; but do we see a similar pattern in provincial squadrons?

Voluntarism certainly played a significant role in national life but was fundamentally rooted in specific regional and local contexts, and it is here that a military tradition of voluntarism was most deeply rooted. There is a long tradition in British society that mistrusts standing armies, seeing them as dangerous forces that might be foisted on a nation and used to oppress it. In place of the standing army, it has celebrated the virtues of a citizen army made up of volunteer units recruited and operating in specific localities, willing and able to defend their families and communities when the need arose. The ideal of the citizen army was an expression of community solidarity, recruited from a local population, taking its identity from a particular region and enjoying – at least in theory – a close and almost organic relationship with that community. The AAF was formed according to the ideals of this enduring tradition.

Conclusion

The key focus of this chapter therefore was the way in which men joined the AAF, SR and RAFVR. The chapter has also looked at what kinds of men were selected as officers and also what influence social class had upon recruitment. Therefore, men joining the SR applied directly to their local squadron. Here those men who wanted to fly were trained and those who wanted to become airmen had to be skilled tradesmen. Men joining the AAF were recruited through the local Territorial and Auxiliary Air Force Association, those men wanting to become pilots had to already be able to fly, whilst those wanting to become airmen could select any trade and they were given skilled training. Men volunteering for the RAFVR had to be educated up to School Certificate, and were enlisted as airmen before being promoted to sergeants when they began their flying training at civilian flying schools.

Recruitment into the SR and AAF was largely based upon someone knowing somebody suitable, as well as background and suitability with the interview process taking on a social test as well. In theory, those joining the RAFVR would face no social barriers, as background and status were not to be obstacles to enlistment. This chapter has analysed the ideal way to be recruited into one of these three organisations. The question that the next chapter will answer will be, does the research support the current literature which suggests that the AAF was a gentleman's flying club and the RAFVR a citizen's air force?

Chapter 3

The Social Composition of the Territorial Air Force Prior to 1939

Introduction

This chapter will examine the social composition of the Territorial Air Force (TAF). The prevailing thesis is that the Auxiliary Air Force (AAF) was a "gentleman's flying club", and that it was so rigid in its recruitment processes that there were never enough men to fulfil its needs. Subsequently, a new reserve, the Royal Air Force Volunteer Reserve (RAFVR), was then developed to remove the social and class barriers to recruitment which those choosing to enter the AAF faced by creating what was to be a "citizen's air force". Analysing the data in this chapter will allow these assumptions to be tested.

This chapter contains all of the research data in the form of both discussion, and in the form of tables. The data was collected over a five-year period. The research began by using the *London Gazette* to identify all men within the AAF, (including those of the five SR Squadrons which were merged into the AAF in 1936) who were commissioned between the years of 1925 and 1939. Once each squadron had been identified, its members were listed together with the date of their commission. Each squadron and each individual name were then cross-referenced with *The Times* Digital Archive. This gives a list of all of the news articles featuring the individual's name. Each newspaper article was then read to retrieve any biographical information about the newly commissioned officer. Ten categories were selected by the author as representing the activities of a young man from a specifically high- or middle-class group. The categories selected were as follows:

Attending a public school.
Attending Oxford or Cambridge University.
Attending any other university.

Taking part in elite sport – defined as rowing, yachting, fencing, horse riding/hunting, shooting, archery.
Marriage announcement in *The Times*.
Birth announcement in *The Times*.
Death announcement in *The Times*.
Profession, business or industry.
Family business.
University Air Squadron (UAS).

It was decided that these ten categories could be measured and could be used to suggest the social status of a young officer recruit. Moreover, these categories could in fact be used to measure status across the civilian population during this period too. A Google search of the man's full name was also undertaken which threw up individual squadron web pages as well as the Commonwealth Graves Commission and the research of other individuals. Finally, squadron histories were also used to try to find out biographical information about all of the men who had been identified. This method of identifying men and then discovering their own individual information was used across the AAF and the RAFVR. This chapter, along with Chapter 5, will help to provide an answer to the question which asks whether the TAF squadrons across the United Kingdom were different according to region. It will also go some way to decide whether or not the experiences, social make-up and exploits of the two London squadrons, to whom most of the literature pertains, were mirrored by other squadrons and in particular, the case study squadron, across the United Kingdom.

When looking at the social composition of the TAF, it is important to distinguish between the AAF, which was made up of the AAF and the five squadrons of the SR, which had been merged into the AAF in 1936, and the RAFVR, which was created in 1936 to cope with the recruiting problems of the AAF. Indeed, Ian White in his history of 604 (County of Middlesex) Squadron noted that:

"The Air Force reserves underwent significant changes in 1936. Experience with the Special Reserve and AAF units had shown that in terms of economy, recruiting success, professional standards, morale and popularity, the auxiliary squadrons out-performed those of the Special Reserve. The AAF was less expensive to operate due to it having fewer regulars in its establishment, recruitment was easier as there were fewer constraints on the volunteers, professional standards were regarded as being higher, morale was also higher because each squadron was seen to belong to its members and in terms of popularity, several County Territorial Associations were keen to establish more."[1]

The chapter is divided into two sections so that the differences between the social composition of the AAF and the RAFVR can be identified.

The Auxiliary Air Force and Special Reserves

Available literature surrounding the AAF focuses on the experiences and composition of 600 and 601 Squadron, located in London, and presents an image of the pre-war AAF as a "gentleman's flying club." This research has found biographical information for a significant number of men who were enlisted as AAF and SR officers.

Table 3: Auxiliary Air Force and Special Reserve Initial Data

Squadron Number	Total of Identified Men	Total Men With Biographies	Percentage %
600	69	26	38
601	72	44	61
602	40	23	58
603	45	38	84
604	38	13	34
605	52	8	15
607	25	11	44
608	32	20	63
609	20	15	75
610	17	11	65
611	18	11	61
612	20	11	55
613	5	3	60
614	19	12	63

Squadron Number	Total of Identified Men	Total Men With Biographies	Percentage %
615	17	10	59
616	5	4	80
500	27	15	56
501	17	7	41
502	17	13	76
503	8	4	50
504	22	17	77
TOTAL	**585**	**316**	**55 (Average)**

Many of the young men who were approached by newly formed squadron Commanding Officers were from similar backgrounds, and these men often knew each other from their school days, or through their own family connections. This becomes apparent when each individual squadron is studied separately. Where possible, the backgrounds of the pre-war officers are presented and then contrasted to the backgrounds of the post-war officers to assess the degree of difference in recruitment procedures and social composition. Is there evidence of a shift from a social elite to a more technocratic and democratic organisation following the impact of the Second World War? Are there regional variations in the social backgrounds of officer elites?

Detailed information on the backgrounds of officers recruited to join some of the auxiliary squadrons is often lacking, due primarily to the lack of existing detailed research on these squadrons. Furthermore, it has been virtually impossible to trace the backgrounds of those men who served in AAF squadrons who were not officers. All of the Squadron Associations have been contacted and supporting information has been used to help clarify the picture. Where information has been located there has been more of it available for officers than airmen.

Much of the evidence suggests that during the 1930s men were recruited into the Auxiliary Air Force on the basis of their social backgrounds. These qualities varied considerably across the country and depended in many cases upon the personal preferences of the commanding officer. Whilst some common attributes were shared by everyone, others were more specifically linked to regions of the UK, providing an insight into the contrasting business and industrial interests of the regions as well as between the metropolis and the provinces.

Mansell[2] in discussing the pre-war Auxiliary's notes:

> "The Auxiliaries represented *par excellence,* that powerful
> amateur tradition which characterised so much of British life
> before the war…to be an Auxiliary, it was essential to be the right
> person from the right background. The expense of the Auxiliary
> lifestyle saw to that if nothing else did…The AAF was reluctant
> to sacrifice its exclusive character to serve wider interests."[3]

Southern Squadrons

The two London squadrons form the basis upon which most historians
have made judgements about the AAF. 600 (City of London) Squadron was
formed on 15 October 1925 at Northolt, before moving to Hendon in 1926;
it was affiliated to the City of London Territorial Association, and most of
its members worked in the City at Lloyds, the Stock Exchange, or in other
financial firms and legal institutions. Hans Onderwater suggests that they
considered flying to be the young gentleman's new pleasure and the sky his
new hunting ground.[4] *The Times* in 1929 noted that "this City of London
Squadron is largely recruited from the men of London who are engaged in
banks, big business houses and offices, and the fact that it has reached its
present efficiency is a notable testimony to their keenness and intelligence."[5]

There was a great deal of publicity surrounding the creation of the new
squadron and articles in the national press helped with recruiting. The
first Adjutant and Flying Instructor of the squadron was The Hon James
H.B. Rodney MC, considered by the Commanding Officer (CO) to be "the
right man". Several of the young men who were recruited as officer pilots
for 600 Squadron had similar backgrounds. Freddie Guest, Roger Nathanial
Frankland, Robert Francis Gore Lea, Anthony Henry Hamilton Tollemache
and George Dawson Damer had family links to the aristocracy. Many of
the young men had been to public schools such as Eton or Winchester,
and then moved on to either Oxford or Cambridge, including Anthony
Henry Tollemache, Samuel Charles Elworthy, and Edward Colbeck-Welch.
Some had political interests; for example, Freddie Guest was a Liberal
Party MP and George Ambrose Lloyd, Lord Lloyd of Dolbran was MP for
West Staffordshire. Many of the men had elite sporting interests such as
motorcar racing, athletics, skiing and rowing. Others worked in the City
such as Charles Gambier Jenyns, who worked at the Stock Exchange,

or Ralph Hiscox who worked at Lloyds, or Samuel Charles Elworthy who worked in the legal profession.

Summer camp was considered to be the highlight of the auxiliary officers' life, two weeks of constant flying and camaraderie; in 1932, 600 Squadron's annual camp was at Tangmere. One requirement of summer camp was that although men were allowed to wear plain civilian clothes off duty, the wearing of hats remained compulsory:

> "It was a regrettable fact that the well-dressed citizen airman off duty might have possessed only a bowler and that this hat would take a lot of space in the issue kit. Pretty soon the squadron cricket team had been persuaded to hand over their caps for the common good and in no time a system was organised whereby a gent in plus fours and cricket cap would clock out of the guard room and pass his hat back through a hole in the hedge."[6]

High jinks were also apparent at the camp, particularly at the end of a day's work when the officers would head down to Bognor.

The famous Mr Butlin had even then a fun fair at Bognor, and it is a fact that an undeclared state of war existed between his attendants and 600 Squadron. Butlin's was subjected to a series of sporadic but highly co-ordinated raids for the express purpose of capturing the current collector arms of the Dodgems, in effect, the enemy's colours. Surprise was the order of the day, one moment of relative peace, the next thing a grand melee with protagonists locked in battle on individual Dodgems.[7]

"The Millionaires Mob", otherwise known as 601 (County of London) Squadron was born in White's Club, St James's, W1, the idea of Lord Edward Grosvenor who very much wanted to create a civilian air force. It was formed on 14 October 1925, and based at Northolt, before moving to Hendon. Grosvenor chose his officers from gentlemen who themselves had confidence and the right social background to ensure that they were not over-awed by him.[8] As in 600 Squadron, this confidence and social background often came from men who had been educated in private schools such as Eton and then moved on to Oxford or Cambridge. Grosvenor enjoyed eating, drinking and White's Club, an exclusive gentleman's club in the St James area of London. On the whole he preferred potential officers who would fit naturally into the setting of White's. He liked to see initially whether their social training had equipped them to deal with the large glasses of port he would pour for them at his Eaton Square home, and if they responded satisfactorily, he would take them to White's for even larger gins.[9]

THE SOCIAL COMPOSITION

Following Grosvenor's death in 1929, the new Commanding Officer of 601 Squadron was Sir Philip Sassoon, a man with family connections to the aristocracy and a political career. Other members included Edward Bulwer-Lyton - Viscount Knebworth; Max Aitken, who was the son of Lord Beaverbrook; Henry Norman, the son of Sir Hendry Norman; Peter Clive, the son of Sir Robert Clive; Nigel Seely, son of Sir Charles Seely and Robert Forbes-Leith, the son of Sir Charles and Lady Forbes-Leith of Fyvie Castle. Other links to the aristocracy came from Stanley Beresford-Collett, Richard Stephen Demetriadi, Robert Arthur Grosvenor, Edward Ward and Wiliam Drogo Sturges Montagu. Roger Joyce Bushell, who along with Max Aitken, Carl Davis, Edward Whitehead Reid, Guy Rawston Branch and Edward Bulwer-Lytton, had attended Cambridge University and public school. All these men were keen athletes, skiers and members of the university rugby, soccer and golf clubs; Aiden Crawley and Michael Peacock had both been to Winchester and then Oxford University, and shared a passion for skiing and cricket, while Willard Whitney Straight was a millionaire racing driver. Legal backgrounds were common with Roger Bushell, James Hayward Little, Robert Forbes-Leith and Michael Peacock, all acting as barristers or solicitors; whilst other members of the squadron had interests in aviation, such as Henry St Valery Norman.

The social status of the kind of gentlemen who joined the squadron in the late 1920s and early 1930s meant that there was pressure to personalise their AAF uniform to reflect their positions. Subsequently, many of the officers ensured that their uniform jackets were lined with red silk, to set them apart from other Auxiliary squadrons, and many wore red socks or red scarves.[10] This helped gain the squadron its characteristic notoriety, and their exclusivity was even known to the Germans who saw the squadron partly as a voluntary cohort of patriotic aristocrats (which they admired) and also as a bunch of flippant pleasure-seekers (which they deplored).[11] The social activities of the officers from 601 Squadron reflected the hedonistic nature of the young, rich aristocrats and their desire to be seen fulfilling their patriotic duty by volunteering to serve their country whilst still enjoying a light-hearted, somewhat devil-may-care attitude to the job, an image which they were more than happy to convey.

Indeed, games played within the officers' mess were known to further stimulate the rivalry between the two London squadrons, who were both based at Hendon and subsequently shared the same officers' mess:

"The rivalry between 600 and 601, both of whom were commanded by Right Honourables 'Freddy' Guest and Philip

41

Sassoon, was intense. Known collectively as the 'Berkley Boys' in deference to the black and light blue old school tie of Eton attributed to many of the squadrons' officers, the two London Auxiliary Squadrons' behaviour in the Hendon Officers' Mess was described as 'bloody.'"[12]

The squadron continued to attract young men, "they came in their own small aircraft, sometimes literally held together by string and sticking plaster, to fly bombers at Northolt each weekend."[13] Len Deighton confirms their connections with the city:

"At the outbreak of war, the 'millionaires' were so concerned about the prospect of petrol rationing and how it would affect their private transport an officer was assigned to the task of buying petrol. He came back having bought a service station but announced that the pumps there were only half-full. This situation was remedied when another pilot remembered that he was a director of Shell. His secretary arranged a delivery."[14]

It is apparent that political and aristocratic connections, coupled with a background in financial or legal institutions, were prerequisites to membership. The selection of the upper middle class, who had developed networks from either public school or university, meant that in many ways, volunteering for these squadrons was based primarily on family and social connections rather than technical skills. However, it is also clear that these gentlemen were not simply playboys but also had responsibility for managing staff; Roger Joyce Bushell, for example, was a lawyer; Henry Norman was an architect; Edward Bulwer-Lytton worked for the *Daily Mail;* Raymond Davis was an engineer; Max Aitken was manager of the *Sunday Express*; Stanley Beresford Collett worked as Assistant Company Secretary of Great Western Railways, whilst Edward Whitehead Reid was a doctor and Simon Gilliat was a stock and share broker. In many ways, they were ideal candidates for officers within a voluntary military hierarchy. They had been educated, in the main, within the public-school sector and had been groomed to fulfil leadership roles.

Of the 141 identified officers attached to these two well-publicised squadrons, seventy have been found using a range of available records, including seventy-seven references from *The Times,* seven references from Peerage Records and sixteen references from miscellaneous websites. No records could be located for the remaining seventy-one officers, representing 50 per cent of the total. The records rarely followed a predictable structure or form: sometimes family backgrounds of officers would be given, sometimes not; often there would be details of educational backgrounds, but not always; mention of sporting activities might or might not be included, and so on.

The officers who could be tracked in this fashion, together with the impressionistic nature of the information, poses problems in terms of building a typical social profile of AAF officers in these elite squadrons. However, for all their limitations, these new records do provide interesting and significant insights into the social world of the AAF.

Data for 600 and 601 Squadron combined: 141 officers were identified of which there were seventy biographies. This means that the percentage of officers with biographies is forty-nine.

Table 4: 600 & 601 Squadron combined data by category

Category	Total	Percentage of Men with Biographies
Public School	24	34%
Oxbridge	23	33%
University	5	7%
Elite Sport	13	19%
Marriage Announcement	12	17%
Birth Announcement	4	6%
Death Announcement	23	33%
Profession	32	46%
Family Business	3	4%
University Air Squadron	2	3%

Of the seventy available records, at least 21 or 47 per cent make specific reference to titled backgrounds and this figure, like most figures that can be derived from such a methodology, is almost certain to be an underestimate. Where educational backgrounds are mentioned, almost all refer to a classic trajectory of public schools (Eton, Winchester, Harrow, Westminster) leading to Oxbridge colleges, with a significant weighting towards Cambridge rather than Oxford. The relatively large number of references in *The Times* – usually in the form of marriage and engagement announcements or obituaries – carries its own social significance.

The occupations of these men offer a predictable profile: 18 per cent of them were engaged in Law; over 25 per cent in the City (the stock exchange; Lloyds Insurance; large national companies); at least five in the national media; six were actively engaged in national politics, and 3 per cent occupied important posts in government. Whenever leisure activities were mentioned, they invariably included the mix of elite activities including private flying, racing, racing car driving, polo, big-game hunting, rowing, cricket, fencing, yachting, golf, rackets and skiing.

Other southern squadrons included 604 (County of Middlesex) Squadron, formed on 17 March 1930 at Hendon. Its CO was Lieutenant Colonel A.S.W. Dore, DSO, TD, a former soldier in the Worcester Regiment who had transferred to the Royal Flying Corps in 1917. His concerns on being approached to set up the new squadron reveal much about his social background: "Was it fair to my family? I should have to give up much of my leisure, my holidays, my golf and tennis at weekends."[15] However, the fact that Dore accepted the job suggests that ideals of voluntarism were very much alive in the context of the 1920s. It was his job to select the officers who would serve within his new squadron. His selection techniques mirrored those of Grosvenor in that, as mentioned earlier, each applicant was given marks for his school record in scholarship and athletics; and if he could ride a horse, or drive a car or motorcycle, or sail a boat, or ski or play the piano he was given more marks.[16]

Officer candidates for 604 squadron included Roderick Aeneas Chisholm, who was educated at Ampleforth College and then worked in the oil industry prior to joining the AAF in 1935, John Cherry, the son of Sir Benjamin Cherry, John Davies, son of Colonel Sir Alfred Davies, Alan Loader Maffey, son of John Loader Maffey, Lord Rugby; Edward Prescott, son of Lieutenant Colonel Prescott and Michael Montagu, the stepson of Lord Kimberley, who worked as a post office engineer. Philip Wheeler was educated at Uppingham and New College, Oxford, with a background in point-to-point racing, whilst Philip Lawton was educated at Westminster School and was a lawyer. Finally, Robert Nimmo was a stockbroker. Other young officers often had their marriages announced in *The Times* which reflected their upper class or upper middle-class status.

On 1 December 1932, 604 Squadron won the Esher Trophy for Auxiliary Efficiency and their behaviour in the mess mirrored that of 600 and 601 squadron:

> "We were sitting in the Mess when Air Commodore McNeece Foster, commanding the Auxiliary Group – who by his keenness and personal knowledge of almost every auxiliary officer, led us on to greater effort – telephoned

the good news and his congratulations. There was a whoop of joy from the boys. I ordered half a dozen Veuve Clicquot and when I left, discreetly, the celebrations had reached the stage of nose-diving over the sofas and chairs."[17]

Out of the ten identified officers for 604 Squadron, 60 per cent attended public school, and 40 per cent of those attending public school went on to Oxford or Cambridge University. Furthermore, 30 per cent of the officer recruits went on to work in professional jobs compared to no recruits working in family businesses. Thirty per cent of them had their engagement or marriage printed in *The Times*.

605 (County of Warwick) Squadron were formed on 5 October 1926 at Castle Bromwich, Birmingham. Aristocratic links for officer personnel were not as apparent as those personnel that were associated with 600 and 601 Squadrons, but other candidates had similar backgrounds in terms of public schools, elite sports and business connections. For example, Ralph Hope was educated at Eton and New College, Oxford, an outstanding oarsman and the nephew of Neville Chamberlain; Baron Willoughby de Broke was a member of a hunting family,[18] whilst Ron Noble was the son of an army officer and worked for Cornhill Insurance; Christopher Currant was the son of a hatter and worked in research and development in the engineering industry and Walter Barnaby was a building contractor from Wolverhampton. Like many officers in 600 and 601, Nigel Stuart Graeme was sufficiently important to have his marriage announced in *The Times*. There was still a recognisably elite culture at work here, but with its own distinctive provincial character compared to the well-publicised London squadrons. Engineering and building occupations, for example, tended to characterise provincial squadrons as opposed to the financial, legal and media occupations of many officers in London.

Fifty-two officers were identified for 605 Squadron, and eight officers had biographies. Thirty-eight per cent of them had attended public school and 13 per cent of them had gone on to Oxford or Cambridge University. Furthermore, 50 per cent of them worked in professional jobs compared to 13 per cent who worked within family businesses.

610 (County of Chester) Squadron was formed in 1936 at Hooton Park, "most of the pilots took private flying lessons to qualify. One person said never have I seen so many Rolls Royce cars in one spot at the same time – an indication of the pilots' social status."[19] Some of its members included Gerald Kerr, who had been educated at Leeds Grammar School

and won an Eldon Scholarship at Oxford for Natural Sciences in 1927. Mark Topham was a director of Tophams Ltd from Liverpool, who managed Aintree Racecourse; William Cromwell Warner was the son of Sir Lionel Warner, and Graham Lambert Chambers studied at Cambridge University. Several of its members warranted marriage announcements in *The Times;* for example, Douglas Strachan Wilson, Charles Ross Pritchard and Allan Graham.

Further away from London, there is a marked decrease in the number of men who can be identified, and who also follow the same educational route as many recruits of 600/601 Squadron. For 610 Squadron, of the eleven officers with biographies, 11 per cent went to public school; however 22 per cent went to Oxford or Cambridge University. Similarly, 22 per cent of the men had their engagement or marriage mentioned in *The Times* newspaper.

614 (County of Glamorgan) Squadron was formed on 1 June 1937 at Llandow in Wales. Nineteen officers who were commissioned to 614 Squadron have been identified, and of these nineteen, some background information has been found for twelve, which equates to 63 per cent. Martin Llewellyn Edwards and Norman Stuart Merrett were educated at Marlborough College and Clifton College respectively, whilst Martin Llewellyn Edwards also attended Lincoln College, Oxford University. He also had a marriage announcement in *The Times*, as did Phillip Michael Vaughan Lysaght, and John Dudley Rollinson, whilst Richard Edward Charles Cadman, Richard Owen Rhys and Phillip Michael Vaughan Lysaght had their children's births recorded in *The Times*. Martin Llewellyn Edwards was a solicitor and Alexander Glen Pallot was an accountant. Finally, Norman Stuart Merrett played rugby and also international hockey.

Another southern squadron was 615 (County of Surrey), formed on 1 June 1937 at RAF Kenley. Again aristocratic links can be identified with candidates for pilot training; for example, John Gayner, the son of Dr Gayner, and John Lloyd, son of Lieutenant Colonel Sir John and Lady Lloyd of Dinnas. But mixed in among these elite families were one or two other men who had more modest backgrounds such as Bernard Brady, who left school at fourteen and joined the Royal Navy as an able seaman, eventually training as a pilot with the Royal Flying Corps. He set up his own business as manager of Aircraft Exchange and Mart located at Hanworth Air Park in Middlesex. Between Brady and the more middle-class recruits, there was Anthony Eyre, son of Mr G.W.B. Eyre of Purley, educated at Whitgift School in Croydon and Walter Stern who worked for the London Metal Exchange. Again, several young pilots had their marriages announced in *The Times*; for example, John Richard Hensman Gayner, Peter F Cazenove and Anthony Eyre.

In percentage terms, eight men were identified for 615 Squadron, of which 13 per cent of them went to public school, whilst none of them went on to Oxford or Cambridge University. Moreover, 25 per cent of the officer recruits worked in professional jobs and none worked in family businesses. However, 38 per cent of the men had their engagement or marriage announced in *The Times*, and 25 per cent of these men also had the birth of their children announced in *The Times*.

500 (County of Kent) Squadron was formed at RAF Manston on 15 March 1931 as a Special Reserve Squadron. Officer recruits included Stanley Dudley Pierce Connors, personal assistant to Air Commodore J.C. Quinnell, and several young men whose backgrounds are revealed in marriage notices published in *The Times,* for example, Arthur Cousins, son of Lieutenant Colonel Cousins of Bix Manor, Henley on Thames, Charles Elgar, son of Walter Robinson Elgar, JP, William Heath Corry, son of Mr and Mrs H.W. Corry of Yaldham Manor, Kemsing and George Geoffrey Stockdale, son of Mr and Mrs G Holmes Stockdale.

Of those officers with biographies none of the officer recruits went to public school, or went on to Oxford or Cambridge University, but 8 per cent of them worked in a professional job, compared to none working in family businesses, and 73 per cent of them had engagement or marriage announcements in *The Times*.

501 (County of Gloucester) Squadron was formed at Filton on 14 June 1929 as a Special Reserve Squadron. Many of the first officer candidates also had their marriage notices announced in *The Times,* for example, Cautley Nasmyth Shaw, son of Oliphant Shaw of Woorwyrite, Victoria, Australia, John Anthony Warren, a test pilot; and Camille Enright Malfroy, son of Mr and Mrs C.M. Malfroy of Wellington, New Zealand. Of the seven identified officers with biographies, 49 per cent of them worked within the professions and 29 per cent had their engagements or marriages announced in *The Times*.

503 (County of Lincoln) Squadron was formed at Waddington on 5 October 1926, and initial recruits included John Bell, educated at Charterhouse and Christ's College Cambridge, the son of Mr and Mrs H.A. Bell of Lindum, and Robert Higson Smith. Of the officers who were identified with biographies, both went to public school and then on to either Oxford or Cambridge University.

504 (County of Nottingham) Squadron was formed at Hucknell on 26 March 1928. Officer candidates included Philip Parsons, educated at Charterhouse and Downing College, Cambridge, who worked for Rolls-Royce Limited as an engineering pupil. Other young men who joined the squadron had their prospective marriages announced in *The Times*, for example, Gilbert Darwin, son of Colonel Charles Waring Darwin CB, of Elston Hall, Newark; Rupert Hartley Watson, son of Lieutenant Colonel and Mrs G Hartley Watson of Powderham near Exeter; Reginald Broadhead, a property dealer from Ockwells Manor, Maidenhead, Michael Rook, son of Colonel and Mrs W.R. Rook of Edwalton House and Sir Hugh Michael Seely Bart MP, the son of Sir Charles Seely, MP for East Norfolk and High Sheriff of Nottinghamshire. Consequently, of the fifteen officers with biographies, 6 per cent went to public school and 5 per cent of them went on to Oxford or Cambridge University. Thirteen per cent of the recruits worked within the professions and a further 13 per cent had either their engagement or marriage announced in *The Times*.

When the southern squadrons are considered as a whole, it is apparent that 600 and 601 squadron represented men with aristocratic or upper middle-class backgrounds, who had attended the same public schools and universities whereas, 604, 605 and 615 squadrons recruited men from a wider spectrum of upper- and middle-class society.

Of the 368 officers identified who served in southern AAF squadrons during the 1930s, background information has been found on 49 per cent or 180 of the men. These officers have been identified using press, oral testimony and AAF records. Generally, over 61 per cent worked in financial or legal institutions and in public companies, with only 9 per cent working in family businesses. They tended to be prominent within their local community and over 39 per cent of them had been educated at public school, followed by either Oxford or Cambridge University. It also becomes evident that many of them had forged friendships and social networks in elite athletic clubs ranging from cricket and golf through to rowing and yachting, with over 16 per cent of the available records mentioning some form of sporting prowess. It is also apparent that for the southern squadrons which are further away from London, the number of officers with biographies falls, as does the percentage of men attending public school or an Oxbridge University. This must be taken into account because the less officers identified with biographies, the higher the percentage will be for each of the categories:

Table 5: Auxiliary Air Force and Special Reserve southern squadrons showing percentages of men with biographies

Squadron Number	Number of Identified Men	Number of Men With Biographies	% of Men With Biographies
600	69	26	38%
601	72	44	61%
604	38	13	34%
605	52	8	15%
610	16	11	69%
611	18	11	61%
613	5	3	60%
614	19	12	63%
615	15	10	67%
500	25	15	66%
501	17	7	41%
503	5	4	80%
504	22	16	73%
TOTAL	**368**	**180**	**49%**

Northern Squadrons

Membership of the northern AAF squadrons shows some similarities to the southern squadrons but also some significant differences.

602 (City of Glasgow) was formed on 15 September 1925 at Renfrew, with Captain J.D. Latta as Commanding Officer. A wooden hut was set up as the new recruiting centre, and within the first week more than 200 men had applied to join. Three men, H.G. Davidson, James Pearson Drew and Colin Alfred Stuart Parker, had also begun training for their pilots licences which were necessary for pilot entry into the Auxiliary Air Force. By 1926 David Fowler McIntyre had passed his flying training and was joined by Pilot Officer Douglas Douglas-Hamilton, Andrew Douglas Farquhar and Robert Faulds. In January 1933 the squadron moved to a new airfield at Abbotsinch and the squadron made history when Squadron Leader Douglas Douglas-Hamilton, with an observer, and Flight Lieutenant McIntyre, with a photographer, became the first men to fly over Mount Everest. Both men received the Air Force Cross. Empire Air Day in 1935 saw a crowd of 1,500 people visit the squadron to watch the air displays. On 12 December 1937, fifteen officers provided the guard of honour at the wedding of the Marquis

of Clydesdale, Douglas Douglas-Hamilton to Lady Elizabeth Percy at St Giles' Cathedral Edinburgh. A significant event took place in April 1939 when Leading Aircraftsman Phillips began pilot training, the first volunteer for the new post of NCO-pilot. May 1939 saw a crowd of 20,000 come to the aerodrome for Empire Air Day. When war began twenty-two AAF officers and 174 AAF airmen were embodied into the Royal Air Force for the duration of the war.

Of the forty-six officers who were identified as being gazetted into 602 Squadron, information about individual backgrounds was found for twenty-seven of them. This equates to 59 per cent. Of these individual officers, 11 per cent attended public school, including Douglas Douglas-Hamilton and Colin Alfred Stuart Parker who attended Eton, and William Harold Mitchell who attended Sedbergh School. Six per cent of men attended Oxford or Cambridge University, including William Harold Mitchell, while 2 per cent of men attended universities such as Charles Hector MacLean. Six per cent of the men took part in elite sports such as rowing, rugby, boxing and yachting, whilst 8 per cent took up work such as law or politics, such as Douglas Douglas-Hamilton who was MP for East Renfrewshire and Charles Hector Maclean who was a lawyer. A further 7 per cent worked for family businesses. Twenty-six per cent of the men had engagement announcements in *The Times* and a further 11 per cent also had the birth of their children announced in *The Times*.

603 (City of Edinburgh) Squadron was formed on 14 October 1925 at RAF Turnhouse as a day bomber squadron with an establishment of twenty-three officers and 158 airmen. The first Commanding Officer was Squadron Leader James McKelvie and David Ross, author of 603 (City of Edinburgh) two volume squadron history found that:

> "The initial influx of officers into the squadron consisted of professional businessmen from Edinburgh and the surrounding districts, and the airmen were of various trades and callings, from corporation employees and civilian industry to students from the university."[20]

Furthermore, David Ross pointed out that:

> "The wealthy young professionals and students who joined 603 Squadron after it was founded in 1925 were the cream of society, the 'young tearaways' of their day who could afford to pay for flying lessons to indulge their love of aviation."[21]

The squadron headquarters were at 25 Learmouth Terrace, and when the first training camp took place, the squadron was represented by three officers and fifty-five airmen. By December 1926, the squadron establishment was four officers and sixty-four airmen, this had risen to seventeen officers and 155 airmen by the end of 1928.

Would-be pilots had to face preliminary hurdles. If a vacancy occurred, serving officers of the squadron were asked for recommendations. They were first interviewed by the adjutant. If he felt they were suitable, he sent them to Comiston House, Squadron Leader McKelvie's home, to be vetted by the CO and his wife. The survivors then faced the stiffest test of all – a trial flight with the adjutant. In 1929, ten candidates got as far as the test flight, but only one of these got through.[22]

Each officer was required to buy RAF service dress. They were given a uniform allowance of £40. Also, officers could buy mess kit at their own expense, "as a mark of distinction, 603 Squadron obtained official permission to wear red silk linings in their tunics and greatcoats."[23]

This mirrors the behaviour of 601 (County of London) Squadron who also personalised their uniforms. Moreover, "joining 603 Squadron in the 1930s was something of a family affair with brother following brother, or teenagers following their old school chums".[24] In 1931, Squadron Leader McKelvie retired and Squadron Leader Hylton Murray-Philipson, who owned an estate at Stobo, took over. He was also a magistrate and a parliamentary candidate who was elected as Member of Parliament for Twickenham. On 30 June 1931, Lord George Nigel Douglas-Hamilton joined the squadron, and he became commanding officer in 1934 following the death of Squadron Leader Hylton Murray-Philipson. In 1938, Lord George Nigel Douglas-Hamilton relinquished his commission and was replaced as CO by Squadron Leader Ernest Hildebrand Stevens, a lawyer by trade.

Forty-seven officers were identified for 603 Squadron, and of those men, forty, or 87 per cent have short biographies. Fifteen per cent of the young men attended public school, for example both George and Malcolm Douglas-Hamilton attended Eton, whilst Patrick Gifford attended Sedburgh School. Ten per cent of the officers attended either Oxford or Cambridge University, for example, Donald Kenneth Andrew Mackenzie attended Cambridge University, as did George Lovell Denholm, whilst George Nigel Douglas-Hamilton attended Oxford University. Ten per cent of the young men attended Edinburgh University, such as Patrick Gifford. Fifteen per cent of the men had professional jobs, such as Patrick Gifford, who was a lawyer and James Lawrence who was a banker, whilst Malcolm Avendale Douglas-Hamilton was the MP for Inverness. Twenty-five per cent of the officers had their engagement announced, such as Alastair Henry Bruce, Thomas Clark Garden and Ivone Kirkpatrick. Eight per cent had their children's births announced in *The Times*, for example, Edward Stanley Viner Burton. Finally, 15 per cent of the men worked for family businesses, such as George Lovell Denholm whose family business was coal exporters and pit prop importers, and Thomas Usher of Tom Usher and Son Ltd Brewery.

607 (County of Durham) Squadron was formed at Usworth on 17 March 1930. It was comprised of officer recruits who shared some similarities to the southern squadrons, including William Whitty who attended Liverpool University studying to become an electrical engineer; George Craig who had attended Aysgarth School, followed by Winchester School and then Pembroke College, Cambridge where he gained a soccer blue and an MA in Law Studies, working in Durham as a solicitor; Leslie Runciman, the eldest son of Viscount Runciman, who had been educated at Eton, before moving to Trinity College Cambridge to study to become a chartered accountant; William Francis Blackadder who attended Cambridge University and in later life was a director of Moor Line. Many of the recruits worked in family businesses rather than large companies; for example, Leslie Runciman worked for the family shipping company called The Moor Line; Launcelot Smith was the Chairman of the Board of Directors at his family business called Smiths Dock Repairing Company; Joseph Robert Kayall worked for the family timber business, Joseph Thompson and Co Ltd. Two of the original recruits worked for larger companies; Maurice Irving was an engineer at Vicker Armstrongs and John Sample was the land agent for the Duke of Portland Line. Both Leslie Runciman and William Blackadder had the sporting interests of most AAF recruits; Runciman as a transatlantic yachtsman and Blackadder as a Scottish rugby player. Thomas Templer Richardson and Kenneth Stoddart both had their marriages announced in *The Times*.

Of the ten officers with biographies, fifty per cent of them attended a public school and 20 per cent of them attended Oxford or Cambridge University. Furthermore, 60 per cent of them worked in a professional capacity compared to 20 per cent who worked in family businesses. Finally, 20 per cent of them had their engagement or marriage announced in *The Times*.

608 (North Riding) was formed on 17 March 1930. It was assigned to No 6 Auxiliary Group as a bomber squadron and located at Thornaby. It is evident that there were social links between young men who were selected to join 608 Squadron as officer recruits. These included a common university background, sporting activities, and membership of a UAS; in many cases there were also

business links. These kinds of social links do not usually exist between the airmen or the NCOs and decisions to volunteer for the AAF were clearly different. Another reason for volunteering was to pre-empt conscription in a potential war that many men felt was likely to occur following the appointment of Hitler as Chancellor of Germany in 1933. Twenty-seven per cent volunteered simply because their friends did. Thirty-two officers were identified, and of these men, twenty had biographies, which equates to 63 per cent.

In many cases, the young officers knew each other and this was seen as vital in ensuring that an extended family atmosphere existed within the squadron. Camaraderie was important because it meant that the young men could train and live together on a weekend, would be able to get on with each other and know what was expected of both themselves and their fellow officers. It also supported the principle that their local communities would adopt AAF squadrons and thus foster some sort of local pride in them. Young middle-class gentlemen were also keen to volunteer because it meant that they were able to fly without being members of a flying club in the local area, an example being the activities of Geoffrey Shaw who entered the MacRobertson Air Race in 1934.[25]

Fifty-five per cent of the pilot recruits worked within family businesses and the reason for this appears to be that family concerns could often be more flexible in releasing family members. These families were also prominent within the local area and seen as its social leaders. This is clear from the evidence in the local press reporting on engagements and weddings of eminent young men who joined the AAF in the period up to the start of the Second World War. Several of them, most notably, Squadron Leader Geoffrey Ambler, Geoffrey Shaw and Keith Pyman, owned their own aeroplanes.[26] This is a significant factor in determining the financial standing of these young men and their families since the average cost of an aeroplane during the mid-1920s was £830. Another indicator of their financial status was that 74 per cent of the young officers had their own cars. Motorcars at that time cost upwards of £350 at a time when the average wages for young men would be less than £2 a week. This level of wealth, whilst not matching the super-rich families associated with 600 and 601 squadron, stood in particularly stark contrast to the wider economic climate of Teesside where anywhere between 20 per cent and 40 per cent of the adult insured workforce were unemployed in Stockton and Middlesbrough during the same period.[27]

It is probable therefore that the officer recruits to 608 Squadron, in keeping with officers in other AAF squadrons, had knowledge of each other through either their working environment or through their family connections.

For example, William Howard Davis lived in Saltburn and his family knew the Appleby-Browns and the Shaws;[28] Henry Charles Newhouse's family knew the Clayton, Wilson and Wright families through business links,[29] whilst the Appleby-Brown and Shaw families knew the Baird and Phillips families.[30] Vaux, Robertson and Pyman also had links through land owning.[31] Twenty-five per cent of the officer candidates had been to public school; for example Geoffrey Ambler, Phillip Lloyd-Graeme, Geoffrey Shaw and Peter Vaux. Forty-five per cent had been to university, including Ambler, Shaw, Newhouse, Appleby-Brown, and Vaux who attended Cambridge; Phillip Lloyd-Graeme and Paul Kennedy were Oxford men. Other common links between the young officers were UASs and elite sporting activities. However, it is apparent that none of these 1930s recruits to 608 Squadron had quite the elevated social backgrounds or connections associated with recruits to London's 600 and 601 Squadrons. Fifty-five per cent of 608 Squadron officers for example, came from local businesses and tended to socialize in a middle-class culture that lacked the titled aristocratic and landed connections found amongst 600 and 601 men. That said, they shared a common experience of private education and Oxbridge, as well as subscribing to an increasingly unified middle-class culture promoted through print culture and education. Whilst many of the 608 officers might have struggled to hold their own in the social tests favoured by 600 and 601, they nonetheless exerted considerable social authority in their own localities.

For example, Geoffrey Ambler was the nephew of Sir James Hill, who was the owner of James Hill & Sons Ltd, the largest private wool merchants in the country, and also Liberal MP for Bradford Central. Geoffrey's father, Frederick Ambler, owned Midland Mills in Bradford, his mother, Annie Hill, was the sister of Sir James Hill. Geoffrey was born at Baildon in 1904 and was educated at Shrewsbury and rowed for the school at Henley in 1922. He attended Clare College, Cambridge where he obtained his BA degree and rowed in the winning university crews of 1924, 1925 and 1926. By 1930 he was Director of Fred Ambler Limited of Bradford, his father's woollen firm. A member of Yorkshire Aeroplane Club, he already had his pilot's licence and owned his own plane.

Geoffrey Shaw came from Nunthorpe and his family owned W.G. Shaw Engineering Co in North Ormesby. His father, W.G. Shaw, was the President of the Middlesbrough branch of the Institute of British Foundry men. Geoffrey was educated in Scotland but then attended Cambridge University where he learned to fly as part of the UAS. He also owned his own aeroplane which he used for long business trips. He took part in the MacRobertson Air Race from England to Australia in 1934.

Henry Charles Newhouse came from one of the villages outside Middlesbrough, attended Cambridge University and was part of a family that owned Newhouses Department Store in Middlesbrough. William Appleby-Brown was from Saltburn; his father, James Brown, worked for the family firm J Brown and Co who were builder's merchants at Queens Square in Middlesbrough. The Brown family was prominent in Middlesbrough and included Alderman John Wesley Brown, who was MP for the town in 1921.

William attended Cambridge University where he learned to fly as a member of the UAS. After university, he then joined the family firm. His family also had a shipping company called Lion Shipping that imported iron ore from Spain and timber from the Baltic States. They were very friendly with the Baird, Wrightson and Crosthwaite families. By the same token, the Appleby-Browns often visited the home of Sir Thomas Wrightson at Neasham and Eryholme.

Dennis Baird came from West Hartlepool and his family business was importing various timber from the Baltic and Russia. Harry Clayton's family owned a well-known retail business in Middlesbrough and finally the families of Anthony Neville Wilson and Cosmo William Wright were clothiers in the Tower House in Middlesbrough.

Links with the aristocracy may have been thin on the ground, but 36 per cent of the officers in 608 had landed connections. For example, Peter Vaux was born in Grindon near Sunderland, went to school at Harrow, then went to Cambridge where he joined the UAS and learned to fly. He was commissioned into the Auxiliary Air Force in July 1933 and lived at Piercebridge in County Durham. He was the son of Colonel Ernest Vaux of Brettanby Manor, Barton. He was also an amateur jockey who rode in the Grand National, took part in various point-to-points, and rode with the Zetland and Bedale Hunts. At a lower level of landed society, George Williams, another pre-war pilot with 608 Squadron, born in Shrewton, near Salisbury in 1917, attended St Probus Prep School in Salisbury and then went on to boarding school in Cornwall, before studying at Cambridge University. His father was a gentleman farmer who was also a district and county councillor and Justice of the Peace. Similarly, Keith Pyman lived outside Yarm where his family were gentlemen farmers, and James Robertson from Saltburn also came from a farming family.

Other young recruits came from landed backgrounds but then worked for major companies or professions; for example, Philip Lloyd-Graeme, later Sir Philip Cunliffe Lister, was a member of the Lloyd-Graeme family from Sewerby Hall and estate in the East Riding of Yorkshire. His father-in-law was Sir John Cunliffe-Lister, Baron of Masham and chief shareholder in Manningham Mills. Philip was educated at Winchester and University College Oxford. Later he was a barrister, Conservative MP and was three times President of the Board of Trade.

The spectrum of middle-class backgrounds continued with 50 per cent of officers from the squadron having links to local industry. William Howard Davis was the son of R.W. and J.P. Howard Davis of Elton House, Darlington. He lived in Saltburn and worked as Chief Accountant to Dorman Long. John Sherburn Priestly (Pip) Phillips was born in Dublin in November 1919; his father, John Skelton Phillips, was in the army whilst his mother was related to J.B. Priestly. He attended St Olave's School in York before moving to the senior school, St Peter's School in York, on 23 January 1933 where he was a full boarder. He left the school in July 1936 and moved to Crooksbarn Lane in Norton, Stockton on Tees. He was a successful rower for the school and a cadet in the OTC. He worked as an engineer in Darlington, employed by the London North Eastern Railway, joining 608 Squadron in 1937 at the age of eighteen. P Kennedy came from Middlesbrough and attended Oxford University; he was an accountant at ICI. Ivo W.H. Thompson was the son of Sir Wilfrid and Lady Thompson of Old Nunthorpe.

Class not only dictated patterns of recruitment but also the way men spent their leisure time in the AAF. The hierarchy of the AAF meant that officers were kept separate from airmen. They were accommodated at the Officers Mess in Thornaby Hall, where most of their social activities took place. The sergeants had their own mess, as did the corporals and other ranks. Officers did not go to any of the other messes unless they were officially invited. To reinforce this point, Mrs Appleby-Brown noted:

> "The Officers Mess was at Thornaby Hall and it was a long long way from anything else. The officers had no interest in Thornaby and the town. If you come from a distance away you had no interest in Thornaby and the town, you merely wanted to fly. No, there would be no mixing. There would be no reason for them to mix."[32]

This sense of social distance played its own part in creating a division between the squadron and the town and in some ways meant that the young officers preferred to stay in the mess and would often engage in various games and high jinks - walking on the ceiling, high-cock-a-lorum, a violent form of leapfrog, and another game where they were on 'piggy back' and fought each other with rolled up newspapers.[33] It was a pattern that matched closely with the antics of 600 and 601 Squadron. All the social activities for young officers revolved invariably around the consumption of large amounts of alcohol followed by games that had their origin in public school common rooms. If the young officers ventured out of the mess they would go to pubs around the area, such as "The Pathfinders" at Maltby or the "Bluebell" in Yarm, but would remain as a group rather than interacting with the locals. This tended to be during the earlier part of the evening before returning to the officers' mess.

It is evident that the social backgrounds and activities of officers from London squadrons and those from 608 Squadron were not identical. The common link was public schools and universities where a shared culture was promulgated and kept alive in the confines of the officers' mess. Organised sport played a major role in the life of both Oxford and Cambridge university students, in the shape of boat races, inter-university cricket matches, athletics and inter-collegiate competitions; these helped keep young men physically fit and familiar with team ethics, and fed effortlessly into the life of the typical AAF officer. Also membership of either UAS was common amongst AAF recruits with 17 per cent having been part of these squadrons during their time at university, an experience that laid the foundations for an AAF career.

Another comparable northern squadron was 609 (West Riding) formed on 10 February 1936 at Yeadon near Leeds. Its CO was Squadron Leader Harald Peake. With a similar background to Dore, he was a retired officer of the Yorkshire Dragoons Yeomanry. Yorkshire had been heavily industrialised during the nineteenth century although still retained many large country estates. Officer candidates tended to reflect this mix, with sons of fathers who worked in industry mixing with sons of landed families.

Peake was both late Master of the Rufford Hounds on the one side, and a member of a Yorkshire colliery-owning family on the other. Indeed:

"The person mainly responsible for Harald Peake's appointment had been Major General The (10th) Earl of Scarborough, chairman and driving force of the West Riding Territorial Army Association. Looking for a man of local influence to attract and select the best human material for its new winged offshoot, he was no doubt pleased to find that no one was better qualified than his own neighbour. For Harald Peake had been a Territorial already, flew an aeroplane, had rowed for Eton, Cambridge and England, and possessed a drive and ability that later would win him the chairmanship successively of the London Assurance, the Steel Company of Wales and Lloyds Bank Ltd."[34]

Some of the original officer recruits came from similar backgrounds to those of 607 Squadron: Stephen G Beaumont was a graduate from Oxford University, as was John Dundas, who was an aristocrat, athlete and journalist on the editorial staff of the *Yorkshire Post*, while Geoffrey Ambler had been educated at Cambridge; Stephen Beaumont and Bernard Little were solicitors while Dudley Persse-Joynt worked for an oil company; Philip Barran was a trainee mining engineer and manager of a brickworks owned by his mother's family; Desmond Ayre was also a mining engineer. Textile backgrounds included A.R. Edge who worked for I.G. Dyestuffs Ltd, Joseph Dawson, son of Sir Benjamin Dawson who came from one of Yorkshires leading textile families "and used to arrive for training in a Lagonda".[35] Jarvis Blayney and Geoffrey Ambler came from local textile families. Ambler, who had been commissioned into the AAF in 1931, joined 608 Squadron at its outset and became Commanding Officer on 30 December 1934. In November 1937 he took up command of 609 (West Riding of Yorkshire) Squadron.[36] Philip Henry Barran, William Humble and Peter Richard Nickols all had their forthcoming marriages announced in *The Times*. When officers from the squadron attended a "war" course at the Flying Training School, Little Rissington in Gloucester, Ziegler notes:

> "The entire intake for this course consisted of Auxiliary officers and like-minded former members of University Air Squadrons. When Peter Dunning-White of 601 Squadron drove up in a Rolls-Royce, complete with valet, John McGrath of the same squadron in an Alvis Speed-Twenty, and even Michael Appleby of 609 in a drop-head Hillman, the rule about no private cars was quietly waived."[37]

Of the thirteen identified officers with biographies in 609 Squadron, 23 per cent of them attended a public school, whilst 38 per cent of them attended an Oxbridge University. Sixty-two per cent of them worked within a professional job as compared to 23 per cent who worked in a family business. Furthermore, 23 per cent of them had their engagement or marriage announced in *The Times*.

611 (West Lancashire) Squadron was formed:

> "In name only on 10 February 1936 at RAF Hendon, London, five days after the Liverpool City Council had granted a tenancy to the Air Ministry of five acres of land to the East

of the Chapel House Farm, Speke, on which the tenant was to construct roadways and erect temporary buildings. The squadron moved to the local Territorial Army Headquarters in the centre of Liverpool on 1 April 1936 prior to moving to Speke airfield on 6 May 1936."[38]

Squadron Leader Geoffrey Langton Pilkington was appointed to command it. Educated at Broadstairs, Eton and Magdalen College, Oxford, he was a member of the Pilkington Glass family who employed several officer recruits such as W.L. Lang and John Noel O'Reilly Blackwood. He became a sub-director of the family firm in 1910 and a director in 1919. Other officer recruits shared similar university and sporting backgrounds, such as William Johnson Leather and Kenneth Douglas Stoddart, who both attended public school before going to Cambridge where they played rugby. Arthur Westley Richards had attended Liverpool University and worked as a solicitor, whilst both David William Southam Howroyd and Kenneth Douglas Stoddart worked for their own respective family businesses; Howroyd within a family chemical business and Stoddart as part of a family firm of ship suppliers. Ralph Kenyon Crompton had attended Charterhouse School and was a hunting man with the Cheshire hounds.

This indicates that 36 per cent of the officer recruits attended public school and 55 per cent attended Oxford or Cambridge University. Thirty-six per cent of them worked in a professional job whilst 27 per cent worked in a family business. Finally, 36 per cent of the young men had their engagement or marriage announced in *The Times*.

612 (County of Aberdeen) Squadron was formed on 1 June 1937 at Dyce Aerodrome as an army co-operation unit. It trained in aircraft called Avro Tutors and in December 1937 it had received two-seat Hawker Hectors which were used by army cooperation squadrons. The squadron converted to a General Reconnaissance squadron in 1938, and in July 1939 the squadron received Avro Anson aircraft which had room for four crew members and had a much better range, making them better suited for the reconnaissance role. The first few auxiliary pilots who were successful in gaining their flying badges were George Reid Thomson, Alan Milne Scott, Stewart Adjio Middleton, Douglas Gordon Emslie Benzie, Harry Bethune Gilchrist, Ramsay Roger Russell and Ian George Flaxington Stephen. By April 1938, fifty-four airmen had been recruited as ground crew. In August the squadron was transferred into No 18 (Reconnaissance) Group of Coastal Command flying Avro Anson's. The 20 May 1939 saw 5000 people coming to the aerodrome for Empire Air Day.

Of the twenty-one identified officers within the squadron, twelve of the young men have some biographical information about them, which represents 57 per cent. Only 8 per cent of the young men went to public school, for example, Herbert Oswald Berry attended Harrow, and similarly, only 8 per cent attended an Oxbridge University and this was Herbert Oswald Berry who attended Pembroke College Oxford. Thirty-three per cent of the young men worked within the professions, for example, Douglas Gordon Emslie Benzie was an accountant, whilst Harry Bethune Gilchrist was a lawyer. Only 17 per cent of the men placed engagement announcements in *The Times* and only 8 per cent of the men had birth announcements.

613 (City of Manchester) Squadron was formed at Ringway on 1 March 1939, the last of the original AAF squadrons to be formed before the start of the Second World War. As a result of the lateness in its creation, many of its original recruits were from the RAFVR. For example, Patrick Peter Colum Barthropp was born in Dublin in 1920 and was educated at St Augustine's Abbey School in Ramsgate, St Joseph's College near Market Drayton and Ampleforth College, North Yorkshire; after leaving he went to Rover's on an engineering apprenticeship, but, since he was able to fly, he volunteered for AAF and joined 613 squadron in May 1939. As there was only one named officer recruit for 613 Squadron the percentages show 100 per cent for most of the categories.

616 (South Yorkshire) Squadron was formed on 1 November 1938 at Doncaster. Squadron Leader the Earl of Lincoln was posted in from 609 Squadron to command the unit. Lionel Harwood (Buck) Casson, who was the son of a steel buyer, was one of the first officer candidates. Educated at Birkdale School and then the King's School, Ely, he worked in the steel industry in Sheffield before and after the war. Similarly, with only one officer located with a biography, the percentage shows as 100 per cent for public school and working in a professional job.

502 (Ulster) Squadron was formed on 1 May 1925, as the only Irish Special Reserve squadron, commanded by Squadron Leader R.D. Oxland. A recruiting office was set up in the Old Town Hall Street. The first of December saw Pilot Officer Robert McLaughlin becoming the first SR pilot, and by the end of 1925 there were fifty airman recruits, who had been recruited by visiting local factories and employers to raise interest in the release of men for part-time duties. In September 1927 a new headquarters was found in Donegal Square South, which had workshops, a gym and social facilities which boosted recruitment, including three new SR officers. The Bank of Northern Ireland became the first employer to offer staff leave

on half pay if they gained commissions and this led to 2,500 applications for vacancies within the squadron. By 30 June 1928 502 Squadron had an establishment of thirteen officers and ninety-seven airmen. On 1 July 1937, 502 (Ulster) Squadron was transferred into the Auxiliary Air Force and Squadron Leader L.R. Briggs took on the role of commanding officer. Avro Anson aircraft arrived as the squadron was converted to a general reconnaissance squadron as part of No 18 Group of RAF Coastal Command.

Of the eighteen officers identified for 502 Squadron, information was found on fourteen of them, which equates to 78 per cent. Of these men, 28 per cent attended public school, for example, Brian George Corry and Robin Terance Corry. Fourteen per cent were employed within the professions, including William Morrisson May who was an accountant. Finally, only 16 per cent of men had their engagements announced in *The Times*, such as Joseph Cecil Gosselin Bell.

Table 6: Auxiliary Air Force and Special Reserve northern squadrons showing percentages of men with biographies

Squadron Number	Number of Identified Men	Number of Men With Biographies	% of Men With Biographies
602	46	27	59%
603	47	40	85%
607	24	10	42%
608	32	20	63%
609	21	13	62%
612	21	12	57%
616	2	1	50%
502	18	14	78%
TOTAL	**211**	**137**	**65%**

Of the 211 officers identified who served in northern AAF squadrons prior to the start of the Second World War, background details has been found on 65 per cent or 137 of the officers. It is evident that the young officer candidates from the northern AAF squadrons shared similar social backgrounds to their southern counterparts; over 33 per cent came from landed backgrounds or from family-owned businesses, particularly in textiles, collieries, shipping, timber and glass. Sixteen per cent enjoyed elite sports like foxhunting, yachting, rowing, rugby or cricket. A virtually equal number of northern officer candidates attended Oxford or Cambridge, which is around 38 per cent. Furthermore, social connections remained important and a national system of networking, starting at public school and then continuing through sporting and social links, found a new expression in the AAF. It is a case of class identities and solidarities transcending regional differences.

It is evident that the social backgrounds and activities of officers from London squadrons and those from other AAF squadrons were not identical. The common link was public schools and universities where a shared culture was promulgated and kept alive in the confines of the officers' mess. Organised sport played a major role in the life of both Oxford and Cambridge university students, in the shape of boat races, inter-university cricket matches, athletics and inter-collegiate competitions; these helped keep young men physically fit and familiar with team ethics, and fed effortlessly into the life of the typical AAF officer. Also, membership of either UAS was common amongst AAF recruits with 17 per cent having been part of these squadrons during their time at university, an experience that laid the foundations for an AAF career.

Clearly a hierarchy existed within the AAF between the officers and the airmen and the research shows that there was little contact between the two in terms of social activities. However, it is apparent that this division was a crucial part of the AAF as a military organisation. It allowed for the AAF to maintain its image as a "gentleman's flying club" which gave it a certain aura of social exclusivity. This enabled it to attract the "right sort" throughout the 1930s. This elitism was diluted during the war as major changes in the personnel of the AAF took place, some of which were a direct consequence of the creation of the RAFVR, and others as a result of dilution of the AAF. It became increasingly necessary to place regular RAF personnel and RAFVR men in the AAF squadron in order to replace casualties and fatalities; in effect, the previously elite officer class had to be supplemented with non-commissioned pilots to enable the squadrons to function effectively. A final contributory factor to this loss of social exclusivity within the AAF were technological advances in aircraft design and size; more men were necessary to crew the planes, and the pilots themselves needed to have a wider range of skills to fly safely at greater speeds. Social background became increasingly less important.

Furthermore, as the war developed, sergeants were being used increasingly to fly aircraft. Clearly as the war progressed, there were fewer local officers available to fly, either because of fatalities, injuries or postings to other squadrons, and men from lower ranks filled the gaps. Moreover, as the planes used by Coastal Command increased in size, they needed more men to crew them, and there were not enough officers to do this. Thus, changes in aircraft technology were a crucial factor in enabling lower-ranking airmen to fly; a situation that would not have been tolerated during the 1930s when social exclusiveness dominated the officers' mess.

Technological advances in aircraft design and production also resulted in large bombers requiring increasingly large crews. Aircraft such as the Lockheed Hudson required a crew of six, as crew size increased, some of the rear gunners and navigators became airmen. A co-pilot was also needed because the aircraft had a much longer range for flying. In the first instance, a second officer filled the co-pilot's role, but as the war progressed, a shortage of officers led to more NCO pilots being used, first as co-pilots then as pilots themselves. These technological advancements – increases in maximum speeds and range, amounts of weaponry and crew – reinforce the view that the AAF pool of officers could not supply the necessary manpower for these planes on a regular basis, and this transformed the structure and culture of the squadron.

The Royal Air Force Volunteer Reserve

When looking at the officers of the RAFVR, making statements about the social composition is much harder. In the first instance, men volunteered to join the RAFVR as an organisation, rather than individual squadrons as in the Auxiliary Air Force and Special Reserve Squadrons. Moreover, since the RAFVR was not fully operational until late 1936, this study only focuses on those volunteers who enlisted between 1937 and the middle of 1939. It is quite clear that there were no significant problems with recruitment.

Table 7: Royal Air Force Volunteer Reserve Initial data

Number of Identified Men	Number of men with Biographies	% of Men With Biographies
320	252	79%

From 30 July 1936, volunteers were able to enlist in the RAFVR, no experience was necessary, so this was far different from the AAF where officers had to be able to fly before they joined. The RAFVR was to be "a Citizens Air Force", where airmen would be paid all of their expenses for food, travel and accommodation, as well as an annual bounty.

Selection was different to the AAF too, candidates had to go before a selection board and they had to get through a medical examination. This selection process was designed so that every man could get through, unlike that of the AAF which looked for a certain "type" of young man. It also must be remembered that these new pilot recruits were enlisted as Leading Aircraftsmen, and during their training they were promoted to sergeant; they were not officers which meant that the net could be much more widely spread. In 1934 an Expansion Scheme for the RAF had been approved, increasing the number of Home Defence squadrons from fifty-two to seventy-five, but the RAF was only recruiting sixty pilots each year, in fact, it needed 800 more pilots each year, and the job of providing these pilots fell to the RAFVR. The aim was to appeal to the widest spectrum of young men.[39]

In December 1938, a new scheme came into place to recruit 6,600 skilled and semi-skilled airmen. Those who wanted to be aircrew would be trained to join existing squadrons rather than using them to create new units such as the auxiliary squadrons who had links to towns and counties. This was never the idea of the RAFVR. By January 1939 the RAFVR had produced 2,500 pilots in half of the anticipated time, and by June 1939, it was decided that all new recruits into the Royal Air Force would be taken in through the RAFVR. When war was declared in September 1939, there were 6,646 pilots, 1,623 Observers and 1,948 Wireless Operators/Air Gunners.[40]

Air Marshal Sir Denis Crowley-Milling noted that:

> "I was an apprentice at Rolls-Royce in 1937, having gone there straight from school. I was working on the Merlin engine when we heard that there was to be a new reserve called the RAFVR and that we could learn to fly for free. It was almost unbelievable. None of us could have afforded it. We could become pilots and be paid for doing so, and they would even pay your travel expenses. Becoming a pilot was something I could never have been able to pay for. I was earning thirty shillings a week. It was a terrific opportunity and we all thought how tremendous."[41]

He also highlighted the difference between the AAF pilots and the RAFVR pilots when he noted:

> "I was called up on 3 September 1939, I had my wings, and 150 hours in my logbook. I was a sergeant pilot. We were called 'phoney sergeants' by the regulars, because we had not been through the ranks. I didn't mind what I was called,

it was good natured anyway. The important thing to me was that I was a VR pilot. Then we trained alongside Auxiliaries of course and I think a lot of the VRs would have liked to have been Auxiliaries, with their red silk lined uniforms and their famous squadrons. They were officers of course. Their parents had paid for them to learn to fly. We had not developed our own set of traditions but we were very, very proud of the RAFVR."[42]

The results of the research will be compared in the same way as those for the AAF and SR squadrons.

Table 8: Royal Air Force Volunteer Reserve Data by category

Category	Number of Men	% of Men
Public School	99	39%
Oxbridge	135	54%
University	18	7%
Elite Sport	72	29%
Marriage Announcement	65	26%
Birth Announcement	22	9%
Death Announcement	79	31%
Profession	28	11%
Family Business	8	3%
University Air Squadron	27	10%

Table 9: Auxiliary Air Force and RAFVR actual numbers as a direct comparison by category

Category	AAF No of Men	AAF %	RAFVR No of Men	RAFVR %
Public School	62	20%	99	39%
Oxbridge	71	19%	140	54%
University	5	7%	18	7%
Elite Sport	29	11%	64	29%
Marriage Announcement	56	26%	72	28%
Birth Announcement	5	4%	19	9%
Death Announcement	82	27%	79	31%
Profession	63	24%	36	14%
Family Business	30	12%	2	1%
UAS	7	2%	27	10%

Tracing backgrounds of men who served in the AAF and SR squadrons across Scotland, Ireland and Wales proved somewhat easier than in some of the English squadrons. Many of the individual squadrons had their own histories written by local enthusiasts, which helped with the research in that they did identify individual officers which enabled more detailed research to be done. However, often these non-academic texts did not name individual recruits apart from the squadron commanding officers. These individual book details can be found in the bibliography, individual squadron histories exist for squadron numbers 600, 601, 603, 604, 605, 607, 608, 609, 610, 611, 616, 500 and 501.

When all of English squadron members have been analysed, the results are not on the whole what would have been expected. Given that most of the limited research focuses on the exploits of the two London squadrons, 600 and 601, their pre-war members do not seem to have been as privileged as was first thought when compared to those members of other AAF squadrons. For example, analysis of 600 (City of London) Squadron recruits show that only 32 per cent of their officers came from a background of public school and an Oxbridge university, whereas 50 per cent of officer recruits from 504 squadron came from the public school/Oxbridge background and 75 per cent of 503 squadron officer recruits came from the same background. However, it is apparent that 47 per cent of 600 squadron recruits worked in the City, and this is not matched by other squadrons.

When occupation is considered more of the men in the northern squadrons worked in family businesses as compared to those in southern squadrons. For most men, recruitment to the AAF and SR squadrons took place directly through the squadron as only 616 Squadron had a 25 per cent take up from UASs. 616 (South Yorkshire) Squadron also stands out as an anomaly as 50 per cent of its officer recruits had come from public school and 75 per cent of them worked in professions.

RAFVR

When analysing the results for the RAFVR certain points need to be considered before the results can be discussed. In the first instance, recruitment into the RAFVR was not via the individual squadron, and this made the identification of officer recruits much more difficult. Thus the *London Gazette* Archive was used to search for names of recruits to the RAFVR, and took a significantly longer time to identify the individual names, before *The Times* Digital Archive and other web pages could be used to build up a biography of each man. However, though the process took a longer amount of time, it was more successful than the AAF as 81 per cent of recruits for the RAFVR were identified.

By analysing the results using the same categories as used for the AAF and SR squadrons, the results can be compared. The RAFVR was to be a "citizens air force", where recruits were to come from a much less privileged background, and this would help to relieve the pressure on the AAF and the SR squadrons, where recruiting was more difficult due to what the AAF believed was its exclusivity.

The RAFVR had a higher percentage of candidates attending public school and a significantly higher percentage of people attending Oxford or Cambridge University and being a participant in elite sports such as rowing, fencing and boxing. *The Times* announcements such as marriage, births and deaths remain as similar figures. More candidates from the RAFVR joined UAS's, whilst those from family businesses are similar. The number of RAFVR recruits who attended Oxford or Cambridge is virtually double with 140 as compared to the AAF and SR figures which are seventy-one. Eighty-eight RAFVR candidates had attended public school compared with sixty-two for the AAF and SR squadrons. Sixty-four RAFVR recruits had been involved with elite sports as compared to twenty-nine from the AAF and SR. Only seven candidates had been involved in the UAS as compared to twenty-seven in the RAFVR, however, the AAF/SR squadrons had sixty-three men in the professions as compared to thirty-six in the RAFVR, and thirty working in family businesses compared to two in the RAFVR. So, what does this show? From the analysis of the results it is clear that the idea of a citizen's air force in terms of simple entry into the RAFVR did not come to fruition. Significantly more recruits to the RAFVR had come from a public school/Oxbridge background than the AAF. Furthermore, the findings are not what was expected when the research began. The results that were expected were that the AAF/SR squadrons would have considerably higher candidates for the public school/Oxbridge/elite sport background and this is clearly not the case.

When we compare the figures for the RAFVR with the same figures for the AAF and SR squadrons the evidence shows that in many ways, the exclusivity of the AAF was matched by the recruits of the RAFVR, regardless of the organisation's intentions when it was first developed. For example, 18 per cent of men in the AAF went to public school, whilst 39 per cent of the RAFVR recruits attended public school, and this pattern is followed by the 19 per cent of AAF recruits who went to either Oxford or Cambridge University compared to 54 per cent of RAFVR recruits. It must also be pointed out that for the RAFVR, the figures represent a much smaller time span for the RAFVR, that is between 1937 and the middle of 1939, whereas the AAF figures reflect the period 1925 to the middle of 1939.

Conclusion

An analysis of the pre-war data suggests that perhaps the Auxiliaries were not as exclusive as they wanted to portray themselves. Indeed the concept of the AAF as a "gentleman's flying club" does not hold true when all of the squadrons across the United Kingdom are taken into account. Moreover, the concept of the RAFVR being a "citizens' air force" does not hold true either. The detailed data analysis shows that 20 per cent of the men in the AAF attended public school and only 19 per cent attended an Oxbridge University, whereas, 39 per cent of men in the RAFVR attended public school and 54 per cent of them attended an Oxbridge University. Furthermore, when the two different types of data are compared, the results also show that those recruits to the RAFVR used *The Times* newspaper to make family announcements more than those men in the AAF. The research therefore challenges the existing historiography and provides a new contribution to knowledge by showing that the pre-war TAF was different to what had previously been thought. The Auxiliaries were less exclusive than previously suggested while the RAFVR were in fact more exclusive than had been thought.

Chapter 4

The War Years

September 1939 saw Germany invade Poland and Britain responding with a declaration of war. The Second World War played a major role in "damping-down" class tensions within the Territorial Air Force. Officers and airmen were united against the external enemy and it is apparent that the sheer pressure of winning the war pulled people of all ranks and social backgrounds together. In August 1939 members of the AAF and RAFVR were embodied into the RAF. There were twenty Auxiliary Air Force squadrons at the outbreak of war, fourteen squadrons who were fighter units, four squadrons who operated under the control of Coastal Command and two squadrons whose duties were army co-operation. Shores notes:

> "At this stage, as the AAF was being mobilised, all units were undoubtedly at their most 'pure' as 'auxiliary' squadrons. Certainly their ground crew personnel were essentially those who had faithfully served their chosen units throughout much of the 1930s and who were all enlisted under provisions which allowed the AAF personnel to refuse a posting to any other unit."[1]

A major change in recruitment took place in 1939 when a committee under the chairmanship of Sir James Barnes, Under Secretary of State for Air recommended increases in pay and allowances for the AAF and also required them to accept airmen pilots, first by training some of their own ground crew and then by taking in direct-entry men. Many AAF squadrons reacted violently to this order but were forced to comply and this resulted in a handful of AAF sergeant pilots in British AAF squadrons. On enlistment, recruits for other ranks were guaranteed that they would never be called upon to serve further than five miles from their home airfield. Once their term of enlistment was finished, they were then required to transfer into the RAFVR. By the end of the war, the original twenty-one AAF squadrons "became increasingly indistinguishable from all of the other squadrons fielded by the wartime RAF,"[2] due to an influx of pilots and aircrew from the RAFVR, the RAF and aircrew from allied forces and original members of the AAF being posted out to different squadrons.

Auxiliary Air Force

600 (City of London) Squadron were involved in the defence of the United Kingdom and, as part of Fighter Command, were active in the Battle of Britain. In November 1942 they flew out to North Africa before being posted to Malta, Sicily and finally Italy. One of its original members, Jack Elkan David Benham was reported missing whilst on air operations in January 1942 and by November of the same year he was presumed killed in action. He was the only son of Mrs M Benham of Bentinck Mansions, W1. His name is commemorated on Runnymede Memorial, Surrey, on Panel 64.[3] Another original member, Arthur Hammond Dalton was reported killed on active service on Thursday, 31 July 1941. The son of William and Catherine Dalton, and the husband of Eileen Dalton of Henley, Oxford, Anthony Henry Hamilton Tollemache was awarded the George Cross for bravery. On the 11 March 1940 at Manston in Kent, he was involved in the incident that led to the award of the Empire Gallantry Medal. Tollemache, of 600 Squadron, was pilot officer of an aircraft when it hit a tree and crashed into a field, bursting into flames. Tollemache was thrown clear, and his gunner LAC Smith was able to escape. However, realising that his passenger, Second Lieutenant Phillip Sperling, was still in the wreck, Tollemache, with complete disregard for the exploding ammunition, endeavoured to break into the forward hatch and rescue him. He persisted in this gallant attempt until driven off with his clothes blazing. His efforts were in vain however, as sadly Sperling died. Tollemache suffered horrendous burns in the incident and was saved by the pioneering work of Sir Archibald McIndoe. He recovered from his injuries, and the Empire Gallantry Medal was converted to a George Cross only a few months later.[4]

Squadron Leader Charles Arthur Pritchard was awarded a DFC (gazetted 24 June 1941). Pritchard was reported at the time to be the first Australian night fighter pilot to receive the award. His citation stated that; "This officer has displayed considerable skill as a night fighter pilot. His untiring devotion to duty, combined with great persistence and determination in his attacks against the enemy, have enabled him to destroy at least two and damage a further three of their aircraft at night. His example has been a source of encouragement to his fellow pilots."[5] Flying Officer Thomas Norman Hayes also received a DFC, gazetted on 24 May 1940. On 10 May 1940 Hayes flew one of six Blenheims which attacked Waalhaven airfield at Rotterdam in daylight. In company with the CO, he shared in the destruction of a Ju52 on the ground by machine-gun fire. Climbing away, the Blenheims were attacked by twelve Me110s, which Hayes, instructed by his gunner, Sergeant G.H. Holmes, evaded. Afterwards he saw a Ju52 and in spite of being harassed by enemy aircraft and with his own aircraft damaged, he attacked and sent it down with an engine on fire. Hayes evaded his attackers and headed for home but encountered three He115s, upon which he expended his remaining ammunition, breaking up their formation. He then got safely back to base, the only one of the six Blenheims to do so.[6] Finally, Samuel Charles Elworthy received the DSO, he flew Blenheims on operations over north-west Europe in 1940-41. "By his magnificent leadership and complete disregard of danger," his DSO citation read, "he brought his squadron to the highest peak of war efficiency."[7]

601 (County of London) Squadron spent the first part of 1940 helping with the Evacuation of Dunkirk and then defending their country during the Battle of Britain. They remained in the United Kingdom, involved in home defence until April 1942 when they relocated to Malta and then on to Egypt and Libya during that year. February 1943 saw them move to Tunisia and then back to Malta, Sicily and then to Italy in October 1943 where they remained until the end of the war. Some of the original members of the squadron were awarded DFCs and DSOs. John William Maxwell Aitken destroyed a He111 off Brighton during the night of 25/26 June. For this and his victories in France in May he was awarded the DFC (gazetted 9 July 1940). As Commanding Officer of 68 Squadron, he was also awarded a Czech Military Cross in August 1942, a DSO in August 1942 and the Air Efficiency Award in January 1943.[8] Gordon Neil Spencer Cleaver was awarded the DFC in September 1940 for the destruction of two Me110s in the Dunkirk area, followed a month later by a Ju87 and a Me109 destroyed on the twenty-sixth, an Me109 and an Me110, both probably destroyed on 11 August and an Me110 probably destroyed on the thirteenth. Two days later he was shot down in combat over Winchester. When his hood was shattered by a cannon shell Cleaver's eyes were filled with Perspex splinters. Somehow he managed to bale out and parachuted down at Lower Upham outside Southampton. He was taken to hospital in Salisbury. He would not

fly again, being now blind in the right eye and with seriously reduced vision in the left eye.[9]

Charles Patrick Green was a member of the English bobsleigh team in the 1936 Olympic Games. He was awarded the DFC in April 1941 for shooting down enemy aircraft over France and the DSO in August 1943 for shooting down enemy aircraft over the Mediterranean Sea whilst based in Malta, Sicily and Italy. Roger Joyce Bushell will be remembered for being imprisoned in Colditz camp, where he took on the role of escape officer and took part in the "Great Escape" where he was recaptured and murdered by the Germans. Also, Simon Howard Gilliat, Vivian Allen William Rosewarne and Julian Langley Smithers who also served as members of the squadron and were killed in action in 1940.

602 (City of Glasgow) Squadron remained in the United Kingdom throughout the early years of the war, concentrating on the defence of the country before moving to France in June 1944 and then Belgium in September of the same year. They then returned to England until the war ended in 1945. Robert Findlay Boyd was awarded the DFC on 24 September 1940, he "has led his flight into action on all possible occasions and by his initiative and accurate shooting has personally destroyed nine enemy aircraft. He has displayed cool judgment and a keen desire to engage the enemy irrespective of the odds against him."[10] He was also awarded the Bar to the DFC on 25 October 1940 and a DSO on 10 April 1942. Andrew Douglas Farquhar was awarded a DFC in recognition of gallantry during February 1940. Archibald Ashmore McKellar was credited with the downing of the first enemy aircraft to fall on British soil. He was awarded a DFC on 13 September 1940 and the Bar to the DFC on 8 October 1940. He was shot down and killed on 1 November 1940 and was later awarded the DSO for destroying twenty enemy aircraft. Marcus Robinson was awarded the Air Force Cross on 30 September 1941, as was another member of the squadron, Norman Stone. The Commanding Officer of 602 Squadron between 1940 and 1941, Alexander Vallance Riddell Johnstone, was also awarded a DFC and the Air Efficiency Award.

603 (City of Edinburgh) Squadron concentrated on the defence of Great Britain between September 1939 and March 1941, being actively involved in the Battle of Britain. In April 1942 they moved to Malta before moving to Egypt until December 1944. They finished the war back in England. John Laurence Gilchrest Cunningham died in the Battle of Britain when his Spitfire was shot down by a Me109 over Dover on 28 August 1940.

Malcolm Avendale Douglas-Hamilton was awarded a DFC in 1945 whilst his brother George was twice mentioned in dispatches and was awarded the Air Force Cross in 1938. Another squadron member, Patrick Gifford, was killed in action on 16 May 1940 and his body was never found. He was awarded the DFC for gallantry in flying operations. Several original squadron members were killed during the war, including Claude Eric Hamilton, Graham Cousin Hunter, Harold Kennedy MacDonald, Donald Kenneth Andrew Mackenzie and Donald Kennedy MacDonald.

604 (County of Middlesex) Squadron concentrated on the defence of the United Kingdom between September 1939 and July 1944, taking a key role in the Battle of Britain. They spent a month in France before returning to England in September 1944 until the end of the war. Roderick Aeneas Chisholm was awarded the DFC in March 1941; "This officer has completed many hours operational flying at night. He has at all times shown the greatest keenness and determination to seek and destroy the enemy and, during one night in March, 1941, he succeeded in destroying two Heinkel 111s."[11] And a second DFC in July 1941: "Since being awarded the Distinguished Flying Cross in March 1941, this officer has destroyed five enemy bombers at night, thus bringing his victories to seven destroyed. By his exceptional skill, Squadron Leader Chisholm has been largely responsible for the high standard of efficiency shown by his flight."[12] Followed by a DSO in 1944: "This officer has completed an extremely large number of sorties at night during which he has destroyed nine enemy aircraft. He has displayed exceptional skill and keenness and, both in the air and on the ground, his outstanding qualities and personal example have contributed materially to the efficiency of the unit he commands."[13] John Cunningham also ended the war with three DSOs, two DFCs and an Air Efficiency Award. Alan Sidney Whitehorn Dore was also awarded a DSO, whilst Philip Charles Fenner Lawton and Hugh Speke were both awarded DFCs. Michael Duke Doulton was shot down over the Thames Estuary on 31 August 1940 and was reported missing at the age of thirty-one. In August 1984 his aircraft was excavated near Romford in Essex and his remains were still in the cockpit.

605 (County of Warwick) Squadron were involved in the Evacuation of Dunkirk and the Battle of Britain, before being based in Malta in March 1942, and then moving on to Batavia, Java and Netherlands East Indies. Within the original squadron, Christopher Frederick Currant was one of the most successful fighter pilots. He "was twice awarded the DFC during

the Battle of Britain being credited with destroying at least thirteen enemy aircraft."[14] In July 1942 he was awarded the DSO, being described as "a most courageous pilot and a brilliant leader".[15]

607 (County of Durham) Squadron were part of the British Expeditionary Force and played an important role during the Battle of Britain. In May 1942 they were sent to India and served in Bengal before moving to Burma in 1945. James Michael Bazin was awarded the DFC in October 1940 and the DSO on 21 September 1945. Patrick George Leeson was a prisoner of war at Stalag Luft III and was one of the prisoners involved in the "Great Escape," although he was number 230 and only the first seventy-seven got out. Joseph Robert Kayll was awarded a DFC and a DSO in 1940. He was taken prisoner in 1941 and was also taken to Stalag Luft III where he took on the role of escape officer. He organised the "Wooden Horse" break out, but stopped organising breakouts after the "Great Escape" in 1944 when fifty prisoners who were recaptured were shot on Hitler's orders, including Roger Bushell of 601 Squadron. He was awarded the OBE in 1945 for his escape work in the camps. Montague Henry Brodrick Thompson was killed in action in Belgium on 13 May 1940.

608 (North Riding) Squadron were part of Coastal Command during the war and spent much of their time protecting shipping convoys around Scotland and the North East coastline. They went to Blida in Algeria in October 1942, before moving to Tunisia, Sicily and Italy in 1943. John Sherburn Priestly Phillips was awarded the DFC on 22 October 1940. The first operational flight of 608 Squadron was on the 21 September 1939 when an anti-submarine patrol left Thornaby on what proved to be a false alarm.[16] The number of operational sorties increased month by month so that by April 1940 the monthly total was 131. These consisted of convoy escorts, anti-submarine patrols, air-sea rescue missions and coastal patrols searching for sight of possible German invasion forces.[17] On 5 October 1939, after one months training, 608 (NR) Squadron became operational and on 27 October the squadron suffered its first operational casualties when Anson N5204 was shot down into the North Sea by a Hurricane from Digby. On 1 November 1939, King George VI, accompanied by the Chief of Air Staff, arrived to inspect 608 Squadron.[18] Following the inspection, planes were dispatched to search the coast looking for signs of enemy warships or merchant ships which were suspected of dropping raiding parties on to the North East Coast.[19] The rest of November and December

showed little activity due largely to poor weather and bad visibility. Over ten inches of snow fell in January 1940 making the aerodrome virtually unusable. Indeed, most of the early months of 1940 saw flying hampered by poor weather conditions.[20] An escort of planes from 608 Squadron helped to deliver the torpedoed destroyer HMS Kelly back into the River Tyne after it had fought off German E-Boats in an encounter off Heligoland, an engagement which had cost the ship twenty-seven deaths. This job was completed on 13 May 1940.[21]

In the *North Eastern Daily Gazette,* on 29 March 1941, the reporter talked of "Teesside weekend fliers making war history". He gave individual accounts of original members of 608 Squadron who had been posted to Fighter and Bomber Command, but generally speaking, the war record of this squadron will be a tale of hard slogging on general reconnaissance work in good weather and foul, at all times of the year, of nerve-wracking hours spent at tugging controls while shepherding convoys along the North East coast, or patrolling enemy coastlines ever conscious of the German fighters waiting to pounce.[22]

The writer went on to claim the important place the squadron held in local people's minds, although one wonders what many Thornaby residents made of this, but went on to describe how "other non-local personnel were now making up the squadron, it will be as gratifying to the people of Teesside as it was encouraging to the members of the squadron that all the vital work had not escaped the eyes of the Air Ministry, and the unit has four times been mentioned in despatches, and there have been two Distinguished Flying Crosses awarded. Few of the original members of the 608th Squadron now remain with the unit. There has been the inevitable toll of warfare, and many are playing a heroic part with other squadrons. But the tradition of the unit still remains, and when the exploits of each section are fully revealed, they will make an outstanding contribution towards the great part Teesside is playing in winning this war."[23]

During 1941, the squadron was re-equipped with Lockheed Hudson aircraft with their airborne radar. They carried out offensive missions off the Norwegian and Dutch coasts and dropped leaflets over Denmark, which urged the Danish people to continue their resistance to the Germans, and on 3 October the squadron bombed the enemy airfield at Aalborg.[24] In January 1942, 608 Squadron moved base from Thornaby to Wick in North Scotland. Their brief was to continue coastal reconnaissance and also to hunt for German U-Boats. They were involved in hitting a tanker, attacking U-Boats and attacking the German cruiser, *Prince Eugen.*[25] On 5 August 1942 the squadron moved up to the Shetland Islands to Sumburgh with a brief to attack targets off the Norwegian coast and to help protect convoys moving to North Russia.[26] However, on 25 August 1942 orders were received to move to Gosport. The main air party left on 25 August 1942, and the move had been completed by 27 August.[27] By 1 November, the squadron were on board HMT *Strathmore*, a P & O liner that had been commandeered as a troop ship. 608 Squadron's Operational Record Book states that "eight officers and 400 other ranks left Gourock for an unknown destination, which was later revealed that the squadron was to take part in the occupation by American and British forces of French North Africa. The ship's destination is the Port of Algiers."[28]

November 1942 was a busy month for the squadron as it provided anti-submarine cover for Allied shipping transporting the invasion force to North Africa. During the course of five consecutive days, it depth-charged eleven U-Boats, and such was the threat posed to the invasion life-line that 608 was moved to Blide in Algeria to enable them to have better coverage of the Straits of Gibraltar and the Western Approaches.[29] A detachment was also stationed at Bone, and from the two airfields the North Riding Squadron carried out 334 sorties over the next two months. Four U-Boats were attacked.[30] In February 1943, Wing Commander C.M.M. Grece DFC took over command of the squadron. It then switched its attention to the enemy supply routes feeding into Tunisia, firstly Protville and then Bo Rizzo being used as bases.[31] In August 1943, it moved to Augusta in Sicily from where it flew convoy escorts for Allied shipping that was building up for the campaign on the Italian mainland. Wing Commander D Finlay OBE took over as Commanding Officer of the squadron and its main base was moved to Grottaglie, with a detachment at Guado to provide constant anti-submarine patrols for the convoys servicing the Anzio beachhead.[32] By February 1944, the squadron had again moved its main base to Montecorvino, with a detachment at Bo Rizzo. Volcanic activity in March 1944 caused 608's Hudsons to be grounded after they were covered in volcanic dust from Mount Vesuvius; however, they eventually resumed their convoy duties until 7 July 1944 when the squadron was withdrawn from active duty. They were disbanded at Montecorvino on 31 July 1944.[33]

609 (West Riding) Squadron spent the war years within the United Kingdom, apart for helping with the Evacuation of Dunkirk and the Battle of Britain in 1940. Paul Richey was awarded the DFC and Bar during 1942 for his courage and determination in France. George Desmonde Ayre was killed

at Dunkirk on 30 May 1940 and John Curchin was reported missing on 4 June 1941 and later presumed killed in action.

610 (County of Chester) Squadron spent the war between United Kingdom bases apart from a short stint in Belgium in December 1944. Paul John Davies-Cook, John Kerr Wilson and Allan Delafield Graham were all killed on active service, while Cyril Stanley Bamberger was awarded the DSO and Bar in 1944 and James Anthony Leathart was awarded the DSO.

611 (West Lancashire) Squadron were involved in the Evacuation of Dunkirk and the Battle of Britain and remained on United Kingdom bases throughout the war. John Noel O'Reilly Blackwood was killed in action on 25 January 1940 and a killed in action notice was also given for Ralph Kenyon Crompton. Francis David Stephen Scott-Malden was awarded the DFC in August 1941, Bar to the DFC in June 1942 and the DSO in September 1942.

612 (County of Aberdeen) Squadron worked from bases in the United Kingdom throughout the war. Douglas Gordon Emslie Benzie was awarded a DFC in 1941. Stewart Audjo Middleton was awarded the DFC in 1940. Ronald Bain Thomson was awarded the DSO in 1943 and the DFC in 1943 also. Charles Chamberlain MacCulloch was killed on 25 April 1941 when his aircraft collided with a hospital. David Alexander Sadler was killed on active service in a Botha L203 on 28 August 1940, as was Alan Milne Scott who was killed on 5 November 1940 aged twenty-six.

613 (City of Manchester) Squadron was involved in the Evacuation of Dunkirk in 1940 and remained at bases throughout the United Kingdom for the remainder of the war. A.F. Anderson was awarded the DFC, DSO and the Bar to the DSO. Allen Laird Edy was awarded the DFC, and was killed on 5 December 1941 when his Spitfire caught fire. He baled out but was too close to the ground for his parachute to open.

614 (County of Glamorgan) Squadron remained on bases within the United Kingdom until November 1942 when they went out to Blida in Algeria, and then in August 1943 they moved on to Sicily before spending the last year of the war in Italy. Martin Llewellyn Edwards saw distinguished military service during the war in both the Auxiliary Air Force and the RAF. John Dudley Rollinson was awarded the DFC in January 1942 but was reported missing from air

operations in January 1944 with 630 Squadron and was presumed killed. David Smyth was reported missing on 18 November 1943, presumed killed, as was Philip Michael Vaughan Lysaght who was reported missing, presumed killed in action and Herbert Charles Wilson Miles who was also killed on active service.

615 (County of Surrey) Squadron were part of the British Expeditionary Force in France and were then involved in the Battle of Britain. In 1942 they went out to Bengal and then in June 1945 they went to Burma. Peter Collard was killed in action, as was John Richard Lloyd. Peter Norman Murton-Neale was killed in action over Belgium on 14 May 1940.

616 (South Yorkshire) Squadron took part in the Evacuation of Dunkirk and the Battle of Britain and then stayed on bases in the United Kingdom before leaving for Belgium and Germany in 1945. Lionel Harwood Casson was shot down over France and was captured near St Omer and sent to Stalag Luft III. He was awarded a DFC. Ralph Roberts was shot down over Calais in Spitfire K9964, he too was captured and sent to Stalag Luft III where he remained until the camp was freed in May 1945. Henry Spencer Lisle Dundas was awarded a DFC in August 1941 and the DSO in 1944.

500 (County of Kent) Squadron were involved in the Battle of Britain in 1940 and remained in the United Kingdom until November 1942 when they were sent to Algeria, followed by Corsica in 1943, Italy in 1944 and finally Kenya in 1945. James Peter Henry Balston was killed in action in April 1940, in September 1940 Stanley Dudley Pierce Connors was also killed in action. Dennis Guy Mabey was killed in action on 23 October 1939 and Andrew MacDonald Paterson was killed in action on 13 October 1939. Patrick Green was awarded the DFC on Monday, 14 April 1941.

501 (County of Gloucester) Squadron were involved in the Battle of Britain in 1940 and then remained on bases throughout the United Kingdom for the rest of the war. John Ryan Cridland was killed on active service on 12 June 1943, Allan Frederick William Miles was reported missing, presumed killed, on 20 December 1941, Peter Herbert Rayner was killed in action on 20 May 1940 and Michael Fauconberge Clifford Smith was killed in action on 12 June 1940.

502 (Ulster) Squadron served on bases across the United Kingdom during the war. Samuel John Harrison was awarded the DFC. James Charles

Barclay had previously been reported as a prisoner of war but was later reported missing believed killed in action on 3 November 1941. Arthur Peter Buckley Holmes died on 23 January 1941 aged thirty-two and Mervyn John Cameron Stanley was reported missing on 1 May 1942.

503 (County of Lincoln) Squadron were disbanded in January 1938 and became 616 (South Yorkshire) Squadron, but some of the original members deserve mention. John Swift Bell was killed on active service on 4 September 1940. Edward Fitzroy St Aubyn was killed in action in May 1943 and Roger Hargreaves Maw was shot down and is famous for designing the wooden vaulting horse which was used by his fellow prisoners of war to escape.

504 (County of Nottingham) Squadron were involved in the Battle of Britain in 1940 and then remained on United Kingdom bases for the remainder of the war. John Michael Godfree Brown was killed in action on 16 October 1939, John Samuel Owen was killed in action on 15 November 1940 and Rupert Hartley Watson was killed in active service on 13 May 1940.

Auxiliary Squadron roles throughout World War II

Squadron number	War Command	Wartime Postings
600 (City of London) Squadron	Fighter Command	Home defence including the Battle of Britain North Africa Malta Sicily Italy
601 (County of London) Squadron	Fighter Command	Home defence including the Dunkirk Evacuation and the Battle of Britain Malta Egypt Libya Tunisia Sicily Italy
602 (City of Glasgow) Squadron	Fighter Command	Scotland England France Belgium England

Squadron number	War Command	Wartime Postings
603 (City of Edinburgh) Squadron	Fighter Command	Scotland England Malta Egypt United Kingdom
604 (County of Middlesex) Squadron	Fighter Command	Home defence including the Battle of Britain France England
605 (County of Warwick) Squadron	Fighter Command	Home defence including the Dunkirk Evacuation and the Battle of Britain Malta Batavia, Java Netherlands East Indies
607 (County of Durham) Squadron	Fighter Command	Home defence including the British Expeditionary Force in France and the Battle of Britain England India Burma
608 (North Riding) Squadron	Coastal Command	Thornaby Scotland Blida, Algeria Tunisia Sicily Italy
609 (West Riding) Squadron	Fighter Command	Home defence including the Dunkirk Evacuation and the Battle of Britain United Kingdom
610 (County of Chester) Squadron	Fighter Command	United Kingdom Belgium United Kingdom
611 (West Lancashire) Squadron	Fighter Command	Home defence including the Dunkirk Evacuation and the Battle of Britain United Kingdom

612 (County of Aberdeen) Squadron	Coastal Command	United Kingdom
613 (City of Manchester) Squadron	Army Co-operation Unit	Home Defence including the Dunkirk Evacuation United Kingdom
614 (County of Glamorgan) Squadron	Army Co-operation Unit	United Kingdom Blida, Algeria Sicily Italy
615 (County of Surrey) Squadron	Fighter Command	Home defence including the British Expeditionary Force and the Battle of Britain Bengal Burma
616 (South Yorkshire) Squadron	Fighter Command	Home defence including the Dunkirk Evacuation and the Battle of Britain United Kingdom Belgium Germany
500 (County of Kent) Squadron	Coastal Command	Home defence including the Battle of Britain United Kingdom Algeria Corsica Italy Kenya
501 (County of Gloucester) Squadron	Fighter Command	Home defence including the Battle of Britain France United Kingdom
502 (Ulster) Squadron	Coastal Command	United Kingdom
503 (County of Lincoln) Squadron	Re-numbered 616 Squadron in January 1938	N/A
504 (County of Nottingham) Squadron	Fighter Command	Home defence including the Battle of Britain United Kingdom

Royal Air Force Volunteer Reserve

When war was declared on 3 September 1939 the RAFVR became the organisation through which all entrants to the Royal Air Force had to pass for training. As mentioned in earlier chapters the RAFVR was not allocated specific squadron numbers which makes it much more difficult to identify and track officer recruits. Also, the reserves, per se, did not exist once war began, as all reserves were embodied into the Royal Air Force for the duration of the hostilities. However, men who were identified as being in the RAFVR prior to the commencement of war have been followed for the purpose of this chapter and information about some of them has been found and is presented here.

Name	Date of Commission	Information
Christopher John Drake **Andreae**	01/02/1938	Failed to return from a combat with Me109s over the English Channel. He was 23-years-old.
John Frank Hough **Andrews**	16/11/1937	Killed on active service 24 January 1944.
Robert Howard **Angas**	20/12/1938	DFC awarded 4 December 1942.
Leslie Longmore **Bache**	16/11/1937	Served with 41 Squadron from August to October 1941 where he was killed in action aged twenty-eight.
James Peter Henry **Balston**	01/02/1938	Reported missing believed killed on active service aged twenty-six.
Clifton Charles Joseph **Barritt**	01/02/1938	Air Force Cross awarded.
Nathanial John Merriman **Barry**	15/11/1938	Hurricane V6800 was shot down by Me109s. He was twenty-two.
Maurice Edward **Blackstone**	31/05/1938	King's Commendation for Valuable service in the air. Awarded the DFC.
Arthur Thomas **Brock**	15/03/1938	Awarded DFC in August 1944.
A R **Brodie**	02/08/1938	Awarded DFC.
Kenneth Douglas **Bruce**	29/03/1938	Pilot with 48 Squadron killed on 11 April 1942.

Norman Whitmore **Burnett**	01/02/1938	Called up on 1 September 1939, he was with 266 Squadron at Wittering in June 1940. On 25 July he was posted to 46 Squadron at Digby. He crashed at Hollingbourne on 8 September following a combat over Sheppey. Admitted to hospital wounded having written off his plane. Following his recovery, he rejoined 46 Squadron and sailed for the Middle East in the aircraft carrier HMS *Argus*. In Gibraltar the pilots and aircraft were transferred to the carriers HMS *Ark Royal* and *Furious*. On 6 June 46 Squadron flew off to Halfar, Malta. Five days later he was flying Hurricane Z2480, when he was shot down by an MC200. A search to within sight of the coast of Sicily failed to find any trace of him. He is commemorated on the Malta Memorial.[34]
Davis Stuart Harold **Bury**	21/12/1937	Killed in action 9 April 1942.
Kenneth **Campbell**	23/08/1938	Posthumously awarded the Victoria Cross for an attack which damaged the German battle cruiser *Gneisenau*.
John Nemours **Carter**	06/09/1938	His plane crashed in Suffolk in bad weather returning from a leaflet drop. He and all his crew were killed on 3 March 1940.
Mark Medley **Carter**	01/02/1938	Killed on 15 May 1940 aged twenty-seven when he was shot down in Hurricane N2534.
John Champion **Carver**	16/08/1938	Attended Christ Church College, Oxford University.[35] Reported missing from operations, June 1942, Squadron Leader J.C. Carver RAFVR, third son of the late S.R.P. Carver.[36]

Name	Date of Commission	Information
Alexander Brise Travers **Cazalet**	28/06/1938	Killed on 9 September 1940.
Geoffrey Leonard **Cheshire**	16/11/1937	He was awarded the DFC, two bars to the DSO and, after completing the unique total of 100 missions, the Victoria Cross.[37]
Ralph Campbell **Chopping**	01/02/1938	Reported missing from 75 Squadron operation over Brest aged twenty-nine.
H A **Clark**	10/03/1939	DFC and DSO awarded
Alexander William Locke **Cobbe**	27/09/1938	Missing officially presumed killed in flying operations against the enemy on 8 September 1940.
L W **Coleman**	03/01/1939	DFC awarded November 1940, Bar to DFC awarded May 1941.
Denys Geoffrey Graeme **Coles**	08/11/1938	Missing presumed killed.
Kenneth Crossley **Cooke**	24/05/1938	62 Squadron killed in action 8 December 1941 aged thirty-one.
Hugh Christopher **Corbett**	18/10/1938	Killed on active service aged twenty-two. August 1940.
Philipp Richardson **Crompton**	05/04/1938	Awarded bar to the DFC in December 1942.
Thomas Edward Stafford **Crossman**	28/12/1937	Killed on active service aged twenty-two. June 1940.
Denis **Crowley-Milling**	04/05/1937	Awarded DFC in 1941, Bar to the DFC in 1942 and DSO in 1943.
Kenneth Fraser **Dacre**	03/01/1939	He was reported missing in September 1943 as a result of operations over north-west Germany and was presumed to have lost his life.[38] He was awarded the DFC in October 1943.
Peter Brian Newsom **Davis**	01/02/1938	Reported missing but killed in action on 19 September 1944. Previously awarded the DSO.
Archibald Ian Scott **Debenham**	01/02/1938	DFC awarded November 1943.

Gordon Alfred **Denby**	02/08/1938	Awarded DFC in April 1941. Reported missing in December 1942 and presumed to have lost his life. Actually killed on 10 December 1942.
Eric **Deville**	27/07/1938	Reported missing August 1943.
Denis Herbert **Dey**	01/02/1938	Died pm 6 October 1941 aged twenty-seven.
David William **Donaldson**	01/02/1938	DFC awarded November 1940, DSO awarded May 1943.
Alfred Graham **Douglas**	01/02/1938	Reported missing now presumed killed in action June 1941.
Michael Peregrine **Fellowes**	14/12/1937	Awarded DSO and DFC.
Basil Mark **Fisher**	26/07/1938	Killed in action 15 August 1940.
Frank John **French**	29/03/1938	DFC awarded April 1944.
Anthony Ellerton Ryan **Fry**	19/04/1938	DFC awarded in 1941.
Frederick Thomas **Gardiner**	22/02/1938	Awarded DFC on 10 March 1944.
Robert **Gray**	04/01/1938	Death announcement October 1942.
Christopher Harold **Hartley**	02/09/1938	DFC awarded January 1945.
Barry **Heath**	26/07/1938	Flew in the Battle of Britain and awarded the DFC.
James Jewill **Hill**	16/11/1937	Lost returning from Germany 29/30 October 1940.
Michael Rowland **Hill**	18/10/1938	Reported missing September 1945.
David Henry Thoroton **Hildyard**	19/04/1938	Awarded DFC in 1943.
Richard Hope **Hillary**	18/10/1939	3 September 1940 he was shot down by a Messerschmitt Me109 and suffered extensive burns. Returned to service with 54 Operational Training Unit. He died on 8 January 1943 when he crashed his Bristol Blenheim aged twenty-three.

Name	Date of Commission	Information
Richard Adrian **Hopkinson**	01/02/1938	Reported missing in air operations over Norway in July 1940 aged twenty-four.
Edward Gordon **Hughes**	04/07/1939	Awarded DFC September 1941 and DSO in November 1943.
Alec **Ingle**	21/05/1937	Badly burnt September 1943 after his plane was shot down over Northern France. Sent to Stalag Luft III.
James Fraser **Inkster**	01/02/1938	Commanding Officer of 515 Squadron from July 1943-January 1944.
Sidney Packwood **Jackson**	01/02/1938	AFC awarded August 1943.
Alfred William Douglas **James**	03/05/1938	DFC awarded.
George Herbert Arthur McGarel **Johnston**	04/01/1938	Awarded DFC in late 1942 and a DSO and Bar to his DFC in late 1944.
Michael Thomas **Judd**	16/11/1937	Awarded DFC in November 1942 and awarded Air Efficiency Award.
John William Rolfe **Kempe**	21/12/1937	Served in North Africa and Malta as well as with 602 Squadron.
John **Kershaw**	25/10/1938	Died during air operations in July 1940.
Dennis Maurice Gerald **Kilralfy**	22/11/1938	Killed on active service.
Benjamin Edward **Knight**	01/02/1938	16 May 1944 his Mosquito M1988 crashed when the bomb doors opened in error leading to a sudden loss of height.
Jack **Korndorffer**	06/09/1938	Received AFC April 1943.
Robert Charles Ewan **Law**	21/02/1939	Awarded DFC and DSO.
John Edward Seaton **MacAllister**	01/12/1938	Killed on 13 June 1940 aged twenty-seven.
Malcolm Robert **MacArthur**	25/10/1938	DFC awarded.

Michael John Colville **Marks**	29/11/1938	Killed in action September 1941.
Walter Ronald Price Knight **Mason**	01/02/1938	Reported missing 29 June 1940 now presumed killed in action during bombing operations over Libya.
Denys Mowbray **Maw**	01/02/1938	Awarded AFC November 1942.
Charles George Buchanan **McClure**	01/02/1938	Air Force Cross awarded September 1944.
George Goodhart **McLannahan**	01/02/1938	Air Efficiency Award January 1943.
Ernest Reginald **Meads**	01/02/1938	DFC awarded August 1943.
Charles Michael **Miller**	23/08/1938	Awarded DSO, DFC and Bars.
Leonard John **Oldacres**	01/02/1938	Based at Lille-Ronchin with No 4 Squadron when his plane was attacked and shot down on 5 May 1940.
Edward **Ostlere**	07/12/1937	March 1941 killed on active service.
Denis Geach **Parnell**	01/02/1938	Killed on 18 September 1940 when his Hurricane V6685 was shot down over Gravesend.
Cyril Wolrich **Passy**	16/11/1937	Crash landed his hurricane on 15 August 1940 after combat.
Arthur Peter **Pease**	01/02/1938	Killed in action, September 1940.
Arthur Docray **Phillips**	09/08/1938	DFC awarded October 1939, DSO awarded March 1944.
David John Colin **Pinckney**	06/12/1938	Reported missing believed killed during air operations in Burma aged twenty-three.
Geoffrey Frederic **Powell**	01/02/1938	DFC awarded in November 1943. DSO awarded December 1943.
John Rankin **Rathbone**	14/06/1938	Reported missing now presumed to have lost his life in operations against the enemy, December 1940.
Colin Guy Champion **Rawlings**	01/11/1938	Awarded DFC February 1941.

Name	Date of Commission	Information
William Ronald **Ross**	31/05/1938	On 14 November 1939, killed as a result of a flying accident, aged twenty-seven.
Kendrick Herbert **Salusbury-Hughes**	01/02/1938	Did not return from night operations over Italy, 21 July 1943.
Terence Lindsay **Sandes**	27/09/1938	Awarded DFC January 1943.
Arthur John **Saver**	01/02/1938	Killed in action off the coast of Denmark on 15 February 1944.
William John Morr **Scott**	01/02/1938	Killed 8 September 1940 in Spitfire R6756.
Douglas. Frederic Ommanney **Shelford**	16/11/1937	Killed in action in the Western desert in April 1942.
Herbert Arthur **Skeats**	09/11/1937	Died 19 November 1940 aged twenty-five while serving with 206 Squadron.
Clifford Parker Seymour **Smith**	01/02/1938	Killed on active service in March 1940.
Harold Souden **Smith**	01/02/1938	Killed on active service June 1940.
Ian Raitt **Stephenson**	09/11/1937	Killed in action on 26 November 1943.
Arthur Kenneth Lennard **Stephenson**	19/04/1938	DFC awarded July 1944.
Ian Welsh **Sutherland**	08/11/1938	On 4 October 1940, killed as a result of an accident.
Graham Templer **Swann**	26/07/1938	Killed on active service July 1941.
George Holland **Thevenard**	19/07/1938	Killed on 1 August 1940.
William Kelman Burr **Thomas**	12/04/1938	Killed age twenty-six on 4 December 1941 flying as part of 106 Squadron over France.
Walter Briggs **Thompson**	29/03/1938	Air Efficiency Award, Air Force Cross awarded in 1943.
James William Jamesion **Truran**	01/02/1938	Awarded AFC June 1944.
Aidan Boys **Tucker**	01/02/1938	Part of 151 Squadron, shot down by Me109s on 12 August 1940 and crashed his Hurricane into the sea. Rescued with back wounds.

Hugh Beresford **Verity**	08/11/1938	Awarded DSO to go with DFC in August 1943.
William Hugh Maitland **Walker**	01/02/1938	Air Efficiency Award January 1943.
Gerald **Watson**	19/03/1938	Awarded DFC 11 January 1943.
Archibald Nigel Charles **Weir**	04/07/1939	Awarded DFC. Killed in action over the English Channel on 7 November 1940.
Patrick. Hardy Vesey **Wells**	22/02/1938	DSO awarded. With 249 Squadron bailed out wounded on 7 September 1940 when his Hurricane was shot down by return fire whilst attacking some Heinkel He111s.
Harold Raymond **Wheeler**	01/02/1938	Killed on active service August 1940.
Reginald Garton **Wilberforce**	01/02/1938	Awarded AFC January 1945.
Arthur Bernard **Wilkinson**	27/12/1938	Missing over Sicily 13 July 1943.
Trevor L McAlpine **Woods**	27/11/1938	Lost his life returning from an intruder patrol inside Germany on 11 May 1944.
Henry Melvin **Young**	13/09/1938	DFC awarded May 1941. Lost his life on a raid on the Ruhr Dams on 16 May 1943.

Conclusion

The Territorial Air Force played a key role within all the squadrons of the Royal Air Force throughout the duration of the Second World War. However, throughout the period 1939-1945, the TAF did not exist as such, as all of its personnel had been embodied into the full time Royal Air Force. Many of the pre-war auxiliaries chose to wear their brass "A"s on their uniforms to show their pride in their previous auxiliary squadrons. The same can be said for the RAFVR members who were also taken into the full time RAF. The TAF was reformed in 1946, the year after the war had ended, and its story continues in the next chapter.

Chapter 5

The Reconstitution of the Territorial Air Force 1946–1957

Introduction

This chapter will analyse the way in which the Territorial Air Force (TAF) was reformed in 1946, following its amalgamation into the Royal Air Force (RAF) for the duration of the Second World War. Through the use of primary source documents from The National Archives, the discussions between the Air Ministry and the Labour Government, formed after the General Election of July 1945, are identified, therefore enabling an analysis of the way in which the post-war TAF was recreated. Bearing in mind the shortcomings of the pre-war reserves, would the same mistakes be made again, resulting in an organisation which was not necessarily fit for purpose?

National Service is also discussed because of the considerable impact that it had on recruiting, particularly for the Royal Air Force Volunteer Reserve (RAFVR), but also for the Auxiliary Air Force (AAF), and this is discussed later in the chapter. The chapter will identify the recruitment process of the AAF and the RAFVR and will compare it to that of the pre-war highlighting significant differences in the importance of social class in the post-war world. The pre-war data highlighted the necessity of being the "right type" of young man to be recruited as an officer in the AAF, and therefore a question to be considered is the extent to which this holds true in the post-war world. This chapter will also discuss the role of recruitment posters which were used between 1948 and 1957. These posters were deliberately designed to appeal to young men who had the technical qualifications needed to fly or maintain a modern jet aeroplane.

Reconstitution of the Auxiliary Air Force

On 14 November 1945, William Wedgewood Benn, (Lord Stansgate), Secretary of State for Air, made a statement in the House of Lords on the

90

subject of the post-war Auxiliary and Reserve Forces. Following the speech, the approval of the King was granted for the resuscitation of Reserve Command of the RAF, which had been abolished in 1940 when its work, administering the reserves, had ended. He pointed out that "the appropriate joint Territorial Army and Air Force County Associations, with the approval of the Treasury, have been asked to undertake certain preliminary steps towards the reformation of the AAF squadrons which formed part of our first line air defence in 1939, and have since served with distinction in all theatres of war."[1]

Over time there would be twenty new Auxiliary squadrons which would be recreated on their old territorial basis. Recruiting to the AAF was going to be from officers and airmen who served with the RAF during the war. The Ministry of Air document notes that "it is laid down that the new AAF is to be raised by recruiting in the first instance released officers and men who have been trained in the Air Force during the war and who therefore will only require refresher training."[2] In terms of the AAF, the view was that:

> "We have the AAF as a means of augmenting economically the front-line strength of the regular RAF by making use of the voluntary services of young men willing to devote most of their spare time to the work. That a standard of efficiency as high as that to be found in regular squadrons can be attained by the AAF squadrons was amply demonstrated in the opening stages of the war and there is no reason to believe that this performance could not be repeated in the future, provided that the incentive is there."[3]

Throughout the end of 1945 and early 1946 there was a great deal of discussion around the role and classification of the newly reformed AAF squadrons. On 22 February 1946 considerations had been taken into account to determine the final squadron pattern for the AAF. The main points of these discussions were:

1. The squadron should be simple to operate, maintain and administer.
2. The squadron should not be called upon to proceed overseas except in war and should not be required to work mid-week.
3. The squadron should be static and based close to large towns.
4. AAF squadrons in any particular role should not outnumber RAF squadrons allotted to that role.[4]

These considerations led the Air Ministry to decide that:

- AAF squadrons should not be included among the small number needed for roles such as long range fighter and coastal shipping strike.
- Nor should they be included in light bomber squadrons or close support fighter units.
- The unit equipment of long-range strategical bomber, transport and general reconnaissance squadrons are also considered to be too complicated to be operated and maintained by Auxiliary personnel.[5]

There was a belief that demobbed RAF personnel would be keen to join the AAF to maintain their contact with servicemen who were their friends, but that "once that stock had been depleted, it would have to start using inexperienced crews, who would fly relatively infrequently and therefore might not be able to cope with the increasingly complex technology of aircraft."[6] Moreover, Air Vice-Marshal Douglas Macfadyen supported this view by concluding that there would be a major gulf between a man who could fly a modern fighter and a skilled pilot who could operate it effectively.[7] Clearly the shortcomings of part-time pilots and airmen flying and maintaining modern aircraft were apparent as early as February 1946, whilst discussions were taking place to reform the Auxiliary Squadrons. Furthermore, a memo from the Assistant Chief of Air Staff, dated 10 September 1945 noted that "in terms of the proposal to reconstitute a number of AAF squadrons as Night Fighter squadrons, I am of the opinion that it is unacceptable because it is extremely doubtful whether they could be trained to the high standard of efficiency in this specialised role."[8] However, the decision made by the Air Ministry was that the twenty auxiliary squadrons should comprise thirteen day fighter (interceptor) squadrons, three night fighter squadrons and four light/medium bomber squadrons, which were to be the responsibility of Reserve Command. They would ensure the raising and initial training of the reconstituted AAF squadrons which were to be named and located as follows:[9]

Table 10: Reconstituted Auxiliary Air Force squadrons name, classification and location

Squadron Number	Squadron Name	Squadron Classification	Squadron Location
500	County of Kent	Night Fighter	West Malling
501	County of Gloucester	Day Fighter	Filton
502	County of Ulster	Light Bomber	Aldergrove

504	County of Notts	Light Bomber	Syerston
600	City of London	Day Interceptor	Biggin Hill
601	County of London	Day Fighter	Hendon and later North Weald
602	County of Glasgow	Day Fighter	Abbotsinch
603	County of Edinburgh	Day Fighter	Turnhouse
604	County of Middlesex	Day Interceptor	Hendon and later North Weald
605	County of Warwick	Night Fighter	Honiley
607	County of Durham	Day Fighter	Ouston
608	North Riding	Light Bomber	Thornaby
609	West Riding	Night Fighter	Church Fenton
610	County of Cheshire	Day Fighter	Hooton Park
611	West Lancashire	Day Fighter	Speke
612	City of Aberdeen	Day Fighter	Dyce
613	City of Manchester	Day Fighter	Ringway
614	County of Glamorgan	Day Fighter	Llandow
615	County of Surrey	Day Fighter	Biggin Hill
616	South Yorkshire	Light Bomber	Finningley

Over several months there was also a dialogue taking place regarding the training of pilots, in that all fighter pilots, with the exclusion of night fighter pilots, would be trained on single-engine fighters, whilst single seat fighter pilots intended for twin-engine jet aircraft such as the Meteor and the Hornet, would receive their training on twin-engine aircraft:

Table 11: Reconstituted Auxiliary Air Force pilots in training – aircraft and percentage of pilots

Type of Aircraft	Percentage of Pilots
Single-Engine	32%
Twin-Engine	48%
Night Fighter	10%

Thus, there would be twenty auxiliary squadrons, thirteen of which would be day fighter (interceptor) squadrons, three would be night fighter squadrons and four would be light/medium bomber squadrons.[10] In September 1946, the Defence Committee decided to allow an active air force reserve of 72,000. Of those, 12,000 would be members of the AAF.[11] Wing Commander Jefford, speaking to the Royal Air Force Historical

Society noted that, "in the event of an emergency the auxiliary units would be embodied and take their places in the front line, as they had done during the Second World War."[12]

Matters become rather more complicated when discussing the post-war auxiliaries as it was decided to include two other type of squadrons within the AAF – the Light Anti-Aircraft ground-based squadrons of the AAF Regiment and the Auxiliary Fighter Control Units. The role of the Light Anti-Aircraft ground-based squadrons of the AAF Regiment was to act as airfield defence, using their Bofors L40/60 gun, whilst the role of the Auxiliary Fighter Control Units was to control air defence through the use of radar and Ground Controlled Interception units, which rotated 360 degrees allowing for the accurate tracking of aircraft over land and sea. Thus, the AAF was to have extra recruits which meant that the original figure of 12,000 had to be revised. The figure was increased in 1946 to 26,400, which had a huge impact on the numbers for the RAFVR which fell from 60,000 to 45,600.[13]

Table 12: Name of individual AAF squadron and new Light Anti-Aircraft Regiment squadron and new Air Defence Unit

Flying Squadron Number	Light Anti-Aircraft Regiment Squadron Number	Air Defence Units
600 (City of London) Squadron	2600 (City of London) Field Squadron AAF Regiment	
601 (County of London) Squadron		
602 (City of Glasgow) Squadron	2602 (City of Glasgow) Field Squadron AAF Regiment	3602 (City of Glasgow) Fighter Control Unit
603 (City of Edinburgh) Squadron	2603 (City of Edinburgh) Field Squadron AAF Regiment	3603 (County of Edinburgh) Fighter Control Unit
604 (County of Middlesex) Squadron		3604 (County of Middlesex) Fighter Control Unit
605 (County of Warwick) Squadron	2605 (County of Warwick) Field Squadron AAF Regiment	3605 (County of Warwick) Fighter Control Unit

607 (County of Durham) Squadron		
608 (North Riding) Squadron	2608 (North Riding) Field Squadron AAF Regiment	3608 (North Riding of Yorkshire) Fighter Control Unit
609 (West Riding) Squadron	2609 (West Riding) Field Squadron AAF Regiment	3609 (West Riding of Yorkshire) Fighter Control Unit
610 (County of Chester) Squadron		
611 (West Lancashire) Squadron	2611 (West Lancashire) Field Squadron AAF Regiment	3611 (West Lancashire) Fighter Control Unit
612 (County of Aberdeen) Squadron	2612 (County of Aberdeen) Field Squadron AAF Regiment	3612 (County of Aberdeen) Fighter Control Unit
613 (City of Manchester) Squadron		3613 (City of Manchester) Fighter Control Unit
614 (County of Glamorgan) Squadron		3614 (County of Glamorgan) Fighter Control Unit
615 (County of Surrey) Squadron		
616 (South Yorkshire) Squadron	2616 (South Yorkshire) Field Squadron AAF Regiment	
500 (County of Kent) Squadron		3500 (County of Kent) Fighter Control Unit
501 (County of Gloucester) Squadron	2501 (County of Gloucester) Field Squadron AAF Regiment	
502 (Ulster) Squadron	2502 (Ulster) Field Squadron AAF Regiment	3502 (County of Antrim) (Ulster) Fighter Control Unit
504 (County of Nottingham) Squadron	2504 (County of Nottingham) Field Squadron AAF Regiment	3504 (County of Nottingham) Fighter Control Unit

The newly formed AAF squadrons maintained much of their pre-war framework and organisation and "were established on a pre-war basis".[14] Advertisements that appeared in the press emphasised the specific requirements and conditions of service to ensure that men who volunteered were highly motivated and understood the commitment that they were making. For example, the *Yorkshire Post* noted on 7 November 1946:

> "Recruiting for the new Auxiliary Air Force of twenty flying squadrons opens tomorrow and will be carried out by the individual squadrons. At present, only officers and men who have served in the Air Force during the war are eligible to join. Vacancies exist for flying members, for personnel for ground trades...officers will be commissioned for five years and airmen will be enlisted for four years. Members must carry out certain training each year, to be undertaken during evenings, at weekends, and at the annual camp, which lasts fifteen days."[15]

The article went on to specify the conditions of service for both officers and airmen. Thus, men who volunteered to join the AAF were supposed to be very aware of their obligations towards the organisation and were fully cognisant of the nature and purpose of the establishment that they were volunteering to join. The social backgrounds of the officers ceased to carry the same weight as before, and this will be discussed in much more detail in the next chapter.

The changing technical demands of both flying and crewing aircraft became even more apparent when jet-engine aircraft became available to AAF squadrons in the late 1940s; aircraft which required large crews became obsolete and were replaced by single-seater fighters that needed high-level technical skills and knowledge to operate. A direct consequence of these technical changes was the acceptance of men as pilots who were not officers.[16] Whilst the initial level of interest was overwhelming, the actual number of men who met the criteria for enlisting was disappointing and reflected the new recruitment restrictions placed on all squadrons. Selection of officers, NCOs and airmen became much more demanding with particular emphasis on previous experience and knowledge.

In 1948 the regular establishment of an auxiliary squadron stood at three officers, five NCOs and thirty-three airmen, a total of forty-one, although HQ

Reserve Command had recently submitted a bid for this to be increased to sixty-four.[17] These demands were relaxed in 1948 to allow any ex-servicemen to join the AAF in an effort to increase recruitment.[18] However, in many ways this action was too late to enable the AAF squadrons to benefit from the immediate post-war wave of enthusiasm which subsequently waned as men successfully re-entered civilian life.

Another significant factor in slowing down recruitment was the conditions of service, which required the attendance for twelve weekends and fifteen days at annual camp, as well as the completion of one hundred hours of non-continuous training. Many potential recruits could not meet this level of commitment. Volunteers had to be prepared to give up a significant amount of their free time in order to fulfil their obligations to the AAF.[19] For airmen, wartime aircrew categories and ground crew classifications were superseded by peacetime ones, sometimes requiring higher qualifications.[20] On 19 January 1948 a memo was sent to all AAF squadrons informing them that in recognition of their outstanding service in the Battle of Britain and in many of the other campaigns, King George VI had conferred upon the AAF, the pre-fix "Royal".[21] This title remained until all of the squadrons were disbanded in March 1957.

Recruiting by the end of March 1948 was at 39 per cent of the establishment figures for the Royal Auxiliary Air Force (RAuxAF) across the country.[22] National attention turned to new conscripts who were being compelled by the National Service Act of 1948 to join HM Forces. Initially the time period of National Service was eighteen months but this was extended to two years following the outbreak of the Korean War in 1950. An agreement was made that 300 National Service conscripts would be selected for flying training each year and these men would fulfil their subsequent reserve obligation by either becoming members of the Volunteer Reserve or of an auxiliary squadron. In this way it was hoped that the poor number of recruits for the RAuxAF squadrons could be boosted.[23]

There was also an undercurrent of thought which was captured in 1949 by Air-Vice Marshal Douglas Macfadyen who was quoted as stating that he was very aware of the gulf that existed "between the man who can fly a modern fighter and the skilled pilot who can operate it effectively".[24] These beliefs were compounded by poor overall recruiting figures, there were significant numbers of pilots, around 73 per cent across England who had served in the AAF during the 1930s and were eager to continue flying, and wanted the opportunity to fly. Many were officers who had attained high ranks or had been decorated for their skill and bravery; others were NCOs who had been able to fly and had enjoyed successful careers. Members from both groups were very willing to re-join the RAuxAF as soon as it was reformed, but these men were in the minority compared to the larger number of ex RAF personnel.

During the mid to late 1940s and throughout the 1950s the auxiliary squadrons struggled to recruit sufficient numbers to maintain efficiency. Indeed, there had been concern about their efficiency since they had been reformed in 1946. By 1948, the Minister of Labour appealed to young men and women to join one of the auxiliary or reserve forces. He also asked employers to give their employees all possible facilities.[25] Lord Pakenham, Minister of Civil Aviation urged more volunteers to come forward, stating that the RAuxAF still needed some 25,000 volunteers. He noted that the country would remain in danger, along with the rest of Europe, until Western Europe was very much stronger both economically and militarily.[26] In early 1949, Arthur Henderson, Secretary of State for Air, noted that to fit the squadrons of the RAuxAF for their role as part of the first line of Britain's defence they were to be re-equipped with jet fighters. He hoped that as a result of special measures to be taken this year a steadily increasing number of auxiliary pilots would be able to gain jet flying experience.[27]

The Auxiliary and Reserve Forces Bill was presented to the House of Commons on 23 May 1949. "It is designed to extend the powers and duties of the territorial and auxiliary forces associations and to facilitate calling out reserve and auxiliary forces to meet either an actual or an apprehended attack upon the United Kingdom."[28] At the end of October 1949 the twenty fighter squadrons of the RAuxAF were transferred to Fighter Command, which emphasized their place in the wartime front line defences of Great Britain. "Since their reforming in 1946, the squadrons have been training and have now reached a sufficiently high standard to be transferred into the command who would control them in a time of war."[29] Throughout this time, recruitment posters appeared regularly in *The Times*.

During March 1950, a new Air Ministry Scheme which enabled the twenty squadrons of the RAuxAF to have combined training with the regular fighter squadrons every month was unveiled. This scheme would enable the auxiliaries to get the most out of their weekend flying by operating under conditions similar to wartime. Each auxiliary unit was affiliated to a regular squadron, and each auxiliary squadron would visit their regular station to help them gain a close understanding and develop a common operating system and technique. The pilots and ground crews would live on the RAF station during their training weekend. "For the auxiliary pilots, the greatest benefit will be that they become accustomed to being directed from the ground, which they cannot do unless they are operating under a Fighter Command sector control."[30]

Towards the end of 1953 a new pilot training scheme was announced to maintain the strength of the RAuxAF. Commanding Officers of auxiliary squadrons were able to select and recommend youths for aircrew training before their national service, if they were willing to transfer to the RAuxAF after completing their two year full-time service, their pilot training would occupy nearly all of the period but the time and expense would be justified by their continued part-time service with an auxiliary service.[31]

National Service

At the end of the Second World War, the General Election resulted in a Labour landslide victory, and a new Prime Minister, Clement Attlee. One of his election promises was to quickly bring home and release over five million men who had fought in the various theatres of war. However, British forces were still involved in clashes in both Italy and Greece, as well as Malaya, Singapore and Hong Kong. These circumstances led the Government to consider reintroducing conscription in the post-war world, to cope with the poor recruiting into the regular armed forces which could not plug the gap left by the huge number of skilled men who were being demobbed.

On 30 May 1946, a White Paper entitled National Service (Call-Up Scheme) was introduced which tentatively put forward the plans for National Service which would be imposed across all of society, not just on public-spirited public schoolboys.[32] A great deal of debate took place primarily on the length of service, which was initially set at eighteen months full time service followed by five and a half years part-time service with the reserve. The National Service Act became law in May 1947. All men living in Britain were liable for National Service between the ages of eighteen and twenty-six. In December 1948 the National Service Amendment Act came into force which maintained the eighteen months full time service, but reduced the part-time service to four years, furthermore, following the onset of the Korean War in 1950, National Service was increased to two years full time service with three and a half years part-time service. Any young man who had a place at university, or who was completing professional articles, or who had accepted an apprenticeship could defer their National Service until they had finished, however, the majority of those chose to do their National Service first before taking up their place. If the young man was going to Oxford or Cambridge University, they were given no choice as the Oxbridge universities had agreed to take men only after their National Service was completed.[33]

Once the young man had registered for his National Service, he would have to attend a medical which was conducted by a civilian panel of GPs, a basic intelligence test and a discussion with an interviewing officer. Tom Hickman, in his *History of National Service,* suggests that, "the Battle of Britain lived on in the imagination of the wartime generation. Many still thought the RAF was the one to go for: discipline was known to be more relaxed than in the army, living conditions were better, and, all things considered, you were less likely to be shot at."[34] Moreover, "there were ways of increasing your chances of getting into the air force or navy. One was to belong to an appropriate cadet corps. Another was by training with the RAFVR or the RNVR."[35] In general terms, out of every one hundred men the army took seventy-two, the Royal Air Force took twenty-six and the Navy took two. One young man who was desperate to do his National Service as a pilot with the RAF felt that his interview had not gone well. "The examiner stood at the window, deep in thought. 'Look at that bloody sports car!' he suddenly yelled. Colin had parked the Allard in front of the building. 'It's mine', he said. 'Crikey! Well, if you can drive that you can certainly fly a plane,' he said and passed him right away."[36]

The National Service Act which came into force on 1 January 1949 imposed a liability for five and a half years' service, which was made up of two years' full-time service and three and a half years part-time service. The Act was for young men between the ages of seventeen and twenty-one. Some men who served their National Service in the RAF went on to take a permanent job with them. Those who signed up to work as aircrew had to agree that after completion of their compulsory two-year full-time service, their reserve service would be taken with the RAuxAF or the RAFVR. Part of the station commander's role was to ensure that National Service men were made fully aware of the opportunities for service in the RAuxAF and the RAFVR. Men were given the opportunity to visit their local RAuxAF station and to speak to the commanding officer. This process was meant to allow the smooth transition into the reserve forces following completion of their two-year full-time service.[37]

Most men who wanted a commission in the air force wanted to be aircrew, with most of those wanting to be pilots:

> "The air force put their candidates through a rigorous examination at RAF Hornchurch that involved written papers, tests of perception and dexterity, eye-hand coordination and acuity of hearing, and a medical which was so tough they almost failed men who had a filling. The failure rate was high, 1,300 men out of the 6000 selected for aircrew training during the national service years failed to get their wings."[38]

Hickman suggests that National Service threw together men from all backgrounds and walks of life and helped to mobilise social change, however, he counters that suggestion by saying that potential officers were whisked away from the rest of the men as if they might be contaminated by the others, and that "getting a commission was all about having an acceptable accent". In the National Service years the air force commissioned just over 9,000.[39] How much National Service influenced social change is difficult to say. Certainly if those wanting to be commissioned were kept away from the other men, then perhaps not. However, one thing that National Service did highlight is the considerably tougher process of being selected for officer training in the Royal Air Force which suggests perhaps that the old system of word of mouth and social status was no longer the key to a commission.

The Post-War Royal Air Force Volunteer Reserve

The RAFVR was reconstituted after the war, with its role being defined as "providing a reserve of flying personnel (pilots, navigators, signallers, engineers and gunners) and of officers and airmen in certain ground branches and trades".[40] It was also expected that the RAFVR would include, and indeed would largely consist of, personnel who had completed their period of compulsory national service and who were still liable to a statutory period of reserve service.[41] In April 1947 a revised set of regulations were approved by the King for the RAFVR. Officers would continue to wear the gilt "VR" badges on their collars whilst airmen would wear the cloth patches on their upper sleeve.[42] A new feature for the RAFVR was the introduction, in June 1947, of women pilots which had been approved by Philip Noel-Baker, Secretary of State, with a ceiling figure of 200.[43]

Immediately after the end of the Second World War, many regular and part-time pilots were keen to enlist in the RAFVR, and were signed up for a period of five years. However, there were never enough pilots and consequently, focus was turned to the National Service men. However, training to be awarded their wings took eighteen months, and in general, men were enlisted only for twelve months. For this reason, the Preliminary Flying Badge, which ensured that trainee pilots would be able to show their skills at a basic level, was introduced, and as time went on and the length of service for National Service men was increased to eighteen months, most pilots had reached a competent level. Furthermore, there were also VR women pilots who had a great deal of experience who would be able to demonstrate their proficiency at Preliminary Flying Badge and beyond.

It was hoped that a figure of 72,000 was going to be adequate for the Territorial Air Force with 60,000 being part of the RAFVR. The remaining 12,000 would be members of the RAuxAF, as mentioned earlier in the chapter. This figure of 60,000 would be made up of 20,000 flying personnel, which would include pilots, navigators, signallers, engineers and gunners. The remaining 40,000 would be made up from ground crew recruits. All of these recruits to the RAFVR would come from veterans who were just leaving the RAF at the end of the war.[44]

On 20 October 1947, Arthur Henderson, Secretary of State for Air said that "this was a difficult period in which to recruit men and women to the reserve forces because patriotic men and women were now putting forward their best efforts to help the country in the economic struggle" that faced the country after the end of the war.[45] This was followed up when it was announced that there would be a special campaign to bring the RAFVR up to strength because of the key positions which the fighter squadrons held in the defence of the country.[46] In February 1949 in the Air Estimates it was noted that the RAFVR was being developed and new centres for training were being opened.[47]

Mr A.M. Crawley, Parliamentary Under Secretary of State for Air opened the new No 81 Reserve Centre in London and spoke of the extent of the need for recruits in the RAFVR. It was hoped to enlist 35,000 recruits throughout the country, but the strength was 8,500 in 1950. He specifically spoke of the need for tradesmen.[48] At least a further 3,000 volunteers were asked for with the greatest need in London being for ground trades such as maintenance, signals and radar.[49] In the Defence Budget of 1952, three more flights were to be formed in the RAFVR at Fighter Command and four new types of training aircraft would be introduced into squadrons, two of which were jets, the Vampire T2 and the Canberra T4.[50]

Typical examples of recruiting posters from the 1950s highlight the need for airmen rather than pilots, and there are a selection of typical advertisements to reinforce the point.

Each recruitment advertisement promotes a slightly different message. Illustration number 1, dated 15 July 1948, is very formal and is specifically aimed at those ex-service personnel who want to join the RAFVR, stating; "At present, pilots, navigators and signallers who have gained their wings in the services, and ground officers of certain branches who served with the RAF during the war are eligible."[51] It moves on to inform prospective recruits what pay and allowances they would expect to receive, and also any allowances for using their own vehicle. Finally, it moves on to explain the training commitments, and explains who to contact for details, should someone reading the advert be interested in joining.

Illustration number 2, which dates from August 1948, targets two groups of readers. Firstly, those who want to do some spare time flying as qualified pilots in the RAFVR, and secondly, those who might be interested in working in the RAuxAF as ground control within the Air Defence Unit. It is split into four distinct areas, and again presents a significant amount of information for those who might be interested in joining. The first two quarters show the 35,000-recruitment target for the RAFVR, and the 25,000 targets for the RAuxAF, and then presents the age limits for joining, the period of engagement, training commitment and pay and allowances for each group. The opposite side of the advert presents the full-time opportunities for both men and boys, and again presents a significant amount of information from age limits to leave, for those who might be interested in a full-time career in the RAF.[52]

Illustration number 3 is aimed at the "air-minded" Auxiliaries and the Reserves. It points out that "here is the perfect opportunity for pilots, navigators and signallers to keep their hands in; and for other enthusiasts to handle and maintain modern aircraft – at no cost to themselves."[53] It then moves on to list several of the different trades open to people within both the Auxiliaries and the Reserves, following on with training commitment and pay.[54]

During 1950, five different advertisements were used to try to encourage recruitment within the RAuxAF and the RAFVR. These adverts took a slightly different approach by presenting a drawing of some aspect of work within the RAF Reserves. Illustration number 4, used in January 1950, shows an aeroplane which is being refuelled from a petrol bowser, and features one man working with the bowser, two men refuelling and one man in the pilot's seat. It does not give a great deal of information about pay and training commitment. Instead it takes a completely different approach by appealing in a different way to those who might wish to join:

> "On odd evenings and at week-ends you'll find gathered together the men and women of the Royal Auxiliary Air Force and the Royal Air Force Volunteer Reserve. They work in offices or factories during the day – and then in their spare time learn to master the new equipment of the RAF. They're friendly people doing particularly vital work. Why don't you join them? They need you."[55]

This is followed by Illustration number 5 which is aimed at the more senior executives in civilian life, showing a picture of two men and a woman in discussion with an aircraft in the background, with the slogan; "Managing directors are proud to be mechanics with these keen spare time airmen."[56] It goes on to say:

> "The spirit of the men and women in the Royal Auxiliary Air Force and the RAF Volunteer Reserve is shown by the numbers who, holding important jobs are well content to spend their spare time as members of these organisations. Whether they are ex-servicemen glad to be back where they feel they belong, or new boys proud to be allowed to join, they are all comrades in enthusiasm. All of them – from the pilot with rows of ribbons to the youngster learning the secrets of radar – share the satisfaction of knowing they are helping to keep Britain 'on top' in the air."[57]

This advert appealed to the patriotism of the reader. Illustration number 6, which appears in May 1950, again has a picture of a member of a ground crew pulling the chocks away from an aircraft wheel. It is aimed at those men who do not wish to fly, which makes it different from the previous advertisements. It states:

> "Membership of the RAF Auxiliaries or Reserves is by no means restricted to men and women who fly. For without the ground staff there would *be* no flying. That is why so many

keen men and women volunteer for ground trades. They enjoy spending their spare time demonstrating their ability as skilled technicians and organisers. They are well satisfied to know they are helping to strengthen Britain's influence for peace."[58]

Illustration number 7 from June 1950 features a pilot sitting in his cockpit talking to an airman on his wing and a Women's Auxiliary Air Force (WAAF) holding a clipboard. The heading is; "Spend flying weekends with these keen spare-time airmen."[59] It then moves on to say:

"Did you wear pilot's, navigator's or signaller's wings? If so you may spend your weekends (and other spare time) in the air – by joining the RAF Auxiliaries or Reserves. You are paid and receive allowances at current RAF rates. You get an annual training bounty of £35. You have the additional satisfaction of knowing you are 'doing your bit – and a bit more'. Flying weekends and annual summer camp are also shared by the part-time ground staff who have the fine and responsible job of keeping the squadrons in the air."[60]

The final recruiting advertisement for 1950 is illustration number 8 which was used in December of that year and asked people to "do a grand job in your spare time".[61] The advertisement uses a picture of a ground crew working on some equipment with a jet aircraft in the background, noting that:

"Air power in reserve helps to keep the peace. An efficient highly trained reserve force, proud of its ability to back up the regular RAF, is the best deterrent to would be aggressors. Men and women who believe that our strength in the air ensures peace are needed now to help maintain the proud status of the RAF."[62]

All of the advertisements of 1950 work hard to put forward the view that Britain has the best air force and its role is to ensure peace is maintained. They appeal to both men and women alike in trying to persuade them that for people from all walks of life, there is a place for them in the RAF Reserves, where they can use their spare time in a constructive and productive way.

Two recruiting posters were used in 1951. Illustration number 9 appeared in January of that year and shows a picture of two men on top of an aircraft working on the engine, with the headline; "Help keep Britain *'on top'* in the air."[63] It then moves on to state that:

"To keep Britain 'on top' in the air is to safeguard world peace. That is a responsibility not only of the RAF, but also of its Auxiliaries and Reserves, the men and women who choose to spend a little of their spare-time serving so great an end. If you are both air-minded and peace-minded, you will find this a grand part-time job. It is at once exciting and rewarding."[64]

The second poster, illustration number 10, appears in March 1951 and shows a picture of a pilot in full flying gear standing next to an aircraft, with a pencilled in pilot and an arrow pointing to him stating, "there's a place for you in the part-time RAF."[65] This poster puts forward the importance of volunteering to undertake the vital work of the RAF Reserves, which will enable the applicant to learn useful new skills and to improve existing ones. It also points out that:

"Whether you choose to serve in the air or on the ground the close association with the Royal Air Force will give you new experiences and fresh companionship that you can gain in no other way."[66]

As in the posters of 1950, both of the recruitment posters for 1951 use similar ways to gain the interest of the reader, and to make them see how important they are to the security and safety of Great Britain.

Two posters appeared in 1952. The first, illustration number 11, which appeared in *Flight* magazine in June shows an airman guiding an airman driving a tractor which is pulling a jet aircraft out of a hanger. It states:

"Much has been said and written about the weekend flyers of the pre-war RAuxAF and RAFVR. They and their ground crews – particularly in the tense uncertain days of the Battle of Britain – helped to make possible our way of life today. To keep this life intact we still need weekend airmen. Why don't you become one of them?"[67]

The second one, illustration number 12, appeared in September 1952, and is exactly the same one that appeared in January 1950, with the petrol bowser and the men refuelling the aircraft. It has the same text, ending with, "they're friendly people doing particularly vital work. Why don't you join them? They need you."[68] The adverts attract recruits by offering them something interesting to do with their spare time.

The final advert, illustration number 13, appeared in *Flight* magazine in March 1953 and shows two photographs, the first one with the caption "Berlin 1943", the second with the caption "and back 1953."[69] This poster highlights the "hundreds of ex-RAF men and women who found they were missing the old friendships are back on the job part-time. At week-ends and summer camps they keep abreast of new techniques and meet old friends."[70] So continues to push forward ideas of comradeship and importance.

It is clear that the RAF used many different ways of trying to recruit members to the RAuxAF and the RAFVR. However, the recruiting figures show that these advertisements were not particularly successful in their job and that could be down to post-war apathy, or the fact that those personnel who had served in the RAF during the Second World War, felt that they had done their bit and did not want to consider re-joining, even on a part time basis. In June 1947 it was noted by Sir Basil Embry, Commander-in-Chief of Fighter Command between 1949 and 1953, that the RAuxAF was "living off the fat" which was represented by the post-war veterans who had joined the RAuxAF in 1946 straight after the end of the war. He pointed out that the RAF needed to face up to the fact that by 1951 at the very latest, this stock of men would have effectively run out and therefore the RAuxAF would have to start using recruits with little or no previous experience, and that, coupled with their lesser attendance and training, was likely to create problems for the organisation as a whole.[71] Moreover, what is apparent from analysing these advertisements is that the focus of the recruiting campaign is on airmen not officers. Since flying was seen by many as the more exciting part of the RAF, there was less difficulty recruiting those men who wanted to fly. It would seem that the people needed in large numbers were the tradesmen and in many ways the key recruiting problems lay here. Neither RAuxAF nor the RAFVR were ever at full establishment strength, and this was due to the lack of airmen, not the lack of pilots.

University Air Squadrons

These squadrons were established within the framework of the RAFVR at seventeen universities. "Their purpose, to promote the flow of candidates for commissions in the regular, reserve and auxiliary air forces; to stimulate interest in air matters; and to promote and maintain liaison with the universities in technical and research problems affecting aviation."[72] In 1946 the Air Ministry had realised the value of the UAS in terms of its training of pilots, which were a great source of recruits to the RAF:

> "The purpose of the University Air Squadrons is to provide training during their university career for members of the universities who wish to prepare themselves for commissioned service in the General Duties branch and the Technical branch of the regular or non-regular air forces."[73]

This shows that the emphasis of the UAS had switched from 'air-mindedness' prior to the Second World War to that of recruiting officers as part of their role within the RAFVR. By 1947, fourteen UASs had been formed, in comparison with the three UASs that had existed before the war (Cambridge UAS, University of London Air Squadron and Oxford UAS). This figure remained the same and in many ways was not particularly affected by the reduction of manpower which affected other areas of the RAF. Recruits were taught to fly at civil flying schools and after completing their degrees, were able to apply directly to the RAF College Cranwell to complete their training. Changes in technology meant that the aircraft which were used for flying training were obsolete, and in 1950 they were replaced by the de Havilland Chipmunk, which became the standard training aircraft for the RAF between 1950 and the early 1970s.[74]

As a result of being in a UAS, recruits were given the opportunity to experience what life in the Royal Air Force would be like and it would ensure a ready supply of officer candidates for the Royal Air Force.[75] Those who decided to join a UAS would be expected to attend training nights which took place during week nights, and also to attend the annual summer camp. Each recruit had to follow the same flying syllabus which involved the recruit undertaking some thirty-one flying sorties so that they were in a position to achieve between ten and fifteen hours of flying. Moreover, the training was built upon with both ground training and adventure training. Once the student pilot had completed the Core Syllabus they were then able to receive the award of the Preliminary Flying Badge, or "Budgie Wings". However, each student was expected to reach solo standard before the end of their second year on the squadron.[76]

Apart from flying, UASs also followed a Ground Training syllabus which included attending Adventure Training expeditions, both overseas and within the UK, learning drill, undertaking a field craft exercise, understanding the principles of air power and developing leadership skills. However, the emphasis and priority remained on flying as the core function of each UAS. UAS Officer Cadets were required to participate in a minimum amount of training: one training night a week during the university term which usually entailed a guest speaker presenting on an aspect of the RAF or the military to develop service knowledge; and a two-week period of continuous training in the summer. Most squadrons also offered camps at Easter, Christmas, and September for Officer Cadets to undertake intensive blocs of sport, flying and adventure training. Additionally, students were offered a limited number of week-long Summer Vacation Attachment at another RAF base, where they were seconded to an active regular RAF unit to learn more about their role.[77] Candidates were also expected to participate in inter-UAS sports competitions and adventure training expeditions, in sports such as the UAS Rugby 7s, hockey, rowing, and shooting. Additionally there were frequent squadron expeditions in areas such as the Lake District, which included rock climbing and canoeing.[78]

The end of the Royal Auxiliary Air Force

In 1953 the "Baker-Carr Report", written by Air Commodore John Baker-Carr, stated that because of the limited amount of flying time that was available to an auxiliary pilot, future aeroplanes would be too complex for them to fly proficiently and the squadrons would therefore have to be manned by ex-regulars. Furthermore, Baker-Carr believed that the auxiliary squadrons should all be disbanded.[79] In 1954 the swept-wing supersonic fighter was created and the argument was put forward that since the nation was hard pressed to maintain its regular forces, the cost of new aircraft was so great that it would be cheaper to re-equip the fighter defence if there were less pilots. Harold Macmillan as Defence Minister gained the nickname "Mac the Knife" in tribute to the sweeping defence cuts he proposed as a solution to Britain's economic malaise. He announced that it would not be possible, or indeed right, for auxiliaries to switch to the expensive new machines, a necessity if they were to remain in the front line of defence. He added that the government had decided to alter the organisation of this force to enable those Auxiliary pilots who could give their time to it to train on the swept-wing aircraft themselves as individuals; not to equip the squadrons with these machines, but to train the men. By this means they would provide reserves behind the regular squadrons in war. Thus, the role of the RAuxAF was questioned and three areas were scrutinised. Firstly, RAuxAF fighter squadrons were called up for three months training in 1951 to prepare them for the Korean War. This upset many employers and the RAuxAF were never called out again. Secondly, when the North Atlantic Treaty Organisation (NATO) was formed in 1949, the Air Ministry had declared all twenty auxiliary squadrons to be fully combat capable, but by 1953 they were no longer regarded as front line units. Finally, people were increasingly giving way to advanced technology.[80]

By 1954 the Air Council and the Auxiliary and Reserve Forces Committee were trying to find ways to sustain the flying squadrons; updating their aircraft was considered a possibility, as was reducing the number of squadrons from twenty to fifteen, however, aircraft technology was so advanced that it was not considered viable to give new aircraft to the RAuxAF squadrons. By mid-1955 the Air Ministry was under increasing pressure to save money and the possibility was again discussed of disbanding the AAF squadrons.[81] By 1956, the Suez affair had strengthened the case for disbandment because of the drain on Britain's gold and dollar reserves. Some newspapers, and particularly those associated with Max Aitken, the former post-war Commanding Officer of 601 Squadron who ran the *Sunday Express,* began to leak details of total disbandment. No official comment came from the authorities resulting in protracted discussion in the press. However, in 1957 there was a major review of defence policy that culminated with a White Paper in 1957 from the Minister of Defence, Duncan Sandys. This was announced in the aftermath of the Suez crisis and showed a major shift in defence policy by enforcing massive cuts in the number of troops and by increasing the dependence of the United Kingdom on nuclear technology. Furthermore, the disbandment of the AAF squadrons would save money immediately. It was decided that "the most effective deterrents for the United Kingdom were V Bombers and surface-to-air missiles".[82]

The RAuxAF leaders tried to fight the decision and formed a committee of the four metropolitan areas of London, composed of Squadron Leader John Cormack of 600 Squadron who was an Esso executive, Tommy Turnbull of 604 Squadron who was a Lloyd's underwriter, Bob Eeles of 615 Squadron who was an ICI executive and Peter Edelston of 601 Squadron, an advertising executive.[83] The aim of the committee was to try to educate people in the role of the RAuxAF in the hope that public opinion could stop the disbandment. They made a television appearance at the Pathfinders' Club in Knightsbridge and answered questions from the BBC air correspondent. They wrote to all Members of Parliament and all national and provincial newspapers. Their letter was therefore published all over the country, highlighting their concern that:

> "The country is throwing away an organisation whose worth is far greater than its face value, employing people whose time is spent productively five days a week and two days a week in the service of the crown. There is no doubt that the Royal Air Force is short of pilots, and disbanding the Auxiliary fighter squadrons means that the country will lose over 300 fully-trained fighter pilots, and in addition more than 2,000 ground crew."[84]

501 Squadron's CO, Squadron Leader Collings wrote to a local newspaper to present his case against the Air Ministry:

> "This is an absolute tragedy. They are throwing away a terrific enthusiasm that has always been the keynote of the Auxiliaries. Farmers, airline pilots, bricklayers, bank clerks, printers and railway workers, who give up their weekends to fly or service the aircraft, working and learning with a rare devotion. Now the thirty officers and seventy-five airmen of 501 Squadron must hang up their flying boots."[85]

As no official comment could be wrung from the authorities, a flood of letters took up the case for the part-timers. Some positive but others breathing a sigh of relief that the petrol wasting joy riders would leave them in weekend peace. "They have made mincemeat of my nerves with their power dives over my chimney pots, and I've grown so tired of ducking every few minutes while trying to dig in my garden."[86] In response someone pointed out that "my heart bleeds for Mr H, he might feel better if he were to go up to the Abbey, look through the Book of Remembrance, and take note of the number of Auxiliary Air Force men who gave their lives for us. They had all been joy-riding young men at weekends."[87]

They lobbied MPs and were always received with goodwill and sympathy, but effectively they were beaten. In January 1957, the announcement was made by the Minister of Defence stating that the RAuxAF was to be disbanded on 10 March of that year. The Air Ministry Notice stated that:

> "In view of the magnificent war record of the auxiliary fighter squadrons, which fully justified the hopes of those responsible for the formation of the Auxiliary Air Force, this decision has been taken with the deepest possible regret…with the growing cost of equipment it has become clear that the auxiliary fighter squadrons could not be retained, even with their present aircraft, at the expense of the regular units which must be regarded as of higher priority."[88]

Thus, the main reason given was partly on operational and partly on economic grounds. Operationally it was argued that it was unrealistic to expect weekend fliers to be able to operate complex modern aircraft. Economically, the cost of training, maintaining the aircraft and keeping up the aerodromes was too much. It was, however, made clear that the RAFVR and the UASs would not be affected by this decision. The intention was to abolish the RAuxAF as such and attach its members to the regular force until the supply of National Service pilots dried up, and the last resistance collapsed with the dissolution of squadron entity. Certainly the squadrons could not survive such a transplanting, for their roots were in their histories, not in the hangers and crew rooms of any aerodrome. To abolish pride of unit was to abolish voluntary service.[89] The decision was made and on 10 March 1957, the twenty Royal Auxiliary Air Force Squadrons were disbanded for the last time.[90]

The editor of *The Aeroplane* noted:

> "It is hard to imagine the poverty of imagination that lies behind the decision to disband the Auxiliaries. In these days when financial reward and material gain are alleged to be the only springs of conduct and employment is there nobody in high places who realises that the spirit behind the Auxiliary Air Force is priceless? Nothing could be madder than to discourage those who wish to allocate their spare time to serving their country."[91]

This comment ties in with illustration number 15 which shows a cartoon, drawn by Russell Brockbank, which appeared in *Punch* Magazine on 30 January 1957. Moreover, it also ties in with illustration number 14 which shows a message from the Secretary of State for Air which was sent to the squadrons of the Royal Auxiliary Air Force on their disbandment. The message, dated 11 November 1957, thanks the members for their "loyal and valuable service" and explains reasons previously stated for the disbandment decision.

With the hindsight of half a century it is possible to see that in the long run the government was right, and that Britain's long devotion to amateur service had run its course and would have to yield to the reality of technology. Flying ability was no less important, but flair and courageous individualism would yield to technical mastery and relentless learning and practice.[92]

By 1953, despite a major recruiting campaign throughout the country, there was still a shortfall of aircrew, from the 7,600 needed there was an establishment of only 6,000. Moreover, Tiger Moths had been replaced by Chipmunks, which meant that the more up to date training aircraft were being used, but, at the time, the RAuxAF and RAF squadrons were training on Vampire jets, consequently the training of pilots in the RAFVR was lagging behind compared to the rest of the RAF. Flying schools, whose role it was to train RAFVR pilots and aircrew, trained personnel at weekends and during the two-week annual camp. Group Captain Peter Harris pointed out that:

> "From a military standpoint, the RAFVR did represent a pool from which individuals could be called up if the need arose, but the post-war auxiliary fighter squadrons were of more immediate use, being equipped with jets and trained to provide a highly skilled reserve for Fighter Command."[93]

In 1997, the RAFVR was merged into the RAuxAF due to the fact that one of their functions was to provide a steady source of aircrew and ground crew for the RAF which were not so important in 2014. RAFVR Officer Cadets and Acting Pilot Officers who are members of the UASs still continue with their training following an extended training syllabus which places a much greater emphasis on the development of military skills, building existing leadership abilities and expanding the officer potential within the current membership.

The RAF Reserves continued to be divided into two distinct reserves, the RAuxAF and the RAFVR, this remains the same even considering the way in which recruitment to the AAF was so poor pre-war. This will be covered in more detail in the following chapter.

Conclusion

This chapter has discussed the reforming of the RAuxAF and the RAFVR at the end of the Second World War, and has looked at the debate which surrounded the process of their reconstitution. It has highlighted the intention of forming the two different reserves and the reasoning behind this decision. There has also been an analysis of the role of national service in the post-war world as this had a major impact on recruiting to both the RAuxAF and the RAFVR. Different recruiting posters have also been included which show the lengths that were gone to in the search for new recruits. Overall there is no doubt that it has been much more difficult to attract people to the TAF following the war than it was before the war and this perhaps tells us that the people of the United Kingdom were tired of fighting and being involved in the defence process. The chapter also examines the reasons given for the disbandment of the RAuxAF in 1957 and questions whether or not it was the case that the belief that a part-time pilot could not hope to achieve enough flying hours to cope with the new technology in aircraft development, was true. The data presented in the following chapter will allow further analysis of whether qualifications and technical knowledge did in fact become more important than social background and class.

Chapter 6

The Social Composition of the Territorial Air Force after 1945

Introduction

This chapter analyses the data that the research has gathered for the period 1946-1957. The same process of collecting the data has been used as for Chapter 3, and the same nine categories used to present the information in both tables. Has the Royal Auxiliary Air Force (RAuxAF) changed and adapted to meet the changes which are taking place in society following the end of the war? This is analysed by presenting the data for the RAuxAF across the whole of the United Kingdom, and then comparing that to the data for the two London squadrons. The chapter also examines whether in fact the changes within the Territorial Air Force (TAF) actually reflected what was taking place in the wider society. By analysing the collected data, conclusions can be drawn which will enable judgements regarding whether or not recruits to the TAF became more technically qualified as opposed to the kinds of recruits who joined the organisation before the war.

The post-war world in which the TAF was reformed was very different from Britain in the 1930s. By the late 1950s Britain was more affluent, living standards had risen and class relations changed. Obelkevich and Catterall argue that in the post-war world "there had been a great deal of upward social mobility...class was a reality, but it was not set in stone. British society did not consist of fixed, monolithic classes, but of porous heterogeneous groupings in which the majority of people had personal or familial links across class lines."[1] This view is supported by Richard Vinen who also noted that "class was not static".[2]

In many ways a person's class was still largely defined by their type of employment, but there were more opportunities for individuals to move across and within social classes rather than being tied to one specific grouping as was more often not the case in the interwar years. Another major factor influencing social change was the industrial structure of Britain.

After 1945 the "decline in primary and secondary sectors of employment and a growth of the tertiary sector"[3] which had begun in the inter-war period now gathered pace. Technological advances, particularly in the secondary sector, which processed or manufactured goods, meant that machines were increasingly replacing employees. Those who worked in the secondary sector were now more likely to work in an office than they were to take manual labour. Furthermore, many industries such as agriculture, coal-mining, shipbuilding, railway engineering and textiles had been in decline since the end of the Second World War, whereas a massive growth was seen in the highly technological industries such as chemicals and electronics. The range of skills required by industry had therefore changed. Furthermore, the growth in non-manual jobs created new complexities in terms of class with the old manual and non-manual divide increasingly irrelevant. These changes were not uniform across the country. Many of the new service industries had grown around London and the south of England, whilst the decline in staple industries such as coal-mining, shipbuilding and textiles, affected employment opportunities in the north of the country dramatically. Thus, in 1951, 38 per cent of all employment was concentrated in the south of England as compared to 26 per cent in the north and 15 per cent in the Midlands, primarily within the manufacturing industry.[4] Many inner-city industries such as docks and railways were in decline whilst there was a major growth in the industrialisation of rural areas by new business parks. Furthermore, as Edward Royle argues, "the growth of consumerism, the expansion of the holiday market and technological advances in transport, especially the opening of Heathrow Airport in 1946 allowing for overseas travel, all helped shape a radically new society".[5]

The wave of patriotism that swept the country during and immediately after the war forms part of an ongoing debate amongst historians as to the role played by the Second World War in creating a sense of national identity and social solidarity. Angus Calder[6] reinforces the traditional view of the role of the war in developing characteristics such as the ability to adapt to difficult situations, a willingness to volunteer, to depend on each other, and a sense of British nationalism. This he argued, brought out the best in British civilians and created a sense of social solidarity that broke down class barriers. However, this view began to be challenged in the early 1990s by historians such as Robert Mackay[7] who looked at the role of morale against the civilian population by studying a range of primary sources including mass observation studies and concluded that "overall, the traditional picture of a spirited and resilient people is a valid one."[8] Furthermore, propaganda was used successfully to stimulate patriotism through the promise of post-war reconstruction, and this sense of national pride played its own part in increasing potential recruits to both the RAuxAF and the Royal Air Force Volunteer Reserve (RAFVR).

Beaven suggests that "in a period of increased domestic and international tensions, employers justified their involvement in their immediate local community on a number of levels,"[9] and it seems that the war strengthened the sense of community not just at national but also at local level. Consequently, it comes as no surprise that local employers supported their employees joining voluntary organisations such as the RAuxAF and the RAFVR.

It is important to be aware that there are some anomalies with the post-war data which are not present in the pre-war data. These are, in the first instance, 173 men who have been identified through the *London Gazette* as having volunteered to join the RAuxAF between 1946 and 1957. These men are all lumped together because the squadron numbers for these men have not been given in the *London Gazette*, only the date of their commissions. The reason for this is not clear, but this has affected the RAuxAF post-war data when compared to the pre-war data. Secondly the impact of National Service on the figures must also not be discounted. All young men over the age of eighteen were identified as having to serve two years National Service. At the completion of this they had to remain in the reserve for four years. Richard Vinen suggests that the number of men conscripted for National Service between 1948 and 1960 was 2,167,884 of which 430,885 were taken by the RAF, giving an overall ratio in the RAF of two-thirds regular servicemen to one-third National Service men.[10] Those men joining the RAFVR after 1948 came in holding different ranks and this may well be due to accrued time which they had built up during their National Service.

The Auxiliary Air Force

Following the cessation of hostilities, the decision was taken to reform the AAF on 2 June 1946 following consultation between the Air Ministry and the local County Associations. The idea was that the reformed Auxiliary Air Force (AAF) would still be a part of the country's front-line defence system, provided that its numbers did not unbalance the overall structure of the Royal Air Force (RAF). The new AAF squadrons were also intended to operate from their Home Stations.[11]

Significantly, there were still recruiting concerns as the initial belief was that RAF personnel who had been demobbed at the end of the war would be keen to join the AAF to maintain their contact with the services as discussed in the previous chapter. The framework remained the same in the reformed RAuxAF as it was in the pre-war AAF. It represented a pan-class organisation that was nonetheless hierarchical in nature. Most significantly, social status and background no longer presented quite the same barrier to joining, and thus, the post-war auxiliaries drew lots of different people together through a shared interest in aircraft, as opposed to shared social, educational and recreational interests based largely on class codes.

All of the auxiliary squadrons were reformed on 10 May 1946, and an official announcement in the Royal Air Force Review during 1946/1947 noted that "reformed after seven years magnificent service with the RAF, the Auxiliary squadrons are now looking for the right type of men from those who are being released from war service to carry on their fine traditions."[12] It explained exactly what was meant by "right type" by explaining that: "Only trained men who gained their skill and experience in the service are being taken on to man the force. There are to be no 'passengers'; every member of the squadron comes in fully trained and able to tackle his particular job from the start, service in the Auxiliaries will keep him up to scratch and abreast of all the latest technical developments and new methods of training as they come into effect."[13]

Individually, some of the reformed squadrons did better than others when recruitment figures are considered. The table below highlights the poor overall numbers of identified men who served as officers in the pre-war AAF and then re-joined the newly reformed post-war RAuxAF:

Table 13: Pre-War AAF officers who re-joined the reformed post-war RAuxAF

Squadron Number	Name	Pre-War	Post-War
600	Thomas Norman Hayes	05/07/1936	17/09/1946
	Ralph Hiscox	03/08/1929	30/01/1952
	Peter Graham Stewart	01/03/1927	11/04/1950
601	Max Aitken	11/09/1935	17/09/1946
	Peter William Dunning-White	27/11/1938	17/09/1946
602	Robert Findlay Boyd	02/11/1935	14/07/1947
	Marcus Robinson	08/05/1934	17/09/1946
603	George Kemp Gilroy	10/04/1938	17/09/1946
	James Lawrence Jack	25/01/1927	15/01/1952
	James Storrs Morton	14/07/1939	17/09/1946

604	John Cunningham	07/05/1936	17/09/1946
	Lewis Edward Alton Healy	06/06/1938	05/06/1950
	Keith Temple Lofts	07/11/1938	27/05/1946
605	Patrick George Leeson	05/12/1936	09/04/1946
607	James Michael Bazin	02/12/1935	05/12/1946
	William Francis Blackadder	01/06/1936	05/12/1946
	George Dudley Craig	28/05/1937	27/07/1946
	Joseph Robert Kayll	01/06/1934	17/09/1946
	Robert Edwin Welford	13/03/1937	26/10/1953
	Pumphrey	23/05/1936	02/08/1949
	George Richard Ardene Wilson		
608	William Appleby-Brown	07/02/1938	01/08/1946
609	-	-	-
610	Cyril Stanley Bamberger	17/06/1936	02/08/1949
	James Anthony Leathart	15/06/1936	03/03/1947
611	William Johnson Leather	14/05/1936	17/09/1946
	Francis David Stephen Scott-Malden	03/10/1940	17/09/1946
612	Ramsey Roger Russell	15/06/1937	17/12/1946
613	-	-	-
614	-	-	-
615	-	-	-
616	Lionel Harwood Casson	02/05/1938	27/02/1951
	Maurice Clarke	07/04/1938	04/05/1949
	Denis Gillam	18/05/1938	09/09/1946
	Kenneth Holden	15/04/1939	18/03/1947
	James McCairns	12/02/1939	09/09/1946
500	Charles Patrick Green	30/11/1935	17/09/1946
501	-	-	-
502	William Hunter McGiffin	01/07/1937	17/09/1946
504	John Crescens Reynolds	15/04/1935	02/08/1949
	Michael Rook	08/08/1938	11/12/1947

As can be seen, 607 Squadron managed to recruit six pre-war officers and this would seem to be the most that any of the individual squadrons recruited, suggesting that the initial requirement to recruit those men who had served before or during the war was an overly optimistic one. Those who had served with the pre-war AAF and were really keen to re-join did so in 1946. From the research this would appear to be eighteen out of a total of thirty-one men, which amounts to 58 per cent of those named officers re-joining. Across the country the initial response was so poor that

119

in December 1946 the Air Ministry announced that recruiting for the AAF would be open to civilian candidates with no previous military experience.

Table 14: Royal Auxiliary Air Force Initial Data

Squadron Number	Total of identified men	Total men with biographies	Percentage %
600	31	11	35%
601	40	16	40%
602	11	8	73%
603	44	13	30%
604	8	8	100%
605	40	13	33%
607	7	5	71%
608	31	19	61%
609	15	11	73%
610	5	4	80%
611	48	19	40%
612	1	1	100%
613	6	5	83%
614	2	1	50%
615	8	8	100%
616	7	4	57%
500	5	3	60%
501	28	13	46%
502	4	3	75%
504	2	2	100%
No Squadron Number Given	173	21	12%
TOTAL	**516**	**188**	**36%**

Southern Squadrons

600 and 601 Squadron were overwhelmed with applications to join the newly formed London squadrons. 600 Squadron was re-established at Biggin Hill. Its new Commanding Officer (CO) was Wing Commander Norman Hayes who, along with many officers who volunteered to join the AAF after the war, accepted a lower rank to take up the post.[14] Three pre-war members of the squadron re-joined, and other new recruits included Jack Meadows,

who became a CO of the squadron and David Proudlove who was a member of the Guild of Air Pilots and Air Navigators. The research has identified thirty-one men who volunteered to join the reformed squadron, and of those identified men, biographies were found for eleven of them, which, in percentage terms, is 35 per cent. When analysing the post-war figures there are some significant changes when compared to the pre-war squadron. Notable changes can be seen with regard to the public school/Oxbridge education that 32 per cent of the pre-war members had. None of the post-war 600 Squadron had a public-school background and only 9 per cent of them had attended Oxford or Cambridge University. There is an increase in the number of men who had their child's birth announced in *The Times* with the post-war figure standing at 27 per cent when compared to the pre-war figure of 11 per cent, whilst the marriage and death announcement figures remain similar. The other significant increase is the number of post-war men who worked within the professions or in business. This figure has risen to 55 per cent compared to the figure of 47 per cent for the pre-war officers.

601 Squadron reformed at Hendon with Max Aitkin, second Baron Beaverbrook, reverting to his 1940 rank to lead the squadron. Three ex-group captains and two ex-wing commanders also dropped rank in order to re-join. For example, Hugh Dundas, who had originally been commissioned into 616 Squadron in 1939 who held the rank of group captain joined 601 as a flying officer and also accepted a job as air correspondent on Aitkin's *Daily Express*. Paul Richey, who had originally been commissioned into 609 Squadron was also a keen recruit, as was Chris McCarthy-Jones who had been commissioned into 504 Squadron before the war. Finally, Peter Dunning-White, who had been a wing commander, accepted the rank of flying officer in order to re-join. Many ex-officers returned to fly as Non-Commissioned Officers (NCO) pilots, and consequently there was an ex-squadron leader and three ex-flight lieutenants in non-commissioned pilot roles. The demand for places was so great that a board was set up, chaired by Squadron Leader Aitkin, to reduce the 400 applicants to pilots with 1,500 flying hours or more.[15] Sir Peter Beckford Rutgers Vanneck, son of Lord Huntingford was also a post-war 601 member, with a public school background; he was a former student of Cambridge University, had been in the Fleet Air Arm and insisted on wearing naval wings on his highly individual uniform. He flew a Vampire to Horsham St Faith in Norfolk for a shoot, emerging from his small cockpit replete with tweeds, gun and spaniel.[16] Both Desmond Norman, co-founder of the crop spraying firm of Britten-Norman Ltd and his brother Torquil, a Cambridge

educated investment banker, were members of the squadron. Subsequent commanding officers included Paul Richey who was a journalist and author and Chris MacCarthy-Jones who was a sales manager. 601 Squadron also had no problem recruiting ground crews, although this process took longer. The squadron bought £100 worth of advertising space in London's tube trains and soon had enough applications to make up establishment. Among the airmen were bus drivers, policemen, a baker, a barrow boy and a lighthouse keeper.[17]

The 601 tradition of exclusiveness continued after the war with summer camp squadron dinners requiring the best silver and mess ornaments being transported from Kensington.[18] One particular episode of high jinks occurred at the Manston summer camp in 1948. During the meal in the mess, an explosion of powerful fireworks under the table caused pandemonium when the room filled with smoke as rockets impaled themselves in the ceiling and showered the diners with sparks. A notice "Quick Quick I'm on fire!!!" was pinned to the Mayor of Margate's back and he was drenched in soda water from powerful siphons. Seventy pounds worth of damage was caused during this incident, which the squadron members paid willingly. The squadron was also famous for car races through London in the middle of the night and for continuous horseplay both in and out of the mess.[19] Other notable post-war recruits were Prince Emanuel Gallitzine, whose father had been aide de camp for the Russian Grand Duke Nikoli Nikolaevich, head of all of the Russian armies, who moved to England in the hope of a better future for his son. Also Arden Merville-Crawley who played cricket for Kent, and was the MP for North Buckinghamshire. Forty men were identified as joining 601 Squadron after 1946, and of those men, biographies have been found for sixteen of them, which is 40 per cent. When comparing the data for the post-war officers the number of men who attended public school remains the same, but the number of men who went on to an Oxbridge university has fallen considerably from 51 per cent before the war to 19 per cent after the war. Also the number of men whose death announcement appeared in *The Times* has fallen from 60 per cent pre-war to only 13 per cent post-war. Finally, again the number of men working in the professions or in business has risen considerably to 81 per cent in the post-war world as compared to 60 per cent before the war.

Combining the data for 600 and 601 Squadron, there were seventy-one officers identified, of which there were twenty-seven biographies. This means that the percentage of officers with biographies is 38 per cent. The table below shows the comparison between pre-war and post-war data.

Table 15: 600 and 601 Squadron comparison of Pre and Post-War initial data

Squadron Number	Pre-War Identified Men	Post-War Identified Men	Pre-War Men With Biographies	Post War Men with Biographies
600	70	31	27	11
601	72	40	45	16

The obvious difference between the pre and post-war figures is the significantly less number of men who have been identified as serving in either 600 or 601 Squadron after the war, which in the case of 600 Squadron is well under half, and in the case of 601 Squadron is just over half. This is similar for the number of biographies that were found, with both squadrons being under half of the pre-war numbers. When the biographies are broken down by category, the results are shown below:

Table 16: 600 and 601 Squadron comparison between pre and post-war data by category

Category	Pre-War 600 Squadron	Pre-War 601 Squadron	Post-War 600 Squadron	Post-War 601 Squadron
Public School	7	17	0	8
Oxford or Cambridge	6	17	1	5
Other University	0	1	0	0
Elite Sport	2	12	0	4
Marriage Announcement	3	10	2	4
Birth Announcement	2	2	3	0
Profession/ Business	7	24	6	14
Family Business	1	4	1	1
University Air Squadron	1	1	1	1

In terms of the profession/business category, 11 or 55 per cent of the men worked in business, 3 or 15 per cent were in the newspaper industry, 2 or 10 per cent were in politics and 5 or 25 per cent were in the professions such as law or medicine. Elite sports which have been included in the post-war era include golf, fencing, yachting and rowing, boxing, cricket and rugby, hunting and horse riding. The two men who were involved in politics were both Members of Parliament. Similar results are shown for the public school category where no members of 600 Squadron were found to attend and in fact all but one of the categories for 600 Squadron show a decrease in numbers. When looking at the numbers for 601 Squadron, again it is apparent that there is a significant fall in numbers for all of the categories. This would appear to suggest that the two squadrons on whom the bulk of the evidence regarding the AAF is based, present an image of a "gentleman's flying club" in the years up to the Second World War, but become much more inclusive in the years after. The discussion will now move on to consider the rest of the squadrons of the AAF to see whether or not they follow a similar pattern to the two key London squadrons.

604 Squadron reformed at Hendon and Group Captain John Cunningham reverted back to the rank of squadron leader. He had graduated from Cambridge University as an aeronautical engineer in 1938 and had immediately joined de Havilland as a test pilot, as well as joining the AAF. Thus, along with Lewis Edward Alton Healy, he had served in both the pre and post-war AAF. Another pre-war officer was Keith Lofts, a pre-war wing commander who was offered the post of flight commander accepting a lower rank of flight lieutenant. In November 1946 posters were put up in the local area to try to attract potential recruits. Many applications were received with most men wanting to fly rather than working in a support capacity. Recruiting and interviewing then took place resulting in the squadron processing over 100 officer pilot applications, thirty NCO pilots and around thirty airmen. Other notable recruits were Brian Cross, who bailed out of a Meteor jet at 20,000 feet and was rescued by an Albatross Amphibian of the US Air Force and Derek Yates who got lost in his Vampire jet over Norfolk and was able to signal SOS with his wing tips to a KB29 air tanker aircraft which guided him to an airfield where he landed safely with enough fuel left for five minutes of flying.[20] Eight men were identified as joining 604 Squadron post-war and biographies were found on all of them. Data for this squadron shows that those men attending a public school fell from 54 per cent to zero and in similar fashion those attending an Oxbridge university fell from 31 per cent to zero. However, those working in business or professions rose from a pre-war figure of 23 per cent to a post-war figure of 38 per cent.

605 Squadron reformed at Honiley with Squadron Leader R John Walker in command. Recruiting was very slow initially with a particular shortage of technicians and ground crew. In 1948, 605 Squadron became the first

auxiliary squadron to be equipped with the new de Havilland Vampire, a jet aircraft. This new arrival did not sit well with the locals, and a vicar of a small village complained that the jets were affecting his parishioners. He complained to the local MP, Sir John Mellor, and asked for a total ban of Sunday flying. The response of the CO was as follows:

> "The auxiliary services have to be maintained and that can only be done by weekend flying. Auxiliary squadrons are composed of personnel who are working in the office and factories during the week and their only opportunity of flying training is at weekends."[21]

Patrick Leeson was the only officer to have served in both the pre and post-war squadron. Notable recruits included John Cecil-Wright who became Conservative MP for Edrington and R.L.M. Smalley who was serving as first officer on a civilian Viking Airliner which went missing in 1961, with a school party of thirty-four 14-year-old boys and their two school masters on board. Information on this squadron was much harder to find and forty men were identified as having joined the squadron as officers, with biographies being found for only thirteen of them, which amounts to 33 per cent. The data for 605 Squadron also has lots of gaps in it. Those attending a public school fell from 25 per cent to 8 per cent, whilst no men attended an Oxbridge university. Marking life events with announcements in *The Times* still continued with marriage announcements staying the same and death announcements falling by 1 per cent. The number of men in business or professions rose from 38 per cent to 54 per cent.

610 Squadron reformed at Hooton Park under Squadron Leader Peter Gilbert Lamb and five men were identified as serving within the squadron. Two pre-war officers signed up to the post-war AAF, Cyril Bamberger and James Leathart. Biographies were found for four of the identified men amounting to 80 per cent. Summer camps were held at Tangmere, Thorney Island, Horsham St Faith and Sylt in Germany, and just before the squadron disbanded in 1957 it was noted that:

> "Of the 610 RAuxAF pilots, fourteen held degrees, and –
> to a man – offered to carry on their flying without pay or
> allowances, a gesture of which the pre-war Auxiliaries would
> have been very proud had they been there to share the genuine
> dismay at the decision to cease this part-time flying."[22]

For 610 Squadron, the data was very poor. It shows that the number of men who had attended public school had increased from 18 per cent to 25 per cent, whilst no men had gone on to an Oxbridge university. No men used *The Times* for family announcements, which was a significant fall from the 55 per cent of the pre-war men whose deaths had been announced. There was however an increase in the number of men working in either the professions or in business from 18 per cent prior to the war to 75 per cent in the post-war world.

614 Squadron reformed at Llandow on 26 August 1947, commanded by Squadron Leader W.H. Irving. This squadron was also particularly difficult to research and searches in *The London Gazette* and *The Times* Digital Archives proved fruitless. Apart from the CO, the only other name that was found was Nigel Palmer who was killed when his Vampire jet collided with another 614 Squadron Vampire over the Isle of Wight in 1954. Overall, the research found two names for the squadron and a biography on one of them which amounts to 50 per cent. There is no data for 614 Squadron, which therefore shows a decrease in the number of men attending public school from 25 per cent to zero, and also going on to an Oxbridge university from 17 per cent to zero in the post-war world. Similarly, *The Times* has not been used to make any family announcements, which again shows a fall from 33 per cent marriage, 25 per cent birth and 50 per cent death to zero. This is again reflected in the fall of business/ professions from 17 per cent to zero.

615 Squadron reformed at Biggin Hill and was commanded by Squadron Leader Ronald Gustave Kellett[23] who had joined the pre-war 600 Squadron in 1934. Interesting names included Neville Duke who was Chief Test Pilot for Hawker Aircraft Limited. He broke the world air speed record in 1954, and of course Ronald Kellett who worked as a stockbroker and enjoyed country pursuits such as hunting and shooting. Eight men were identified, all of whom had biographies. The data for this squadron is better than the previous squadron, showing an increase in the number of men attending public school and an Oxbridge university from zero to 13 per cent. Those using *The Times* for family or personal announcements had changed after the war with a decrease from 60 per cent of men having death announcements in the pre-war world and no one using them in the post-war world. However, again there was an increase in the number of men working in business or the professions from 10 per cent to 63 per cent.

500 Squadron reformed on 23 August 1946 at Maidstone under the command of Squadron Leader Patrick Green, who had previously served in

the squadron from 1936. One story from this squadron shows the high jinks that still went on in the mess:

> "We used to have good 'dining-in' nights at Astley House. The men, I remember, at one time clubbed together to buy a piano that one of them had seen. It cost the princely sum of £5.00 and many thought it would be nice to have a piano in the mess for social evenings. However, not everyone thought alike. Their intention was that the piano should not be played. With a sound like charging Indians, several of the officers descended on this poor piano with axes, hammers and all manner of dreadful weapons. In no time at all the poor piano was demolished and was then burnt ceremoniously in the officers' mess grate, causing black clouds of smoke which rose, but then sank back to earth enveloping the residents houses within 200 yards of the mess."[24]

Only five men were identified for 500 Squadron with three having biographies. Again the data for this squadron is poor, with a slight decrease in the number of marriage announcements in *The Times* from 73 per cent to 67 per cent, with the death announcements falling from 27 per cent to zero post-war. Those in professions and business increased from zero to 33 per cent with those working in family businesses increasing from zero to 33 per cent post-war.

501 Squadron reformed on 10 May 1946 at Filton with Squadron Leader Tom James as CO. The squadron attended summer camps in Malta and trained hard to be able to fly and maintain the new jet aircraft. John Crossley will be sadly remembered for flying under the Clifton Suspension Bridge and crashing into the bank of the river Avon, just hours before the final disbandment parade, whereas Brien Smith managed to come second in the four-lap race of the RAuxAF pilots in 1949. Twenty-eight men were identified and biographies were found for thirteen of them, which amounted to 46 per cent. The data shows that in terms of family announcements in *The Times*, those making marriage announcements increased from 29 per cent to 81 per cent, the birth announcements increased from zero to 81 per cent whilst the death announcements remained the same. Following the trend the number of men working in professions and business rose from 71 per cent to 92 per cent.

Finally, 504 Squadron reformed at RAF Syerston on the 10 May 1946, commanded by Squadron Leader Archie Hook. John Crescens Reynolds and Michael Rook also re-joined having served with the squadron prior to the war. Two men were identified as having joined the post-war squadron with biographies for them both. Again the data here is sketchy with those attending public school remaining stable, whilst in terms of those using *The Times* for family and personal announcements, those making marriage announcements rose from 24 per cent to 50 per cent and those announcing deaths increased very slightly from 47 per cent to 50 per cent.

Table 17: Southern Squadrons showing percentages of men with biographies

Squadron Number	Percentage
600	35%
601	40%
604	100%
605	33%
610	80%
614	50%
615	100%
500	60%
501	46%
504	100%

Northern Squadrons

602 Squadron was reformed on 10 May at RNAS Abbotsinch, under the command of Squadron Leader Marcus Robinson. Marcus Robinson was a pre-war member of the squadron who was demobbed in February 1946 and appointed to command 602 Squadron immediately after it was reformed. Robert Findlay Boyd was the only other officer who had served in the pre-war squadron. Other members of the squadron included Pierre Clostermann who later became a member of the French House of Representatives, Andrew McDowall who worked as a test pilot for Rolls-Royce and Stephen Mackay who had a successful career as managing director of several of the national newspapers, for example, the *Evening Standard*, the *Sunday Times* and the *Daily and Sunday Telegraph*. Eleven men were identified as joining the squadron with biographies found for eight of the men. This equates to 73 per cent. The data for 602 Squadron shows considerable differences from the pre-war data. For example, no identified officers were educated at

public school or at Oxbridge universities. This compares to the pre-war data of 17 per cent and 9 per cent respectively. As with 600 and 601 Squadrons, the number of men whose death announcements appear in *The Times* has increased from 13 per cent to 22 per cent, but again, the biggest change is those men who worked in professions or business, which has risen from 4 per cent to 50 per cent.

603 Squadron reformed on 10 May 1946 at RAF Turnhouse, commanded by Squadron Leader George Gilroy DSO DFC. He had ended the war with the rank of group captain, but was more than happy to re-join the squadron at a significantly lower rank. Here, finding suitable candidates to become officers and members of the squadron meant facing a selection board, followed by "a boozy selection board at L'Aperitif in Rose Street with John Sowerby, 603's Adjutant, Count Stevens and another 603 old boy, both ex group captains".[25] However, recruiting for the squadron was very poor and at the beginning of 1947, the squadron only had three officers and thirty-five airmen. A one week recruiting drive was launched with the support of the main Scottish newspapers – *The Edinburgh Evening News, The Scotsman* and *The Flying Despatch,* which resulted in fifty applications for flying posts and fifty applications for ground positions. But by January 1949 establishment strength was still low with fourteen officers, four airman pilots and fifty other ranks. Yet another recruiting campaign began resulting in a further 150 applications with limited results again highlighting recruiting problems across all of the auxiliary squadrons across the country. Three men, George Kemp Gilroy, James Lawrence Jack and James Storrs Morton, were the only men who had served in the pre-war 603 Squadron and the post-war squadron. Overall, forty-four men were identified for 603 Squadron and biographies were found for thirteen of them, which is 30 per cent. When comparing the data for this squadron, the number of men attending public school is similar, whilst the number of men attending Oxbridge universities has doubled. Those having marriage announcements has fallen to 15 per cent compared to the pre-war figure of 24 per cent. Those having death announcements in *The Times* has also fallen from the pre-war figure of 58 per cent to the post-war figure of 23 per cent. However, as seems to be the post-war trend, the number of men in the professions or business has risen from 18 per cent to 46 per cent.

607 Squadron was reformed at Ouston and was commanded by Squadron Leader Joseph R Kayll, a member of the pre-war squadron, as well as

James Bazin, William Blackadder, George Craig, Bob Pumphrey and George Wilson, all of whom reverted back to pre-war ranks. Only seven men were identified as having joined the squadron with biographies being found for five of the men, amounting to 71 per cent. Those attending public school increased in the post-war era from 30 per cent to 40 per cent, whilst the figure for Oxbridge universities remained similar. Forty per cent of men had their marriage announced in *The Times*, whilst there was another increase in death announcements from 10-20 per cent. Finally, those in professions and business increased from 15 per cent to 40 per cent at the expense of those working in family businesses, who fell from 55 per cent to 20 per cent.

In July 1946, at Thornaby, the new post-war 608 Squadron began to reform, designated as a Mosquito light-bomber unit, but actually receiving the Mosquito NF (Night Fighter) 30 as part of Reserve Command 64 Group, with Squadron Leader William Appleby-Brown DFC as CO, and the Rt Hon Viscount Swinton continuing his appointment as Honorary Air Commodore.[26] On 11 July the *Northern Echo* reported that:

> "A flying start has been made by 608 Auxiliary Air Squadron at Thornaby with recruiting and training and with twelve officers and forty-four airmen now enlisted, the squadron shows the highest returns for all Northern Command reserve squadrons. At the same time it leads all Northern squadrons in the number of flying hours achieved since training began four months ago."[27]

Those who had flown with the Royal Air Force during the war could effectively be offered positions within the AAF as officers based on their technical skills and regardless of their background and social status. However, there was not a rush of recruits. Increased technical demands and a more rigorous selection process served to keep the numbers down. The recruitment process was much more carefully controlled and acceptance into the AAF took much longer than it had before the war when status equated to acceptance. Consequently, in conjunction with most of the other AAF squadrons, 608 struggled to recruit sufficient personnel to reach their establishment, in fact, by July 1947, it had only twelve officers and forty-four airmen enlisted, which amounted to 25 per cent of the station establishment.[28]

The first post-war training camp for 608 Squadron began at Thornaby on 8 August 1947 and lasted for fourteen days. "Training included exercises over Germany and Holland and aircrews were flying Mosquitoes," reported one local newspaper, "local employers have given their full cooperation and the time spent at camp will be in addition to the customary summer holidays."[29] Other comments about the summer camp mentioned "the happy camaraderie which animates all ranks".[30] Again the men attended one night a week, and at weekends. Activities involved lectures, servicing the aeroplanes, working in the control tower, refuelling visiting aeroplanes, and of course, flying exercises. For all of these tasks the auxiliary men worked alongside their regular counterparts. In May 1948 the squadron converted to a day-fighter squadron using Spitfires and NA Harvard T26s. In December 1949, it was then re-equipped with Vampire jets and continued to fly this plane until 2 February 1957. Local sporting events between the squadron and the local community, such as tug of war and football matches, along with squadron open days were meant to help build positive relationships between the squadron and the local community.

All of this came to an abrupt end in 1957 when the government took the decision to cut back on defence spending. It was decided, "the most effective deterrents for the United Kingdom were V Bombers and surface-to-air missiles".[31] On 10 March 1957, along with twenty other RAuxAF Squadrons, No. 608 Squadron was finally disbanded. On 1 October 1958 the airfield was closed to flying and placed on a care and maintenance basis, although the airfield continued to be used for a few months by Teesside's 3608 Fighter Units Radar Control operations.[32] On Sunday, 1 November 1958, in the presence of former officers and airmen, the Standard of No 608 (NR) Squadron Royal Auxiliary Air Force was presented to the 608 (NR) Squadron Association by Air Vice-Marshal G.H. Ambler, who in December 1934, had been the Commanding Officer of the squadron. This took place at RAF Middleton St George at 3 pm. On Saturday, 14 November 1959, the Standard was laid-up in York Minster.[33]

Overall, the research managed to identify thirty-one men as recruits to the squadron, with nineteen of them having biographies. This amounted to 61 per cent. Of the men who joined the post-war 608 Squadron, the occupations of volunteers for officer posts were different from those of the pre-war officers. Forty-two per cent of men worked for ICI undertaking a variety of skilled jobs including draughtsman (Jim Steedman), metallurgist (Harry Bates), analyst (George Joyce), and researcher (Grant Goodwill). All these jobs involved technical training and knowledge and reflected the higher emphasis that was being placed on skill and intelligence in English post-war society, as well as within military institutions. It also demonstrated the fact that technical knowledge did not necessarily have to be acquired through a traditional public-school and university education but could be learned through work experience or other forms of training. Other officer volunteers in the post-war 608 Squadron came from a wider range of occupational backgrounds: Bill Goodrum ran his own building business, Jim Marshall and Dave Stewart worked at Dorman Long, Bill Swainston was an engineer, Alan Clough worked for the Electricity Board and Neil Hancock worked for British Rail.

Eighty-two per cent of the men now came from the large corporate industries such as ICI, and Dorman Long, and this impacted on the relationships that existed between all ranks because many officers and lower ranks knew each other within their civilian jobs. Furthermore, only a small minority of officers, such as William Appleby-Brown, continued to work within family businesses.

Fifty-eight per cent of the post-war officers had served in the squadron prior to the war and were prepared to accept a substantial reduction in rank in order to re-join. This initial willingness to enlist in the AAF was reflected across the country and highlighted the wave of post-war patriotism that swept Britain. This can be seen in the case of Mr Winstanley who, having served in the regular RAF, joined 608 Squadron in 1946 and had to drop two ranks from warrant officer pilot in the regular RAF to sergeant pilot in 608 Squadron. David Stewart also served with 608 Squadron between 1949 and 1952 and was an officer during his time in the RAF but had to re-join 608 Squadron as a warrant officer pilot flying Spitfires and Vampires. Other former RAF personnel, who wanted to join 608 Squadron, were prepared to drop rank in order to be accepted. A local reporter who met a sergeant pilot wearing the ribbon of the Distinguished Flying Cross (DFC) reinforced this point noting that this was an indication that he had dropped rank in order to re-join. John Pollock also served as a sergeant in the RAF but dropped three ranks to be an Aircraftsman Second Class (AC2) when he joined 608 Squadron. Also, the CO, Squadron Leader W Appleby-Brown DFC, had dropped rank from a wing commander, in order to get back in.

However, of those veterans who had served in 608 Squadron during the 1930s and the war, 42 per cent felt that they had "done their bit" and that they did not want to re-join the AAF after the war. Flying was no longer a novelty, it was no longer a sport, it was an accepted symbol of modernity and therefore had in some ways lost its appeal. Whilst the initial level of interest was overwhelming, the actual number of men who met the criteria for enlisting was disappointing and reflected the new recruitment restrictions placed on all squadrons. Selection of officers, NCOs and airmen was now much more demanding, with particular emphasis on previous experience and knowledge. These demands were relaxed in 1948 to allow any ex-servicemen to join the AAF in an effort to increase recruitment.[34] However, this action was too late to enable the AAF squadrons to benefit from the immediate post-war wave of enthusiasm which subsequently waned as men successfully readapted to civilian life. Thirty-seven per cent of the ex-servicemen found it hard to adapt to civilian jobs and life and felt they lacked the interaction and teamwork that had characterised life in the RAF.

Furthermore, increased technical demands and a more rigorous selection process served to keep numbers down. The recruitment process was much more carefully controlled and acceptance into the AAF took much longer than it had before the war. Consequently, in conjunction with most of the other AAF squadrons, 608 Squadron struggled to recruit sufficient personnel to reach their establishment, in fact, by July 1947, it had only twelve officers and forty-four airmen enlisted, which amounted to 25 per cent of the station establishment.[35] Another significant factor in slowing down recruitment was the conditions of service, which required the attendance for twelve weekends and fifteen days at annual camp, as well as the completion of one hundred hours of "non-continuous" training. Many potential recruits could not meet this level of commitment. Aircrews were slightly different in that they were expected to put in one hundred and twenty-five hours flying a year. Volunteers had to be prepared to commit to the conditions of service and therefore had to be willing to give up a significant amount of their free time in order to fulfil their obligations to the AAF.[36] Slow recruiting across the country prompted the Air Ministry to change the recruiting regulations in 1947, but the number of potential recruits slowed down considerably as many men felt that they had served their time during the war, had made the most of their opportunities to work with aircraft and satisfied their desire for travel. In a more expansive modern world, the opportunities that the AAF offered young men were not as appealing as they had been in the 1930s, because there were now new chances to travel or work in more challenging environments in civilian life.

Moreover, despite poor overall recruiting figures, there were significant numbers of pilots, around 73 per cent across England, who had served in the AAF during the 1930s who were eager to continue flying, and wanted the opportunity to fly. Many were officers who had attained high ranks or had been decorated for their skill and bravery; others were NCOs who had been able to fly and enjoyed successful careers. Members from both groups were willing to re-join the AAF as soon as it was reformed, but these men were in the minority compared to the larger numbers of ex-RAF personnel. These national problems were also faced within 608 Squadron. All of the post-war recruits wanted to pursue their interest in aircraft and maintain the comradeship of the war. They were able to maintain their civilian jobs, receive a small second income as a member of the AAF and enjoy weekend camps and summer camps. Sixty-three per cent of men in 608 Squadron and other squadrons talked of it making their lives more enjoyable, enabling them to have some structure within their leisure time, fulfilling their interest in aircraft, and giving them a sense of pride in both country and local community.

Viscount Swinton remained as 608 Squadron's Honorary Air Commodore after the war and continued to be the only real link to the upper middle-class backgrounds of the pre-war officers who had served within the squadron. Although the employment backgrounds of the officers were different, the backgrounds of post-war airmen remained similar to their pre-war contemporaries. All of the men interviewed felt that their employers in civilian life approved and actively encouraged them to join. Furthermore, all the veterans felt a strong sense of patriotism in the aftermath of the Second World War. Interviews with respondents reveal that reasons for joining the post-war AAF were wide and varied. Some volunteered for 608 Squadron after completing their national service. Others noted that following their demob from national service they volunteered for 608 Squadron because "the social side of squadron life was an attraction", while others volunteered to be able to fly. Some men felt that the transition from service life was difficult, to suddenly leave their friends, and then the adverts in the local press gave them the opportunity to become part of it all again.[37]

For all the new openness in terms of recruitment, social activities within 608 Squadron after the Second World War continued to be based upon rank and position. The mess structure within the forces meant that officers had their own mess, which was often shared with the regular officers, as did sergeants, whilst the airmen had the Navy Army Air Force Institute (NAAFI). This hierarchical structure meant that officers and men were still kept separate and this resulted in specific locations where each group of men would go to socialise. Even after the war, the officers kept to themselves. They did not mix with the NCOs unless there was a function in the Sergeants' Mess that they were specifically invited to attend. Similarly, the officers did not mix with the men, nor did the NCOs. Indeed the system of separate messes was standard RAF practice - and still is.

Social life within the squadron held a certain masculine appeal for both officers and airmen, although it is evident that the officers appeared to place a greater importance on social activities in the mess than the airmen. The officers functioned in a completely different way socially within the officers' mess and within the local public houses that they frequented. In the main they still continued to engage in public school boy antics in both social settings; however the mess games were a major part of weekend activities, especially amongst the younger pilots, and it is clear that the older officers would retire to another room to enable the younger element to "let off steam".

All of the officers were clear about the lack of social mixing between themselves and the airmen, and most noted that separation of ranks was a normal part of military life. However, it is apparent that during the two weeks annual camp, when the squadron travelled abroad for training, there was a much more relaxed relationship between the officers and the men and a greater likelihood of the two groups mixing. This was not seen as unacceptable because the camp was meant to be a combination of work and play where the rules of everyday life in the squadron were temporarily suspended. Class and rank were transcended during this period by a common sense of national identity in a foreign country.

In the end, the suggestion that AAF stations and personnel were not equipped to fly modern fighter planes was a common complaint voiced right across the country, and raised wider concerns about the efficiency of the AAF. Undoubtedly the technological advances that were being made in aircraft design meant that auxiliary squadrons sometimes struggled to maintain proficiency when compared to regular personnel. This factor prompted the government to analyse the competence of the part-time personnel, and it was these concerns that ultimately led to the winding down of the AAF in 1957.[38]

Twenty-five per cent of the pre-war squadron members had attended a public school compared to a very small 5 per cent of the post-war members, including Hank Costain, Commanding Officer of the squadron from 1955. Similarly, 45 per cent of the pre-war members had attended an Oxbridge university in comparison to 5 per cent in the post-war, which included William Appleby-Brown, the CO and former pre-war member of the squadron. In terms of family or personal announcements, there was an increase from 10 per cent prior to the war to 25 per cent after the war of men who used death announcements. The main increase between the pre and the post-war world is the increase in the number of men who are either professionals, or businessmen, with an increase from 15 per cent to 68 per cent.

609 Squadron reformed at Yeadon under the command of Squadron Leader Patrick H Womersley. He faced a different set of problems to those faced by Harold Peake in 1936. "With the war won, people were sick of hardship, discipline and uniforms, and the problem now was how to utilise some of the wartime skills and experience in a squadron whose future was both vague and unassured."[39] However, Ziegler also suggests that the attraction of belonging to such an exclusive club as the AAF was still powerful and within a year, 609 had virtually reached establishment numbers. Arthur Hudson, who was CO for four of the six years that he served with the squadron said:

> "Some, a declining number, were influenced still by patriotism – men who could not bear to think of the war having been fought in vain, and who felt it was just as important to win the peace. Others had a liking for the service but not for service life, or missed service camaraderie but wanted a home life too. Amongst the aircrew were many who had flying in their blood and could not bear to give it up, but did not want to make it a whole-time job; while amongst the ground crew were many of the trades who had acquired new skills and wished to preserve and practise them."[40]

The second CO was Roland P Beaumont who had worked in civilian life as a test pilot with the English Electric Company at Warton in Lancashire. Another post-war officer was Peter Hodgson, an ex-Oxford University student who had represented Yorkshire at rugby and "owned a pre-war vintage SS Jaguar that he used to race other officers home after a day's flying."[41]

By 1948 heavy recruiting had been followed by poor attendance and marked inefficiency as some members became disillusioned with the future of the AAF. When Arthur Hudson took over as CO in 1949 he was in charge of a unit that was only one quarter of its previous size. In order to rebuild the squadron, the selection board became more selective as the calibre of the applicants rose. Later members who joined the squadron after 1948 included many men who had completed their two-year National Service, including James Heath, Malcolm Slingsby and Francis Reacroft. Fifteen men were identified through the *London Gazette* as having been commissioned into the squadron and biographies were found on eleven of them, amounting to 73 per cent. The data shows that those attending public

Westland Wapiti's from 608 (North Riding) Squadron Auxiliary Air Force.

Lockheed Hudson.

Avro Anson photograph taken by Peter Vaux of 608 (North Riding) Squadron.

Biplanes "Awaiting orders".

Landed Avro Anson taken by Peter Vaux of 608 (North Riding) Squadron.

Air display c.1950.

Crowds attending open day and air display at Thornaby Aerodrome.

"Trying it out for size" Empire Air Day.

Early biplanes.

Armstrong Whitworth Whitley Medium Bomber.

Hawker Demon with Geoffrey Ambler.

Ground crew and biplane.

Crash of Westland Wapiti Mk II a.

Crash of British Bulldog Mk IIA on 11 June 1935 at RAF Kenley in Surrey which was caught by the wind on landing, and tipped over.

Recovery of crashed Demon Mk 1 which had been low flying around Yarm by pilot Keith Pyman on 5 February 1938.

Bristol 105 Bulldog biplane.

Monty and the King.

Peter Vaux and fellow officers "hanging around".

"Relaxing".

A game of darts in the crew room.

William Appleby-Brown.

Pilot and aircrew.

Refuelling.

Routine maintenance.

Auxiliary airmen off to summer camp.

Auxiliary airmen waiting to board their flight to Malta for annual summer camp.

John Pollock and ground crews performing routine maintenance on Commanding Officer Hank Costain's Vampire jet.

Aircrew and ground staff.

Navigation
discussion.

L-R Harry Bates, George Joyce, not identified, Mac McKenzie, Neil Hancock,
not identified, not identified, Vic Fleming and Hank Costain.

Left to Right Neil Hancock, Mac McKenzie, George Joyce, Bill Goodrum, Hank Costain, Bill Swainston, Judd Marshall, Harry Bates.

Vampires leaving Thornaby Aerodrome for summer camp in Malta.

school/Oxbridge fell from 27 per cent to zero in the post-war period. In terms of family announcements in *The Times*, marriage announcements fell from 20 per cent to 9 per cent, birth announcements increased from zero to 18 per cent whilst death announcements fell from 13 per cent to zero. Also, the number of men working in a professional capacity or within a business environment fell from 46 per cent to 27 per cent, whilst those working in family businesses also fell from 27 per cent to zero.

611 Squadron reformed at RAF Woodvale in Lancashire under Group Captain William Johnson Leather, who had also dropped rank to squadron leader to re-join. Francis Scott-Malden was another pre-war member of the squadron who re-joined in 1946. By the end of 1946 squadron strength was twenty-five airmen and three officers. Adverts were on local cinema screens and in both Liverpool and Southport newspapers, together with talks in local clubs. By March 1947 seven new pilots had been recruited, four of whom held the rank of sergeant, with three flying officers. As more planes flew over the area, so applications for the squadron increased; thus by the end of 1947, squadron strength was equal to 54 per cent of establishment. By 1954 the squadron had nineteen AAF pilots but was still running below strength.[42] Other notable officers were Alec Finlay who worked as a director of British Airways and Colin Hodgkinson who suffered a mid-air collision whilst in the Fleet Air Arm, which resulted in severe burns and the loss of both legs. Strongly influenced by Douglas Bader's story, he joined the RAF as a pilot, but was shot down over enemy territory and spent the rest of the war as a prisoner. Forty-eight men were identified as having been gazetted into the squadron and nineteen of them also had biographies, which is 40 per cent. The data remains steady for those attending public school, but those family or personal announcements which are found in *The Times* show a decrease in both marriage and death announcements and a slight increase in the number of births. The number working in a profession or in business rose from the pre-war figure of 18 per cent to the post-war figure of 42 per cent.

612 Squadron reformed on 10 May at RAF Dyce under the command of Squadron Leader Ramsey Roger Russell, who had also served in the squadron prior to the war. It proved very difficult to identify through the *London Gazette* or *The Times* Digital Archive any men serving in the squadron. Only one man was identified with a biography and that was the previously named CO. Hunt, however, notes that the officers in the squadron included a "master plumber, an agricultural student and an ex-Bomber Command

DFC who was now happy to fly as an NCO".[43] Unfortunately, without first and last names, the task to identify officers is practically impossible. This is reflected in the fact that there is no data to compare with the pre-war numbers.

613 Squadron was reformed at Ringway under the command of James Storrs Morton.[44] Members of the squadron included Frederick Butterworth, who served as a town councillor in Bournemouth in 1965, he bought the Branksome Tower Hotel for £200,000 and then sold it three weeks later for an undisclosed price, stating that his plans had changed and he no longer needed to own the hotel. Seven men were identified and of those men five biographies were found, equating to 71 per cent. The data for 613 Squadron is again rather sketchy, however it tells us that the number of men attending public school was now zero, whilst those attending an Oxbridge university had increased to 20 per cent. Those using *The Times* to make marriage announcements had increased to 20 per cent, whilst no one was found to announce births or deaths in *The Times*. However, again the number of men working in the professions or in business had increased from 33 per cent to 60 per cent.

616 Squadron was formed at RAF Finningley and immediately began a recruiting campaign to attract new members:

> "An immediate emotional response was provoked and ex-airmen from offices and shops, the railways, the banks, the schools, the steelworks, rushed to volunteer. Company directors, commercial travellers, men from all walks, were suddenly reunited in a common desire to see No. 616 Squadron a strong and useful part of our country's defence."[45]

Several of the pre-war veterans joined along with wartime members and Squadron Leader Ken Holden was appointed CO. Other former pilots included Group Captain Denis Gillam, Lional Harwood (Buck) Casson, Jim McCairns and Maurice Clarke, and they were so keen to join that they accepted far lower ranks than they had held during the war. This also applied to ground personnel where ex-officers readily accepted duties as NCOs. Interviews, selection and approval had to take place but within six months the squadron had twenty-three pilots, five navigators and twenty-one ground crew.[46] By 1948, 616 Squadron was still trying to recruit its full quota of auxiliaries.

Over time several pilots had to resign as pressure of work meant that they were unable to complete the necessary levels of continuation training. One way of reducing the shortfall of pilots was to take on ex-National Service pilots as they became available. However, problems of recruiting still remained, although an advertising campaign on the side of Sheffield trams produced a fresh batch of applications. By the time 616 Squadron was disbanded it was still struggling to attract enough new recruits.[47] Ten men were identified, with four having biographies which equates to 40 per cent. Those attending public schools had fallen from 50 per cent to 25 per cent, and the university figures remained at zero. Personal announcements in *The Times* remained stable, whilst those in business or professions fell from 75 per cent pre-war to 50 per cent post-war, with the number of men working in family businesses increasing from a pre-war figure of zero to a post-war figure of 25 per cent.

502 Squadron reformed at RAF Aldergrove, commanded by Squadron Leader William Hunter McGiffin, who had served with the squadron from 1937. Flying Officer W Bowden came first in the aforementioned RAuxAF pilots' race in 1949 with an average speed of 325mph. Only four men were identified as recruits with three having biographies, equating to 75 per cent. From this data the only information that can be gleaned is the increase in men working in business or the professions from 23 per cent to 33 per cent.

Table 18: Northern Squadrons showing percentage of men with biographies

Squadron Number	Percentage of men with biographies
602	73%
603	30%
607	71%
608	61%
609	73%
611	40%
612	100%
613	83%
616	57%
502	75%

At this point an anomaly with the total figures must be discussed. There were 173 men's names given by the *London Gazette* as having been commissioned into the RAuxAF between 1946 and 1957. However, no squadron numbers were given for these men. Therefore they are dealt with collectively, and of these men, only twenty-one biographies were found, which equated to a very poor 12 per cent. Analysing the data for these men it would appear that some used *The Times* to make personal or family announcements, 29 per cent announced their marriages, 10 per cent announced births of new children and 24 per cent announced deaths. The data also shows that 43 per cent of the men worked in a professional or business environment, whilst a further 10 per cent worked within a family business. The reason for these men's names to be given in this way is not clear. It could be that they were men who were coming out of their National Service, and were being commissioned into the RAuxAF, or that they were men leaving the RAFVR and being commissioned into the RAuxAF. The fact is the research has been unable to find a reason for their names to be gazetted in this way. However, when analysing the overall squadron results the 173 men with no squadron numbers given have been taken out of the figures to make the final results comparable with those before the war.

Analysis of the Data

Table 19: Royal Auxiliary Air Force Data By Category

Category	Percentage
Public School	10%
Oxbridge	7%
Other University	2%
Elite Sports	6%
Marriage Announcement	15%
Birth Announcement	6%
Death Announcement	25%
Profession/Business	41%
Family Business	6%
University Air Squadron	4%

The data shows that in total 343 men were identified across all of the RAuxAF squadrons and of those 343 men, biographies were found on 167, amounting to 49 per cent. The research has been able to identify 592 men prior to the war and 343 men after the war. This is a significant difference and perhaps shows a drop in the importance of *The Times* newspaper in sharing key events in a person's life, or perhaps suggests squadrons which are much more diverse in social make-up. The other point which must be considered is the fact that the actual squadron personnel research has produced much smaller numbers. This therefore can make the percentage figures seem much higher than the actual numbers. For example, in 612 Squadron, only five men were identified and biographies were found on three of them, this equates to 67 per cent which appears to be a high percentage. The analysis must take this into account when drawing conclusions. When analysing the data for the northern squadrons as compared to the southern squadrons the picture is slightly different. Overall the northern squadrons have higher percentages for men with biographies as compared to the southern squadrons at first glance. However, it may well be the case that the southern squadrons have more men in each squadron which could buck the figures.

So for many of the squadrons, as discussed earlier, the shortage of data reduces many of the categories to zero. This can also be seen when the men with no squadron numbers actual figures by category are given.

Table 20: Royal Auxiliary Air Force data for men with no squadron number given by category

Category	Total
Public School	0%
Oxbridge	0%
Other University	0%
Elite Sport	0%
Marriage Announcement	29%
Birth Announcement	10%
Death Announcement	24%
Profession/Business	43%
Family Business	10%
University Air Squadron	0%

The data for these officers who had no squadron number given in the *London Gazette* shows that there is no information at all about the education of these men in terms of whether or not they went to public school, and whether or not they attended any university. However, with regard to those men who used *The Times* to share with others key events in their lives, it can be seen that 29 per cent of the men announced their marriages, including Leonard Lee in April 1951, James Birkin in March 1956 and Anthony Barker. Ten per cent of the men used *The Times* to announce the birth of their children, including Arthur Barnes in July 1948 and Paul Richey in November 1946. Finally, 24 per cent of the men's deaths were announced, including Michael Taylor who died on 7 June 2008, Paul Richey in February 1989 and John Jupe on 5 July 1977. In terms of employment, 43 per cent of the men worked within the professions or in business, for example T Appleton was appointed managing director of Balfour Kilpatrick Installations and Arthur Brearley, who was director of post-experience programmes at the University of Bradford. Finally, 10 per cent of the men worked within family businesses, for example, William Evans who was self-employed in the family greengrocers business.

The Royal Air Force Volunteer Reserve

Immediately after the end of the Second World War, many regular and part-time pilots were keen to enlist in the RAFVR, and were signed up for a period of five years. However, there were never enough pilots and consequently, focus was turned to the National Servicemen. Training to be awarded their wings took eighteen months, and in general, men were enlisted only for twelve months. For this reason, the Preliminary Flying Badge, which ensured that trainee pilots would be able to show their skills at a basic level, was introduced, and as time went on and the length of service for National Service men was increased to eighteen months, most pilots had reached a competent level. Furthermore, there were also VR women pilots who had a great deal of experience who would be able to demonstrate their proficiency at Preliminary Flying Badge and beyond.

The main area of shortage therefore fell with the airmen/ground crew, whose role it was to service, maintain and ensure that the aircraft remained in the air. A special recruiting campaign began to bring the RAFVR up to strength because of "the key position which the air defence units and fighter squadrons hold in the defence of our country".[48] In 1950 the extent of the need for recruits in the RAFVR was indicated by Mr A.M. Crawley, Parliamentary Under Secretary of State for Air, who declared that 4000 volunteers were needed – specifically tradesmen – everywhere. The greatest need was for volunteers in the ground branches and trades, especially in maintenance, signals and radar, but there are some vacancies for flyers.[49]

By 1953, despite a major recruiting campaign throughout the country, there was still a shortfall of aircrew, from the 7,600 needed there was an establishment of only 6,000. Moreover, Tiger Moths had been replaced by

Chipmunks, which meant that the more up to date training aircraft were being used, but, at the time, the RAuxAF and RAF squadrons were training on Vampire jets, consequently the training of pilots in the RAFVR was lagging behind compared to the rest of the RAF. Flying schools, whose role it was to train RAFVR pilots and aircrew, trained personnel at weekends and during the two-week annual camp. Group Captain Peter Harris pointed out that:

"From a military standpoint, the RAFVR did represent a pool from which individuals could be called up if the need arose, but the post-war auxiliary fighter squadrons were of more immediate use, being equipped with jets and trained to provide a highly skilled reserve for Fighter Command."[50]

Table 21: Royal Air Force Volunteer Reserve Initial Data

Number of Identified Men	Number of men with Biographies	Percentage
4040	224	6%

The London Gazette identifies 4040 men who were commissioned into the Royal Air Force Volunteer Reserve. However, cross referencing these individual names against *The Times* Digital Archive and individual squadron histories produced biographies for only 224, or 6 per cent of the men. This is such a small number of identified men that it is hard to make assumptions based on the data. However, the table below shows the 224 officers with biographies by category.

Table 22: Royal Air Force Volunteer Reserve data by category

Category	Total	Percentage
Public School	14	6%
Oxbridge	19	8%
Other University	7	3%
Elite Sports	7	3%
Marriage Announcement	94	42%
Birth Announcement	15	7%
Death Announcement	102	46%
Profession/Business	70	31%
Family Business	3	1%
University Air Squadron	5%	2%

When the data in the table is analysed it is very difficult to come to conclusions about the kinds of backgrounds of these men on the basis of such a limited amount of information. However, of the 224 men with biographies, 46 per cent of them had death announcements in *The Times* and a further 42 per cent of them had their marriages announced. For example, the marriage and death was announced for Richard Gordon, whereas the marriage was announced for Michael Martin and the death announced for John Emery. Finally, 31 per cent of them worked in business or in the professions.

The final part of this chapter will put forward a series of comparisons where the pre-war data is compared to the post-war data.

Table 23: Pre-war versus post-war recruiting of the Royal Auxiliary Air Force.

1926-1939 Years	1926-1939 Number of Men	1946-1957 Years	1946-1957 Number of Men
1926	32	1946	71
1927	28	1947	66
1928	26	1948	30
1929	21	1949	30
1930	29	1950	65
1931	26	1951	36
1932	17	1952	52
1933	27	1953	84
1934	34	1954	19
1935	53	1955	21
1936	71	1956	17
1937	98	1957	0
1938	95	-	-
1939	32	-	-
TOTAL	561	TOTAL	491

This table shows a year by year total for the actual number of men recruited to the pre-war AAF and the post-war RAuxAF according to the research data. This, it must be remembered, is based on the number of officers that were commissioned each year via the *London Gazette*. From the table it can be seen that between 1926 and 1934 there were a similar amount of men commissioned each year according to the data. The numbers of officers commissioned increased year on year until 1939 when war was declared and the AAF was merged into the RAF for the duration of the hostilities. With the post-war data it can be seen 1946 and

1947 showed a steady number of recruits, when the RAuxAF was reconstituted in 1946 - perhaps the flush of enthusiasm after the war. The numbers then drop, but pick up again during the period of the Korean War between 1950 and 1953, with 1953 showing the highest number of recruits. After that there is a steady decline in the numbers until disbandment in 1957.

It must also be remembered that in the post-war, the RAuxAF was not only recruiting pilots, aircrew and ground crew, but was also recruiting for the Auxiliary Fighter Control Units and the Royal Auxiliary Air Force Regiment, which is very likely to affect the number of recruits to the RAuxAF as a whole.

Table 24: Pre-war versus the post-war recruiting for the RAFVR year on year.

1937-1939 Years	1937-1939 Number of Men Recruited	1946-1957 Years	1946-1957 Number of Men Recruited
1937	42	1946	5
1938	246	1947	498
1939	36	1948	819
-		1949	1229
-		1950	1229
-		1951	395
-		1952	233
-		1953	195
-		1954	49
-		1955	61
-		1956	46
-		1957	1
TOTAL	**324**	**TOTAL**	**4040**

From this data it can be seen that during the first year of recruitment, only a small number of men were commissioned, bearing in mind of course that recruits to the RAFVR were recruited at the rank of sergeant before being commissioned once they were able to fly. As we can see, 1938 is the best year for recruiting prior to the war with 246 men being commissioned. From 1939 onwards, all recruits into the RAF were trained through the RAFVR, so there is no data available for the war years. In the post-war world recruiting was very strong from 1947-1950 where the data shows 1229 men being commissioned. From then the numbers fall continually until just one commission is found in 1957.

Table 25: Post-war Royal Auxiliary Air Force recruitment compared to the post-war recruitment for the RAFVR.

Year	RAuxAF Number of Men	RAFVR Number of Men
1946	71	5
1947	66	498
1948	30	819
1949	30	1229
1950	65	514
1951	36	395
1952	52	233
1953	84	195
1954	19	49
1955	21	61
1956	17	46
1956	0	1
TOTAL	491	4040

The data shows that the RAFVR was significantly better at attracting new recruits than the RAuxAF. The reason for this is not particularly clear, but is likely to be because of the constant issues surrounding the RAuxAF in terms of the likelihood of a part-time pilot being able to handle a jet aircraft with the few hours of training and flying that they had, as well as discussions around the bases that they operated from and their capability to land jet aircraft. These Air Ministry and Governmental concerns may well have impacted on recruitment, as well as the recruitment to the Fighter Control Units and the RAuxAF regiment.

Table 26: Pre-war AAF recruiting versus the post-war RAuxAF recruiting by squadron.

Squadron Number	Pre-War Recruiting - Number of Men	Post-War Recruiting - Number of Men
600	70	31
601	72	40
602	41	11
603	45	44
604	39	8
605	52	40
607	25	7
608	32	31

609	22	15
610	17	5
611	18	48
612	20	1
613	5	6
614	19	2
615	16	8
616	8	7
500	27	5
501	17	28
502	17	4
504	22	2
No Squadron Number Given	0	173
TOTAL	**592**	**516**

From this data it can be seen that squadron numbers 600-610 all show a lower recruitment figure per squadron after the war. Nos. 611 and 501 Squadrons do not fit this pattern, but the remainder do. Again a key question has to be how much the RAuxAF Fighter Control units and the RAuxAF Regiment took recruits away from the flying arm of the RAuxAF.

Table 27: Royal Auxiliary Air Force Data versus Royal Air Force Volunteer Reserve Data by Category.

Category	RAuxAF	RAFVR
Public School	11%	6%
Oxford or Cambridge	7%	8%
University	2%	3%
Elite Sports	6%	3%
Marriage Announcement	18%	42%
Birth Announcement	9%	7%
Death Announcement	36%	46%
Profession / Business	54%	31%
Family Business	8%	1%
University Air Squadron	4%	2%

The data in this table shows that the findings are not too different for each organisation, but again there are facts that must be taken into account before conclusions are drawn. Firstly, the reliability of the data for the RAFVR must be questioned as so few of the commissioned officers had individual biographies and the data given only represents 6 per cent of all the men

147

who were commissioned between 1946 and 1957. Secondly, the post-war RAuxAF figures may well have been heavily affected by the creation of the other two part-time organisations, the Royal Auxiliary Air Force Fighter Control Units and the Royal Auxiliary Air Force Regiment. Therefore it has proved quite difficult to arrive at the more solid conclusions which have been drawn from the pre-war data.

Conclusion

The data collected for the post-war world for both the RAuxAF and the RAFVR has proved much more difficult to analyse than that of the pre-war. This is largely because of the 173 men of the RAuxAF for whom no squadron number was given, and this number has had a major impact on the final results for the RAuxAF. Moreover, the high number of men's names which have been found for the RAFVR has also affected this data, and has therefore made it much more difficult to draw conclusions. However, what can be seen is that there is much poorer recruitment across the country in the post-war world compared to that of the pre-war. Is this because of post-war apathy, or is it because of the more difficult recruitment processes in the post-war world? What we can see is that both of the two key London squadrons, 600 (City of London) Squadron and 601 (County of London) Squadron have performed in exactly the same way as the case study squadron, 608 (North Riding) Squadron, and all of the other squadrons across the country, and that shows that much of the current historiography, which claims that the RAuxAF were overrun with requests to join the post-war squadrons is in need of reconsideration. Taking the data as a whole it can be seen that the most significant area of increase was in the profession category, which for the RAuxAF increased from a pre-war figure of 24 per cent to a post-war figure of 54 per cent, whilst in the RAFVR the increase in the same category was from the pre-war figure of 14 per cent to the post-war figure of 31 per cent. Perhaps this shows the increasing need for qualifications in the more technical post-war world? The most obvious decline can be seen in the public school and Oxbridge categories which fell significantly in both the RAuxAF and the RAFVR recruits.

Significantly, the type of recruits to both organisations changed in the post-war world and this can be seen by the increased use of recruitment posters as a way of influencing young men's choices of how to spend their spare time. What is clear is the fact that after 1945, as prior to the war, the RAuxAF is not a gentleman's flying club, and nor is the RAFVR a citizen's air force.

Conclusion

The Territorial Air Force (TAF) was created as the reserve contingent of the Royal Air Force (RAF). It was organised as two different sections – the Auxiliary Air Force/Special Reserve (AAF/SR) and the Royal Air Force Volunteer Reserve (RAFVR). Both sections were made up of volunteers from different backgrounds and both are viewed in different ways by historians, the AAF being viewed as a "gentleman's flying club" whilst the RAFVR as a "citizen's air force". This book has challenged the current historiography and presented original data to show that the accepted views of the AAF and the RAFVR are in need of review.

The research aimed to answer several questions. In the first instance there was an analysis of the decisions taken by the government in a bid to discover why two different types of voluntary force, the AAF and the SR, were established. The evidence shows that this was an experiment to determine which type of force was more able to recruit men and would fit the requirements of the RAF. The winner of the experiment was the AAF; it was less expensive to run because it had significantly fewer regular men than the SR squadrons, morale was higher as each squadron was seen to belong to its members and recruitment was easier as there were fewer constraints on the volunteers. When the RAFVR was developed in 1936, the RAF reserves took on a different set up; the AAF was always made up of individual squadrons, whereas the RAFVR was not, and therein lies the problem when it comes to measuring data on the two separate parts of the reserve. Because men were recruited into the RAFVR, once trained they could be sent anywhere in the country to join a regular RAF station. This meant that data could not be shown in the same way as for the AAF, where data could be collected squadron by squadron and then comparisons could be drawn. The numbers recruited to the RAFVR simply had to be shown as a list of names, and therefore the detail of the data found for the AAF, such as north and south, England, Ireland, Scotland and Wales and so on, could not be analysed in the same way. As a result of which, the AAF is much easier to analyse and draw conclusions from than the RAFVR and a final comparison between the two different voluntary organisations is not really possible because the two organisations do not function in the same way.

Secondly, one question related to evaluating the recruitment process for both parts of the TAF and using the data to compare the social composition of the two key London squadrons, 600 (City of London) Squadron and 601 (County of London) Squadron, upon which the main assumptions about the AAF are built. Analysing the research data on these two squadrons and comparing it to the case study squadron, 608 (North Riding) Squadron, and the other eighteen squadrons across the entire United Kingdom produced a picture of recruitment and social class challenged previous assumptions. This new picture enabled the third research question relating to whether or not the AAF squadrons across the United Kingdom were different according to their region to be answered. Finally, the research considered how the new squadrons integrated with their local communities and why these voluntary organisations were wound up in 1957.

The results of the research challenge existing academic thought because when looking at the pre-war data, 55 per cent of the men identified as having been commissioned into an AAF squadron had some sort of biographical information about them. Of the two London squadrons, which form the basis for many of the images of AAF pilots, 49 per cent of the men had some sort of biography and in the case study squadron 63 per cent of the men had some useful data. This compares to 79 per cent of men identified for the RAFVR. Furthermore, when we look at the label given to the AAF of being a gentleman's flying club the data does not support this view, with only 20 per cent of the identified men attending public school and 19 per cent of men attending an Oxbridge University. Comparing those figures to those of the RAFVR, labelled as a "citizen's air force" it is clear that this view does not hold true either, with 39 per cent of the identified men attending a public school and 54 per cent of the men attending an Oxbridge University. Indeed, when all of the pre-war data is analysed, the RAFVR has a higher percentage for seven out of the nine categories. However, when the AAF squadrons are analysed squadron by squadron the image in the pre-war world is slightly different than the view across the whole organisation. On an individual squadron by squadron level, many of the squadrons do present an image of a gentleman's flying club, particularly the squadrons in the south of England. Looking at the post-war figures a different picture emerges. Eleven per cent of the identified men for the Royal Auxiliary Air Force (RAuxAF) attended a public school compared to 6 per cent of those identified for the RAFVR and 7 per cent of the men in the RAuxAF attended an Oxbridge University compared to 8 per cent of those men in the RAFVR. The most significant difference relates to announcements in *The Times* newspaper marking memorable events in a person's life with 18 per cent of the RAuxAF men having a marriage announcement as compared to 42 per cent of the RAFVR, and 36 per cent of the RAuxAF men having a death announcement as compared to 46 per cent of the men in the RAFVR.

Data which perhaps highlights changes in society can be seen when comparing the pre-war data with the post-war data for professions and family businesses. The pre-war figures show that 24 per cent of the men identified in the AAF and 14 per cent of the men in the RAFVR worked within the professions compared to the post-war figures of 54 per cent of the men identified in the RAuxAF working within the professions and 31 per cent of the men in the RAFVR. It can be argued that in some ways class can be defined by employment and in the post-war world there were more opportunities for people to move across and within social classes. Also the decline in primary and secondary sectors and the growth in the tertiary sector, with a large increase in the number of people working in offices as compared to those working down the mines, in textile factories, or ship building. Moreover, the growth in consumerism and the expansion of the holiday market and technological advances in transport all helped to shape a radically new society.[1]

However, the figures must be treated with caution because some problems have been identified. The post-war data shows that for the RAuxAF, 36 per cent of the identified men had biographies whilst only 6 per cent of the identified men for the RAFVR had biographies. This means that certainly the data for the RAFVR is so small that to draw conclusions with it would place us on shaky ground, whereas the data of the RAuxAF is more reliable.

When the pre-war data is evaluated, certain images stand out, for example, the notoriety of 600 and 601 Squadrons members is apparent when the list of identified officers for each of the two squadrons is studied. These men were significantly easier to research than some of the men from other AAF squadrons largely due to the fact that some of their names were well known. Clearly, this reflected their national status and although some other AAF officers across the country also used the paper to announce personal events, it was harder to find material relating to officers in other AAF squadrons and particularly difficult amongst northern squadrons. In this sense, 600 and 601 Squadrons were not typical of the wider movement but only in terms of public profile.

600 and 601 Squadrons recruited primarily from the City of London, with their officer candidates employed in the city's major institutions of banks, insurance companies, the Stock Exchange, legal firms and media organisations; their personnel had, in the main, been educated in public schools such as Eton, and many attended either Oxford or Cambridge. They had a general interest in politics with several following a career as an MP; many had connections to the aristocracy, most excelled at elite sports and invariably engaged in the kind of high jinks within the officers' mess that had characterised public school and university. They were all members of an elite lifestyle. However, analysis of 608 and other AAF squadrons revealed that this pattern repeated itself with surprising regularity right across the movement, but not in sufficient numbers to support the existing view.

These common patterns can be identified when the backgrounds of those from 600 and 601 Squadrons are compared with officer candidates from other southern squadrons, such as 604 (County of Middlesex) Squadron, 605 (County of Warwick) Squadron, 610 (County of Chester) Squadron, 615 (County of Surrey) Squadron, 500 (County of Kent) Squadron, 501 (County of Gloucester) Squadron and 503 (County of Lincoln) Squadron. Differences between them are certainly less significant than was initially predicted. That said, there were some minor but nonetheless interesting regional variations. For example, members of the southern squadrons which operated beyond the glamour of 600 and 601 Squadrons, included lawyers, stockbrokers and engineers, as well as post office engineers, building contractors and the sons of doctors, army officers and hatters. Thus, more modest middle-class backgrounds can be identified within these squadrons which are not as noticeable within 600 and 601. In this sense, Jeffrey Hill's argument that voluntary organisations have "the capacity to bring together a wide social mix"[2] holds true, in the sense that the AAF offered a meeting ground for young men from both traditional landed society and a wide spectrum of men from urban-industrial middle classes. However, Ross McKibbin's counter-argument that "social exclusion and political partisanship might be the chief function of many voluntary associations"[3] also applies in that the AAF offered its officers a sphere of authority and exclusivity that help distinguish them from those below them in the social order.

CONCLUSION

When we turn to the northern squadrons, such as 602 (City of Glasgow) Squadron, 603 (City of Edinburgh) Squadron, 607 (County of Durham) Squadron, 608 (North Riding) Squadron, 609 (West Riding of Yorkshire) Squadron, 611 (West Lancashire) Squadron, 612 (County of Aberdeen) Squadron, 613 (City of Manchester) Squadron, 616 (South Yorkshire) Squadron and 504 (County of Nottingham) Squadron, similarities between them and 600 and 601 are still noticeable in terms of links to the aristocracy, attendance at public school or Oxford and Cambridge Universities, and sporting prowess. However, there are significant differences with regard to the economic and social make-up of the officers. Although some of the young men worked within legal institutions or journalism, many worked within family businesses, including timber, shipping, textiles, glass, farming and mining.[4] The picture that ultimately emerges is of a new elite culture that developed during the nineteenth century between traditional landed classes and new bourgeois groups; it was forged through public schools, universities, clubs and print culture, and by the 1920s, the AAF offered a new focus for this elite culture, giving it a leadership role in key areas of national defense. Along with educational institutions and elite social clubs, the AAF played its own part in reinforcing this class identity and authority. The glamorous AAF squadrons in London represented a heightened version of this elite culture and whilst they were distinctive in many respects, they nonetheless shared many features with other AAF squadrons throughout the country, including 608 Squadron.

It is clear that AAF officers in the early twentieth century were men from prominent local and national families, whereas after the Second World War, recruiting procedures were significantly different resulting in social background playing a less important role in officer selection. Thus, pre-war recruitment was based on elite social networks and word of mouth, whilst post war recruitment was based more on qualifications, skill and experience. Whilst many squadron histories believe that many men from the pre-war squadrons raced to join the reconstituted RAuxAF in 1946, the data does not really support that view with only five men rejoining 600 and 601 Squadrons, one rejoining 608 Squadron, and an overall total of thirty-five men overall rejoining the RAuxAF. This may be due to many having lost their desire to be part of a voluntary organisation and deciding that they had given enough time to serving their country during the war itself.

At the beginning of the research there was an assumption, based on the existing literature, that the findings would reveal that 600 and 601 Squadron were indeed very different from other English AAF squadrons, largely due to their elite membership. As the research progressed however, it became clear that in many areas this was simply not the case. There were indeed interesting regional differences which were largely based on economic structures; but the weight of evidence from 608 Squadron and indeed from all other AAF squadrons showed that there was a national common elite culture within the AAF created by universities and public schools, both of which played a major part in shaping a national elite in which the older landed classes and the new middling classes were melded. AAF squadrons played a significant role in sustaining the authority and social importance of these elites. This buttressing of elite culture was particularly important because it came during the early-to-mid twentieth century at a time when the young men forming the officer classes of the AAF were often losing their traditional authority and power in wider political, economic and cultural spheres.

There is no doubt that there were clearly defined social barriers to becoming an officer within any of the pre-Second World War AAF squadrons. Technical qualifications and skills were never sufficient to warrant acceptance. This seems to have been the same across the country and there was no evidence of significant regional variations. What emerged was a picture that confirmed the elitist nature of the movement. Although 600 and 601 squadrons have always been the two most widely studied AAF squadrons, and their personnel and exploits have helped create a dominant image of the AAF, other lesser known squadrons were largely similar in their recruitment procedures and cultures.

Part of the voluntary military tradition that informed the creation of the AAF was based on the ideal of strong links between volunteer units and their localities. Research of national press records shows that "At Home" days were used by the RAF to create an interest in aerodromes across the country and to encourage local residents to support the different kinds of work undertaken by their men. The press played a key role in maintaining local interest in AAF squadrons and the status of the young officers was reflected in their social lives and activities regularly attracting media attention. In particular, AAF squadrons were meant to play a key role in creating positive attitudes towards the military as a whole.

However, evidence from one particular squadron, No 608 Squadron, revealed significant tensions with its local community, including complaints from local inhabitants regarding the revolver and machine gun practice which took place on Sundays, as well as concern that the valuation of properties had been affected due to low flying planes. Local head teachers complained about intensive flying, whilst others found noise and annoyance due to gun firing to be intolerable. The often strained relationship between 608 Squadron and its surrounding community was not helped by the elitist nature of the squadron and whilst it has not been possible to explore this issue in other AAF units, this class-community tension may have been a more common feature throughout the country than the voluntary ideal would suggest.

Another question involved the importance of voluntarism within the TAF. The first question was the extent to which voluntary organisations retained their importance in a modernising society. Much of the existing historiography suggests that the voluntary traditions of the nineteenth century were declining steadily throughout the twentieth century due largely to the expansion of the state sector and the increase of large corporate businesses, coupled with social and cultural changes which led to a more home-centered lifestyle. The creation of the TAF and its subsequent reforming in 1946 challenges this view by highlighting the importance of a voluntary organisation in the defense of the country and presents the experiences of the many veterans who volunteered to join the service. The findings of the research also support the concept of the mixed economy, and the moving frontier model where the role of the state sometimes extends and sometimes retracts in relation to voluntarism, depending on specific circumstances.[5] Throughout this ebb and flow, voluntary institutions like the TAF continued to play an integral role in the social structure of the country.

Moreover, the question regarding how voluntarism intersected with class considered whether it was possible for a voluntary organisation to encompass a broad social mix of personnel. Although the TAF was a voluntary organisation, it remained throughout its existence a military structure which depended upon a rigid hierarchy in order to function effectively. This hierarchy ensured that a certain amount of class division was fundamental and supports the view of Ross McKibbin that social exclusion and political partisanship might be the chief functions of many voluntary associations. It is apparent from the research undertaken that class was a fundamental issue in terms of volunteers in both the pre-war AAF and the pre-war RAFVR with informal barriers in place to prevent entry to the officer ranks by those who lacked the appropriate social background, whilst class relationships in the post-war TAF were more fluid.

The TAF as a voluntary organisation operated during a period when successive governments placed considerable emphasis on the responsibility of individuals to play a significant role in the defence of the nation.

In this climate, the TAF was able to draw officer volunteers from the aristocratic, gentry and bourgeois families in each of the regions across the country. In effect, the TAF offered those with the "right" backgrounds the arena in which to fulfill their enjoyment of flying whilst at the same time enabling them to play a leadership role within the local community, supporting the public school ethos of "doing their bit" and "setting an example for others to follow". When considering non-officer volunteers, however, there was a steady supply of recruits. Whilst these men encountered class divisions within the TAF and talked openly about the way they functioned on a day-to-day level, their motivations for joining the TAF and methods by which they were recruited were less shaped by class considerations; some sought training in a particular trade; some welcomed the additional wages of a TAF member; most talked about a desire to serve their country. The class divisions encountered once they joined their squadrons were accepted as a fact of life.

Furthermore, the question was also raised as to how rooted voluntary organisations like the TAF were in their local communities. The voluntary military tradition that shaped the TAF was based on the principle of a citizen army formed from local people operating in their local context, and the relationship between AAF squadrons and their surrounding communities was a key issue explored in the book. Because military voluntarism of this kind was rooted in regional and local contexts, the TAF was expected to strengthen bonds between local businesses, large corporations and local communities. However, the study suggested that in particular, AAF recruitment policies in the 1930s restricted recruitment of officers largely by class, and in the post-war era, by experience and technical knowledge. Recruitment of other personnel was more broadly based but the organisation never recruited what can be described as a significant cross-section of local society. The social life of officers and men rarely engaged with the wider social life of the community and despite regular open days in which the local AAF squadron encouraged members of the public to explore its facilities, the recurring flashpoints that took place specifically between the case study squadron, 608 Squadron and its surrounding community, testify to an often troubled relationship, particularly in the inter-war period.

It is clear that the AAF did change throughout its existence between 1926 and 1957. Most noticeably there was a more democratic and technocratic spirit at work after the Second World War, specifically in terms of recruitment procedures and officer-airmen relationships on summer camps. The social exclusivity of the AAF which had existed during the interwar years did not continue after the Second World War to the same extent, although there were still divides between officers and airmen, as well as between NCOs and airmen, but these were now essentially based on the hierarchical nature of military life rather than on wider class structures and relations. Prerequisites were put in place to ensure that technical knowledge and qualifications were necessary to acquire rank and status within the new organization. Word of mouth amongst elite social cliques was no longer enough to guarantee membership. Furthermore, although men were prepared to drop rank in order to re-enlist, their middle class backgrounds were no longer sufficient to guarantee a leadership role.[6] In the post war world, the idea of the AAF as a club seemed to lose its previous cachet since young men now had more opportunities to fill their leisure time. After a brief upsurge of patriotism immediately after the war, patriotic ideals lost some of their previous appeal and thus the ideas of the "volunteer fighters", which had been so important in the early 1930s, were no longer as attractive.

Looking at the local squadrons has helped to map out some wider potential conclusions about the AAF as a whole. It has helped support the view that there were only minor differences between the activities of the officers within these squadrons as compared to those in 600 and 601 Squadrons. Whilst many of the officer candidates in these squadrons did not have the social status and family backgrounds of officers in 600 and 601 Squadrons, they still were well-known families who had a certain degree of status within the local area and subscribed to a recognisably national elite lifestyle. Many had similar backgrounds to the 600 and 601 Squadron officers in that they had been to public schools, universities and were wealthy enough to own their own planes. All engaged in the typical activities that went on in the officers' mess and this was clearly a ritual form of behaviour that was replicated throughout the AAF squadrons in England throughout the 1930-1957 period.

The findings of this research show that looking at individual squadrons, the perception of the AAF, which has been put forward by historians and which has been generally accepted throughout the history of the organisation, is largely correct in the period up to 1939. Thus, the pre-war data shows that right across the country, the AAF clearly was a "gentleman's flying club" made up of English social elites, and the experiences of 600 and 601 Squadron were very similar to other AAF squadrons in terms of the types of young men who joined the organisation, the selection process which controlled entry and the social life of a typical officers' mess. There are some relatively minor regional differences, primarily based upon employment patterns, but these pale into insignificance in the face of a hegemonic elite culture that prevailed right across the AAF movement.

The reformed AAF between 1946 and 1957 was no longer an exclusive club made up of rich young officers. Instead it was an organisation composed of men who had the technical ability and skills to fly the modern jet fighter aircraft and who had earned their rank and status by virtue of past education and experience. Those who reformed the organisation had learned that whilst those chosen to be officers in the pre-war AAF were very capable and performed their jobs well, the kind of men needed in the post-war required new technical knowledge and qualifications.

The other key finding demonstrated that the pre-war RAFVR as a whole did not play the role of a citizen's air force, with a high percentage of volunteers attending public schools across the country and Oxbridge universities, and having key events in their lives marked by announcements in *The Times* newspaper. This shows that in many ways the RAFVR recruited and operated in the same way as the individual squadrons of the AAF. This is clearly not the case when the post-war data is considered. There is little doubt that there is limited research covering the reserve forces of the RAF, and this piece of research has found data which challenges the established historiography and view of the reserves. The term used by the government to describe the RAFVR, the "citizen's air force," has been challenged by this new data and has been shown to be open to question, given the backgrounds of those men who were commissioned into it. Similarly, the exclusive nature of the RAuxAF has been reinforced by the research which has provided data on the backgrounds of the officer recruits across the entire United Kingdom.

This shows that the prevailing thesis of the pre-war AAF being a gentleman's flying club is not supported by the data across the whole of the United Kingdom. Even the data found on the two London squadrons, 600 and 601 Squadrons, do not support the view of the AAF as an exclusive club. This result also holds true across the case study squadron. In terms of the RAFVR being a citizen's flying club, the data found does not support that view either, showing that overall, larger numbers of men who joined the RAFVR came from better backgrounds than those who joined the AAF. Consequently, the research has highlighted differences in the composition of the reserves across the country which the existing historiography does not mention.

In terms of the post-war data, again the data shows that the men recruited to the RAuxAF were from less exclusive backgrounds than their pre-war counterparts. This view is mirrored across the whole country and is supported by the data for both the key London squadrons and the case study squadron. The data also shows that the recruits to the RAFVR are also from less exclusive backgrounds compared to the men recruited prior to the Second World War.

However, it is clear that the post-war data is much poorer than the data from before the war. In particular, when the RAFVR figures are considered there is such a poor number of men with biographical details that it is incredibly difficult to draw effective conclusions. Similarly, the data for the RAuxAF shows smaller numbers of recruits to most of the squadrons, and there is an anomaly in terms of 173 men who were recruited to the organisation but where not allocated to any particular squadron. Again this has thrown the figures out and has meant that the conclusions drawn from the post-war data across the reserves as a whole are less reliable.

In this respect, the research has shown that the old adage, well-known in RAF circles, written by an anonymous RAF writer prior to the Second World War, is no longer true:

There are three kinds of Air Force Officer....
The Regular, who is an Officer trying to become a Gentleman.
The Auxiliary, who is a Gentleman attempting to become an Officer.
And there is the VR, who is neither, trying to become both.[7]

Appendix 1

Service with the

R.A.F. Volunteer Reserve

Who is eligible? At present pilots, navigators and
signallers who have gained their "wings" in the
Services, and ground officers of certain branches
who served with the R.A.F. during the war.
Women pilots with at least 100 hours' solo flying
may enrol on the W.A.A.F./V.R. list. Age limit
for flying duties is 30, but exceptions can be made.

What pay and allowance? Pilots and navigators are
paid an annual flying training bounty of £35 tax
free, signallers £30 tax free, and women pilots
£25 tax free. Pay and allowances at Air Force
rates are paid to all reservists during continuous
training of more than 48 hours. A tax free
training expenses allowance of 1/6 an hour is
paid for non-continuous training and travelling
expenses are also allowed.

How about cars and petrol? Reservists who use their
cars are given petrol coupons for duty attend-
ances and there is a mileage allowance of 3d.
a mile.

What are the training commitments? Training is
done at a number of evenings and weekends each
year and at an annual period of 15 days' continuous training; the 15 days' continuous
training may be broken down into a number of
shorter periods. As far as possible times of
training will suit the convenience of the individual. For flying categories training includes at
least 40 hours' flying each year. Officers of the
ground branches have comparable training
commitments.

For further particulars: Apply to the Commandant
of your nearest Reserve Centre or to:
The S.P.S.O.
Reserve Command H.Q.
R.A.F. White Waltham
Berkshire.

R.A.F.V.R.

and W.A.A.F.V.R.

Service with the RAF Volunteer Reserve. (*Flight*, 15 July 1948)

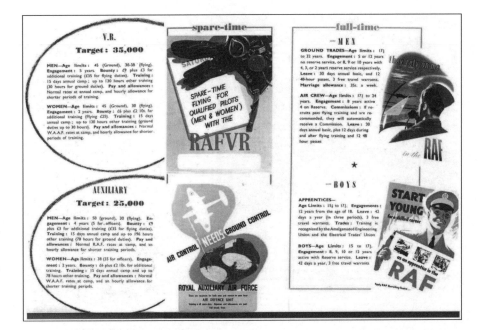

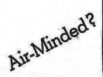

Spare Time. (*Flying Review*, 17 August 1948)

Air-Minded. (*The Times*, 19 January 1949)

There's a place for you
in the part-time RAF.
(*Flight*, 27 January 1950)

Managing directors are proud
to be mechanics. (*The Times*,
4 March 1950)

You don't have to fly to join.
(*Flight*, 27 January 1950)

Spend flying weekends.
(*The Times*, 4 March 1950)

Do a grand job in your spare time. (*Flight*, 22 December 1950)

Help keep Britain 'on top' in the air. (*Flight*, 4 January 1951)

There's a place for you
in the part-time RAF.
(*Flight*, 4 January 1951)

There's a place for you
in the part-time RAF.
(*Flight*, 27 June 1952)

There's a place for you in the part-time RAF.
(*Flight*, 19 September 1952)

Berlin 1943 and back 1953.
(*Flight*, 27 March 1953)

APPENDIX 1

Letter to RAuxAF squadron members from Secretary of State for Air. (TNA, AIR 19/743, 11 November 1957)

R. Aux. A. F.

WHEN we could serve by flying, we gave up our time and flew;
But now, it appears, our country has nothing for us to do.
No doubt the boffins have got it taped; but we'd like to make it clear—
If they ever find anything else for us, they will always find us here.

Punch Cartoon. (*Punch Magazine*, 30 January 1957)

Appendix 2

This is an abridged version of the appendices. It contains the names of all of the officers for whom biographical information was found. The date of commission is next to the name, in brackets. Officers in the Auxiliary Air Force have been listed by squadron number. Officers in the pre-war Royal Air Force Volunteer Reserve have been listed in alphabetical order. Officers in the post war Royal Air Force Volunteer Reserve have been listed by date of commission.

Most of the background information on the officers has been found using *The Times* Digital Archive. Any other information used appears in the end notes. Dates of commission have been found using the *London Gazette* Archive at www.gazette-online.co.uk

Pre-War United Kingdom Auxiliary Air Force Officers

600 (City of London) Squadron
Adams, Harold (29/05/1937) On 30 December 1962, after a short illness, Wing Commander H Adams OBE death announced.

Benham, Jack Elkan David (27/10/1930) Son of Lionel D and Mabel P Benham of Marylebone London. Commemorated on Runnymede Memorial, Surrey Panel 64. Director of John Hunter Morris and Elkan Ltd. Son of Alexander Elkan of Morris and Elkan Ltd, Tobacco Brokers and Cigar and Tobacco Importers.

Brown, Justin Arrowsmith (01/08/1928) The Air Ministry announces that Flying Officer Justin Arrowsmith Brown and No 509359 Leading Aircraftsman John Wood, pilot and passenger, respectively, of a Wapiti aircraft of No 5 (Army Co-operation) Squadron, QUETTA, lost their lives on Sunday as the result of an accident which occurred at Quetta. Obituary – Brown was educated at Clifton and Caius College, Cambridge University. A brilliant rower, he coxed the Cambridge crews in the Boat Race in the years 1924, 1925, 1926 and 1927. Son of Harold and Margaret Brown, IGS, Burma. Died 20 March 1933, aged 28.

Campbell-Orde Ian Ridley (10/12/1929) Born 18 June 1907, Son of Colin Ridley Campbell Orde and Winifred Harriet Stewart.

Colbeck-Welch, Edward Lawrence (21/07/1936) Born in 1914, educated at Eton and Cambridge University.

Collett, Stanley Beresford (06/07/1926) Born 1896. Attended Bishop's Stortford College, then entered The Durham Light Infantry. In 1917 transferred into RFC. Resigned his commission in 1921, then joined the AAF in 1926. Assistant solicitor. Then Assistant Company Secretary of the Great Western Railway. Son of Sir Charles Collett, Chief Mechanical Engineer of the Great Western Railway and Lord Mayor of London in 1934. Obituary in *The Times*. Killed in an RAF display at Hendon when his aircraft was wrecked whilst making a forced landing. He was killed instantly, and could not be extricated from the wreckage before it caught fire, about half a minute after the machine struck the ground.

Dalton, Arthur Hammond (03/09/1926) Born 30 October 1892. Killed on Active service on Thursday, 31 July 1941. Son of William and Catherine Dalton. Husband of Eileen Dalton of Henley, Oxford. Commonwealth Graves Commission.

Dawson-Damer, George Lionel Seymour (15/10/1931) Viscount Carlow, Born 20 December 1907. Son of Lionel George Henry Seymour Dawson-Damer, 6th Earl of Portarlington and Winnifreda Yuill.

Earnshaw, Eric John (25/01/1927) Born on 3 May 1906.

Elworthy, Samuel Charles (15/01/1935) Born 23 March 1911 in New Zealand. Studied Law at Trinity College, Cambridge University. *Times* announcement of Bar results. Called to Bar, Lincolns Inn in 1935. Joined AAF in 1934 and joined RAF in 1936. Awarded DSO.

Frankland, Roger Nathaniel (22/06/1931) Born 11 April 1909, son of Sir Frederick William Francis George Frankland, 10th Bt and Mary Cecil Curzon, Baroness Zouche.

Ferguson, Austin Bruce (01/11/1927) Birth announcement – Ferguson – On 26 March 1943, at The Old Farm House, Knotty Green, Beaconsfield, to Joan, wife of Austin Bruce Ferguson – a daughter. Death announcement – Ferguson – on 9 April 1972, Austin Bruce Ferguson aged 74, at his home. Beloved husband of Joan. Service at Chilterns Crematorium, Whielden Lane, Amersham, at 2.30pm on Thursday, 13 April for close friends and relations.

Healy, E.A. (17/04/1924) Marriage announcement in *Times*, Tuesday, 5 May 1931, Page 17, Issue 45814, Column C. Son of John Edward Healy, Editor of *Irish Times*.

Hiscox, Ralph (03/08/1929) Joined Roberts agency at Lloyd's and started Syndicate 44, writing non-marine insurance in 1938. In 1965 elected chairman of Lloyds. Hiscox company history.

Isaac, John Noel (27/08/1933) The first Briton to die on active service in the Second World War. Whilst practising single-engined approaches and landings, he had spun in on Hendon Old Town and had been killed instantly. The aircraft caught fire and burned three houses, but no civilians were killed or hurt. He had a second class honours degree from Jesus College, Oxford University. He was born on 18 December 1910 in the small village of Dinas Powis, Glamorgan, the son of Wilfred John and Rosalind May Isaac. Before entering Oxford University on a history Scholarship, he had been a pupil at Magdalen College School.

Jenyns, Charles Gambier (06/07/1926) Born 3 June 1899. Worked at London Stock Exchange.

Kellett, Roger Gustave (20/03/1934) Born on 13 September 1909. Educated at Rossall School, worked as a stockbroker for Laurence Keen and Gardner. Died 12 November, aged 89.

Lamplugh, Alfred Gilmer (17/08/1926) Born on 19 October 1895 at Garton on the Wolds, Yorkshire. Educated at King Edwards School and Queens College, Birmingham. Underwriter and principal surveyor for Aviation Insurance Co Ltd. Served in the Royal Flying Corps during the First World War. Member of the Royal Aero Club, Piccadilly, London. Died 2 December 1955, aged 59.

Lancaster, Dent Hugh Turner (02/09/1926) Born on 27 June 1904.

Lea, Robert Francis Gore (22/07/1932) Second son of Sir Sydney Lea and Lady Lea of Dunsley Hall, Stourport, Worcestershire. Marriage announcement in *The Times*.

Lloyd, George Ambrose (16/09/1926) Baron of Dolobran. Born 19 September 1879, a Quaker, educated at Eton and Trinity College, Cambridge, an oarsman. Travelled extensively, became an overseas attaché and ambassador. MP for West Staffordshire. Governor of Bombay in 1918. Left in 1923. In 1925, High Commissioner for Egypt and the Sudan.

Rowe, John Hugh Chitty (03/06/1935) OBE awarded on Tuesday, 1 October 1946. His aircraft was shot down during an attack on a heavily defended airfield in Holland in May 1940. He received severe back injuries which rendered him unable to take part in escape activities. He only recovered into full health in the last year of the war, but by then, he was the key man in the secret communication department and could not be spared to take part in escape activities.

Stewart, Peter Graham (01/03/1927) The memorial service for Group Captain Peter Graham Stewart OBE, will be held at St Bartholomew-the-Great on Tuesday, 25 June at 6pm.

Tollemache, Anthony Henry Hamilton (12/07/1937) Born 3 August 1913. A relation of Lord Tollemache, educated at Eton. Son of Henry and Ethel Tollemache. Awarded the George Cross for bravery. Died 20 February 1977 after a car crash in Paris.

Young, Harold Oswald (26/10/1936) Marriage announcement – on 26 April 1934 at Christ Church, Down Street, Harold Oswald Young, son of the late Mr T.C. Young of Bushey. Birth announcement – on 3 October 1941 at Jennifers, Haslemere, to Joan, wife of Harold Oswald Young – a son. Death announcement – Young – on 19 March, suddenly. Harold Oswald Young of Quarry Garden, Wardour, Tisbury, Wiltshire, aged 80.

601 (County of London) Squadron

Aitken, John William Maxwell (11/09/1935) Born in Montreal on 15 February 1910. Educated at Westminster and Pembroke College, Cambridge. Son of Lord Beaverbrook and later general manager of the *Sunday Express*. Cambridge soccer blue and a scratch golfer as well as heir to the Beaverbrook newspaper title. Keen yachtsman. Won a DFC and a DSO between 1941 and 1943. Obituary in *The Times*.

Bellville, Rupert (10/08/1926) The Salamanca Government today informed the British Embassy to Spain to say that they had received reliable information that Rupert Bellville, the British airman, is imprisoned at Gijon. Mr Bellville landed at Santander Aerodrome in his private aeroplane last Wednesday evening and was taken prisoner by the Asturian Militiamen, who forced him to fly one of their officers to Gijon. Nothing has been heard from him since. On 9 September the authorities in Gijon informed the British Embassy to Spain that they are willing to release Mr Rupert Bellville, and suggest that a British ship should come to Gijon to transport him to France. HM Destroyer *Foresight*, patrolling the Spanish coast, will lie outside the harbour of Gijon at noon tomorrow while the ships cutter goes ashore to pick up Mr Bellville. During the worst storm of the season a boat from the British destroyer *Foresight* picked up Mr Rupert Bellville, the British airman who has been a prisoner of the Asturian authorities since the day before Santander fell. Mr Rupert Bellville put his house, Papillon Hall up for sale. Advert repeated on Tuesday, 31 May 1938. Birth announcement – on 18 June 1939 at San Diego to Jeanette, wife of Rupert Bellville, a son. Bankruptcy notice for Rupert Bellville of 37, St James Street, London, SW1. Rupert Bellville of White's Club, St James's, London SW1, died 23 July 1962. Obituary for Hercules Bellville, a film producer, whose father was Rupert Bellville, an old Etonian and a test pilot who had flown as a volunteer for General Franco in the Spanish Civil War. The family had made their fortune through the mustard trade.

Branch, Guy Rawston (07/05/1937) Educated at Eton. Played rackets for school and was captain of his house. Went to Balliol as an exhibitioner. Obituary in *The Times*.

Bulwer-Lytton, Edward Anthony James (25/08/1931) Viscount Knebworth MP. Eldest son of Earl of Lytton. Godson of King Edward VII. Educated at Eton and Magdalen College, Oxford. Distinguished boxer, boxing for Oxford University. Won in the welter-weight category against Cambridge University in 1924 and 1925. In 1929 he became a director of the Army and Navy Stores. Worked as a *Daily Mail* writer. Obituary in *The Times*.

Bushell, Roger Joyce (10/02/1934) Born in South Africa in 1910, his father was a mining engineer. He was educated in both Johannesburg and England. In 1929 he went to Cambridge University to study law. He was a profound athlete and represented the University as a skier and rugby player. He is famous for being imprisoned in Colditz prison camp and leading a major escape attempt in which he himself was murdered by the Germans. Fluent in German, French and Afrikaans. Obituary in *The Times*.

Carnaby, William Fleming (03/01/1936) Engagement announcement in *The Times*, only son of Mr and Mrs W Carnaby of Dulwich.

Cavendish, Henry Siegel (04/08/1934) Born 29 August 1908. Elder son of Tyrell William Cavendish of Crakemarsh Hall, Uttoxeter.

Cleaver, Gordon Neil Spencer (08/04/1937) Born in Stanmore, Middlesex and educated at Harrow. He was the winner of the *Hahnenkammrennen* in 1931, the only British Skier to win the event. Joined 601 Squadron in early 1937. On 15 August 1940 he was shot down over Winchester. The Perspex canopy of his Hurricane was hit by cannon shells and the fragments shattered into his face and eyes. He bailed out and was taken to Salisbury Hospital where he found out that he had been blinded in his right eye and had seriously reduced vision in his left. He was awarded the DFC. He was sent to Moorfields Eye Hospital under the care of Sir Harold Ridely and had eighteen operations on his eyes and face. During the course of his treatment, Ridley developed the artificial intraocular lens transplant surgery for cataract patients. He died in 1994.

Clyde, William Pancoast (30/07/1935) Born in Sevenoaks on 26 July 1912. His great-grandfather was the founder of the Clyde Shipping Line. He attended Eton and Oxford and then spent three years in Switzerland skiing and representing England. He joined 601 Squadron in 1935. He worked for a London firm of stockbrokers. After the war he worked for Johnson and Johnson Surgical Dressings as Deputy Director, responsible for the company's factories in England, Australia, New Zealand, Canada, South Africa and India. Constant travelling had a bad effect on his health as he suffered from colitis. During six months in Acapulco he became a national figure in dingy sailing. He died on 25 March 1985 in New Orleans, Louisiana, USA.

Crawley, Aidan Merivale (31/07/1936) Kent cricketer, born in 1908 and attended Oxford University. Son of Arthur Stafford Crawley, Vicar of Benenden. Grandfather was an entrepreneur. Educated at Farnborough Prep School in 1917, then Harrow in 1920, then Oxford University. Worked as a reporter on *Daily Mail*. Joined Labour Party and stood as Labour Candidate for North Buckinghamshire. Documentary maker for the BBC. Editor in Chief of ITN. MP.

Davis, Carl Raymond (07/07/1936) Born in South Africa of American parents, he was sent to Sherborne College in Britain. He then went to Trinity College, Cambridge and McGill University in Montreal. He was a qualified mining engineer.

Demetriadi, Richard Stephen (25/07/1938) Younger son of Sir Stephen Demetriadi of Street, Sussex and Lady Demetriadi of Mount Street. Obituary in *The Times*.

Dunning-White, Peter William (27/11/1938) Marriage announcement – Peter William Dunning-White, Auxiliary Air Force, elder son of the late Mr and Mrs E.J. Dunning-White of The Wintons, Bushey Heath, Hertfordshire.

Farquhar, Reginald Arthur (05/11/1932) Son of Captain Sir Walter Farquhar. A well-known hunting man. Marriage announcement in *The Times*.

Forbes-Leith, Robert Ian Algen (17/08/1926) Son of Sir Charles and Hon Lady Forbes-Leith of Fyvie Castle, Aberdeenshire, Thame Park Oxfordshire and 23, St James Place. Marriage announcement in *The Times*. Educated at Hilary College, Law results announced in *The Times*.

Guinness, Thomas Loel Evelyn Bulkely (31/03/1929) Born 9 June 1906. raised in the United States and England he was the son of Benjamin Solomon Guinness, a lawyer from whom he inherited a fortune. Descended from Samuel Guinness, a Dublin goldsmith, the younger of brother of the Guinness brewery's founder Arthur Guinness. In 1940 Loel flew as a fighter pilot, famously buying a petrol station near his aerodrome when his driving was restricted by rationing. He financed the purchase of the *Calypso* for the famous oceanic explorer Jacques Cousteau. He was Member of Parliament for Bath.

Green, Charles Patrick (26/03/1937) DFC awarded. Marriage announcement for Group Captain Charles Patrick Green DSO, DFC, only son of the late Major Charles H Green. Birth announcement – on 4 April 1951, at Johannesburg, South Africa, to Ruth, wife of Charles Patrick Green – a daughter. Deaths – Green – Charles Patrick, born in Pietermaritzburg, South Africa on 30 March 1914. He died peacefully in Owen Sound, Canada on Saturday, 10 April 1999. Paddy attended Harrow and Cambridge and was a member of the Bobsleigh team for England in the 1936 Olympic Games. After the war he settled in South Africa and worked for twenty-six years with the Anglo American Corporation. Paddy emigrated to Canada in 1977. Obituary in *The Times*.

Gilliat, Simon Howard (28/10/1935) Lived at Stanhope Place, Marble Arch. Stock and Share Broker. Killed in action notice in *The Times*.

Grimston, John 6th Earl of Verulam (14/01/1937) Born on 17 July 1912, the son of James Walter Grimston, 4th Earl of Verulam. He was a British peer and Conservative Member of Parliament. He was elected to the House of Commons as MP for St Albans in 1943. Died on 15 April 1973. Marriage announcement for the Hon John Grimston and Miss Marjorie Duncan. Attended Oxford University and was a member of the University Air Squadron. Built up a small company until it was taken over by Delta Metal Combine, and he then became its Managing Director and later, Chairman.

Grosvenor, Lord Edward Arthur (07/05/1937) Obituary in *The Times*. Son of First Duke of Westminster. Born 27 October 1892. Educated at Eton and then obtained a commission in the Royal Horse Guards in 1912. Transferred to Royal Flying Corps at start of First World War. Awarded Military Cross. Married to Lady Dorothy Margaret Browne, eldest daughter of Fifth Earl of Kenmare.

Grosvenor, Robert Arthur (24/07/1928) Only son of Lord Arthur Grosvenor. Born 1895 and educated at Wellington. Obituary in *The Times*.

Hohler, Craven Goring (07/03/1932) Son of Edwin Theobald Hohler from The Court, Stansted Lodge. Solicitor, farmer and sportsman involved in the sport of fencing. Obituary in *The Times*. Nephew of Sir Thomas Hohler.

Hope, Sir Archibald Philip (13/07/1932) Marriage announcement in *The Times*. Son of late Lieutenant-Colonel Sir John Augustus Hope, 60th Rifles of Pinkie House Musselburgh, Midlothian and of the Hon Lady Hope of Donoughmore North Berwick. Awarded OBE in Birthday Honours. Resigned as Director of Airwork Ltd and joined the English Electric Group – appointed to the board of Napier and Son.

Jones, Norman Herbert (20/07/1926) A pilot who flew his Tiger Cub aircraft "when owls were grounded" or in weather unfit for flying. Norman Herbert Jones aged 55, director, of Church Road, Claygate, Surrey, pleaded Not Guilty to four charges of breaking the air navigational rules – failing to satisfy himself at Panshanger, Hertfordshire, that a flight to Redhill, Surrey could safely be made; failing to examine meteorological reports; failing to notify flight plans at Denham, Buckinghamshire and to inform of his landing at Denham. The pilot of a private aircraft was fined a total of £110 at Buckinghamshire Quarter Sessions at Aylesbury. Norman Herbert Jones is a company director of a paper manufacturing company. Members of the Tiger Flying Club have decided to pay the £110 fine imposed on their chairman last week. They will also pay the £150 costs. A club member said that "our members are so appreciative of all that Mr Jones has done to help private aviation in Britain". Death announcement – on 13 April 1991, in Eastbourne, Norman Herbert Jones, very dearly loved husband, father and grandfather.

Little, James Hayward (25/07/1934) Educated Trinity College, Cambridge, Bar examinations results in *The Times*. Born New Orleans. Son of Mr and Mrs John Douglas Little of Ethandune, Hoylake, Cheshire. Marriage announcement in *The Times*. Obituary in *The Times*.

Montagu, William Drogo Sturges (12/02/1930) Son of George Charles Montagu, 9th Earl of Sandwich and Lord Lieutenant of Huntingdonshire. Killed in a flying accident in Scotland on 26 January 1940. Buried in Brampton Churchyard.

Murray, Iain Arthur (17/01/1930) Born 17 September 1904 and educated at Eton and in Switzerland. A founder member of 601 Squadron. Awarded two DSOs during the war. After the war he farmed in Norfolk.

Norman, Anthony Charles Wynyard (25/07/1933) Educated at Magdalen College, Oxford University. Son of Liberal MP for Blackburn.

Norman, Henry Nigel St Valery (20/07/1926) Born 21 May 1897, educated at Winchester and Trinity College, Cambridge. Son of the Rt Hon Sir Hendry Norman PC, JP and was a qualified architect who owned and ran Heston Airport prior to the Second World War. After the war he worked designing airports and was the Director and founder of Airwork Ltd. Obituary in *The Times*.

Parkes, John Joseph (13/07/1926) General manager of de Havilland Aircraft Company. Started his apprenticeship in automobile engineering and worked at Swift Ltd and Rootes Group before joining a group of aviation enthusiasts who formed Airwork Ltd, later to become British United Airways in 1929. He was a test pilot and stayed at Airwork until he joined de Havilland in 1936. Obituary in *The Times*.

APPENDIX 2

Peacock, Michael Fitzwilliam (06/04/1926) South African born barrister, studied at Oxford University, and skied for Britain. Career as a rugby player. Son of Mr and Mrs T.C.H. Peacock of Chalvington, Halshaw. Obituary in *The Times*.

Rhodes-Moorhouse, William Henry (28/07/1937) Son of William Moorhouse and Linda Rhodes-Moorhouse of Parnham House near Beaminster. Owned a 1935 Mercedes-Benz 500K kombination Roadster which sold at auction in 2006 for £285,000.

Reid, Edward Douglas Whitehead (11/05/1926) Born Canterbury 1883, educated at Tonbridge School and Christ College, Cambridge. Then studied medicine at St Bartholomew's Hospital. Obituary in *The Times*.

Riddle, Christopher John Henry (Jack) (14/08/1938) Born on 4 April 1914 and educated at Harrow. He was a member of White's club in London. Joined 601 Squadron and flew with them throughout the war. After the war he worked for an international trading company, buying Baltic timber for the Australian market. Later he set up his own textile company. He died on 8 August 2009, aged 95. He was the son of a GP who had emigrated from the United States. After Harrow he went to Magdalen College, Oxford University where he was excellent at athletics. He went on to the Slade School of Fine Art and then to master portrait painting under the tutelage of Sonia Mervyn ARA. In 1937 he married the daughter of the first Managing Director of Rolls-Royce Ltd and first Secretary of the RAC.

Riddle, Hugh Joseph (31/07/1937) Born on 24 May 1912 and educated at Harrow. Joined 601 Squadron in early 1938. He flew with them throughout the Battle of Britain. After the war, he returned to portrait painting. He painted Queen Elizabeth in 1965 for the RAF Regiment. In 1977 he was commissioned by the Royal Household to paint Prince Edward as a silver wedding present for the Queen and Prince Phillip. He died on 16 April 2009, aged 97.

Robinson, Peter Beverley (05/08/1934) Born on 22 January 1915, he was the son of Christopher Charles Robinson and Isabel Hogins Biggar. He eventually moved to New York and on returning, he was involved in documentary making in London.

Rosewarne, Vivian Allen William (26/08/1937) Killed in Action on 30 May 1940, aged 24. Educated at Dulwich, and at Brentford, where he was head of his house and a prefect. Left school aged 17 to go into business. Joined the AAF in 1937.

Sassoon, Sir Philip Albert Gustave David (13/10/1928) 3rd Baronet, politician, art collector and social host, son of Sir Edward Albert Sassoon, 2nd Baronet and MP, and Aline Caroline, daughter of Baron Gustave de Rothschild. Inherited Trent Park, North London on his father's death in 1912. Renowned for glamorous parties which were held there in the 1920s and 1930s with guests such as Charlie Chaplin, George Bernard Shaw, Winston Churchill, David Lloyd George and members of the Royal Family. He pursued a successful political career becoming the MP for Hythe in 1912 and then the parliamentary private secretary to David Lloyd George in 1920. Between 1924 and 1929 and again from 1931-1937 he served as Under Secretary of State for Air. In 1937 he became First Commissioner of Works, a post which he held until his death two years later. He was a cousin of the poet, Siegfried Sassoon and had a reputation for being one of the most eligible bachelors and greatest hosts in Britain. He built the Port Lympne estate in Kent. He largely re-built his other house and estate at Trent Park, Cockfosters, London.

Schreiber, John Shuldham (14/08/1926) Eldest son of Captain C.S. and the Hon Mrs Sachreiber of Marlesford Hall, Woodbridge. Marriage announcement in *The Times*.

Seely, Nigel Richard William (09/04/1929) Son of Sir Charles Seely and Lady Seely of Kings Manor, Yarmouth, Isle of Wight. Duke of Kent sent a silver cigarette case on his engagement. Marriage announcement in *The Times*.

Smithers, Julian Langley (27/11/1938) Born in Knockholt, Kent on 17 December 1915 and educated at Eton. He entered the City when he went to work in his father's stockbroking firm, and he became a member of the stock exchange in early 1940. He joined 601 Squadron in 1938. On 11 August 1941 he was shot down and killed during a combat off Portland, and crashed into the sea. He was twenty-four. His body was washed up on a French beach. Death announcement in *The Times*. Obituary in *The Times*.

Straight, Whitney Willard (18/07/1938) Born 6 November 1912. Grand Prix racing driver, aviator and businessman. Born in New York. Family moved to England in 1925. Lived at Dartington Hall. Attended a progressive school founded by his parents, then on to Trinity College, Cambridge. Head of the Straight Corporation Ltd. This corporation acquired and controlled twenty-one associated companies. Became first Deputy Chairman and Managing Director of British European Airways in 1946. Chairman of Royal Aero Club. Deputy Chairman of BOAC in 1947. Became Chairman of Rolls-Royce Ltd.

Thynne, Brian Winslow (09/04/1929) Attended Eton, Oxford University, Officer Training Corps and Sussex Yeomanry before moving to the AAF. Had family connections at the highest level. Worked for the families printing firm.[1] Previously reported missing from Air Operations – July 1943, now officially presumed killed in action, Flying Officer Brian Winslow Thynne, elder son of Mr and Mrs Herbert Thyne of Hampton Dene Hereford, who are also remembering the nine members of his crew who were killed.

Ward, Edward Frederick (20/11/1930) Son of the Earl and Countess of Dudley of Himley Hall, Staffordshire. Marriage announcement in *The Times*.

602 (City of Glasgow) Squadron

Bell, Edmund Vivien Norton (01/12/1933) Engagement announcement between Edmund Vivian Norton, only son of the late A.E. Bell and Mrs H.G. Lawson. Marriage of Mr Vivien Bell and Miss Mary Chubb will take place quietly at 2.15 on Thursday, 7 March at All Souls' Langham Place. Owing to mourning in the bride's family, no invitations are being sent but friends will be welcomed at the church. Marriage report. Birth Announcement for Mary, wife of Sqn Ldr E.V.N. Bell, a son. The infant son of the Duke and Duchess of Hamilton and Brandon was christened yesterday. The godparents are Wing Commander E.V.N. Bell and others.

Boyd, Robert Findlay (02/11/1935) Born in East Kilbride in 1915, joined 602 Squadron in 1935 and called up for full time service in 1939. He was awarded the DFC on 24 September 1940. He was awarded the Bar to the DFC on 25 October 1940. He was awarded the DSO on 10 April 1942. After the war he flew charter flights for Scottish Aviation and later tried pig farming and herring fishing and then moved to Skye where he kept the Ferry Inn at Uig.

Farquhar, Andrew Douglas (17/08/1927) Engagement announced Friday, 17 November, Sqn Ldr Andrew Douglas Farquhar, younger son of Mr and Mrs A.W. Farquhar, Hermiston, Bridge of Weir. Guard of honour mounted by fifteen officers of 602 Squadron AAF commanded by Sqn Ldr A.D. Farquhar at the marriage of Wing Commander the marquis of Douglas and Clydesdale, eldest son of the Duke and Duchess of Hamilton and Brandon. Sqn Ldr Lord Nigel Douglas-Hamilton was best man. The King presented Sqn Ldr A.D. Farquuhar AAF with the DFC in recognition of gallantry displayed in flying operations against the enemy. During February 1940 this officer engaged an enemy aircraft while on patrol. Though he expended only a small amount of ammunition, the accuracy of his shooting appears to have put both engines of the enemy aircraft out of action and it effected a forced landing. He also very actively engaged enemy aircraft in October 1939 and has led his squadron with magnificent dash and courage on several occasions.

Faulds, Robert (05/04/1928) Test pilot for Airwork Ltd. Killed in an aircraft crash whilst testing a Percival Gull after work had been done on its Javelin engine. Verdict of accidental death returned at the inquest into the death of Robert Faulds, age 30, in a plane crash. Daughters marriage announcement.

Feather, John Stuart (10/07/1928) Guest at the wedding of Lord Clydesdale and Lady Elizabeth Percy at St Giles' Cathedral, Edinburgh.

Ferguson, Peter John (16/07/1936) Duke of Kent – first member of the royal family flies in a Liberator bomber to Canada. Accompanied on his flight by Flt Lt P.J. Ferguson and Grp Capt Sir Louis Greig.

Hawkes, John Ryder (25/05/1935) Engagement – John Ryder, eldest son of Engineer Commander C.J. Hawkes RN (Retd) and Mrs Hawkes of Gosforth, Newcastle upon Tyne.

Howell, Edward Alexander (09/04/1932) Completion of course at No 1 Air Armament School, Flt Lt E.A. Howell.

Jack, Daniel Macfarlane (08/11/1936) Attended the wedding of Lord Clydesdale and Lady Elizabeth Percy. Brothers marriage – Parents Mr Thomas Jack and Mrs Jack, Ainslie, Kilmalcolm, Renfrewshire.

Johnstone, Alexander Vallance Riddell (11/09/1134) Born in Glasgow on 2 June 1916. Commanding Officer of 602 Squadron during the Battle of Britain. Educated at Kelvinside Academy, he worked in an Edinburgh footwear firm until he joined 602 Squadron in 1934. He was called to full time service in August 1939, aged 24. Posted to Haifa in Palestine in April 1942 and then on to Malta as Station Commander. In the spring of 1943 he returned to Britain. In May 1944 he was promoted to acting group captain on the Allied Expeditionary Air Force operations staff, which was preparing for the D-Day invasion. He took several promotions and postings and eventually retired from the air force in 1968. He served as vice-chairman of the Territorial Auxiliary and Volunteer Reserve. He was secretary of Glasgow Golf Club and head of the National Car Parks Scottish operation. He wrote several books. He was awarded the DFC in 1940, and was mentioned in despatches in 1943. He died on 13 December 2000, aged 84.

Law, David William (06/07/1931) Engagement announcement between Sqn Ldr Donald William Law, eldest son of the late Mr W.T. Law and Mrs Law, late of 6, Huntly Gardens, Glasgow.

Lloyd, David Llewellyn (21/04/1929) D.L. Lloyd attends and completes the specialist armament course at the Air Armament School, Eastchurch. Marriage took place on 12 December between David Llewellyn, seventh son of the late Samuel Jansen Lloyd and Mrs S.J. Lloyd of Pipewell House, Kettering, Northamptonshire. Promotion from Wing Commander to Group Captain. Group Captain D.L. Lloyd to RAF West Kirby to command.

Maclean, Charles Hector (16/05/1936) Born 9 December 1913 in Glasgow, was educated at Cranford School Dorset and the University of Glasgow doing a law degree. He joined 602 Squadron in 1935. On 26 August 1940 he was severely wounded over the Channel but managed to return and belly land his badly damaged aircraft at Tangmere. His injuries resulted in the loss of his right leg below the knee and a lengthy hospitalisation. He was unable to continue flying and became a fighter controller. He retired on transfer to the reserve on 1 April 1950 and relinquished his commission on 2 December 1957. He joined his family's law firm after the war. He died on 19 July 2007, aged 93. Birth announcement on 24 January 1944 at Easter Laggan, Dulnain Bridge, Moray, to Marcia, wife of Sqn Ldr Charles Hector MacClean AAF a son – Marcus.

McKellar, Archibald Ashmore (08/11/1936) Born on 10 April 1912, McKellar was educated at Shawlands Academy and on leaving school he joined his father's construction business as a plasterer. He was commissioned into the AAF as a Pilot Officer in 1936. He is officially credited with the downing of the first enemy aircraft to fall on British soil in the Second World War. He was posted to 605 (County of Warwick) Squadron and moved to RAF Drem in early 1940. He received the DFC on 13 September 1940. He was awarded a Bar to the DFC on 8 October 1940. He was shot down and killed on 1 November 1940, aged 28. A Squadron Leader aged twenty-eight, who won the DFC in September, a bar to it in October and has since been killed in action, has been awarded the DSO in a list of RAF awards which the King has approved. Sqn Ldr A.A. McKellar, who belonged to 605 (County of Warwick) Squadron of the AAF, had destroyed twenty enemy aircraft.

Mitchell, William Harold (01/11/1927) Attended Sedbergh School and played ruby for the school. Gained a maths degree at Oxford University.

Muspratt-Williams, Reginald Typwhitt (16/08/1935) Christening – Daughter of Lord and Lady Malcolm Douglas Hamilton – Godparent is Mr R.T. Muspratt Williams. Attended the funeral of Lt Col The Hon Malcolm Bowes Lyon. Attended the funeral of the Dowager Marchioness of Londonderry. Attended memorial service for Grp Capt Lord Malcolm Douglas Hamilton and Mr Niall Douglas Hamilton.

Parker, Colin Alfred Stuart (06/07/1926) Marriage announcement - marriage will take place in Nairobi between Colin Alfred Stuart Parker CCS, eldest son of Mr and Mrs Evelyn Stuart Parker of The Lawn, Aigburth Liverpool and Little Cumbrae Bateshire, and Daphne Louise, daughter of the late Mr Fichat and Mrs Fichat of Nairobi. Attended Eton and rowed for the Eaton Eight between the years of 1919 and 1920. Attended New College Oxford and rowed for the college rowing team between 1920 and 1924. Nurse required for three children under five to consider diet, health, knitting, needlewoman and teacher who is prepared to go to Nyasaland, central Africa – request by Mrs C.A.S. Parker, Woodbourne, Wenyss Bay, Renfrewshire. Races at Cowes week in 1953. Races at Southsea Regatta in 1955 and Cowes in 1955. Lyme Bay Yacht Race, Ocean racing and Lyme Bay race.

Pinkerton, George Cannon (18/10/1933) Appointed Deputy Lieutenant for the County of Renfrew, Group Captain G.C. Pinkerton of South Houston, Johnstone.

Renshaw, Charles Maurice Bine (30/01/1932) Birth announcement, 17 February 1943 at Ashwater Barton, Devon, to Isabel Popkin wife of C.M.B. Renshaw a daughter. On 17 May 1944 at Ashwater, Devon, to Isabel, wife of C.M.B. Renshaw a son.

Robinson, Marcus (08/05/1934) Born in May 1912, he joined 602 Squadron in September 1933 and in June 1938 he had risen to Flight Commander. He was awarded the Air Force Cross on 30 September 1941.He remained in the AAF and rejoined on 1 August 1946 where he was given command of 602 Squadron. He relinquished his commission on 27 May 1956 and died in March 1988. Marriage arrangements between Sqn Ldr Marcus Robinson, only son of Mr and Mrs Wilson Robinson of Glasgow. Report of the marriage. Daughters engagement announced.

Shewell, John Morland (26/06/1934) Marriage announcement for Flying Officer John Morland Shewell, elder son of Mr and Mrs J.B. Shewell of Arrowside, Alcester, Warwickshire.

Stone, Norman (20/02/1938) On 8 March 1941 at Lindroes Nursing Home Glasgow to Mary Robertson, wife of Flt Lt Norman Stone AAF a son. Air Force Cross awarded to Flt Lt Norman Stone AAF.

Urie, John Dunlop (21/06/1935) A Glasgow pilot is leading one of the squadrons of the wing of the RAF which is now serving in Russia. He is Sqn Ldr John Dunlop Urie. He was one of the original members of the City of Glasgow Squadron and was shot down in action in August of last year after the squadron had gone south to take part in the Battle of Britain. He returned to his own unit in 1940 and was thereafter posted to instruction and administrative duties. First news of the responsible task which he has now undertaken was revealed in Glasgow yesterday at a luncheon in the city chambers attended by RAF officers and members of the Air Training Corps. Squadron Leader Urie is the son of Mr John Urie of the City Bakeries Ltd, Glasgow. He was educated at Kelvinside Academy – the same school attended by his former CO, A.V.R. Johnstone DFC. In civilian life Sqn Ldr Urie was employed by his father's firm. He joined the City of Glasgow Squadron in 1935. The following has been appointed Deputy Lieutenant of the County of the City of Glasgow. Wing Commander J.D. Urie, 21, West George Street, Glasgow.

Webb, Paul Clifford (21/03/1938) Flying Officer P.C. Webb of No 602 Squadron was injured on 9 September 1940 at 1730 hours. He crash landed his Spitfire I (K9910) at Box Grove, Sussex after being attacked by a Bf109 over Mayfield. Wing Commander P.C. Webb (Acting Senior Air Liaison Officer) represented the Air Council and the RAF at the funeral yesterday in Ottowa of Air Chief Marshall Lloyd Breadner. Wing Commander P.C. Webb transferred to HQ Southern Sector for air staff duties. Wing Commander P.C. Webb to Air Ministry for duty in the department of the Chief of the Air Staff. Wing Commander P.C. Webb to Ankara as Air Attaché with acting rank of group captain. Group Captain P.C. Webb to Staff at NATO, Brussels.

603 (City of Edinburgh) Squadron

Bruce, Alastair Henry (09/06/1928) Engagement announcement, Alastair Henry Bruce, only surviving son of Mr and Mrs C Bruce, Kinleith, Currie, Mid Lothian. Marriage announcement – the marriage arranged between Mr Alastair Henry Bruce, Kinleith, Currie and Miss Jean Callander, Ravelrig, Baleino will take place very quietly in St Cuthberts Episcopal Church, Colinton on Thursday, 30 June at 2.15pm. Flt Lt A.H. Bruce relinquishes his commission on completion of service and is permitted to retain his rank.

Burton, Edward Stanley Viner (31/07/1928) E.S.V. Burton resigns his commission (17 November). On 21 May 1946 at Exmouth Nursing Home to Ruth Dorothea, wife of E.S.V. Burton, Indian Forest Service – a daughter. On 6June 1948 at The Cross, Tilehurst, Sussex, to Ruth, wife of E.S.V. Burton, a second daughter.

Cunningham, John Laurence Gilchrist (06/03/1935) Died in the Battle of Britain. Shot down and killed on 28 August 1940 at 1645hrs. His Spitfire was shot down by a Bf109 over Dover. Son of Thomas and Jessie Livingstone Cunningham of Burntisland, Fife. Age 23.

Douglas-Hamilton, Malcolm Avendale (08/06/1932) Wing Commander Lord Malcolm Avendale Douglas-Hamilton was born on 12 November 1909 and was a Scottish nobleman and politician. The third son of the 13th Duke of Hamilton he was educated at Eton College and at the RAF College in Cranwell. He was a fine boxer. He served in the RAF from 1929-1932. He then joined the Auxiliary Air Force. He was made OBE in 1943 and was awarded a DFC in 1945. He was the Unionist Member of Parliament for Inverness from 1950-1954. He was flying with his son Niall when his aircraft disappeared in West Africa. The infant daughter of Lord and Lady Malcolm Douglas-Hamilton was christened Fiona Margaret at Beaulier Abbey Church on Saturday 13th. He attended the marriage of Lord Clydesdale and Lady Elizabeth Percy. The engagement has been announced between Lord Malcolm Douglas-Hamilton OBE, DFC, MP, son of the late Duke and Duchess of Hamilton and Brandon, and Natalie Wales Paine CBE, widow of Edward Bragg Paine.

Douglas-Hamilton, George Nigel (30/06/1931) Born at Merly, Wimborne, Dorset, the second son of the 13th Duke of Hamilton and Brandon. Educated at Eton College, Balliol College, Oxford and Edinburgh University (LLB), and at the University of Bonn, Vienna University and the Sorbonne. He was admitted to the Faculty of Advocates in 1935, taking silk in 1959. He also played cricket for Wiltshire in 1927. He gained the rank of group captain in the service of the Royal Auxiliary Air Force and commanded 603 Squadron between 1934 and 1938. He was mentioned in despatches twice and awarded the Air Force Cross in 1938 and the OBE in 1941. He succeeded as Earl of Selkirk on the death of his father in 1940. He married in 1947 when he was serving as a Scottish representative peer between the years of 1945 and 1963. He was Lord in Waiting to King George VI and to Queen Elizabeth II. He was also the Paymaster-General between 1953 and 1955. He was also Chancellor of the Duchy of Lancaster and served as First Lord of the Admiralty. He became UK High Commissioner for Singapore and Commissioner General for South East Asia. He was appointed a Privy Counsellor in 1955 and awarded the GCMG in 1959 and the GBE in 1963. He was appointed Knight of the Thistle in 1976.

Fosbrooke, John Malcolm (31/05/1927) Flight Lieutenant J.M. Fosbrooke resigned his commission and is appointed to a commission in the Reserve of Air Force Officers. Flying Officer J.M. Fosbrooke MB, CHB relinquishes his commission on completion of service (May 31).

Garden, Thomas Clarke (13/01/1935) Attended the wedding of Lord Clydesdale and Lady Elizabeth Percy. Engagement announcement for only daughter of Mr and Mrs T.C. Garden, South Esk Lodge, Temple Midlothian. Engagement announcement for their eldest son Edward James Clarke. Engagement announcement for younger son, Kenneth John. On 14 February 1978, suddenly at South Esk Lodge, Temple, Midlothian, Thomas Clarke Garden, husband of the late Jean Mallace and father of Teddy.

Gifford, Patrick (30/06/1931) Squadron Leader Patrick Gifford, DFC was killed in action. He was the only son of Mr and Mrs Gifford of Forneth House, Castle Douglas. Educated at Melrose, Sedburgh and Edinburgh University, he was a qualified solicitor, Procurator Fiscal, Deputy Clerk of the peace, secretary of the local NFU and a member of the town council. A good all round sportsman who was involved in tennis, cricket and rugby, he was also an excellent skier and rifle shot. He was well known for driving high speed sports cars between Castle Douglas and Edinburgh. He was granted a commission in an Edinburgh squadron of the AAF on 30 June 1931, and promoted to Flt Lt in April 1938. He is credited with shooting down the first German plane over Britain on 16 October 1939 whilst flying his Mark I Spitfire from RAF Turnhouse. He attended the wedding of Lord Clydesdale and Lady Elizabeth Percy. In November 1940 he was awarded the DFC for gallantry in flying operations. In the previous month he had led his section against enemy bombers off the coast and on two occasions had continued pursuit with skill and determination until the enemy had crashed into the sea. He died on 16 May 1940 and his body was never found.

Gilroy, George Kemp (10/04/1938) Born 1 June 1914 he was a shepherd before he was commissioned into the AAF in 603 Squadron. On 1 September 1940 he bailed out of a burning aircraft and was nearly lynched by the Home Guard. On 19 July 1941 he was posted to command 609 Squadron. He fought in East Africa, North Africa, Sicily and Southern Italy. He was promoted to Group Captain in November 1943 and returned to England. He left the RAF at the end of the war and re-joined 603 Squadron as Commanding Officer in 1946 in the reformed Royal Auxiliary Air Force. He also continued to be a shepherd. He was awarded the DFC in September 1940 and was mentioned in Despatches in January 1941. He received the DFC in June 1942, the DSO in March 1943 and the DFC in November 1944. Marriage announcement for Susan, stepdaughter of Group Captain G.K. Gilroy, Crofts, Castle Douglas, Kirkend, Brightshire. Marriage announcement for Gillian, daughter of Group Captain and Mrs G.K. Gilroy of Auchencairn House Kirkend, Brightshire.

Haig, John Galloway Edward (11/06/1932) Engagement announced between John Galloway Edward Haig, son of Mrs H.E. Haig of Clayton, Dairsie, Fife.

Hamilton, Claud Eric (10/07/1939) Claud Eric Hamilton of Cairns, Midlothian was commissioned into the AAF in 1939. In Mid-November he sailed from Gibraltar on the carrier HMS *Argus*. He was in the first flight of six hurricanes which flew off on 17 November to Takali, Malta, where he joined 261 Squadron. 261 Squadron was disbanded on 12 May 1941 and he was attached to 185 Squadron. He was shot down on the fourteenth in Hurricane Z2901 and fatally wounded. He was 20-years-old and is buried in Malta.

Hunter, Graham Cousin (11/10/1938) RAF Roll of Honour. Killed in Action.

Jack, James Lawrence (25/01/1927) James Lawrence Jack, MBE MC retained the rank of Wing Commander. He was a banker and was manager of Drumsleugh branch of the Commercial bank of Scotland. [2]

Kirkpatrick, Ivone (07/01/1931) Engagement announcement between Ivone Kirkpatrick, son of the late James Ivone Kirpatrick, CA and stockbroker and Mrs Kirkpatrick, 25, Morningside Park, Edinburgh.

Kynaston, Roger Ian (12/11/1928) Pilot Officer R.I. Kynaston resigns his commission 9 March 1930.

MacDonald, Donald Kenneth Andrew (11/05/1939) Attended Peterhouse, Cambridge University. Son of James Harold and Isa May Kennedy MacDonald of Murrayfield, Edinburgh. Brother of Harold Kennedy MacDonald. Died 28 August 1940, age 22.

APPENDIX 2

MacDonald, Harold Kennedy (04/03/1935) Born on 24 February 1912. He graduated from Cambridge University. He joined 603 City of Edinburgh Squadron and took part in the Battle of Britain. On 28 September 1940 he was killed while meeting an enemy attack over the Thames Estuary. When his aircraft had been hit and was about to crash, although he might have bailed out, with complete disregard for his own safety he remained in the machine in order to bring it down clear of any buildings. He crashed close to a crowded barrack room which, but for his action, would have been hit. For this gallant deed, which cost him his life, he was mentioned in despatches.

Flt Lt MacDonald, 603 Squadron died 28 September 1940 age 28. Son of James Harold and Isa May Kennedy MacDonald of Murrayfield, Edinburgh. Brother of Donald Kennedy MacDonald who died 28 August 1940, age 22.

McKelvie, James (01/08/1925) First Commanding officer of 603 Squadron, he was an experienced pilot who had commanded 22 Squadron in the First World War flying Bristol Fighters. He left the squadron on 14 April 1931.[3]

McNeil, Thomas Menzies (30/07/1929) Engagement announced between Thomas Menzies McNeil OBE TO WS, son of the late Mr Allan McNeil SSC and Mrs McNeil, 26, Learmouth Terrace, Edinburgh. Attended the marriage of Lord Clydesdale and Lady Elizabeth Percy on Thursday, 2 December 1937.

Miller, Alexander Robertson Hunter (01/02/1927) On 3 August 1930, the engine in an Avro flown by C Flight Commander, Flight Lieutenant A.R.H. Miller failed and contrary to the strict instructions from his adjutant, Flight Lieutenant Walmsley, he tried to turn back to the aerodrome. The aircraft stalled, crashed and Miller was killed.[4]

Mitchell, Alexander Maclaine (29/09/1928) Engagement announced between Alexander, eldest son of Mr and Mrs A Maclaine Mitchell, 22, Learmouth Terrace, Edinburgh. Engagement announcement between Douglas, younger son of Mr and Mrs Alexander Maclaine Mitchell of Bermuda and Scotland.

Morton, James Storrs (14/07/1939) Mentioned in Dispatches. Engagement announced between Flt Lt James S Morton DFC, AAF, eldest son of Dr H.J.S. Morton of 28, Belsize Avenue, Hampstead. Marriage announcement 8 December 1941 at St Mary, Oatlands, Weybridge. Bar to DFC. He became an instructor before retiring from the service with the rank of wing commander in 1946. He joined the RAuxAF from November 1946 to March 1951. He died in 1982 having had a heart attack on his driveway. He started a successful engineering business until he and his family moved into Woodcote Manor with 100 acres of farmland and he gradually began the transition from engineering to farming.[5]

Peel, Charles David (25/02/1938) Flying Officer Charles David Peel of 603 Squadron died on 17 July 1940. He was flying a Spitfire (K9916) on 17 July when he was reported missing, the details of which are not known. He took off from Turnhouse and was not seen again.

Reid, George Alfred (17/03/1931) Attended St Andrews College, Edinburgh, between 1921 and 1927. Commanded 46 Squadron in May 1942. Killed on Sunday, 3 October 1943 in a Beaufighter.

Rushmer, Frederick William (19/10/1934) Born in Sisland, Norfolk on 12 April 1910. He joined 603 Squadron and was called into full time service in 1939 with the squadron. He made a forced landing at Bossingham in his Spitfire after combat over Deal and he was slightly injured. On 5 September 1940, he failed to return from combat and in later years his Spitfire was found at Buckman's Green Farm, Smarden, Flt Lt Frederick William Rushmer now presumed killed, was commissioned as a pilot officer in the AAF on 19 October 1934 when he was posted to the City of Edinburgh Squadron. He attended the wedding of Lord Clydesdale and Elizabeth Percy.

Shields, Iain Douglas (23/03/1931) Avro Anson Mark I L9153 of No12 Elementary and Reserve Flying Training School, Prestwick, crashed on Corserine on 9 January 1939. Flying Officer Iain Douglas Shields, pilot, was killed. The aircraft had left Prestwick for a navigation training flight. The burnt out wreck was discovered the following day by a shepherd on the lower slopes of Corserine.

Shields, John Temple Lyall (22/07/1927) As the result of an accident at Corstorphine to an Avro machine, Pilot Officer John Temple Lyall Shields, the pilot and sole occupant of the aircraft was killed.

Somerville, James Alexander Brownlie (12/02/1937) Flying Officer James Alexander Brownlie Somerville was commissioned as a pilot officer in the AAF on 12 February 1937. He was promoted to Flying Officer on 14 August 1938 and was killed on active service on 1 October 1939. Son of James Alexander and Ann MacDonald Somerville. Husband of Margaret Somerville of Canon Bridge, Ross Comarty. Buried in Corstorphine Hill Cemetery, Edinburgh.

Sorel-Cameron, Robert (23/06/1930) Born 27 November 1911, achieved the rank of Air Commodore, and retired on 27 November 1962. Awarded the AFC on Monday, 29 April 1944 and a CBE for his work in the Far East on 11 February 1947. After retiring he joined HM Diplomatic Corps and from 1959 until 1971 he was the Queen's Messenger. Engagement announced between Sqn Ldr R Sorel Cameron, younger son of Lt Col and Mrs G.C.M. Sorel Cameron of Gorthleck House, Inverness. Notice of marriage at Church of St John the Evangelist, Forres, Monmouthshire, a quiet event due to the war. On 27 July 1940, at Fulmer Chase, Slough, Bucks, to Jane, wife of Sqn Ldr R Sorel-Cameron RAF, a son. On 13 October 1943, at Bradfield Hall, Berks, to Jane, wife of Wing Commander R Sorel-Cameroon, a daughter.

Stevens, Ernest Hildebrand (07/01/1931) Born 2 June 1909 to Mr and Mrs E.G.C. Stevens of Kuala Lumpur, FMS and Hermand, West Calder. His father, Ernest John Carwithin Stevens was an accountant in Malaya and his mother came from a family which had gained its wealth from the coal mines of West Lothian. He was educated at Merchiston Castle School and Edinburgh University. He gained an LLB and was a member of the university rowing team. He was an experienced shot and fencer and was a member of the Scottish Amateur Fencing Union. On leaving university he was apprenticed as a writer to His Majesties Signet to W.J. Guild from 1935-1937. He was eventually admitted to the Society of Writers to His Majesties Signet on 20 December 1937, after three years as an apprentice. He was well-known in service and civil flying circles and was Chairman of Edinburgh Flying Club. He became Commanding Officer of 603 Squadron on 16 October 1939. Commanding Officer of 603 Squadron – his close friends knew him as "Steve" but more popularly as "Count" due to his apparent aristocratic appearance and professional standing as a lawyer. Later he became Group Captain Stevens OBE. He left the AAF in 1946 and became a partner of W.J. Guilds, becoming responsible for Guilds court work. During the latter stages of the war he had become involved with Olga Blakelock who had previously been seeing Logan John Beveridge who had served in Italy and was a prisoner of war. When Beveridge was released and returned to the UK, he resumed his relationship with Olga, much to the distress of Stevens. At the couple's engagement party, Stevens went to get his gun and confronted the couple in an upstairs bedroom. He opened fire with his automatic pistol. The couple fell to the floor and then Stevens turned the gun on himself. He was pronounced dead thirty minutes later. Beveridge was wounded by a shot in the shoulder.[6]

Thomson, Cecil Alexander Grove (09/01/1935) Killed 26 March 1938.

Usher, Thomas (10/11/1925) Tom Usher and Son Ltd Brewery, Edinburgh, Scotland. Tom Usher resigns his commission on 9 December 1928.

Waterson, Robin McGregor (31/02/1937) Born in Edinburgh, his father was Chairman of George Waterson and Sons, master printers and stationers. His mother was a Norland nurse. Robin was seventh out of eight children. He left school and went straight into insurance but hated it, so he went to Edinburgh University to study engineering. He bought a two seater Wolseley for £4 as he loved fast cars and motorbikes. He joined Edinburgh University Air Squadron. He loved flying, rugby, golf and fishing. Flying Officer Robin McGregor "Bubble" Waterson tragically lost his life during the early evening of Saturday, 31 August 1940 when he was shot down in his Spitfire X4273, which crashed in Repository Road outside the Barrack gates.[7]

Watson, Irvine Ewart Chalmers (22/07/1927) Left 603 Squadron to join the RAFVR as the units Chief Flying Officer as appointed by Scottish Aviation Ltd in 1940.[8]

White, Myles Hemingway Gleeson (25/06/1928) Flying Officer M.H.G. White resigns his commission. Flying Officer M.H.G. White is granted a commission in his present rank on resigning his commission in the AF (26 Oct).

Winkler, William Otto Brash (02/02/1936) Born on 7 July 1895, he was the proprietor of Russ and Winkler furriers. He was a former president of Edinburgh Rotary Club and a founder member of 603 Squadron. Born in Edinburgh and educated at Merchiston Castle School, he was a pilot in the Royal Flying Corps during the First World War. He was shot down in France and a prisoner of war for two years. He was interested in radio and was one of the first wireless experimenters. Secretary of the Edinburgh and District Radio Society. He was a member of the Edinburgh Company of Merchants and for a time he was Chairman of the Retail Trades section of the Edinburgh Chamber of Commerce. He joined the well-known firm of Russ and Winkler after the First World War, a firm which had been founded by his father. He resigned his commission on 9 December 1929.

Wynne-Powell, Geoffrey Trevor (19/06/1935) SOS for "Missing Plane" was answered by the pilot himself. Flying Officer G.T. Wynne-Powell was due to arrive at Kenley Surry from Waddington, Lincolnshire, having landed there on a flight from Edinburgh. Later the BBC announced that Flying Officer Wynne-Powell had landed at Kenley but the aeroplane could not be found. In fact he had landed at Biggin Hill and went on to London accompanied by his passenger thinking that he had landed at Kenley! On 30 January 1945 at Putney Hospital to Sheila, wife of Wing Commander G.T. Wynne-Powell DFC AAF, a son. G.T. Wynne-Powell to RAF Cardington for admin duties.

604 (County of Middlesex) Squadron

Cherry, John (19/08/1930) Son of Sir Benjamin Cherry of Lincoln's Inn. Marriage announcement in *The Times*.

Chisholm, Roderick Aeneas (16/03/1931) Educated at Ampleforth College and then worked in the oil industry. Author of *"Cover of Darkness"*. Born on 23 November 1911, and also educated at the Imperial College of Science and Technology where he read chemistry. In 1932 he joined the Anglo-Iranian Oil Company as a research chemist. He had also joined the AAF, and when war broke out he was a pilot in 604 Squadron. In March 1941 he was awarded the DFC and in July of the same year he was awarded his second DFC. In 1944 he was awarded the DSO. After the war he became personnel manager for Kuwait Oil. He retired in 1970, and died on 7 December 1994, aged 83.

Cunningham, John (Cat's Eyes) (07/05/1936) Born on 27 July 1917, educated at Whitgift School. He joined 604 Squadron in 1936. He had an uncanny ability to hunt out the enemy at night, hence his nickname, Cat's Eyes. He ended the war with three DSOs, two DFCs and the Air Efficiency Award. He received the Order of the Patriotic War from the Soviet Union, and the Silver Star from the USA. After the war he resumed his job at de Havilland as a test pilot. He died on 21 July 2002, aged 84.

Davies, John Alfred (10/03/1935) Son of Colonel B Sir Alfred and Lady Davies of The Eagles, West Hill, Highgate. Marriage announcement in *The Times*.

Dore, Alan Sidney Whitehorn DSO (19/03/1930) Born on 16 September 1882, educated at Mill Hill and Jesus College, Cambridge, where he took first class honours in the Natural Sciences Tripos. Joined the Worcester Regiment who had transferred to the Royal Flying Corps in 1917. Gained the DSO. Chosen in 1930 to command the newly raised 604 Squadron. From 1945-1951 he was chairman of the Middlesex Territorial and Auxiliary Forces Association.

Doulton, Michael Duke (29/09/1931) Engagement announcement, second son of Mr and Mrs Orrok Doulton of 37, DeVere Gardens, W8. Son of the famous pottery family, he was shot down over the Thames Estuary on 31 August 1940. Joined 604 Squadron on 1931, as a trained mechanical engineer. He was reputed to be the tallest pilot in the whole of the RAF. He went on to the Reserve in September 1936, but because of his engineering background, he transferred to the Air Ministry in 1938 to prepare car factories to convert rapidly to shadow factories for the production of aero-engines. He was called up to full time service with 601 Squadron on 24 August 1939. He was shot down on 31 August 1940 in action over the Thames Estuary and reported missing. He was 31-years-old. An aircraft excavated south of Wennington Church near Romford, Essex, on 27 August 1984 proved to be Hurricane R4215, and Pilot Officer Doulton's remains were still in the cockpit. Son of Orrok Mills Doulton and of Catherine May Doulton and husband of Carol Doulton of Vinehall in Sussex.

Healy, Lewin Edward Alton (06/06/1930) Death announcement in *The Times* – On 17 July, peacefully after a long illness borne with strength and humour, Lewin Alton Healy, OBE, 604 Squadron AAF.

Lawton, Philip Charles Fenner (04/07/1936) Born on 18 September 1912 and educated at Westminster School and Law Society School. Solicitor articled to Mr W.W. Hargrove of London. Joined 604 Squadron in 1934. Awarded DFC in 1941. At the end of the war he went back to the solicitors firm to work, but was restless and following an interview with Sir Harold Hartley, chairman of the new British European Airways, he was invited to join the company as secretary and commercial manager, where he remained until he retired in 1973. He died on 8 December 1993, aged 81.

Lofts, Keith Temple (07/11/1938) Memorial Service Announcement.

Montagu, Michael Richard (05/11/1935) Stepson of Lord Kimberley. Post Office Engineer. Son of Mr James Fountayne Montagu of Papplewick Hall, Notts and Coldoverton Hall, Oakham. Born 1915, educated at Eton and Magdalene College, Cambridge. Flew across Africa.

Nimmo, Robert Louis (08/12/1931) Son of J.D. Nimmo of Bushey Heath. Educated at Uppingham and Emmanuel College, Cambridge, he became a member of the Stock Exchange with the firm De Zoete and Garton. He took his pilot's licence in June 1931, and joined the AAF in December 1931. He lived at Gresham House, EC and Chalfont St Giles. Left an estate of £170,924 gross. Death in *The Times*. Obituary 9 August 1935.

Prescott, Edward Neville (19/09/1934) Son of Lieutenant Colonel Prescott of the Clock House, Salfords, Surrey. Marriage announcement in *The Times*.

Speke, Hugh (10/07/1937) Born in South Africa on 17 April 1914, and following the early death of his parents, he was brought up in Northumberland by relatives. He joined 604 Squadron in 1937. He was killed on 26 July 1941 on a routine night flying test. He was 27-years-old. He was awarded the DFC on 29 July 1941.

Wheeler, Philip Clifton (10/08/1935) Educated at Uppingham and New College, Oxford. Good rider, winning point-to-point races. Joined Oxford University Air Squadron in 1932.

605 (County of Warwick) Squadron

Aldridge, George Herbert (17/07/1928) Articled pupil to a firm of surveyors in London.

Barnaby, Walter Collinson (15/07/1931) Building contractor from Wolverhampton.

Currant, Christopher "Bunny" Frederick (02/06/1937) Born on 14 December 1911 in Luton, Bedfordshire, his father was a hatter. He was educated at Rydal School and after various jobs and apprenticeships he joined 605 Squadron in 1937. He was one of the most successful fighter pilots and retired from the RAF with the rank of Wing Commander in 1960 and joined Hunting Engineering where he undertook research and development on weapons for the RAF.[9]

De Broke, Baron Willoughby (01/03/1936) A member of a hunting family. Born John Henry Peyto Verney, 20th Baron Willoughby de Broke. Born 21 May 1896, died 1986. Educated at Eton and Sandhurst. Chairman of Wolverhampton Race Company Ltd.

Graeme, Nigel Stuart (29/10/1937) Second son of Colonel and Mrs J.A. Graeme of Fourwinds, Farnborough. Death announcement in *The Times*.

Hope, Ralph (11/06/1938) Youngest son of Mr and Mrs D Hope of Mosely, Birmingham. Educated at Eton and New College, Oxford. Outstanding oarsman. Nephew of Neville Chamberlain. Obituary in *The Times*.

Knox, Cecil Leonard VC (23/11/1926) Born on 9 May 1888, a civil engineer. Joined AAF between the wars. Suffered a serious parachute accident and so left and joined the Home Guard.

Leeson, Patrick George (05/12/1936) Only son of Mr and Mrs G.W. Leeson of Brendan, Malvern. Marriage notice in *The Times*.

607 (County of Durham) Squadron

Barnes, Wilkinson (02/08/1938) Born in Sunderland on 13 July 1913 and educated at Tunstall Boys School, Sunderland and Durham School. Trained as a Charted Surveyor and Auctioneer and then joining the family firm, becoming a partner in 1937. Joined 607 Squadron in 1938. Involved in an aircraft accident on 28 October 1942 and was severely injured, remaining in hospital for eight months. Invalided out of the forces in March 1944. He rejoined the family firm and retired in 1978. He died in Sunderland on 19 May 1980.

Bazin, James Michael (02/12/1935) Born 1915 in Kashmir, India, but was brought up in Newcastle upon Tyne. Joined 607 Squadron in May 1935. Awarded the DFC in October 1940, and the DSO on 21 September 1945. After war he returned to the engineering industry. Re-joined 607 Squadron in 1946 and commanded it until 1952. He died on 9 January 1985.

Blackadder, William Francis (01/06/1936) Scottish rugby player who had attended school in Edinburgh and then moved on to Cambridge University. Press cuttings from *The Times*.

Craig, George Dudley (28/05/1937) Son of Mr and Mrs R.D. Craig, The Six Lords, Singleborough Bucks. George Dudley Craig OBE of Corbridge was born on 13 September 1913 in Bangkok, the son of R.D. Craig, a member of the Diplomatic Corp and Sarah Louise Craig. He was educated at Aysgarth Public School followed by Winchester School and then Pembroke College Cambridge where he gained a soccer blue and an MA in Law Studies. Prior to the Second World War he earned his living as a local solicitor. Marriage announcement in *The Times*.

Irving, Maurice Milne (10/03/1934) Born in 1911, one of two sons to Benjamin and Katherine Irving. Death announcement in *The Times*. Worked for the locomotive division of Armstrong Whitworth Engineering Works in Newcastle.

Kayll, Joseph Robert (01/06/1934) Born 12 on April 1914 and educated at Aysgarth and Stowe, he worked in the family timber business in Sunderland after leaving school. In 1934 he was commissioned into the AAF, and begun flying with 607 Squadron. He was awarded both the DFC and the DSO in 1940, before the Battle of Britain had begun. Taken prisoner in 1941, he was taken to Stalag Luft III, where he took up the role as escape officer. He famously organised the "Wooden Horse" outbreak in which three men escaped to Sweden and England. He organised other breakouts, but stopped after the Great Escape in 1944 when fifty escapees were shot on Hitler's orders. He was appointed OBE in 1945 for his escape work in the camps. He was demobbed in 1946, and immediately rejoined 607 Squadron Royal Auxiliary Air Force as its Commanding Officer. He also rejoined the family timber business. He died on 3 March 2000, aged 85.

Leeson, Patrick George (05/12/1936) Engagement announcement in *The Times*. Only son of Mr and Mrs G.W. Leeson of Brendan Malvern. He was a prisoner of war at Stalag Luft III, and as a known escape artist, he was one of the prisoners involved in the Great Escape. He was number 230, and only the first seventy-seven actually got out.

Runciman, Walter Leslie (13/06/1930) Eldest son of Walter Runciman who later became Viscount Runciman, a member of Asquith's Cabinet. His mother was also a liberal candidate for St Ives. Born in Newcastle upon Tyne on 26 August 1900 and educated at Eton, before moving to Trinity College Cambridge. He worked at Deloitte as a chartered accountant in London and later worked for the Liverpool shipping company of Holt. On the death of his father in 1949 he became known as the second Viscount. He returned to Newcastle to take a position in the family shipping company, The Moor Line. Obituary in *The Times*.

Sample, John (27/04/1934) Born at Longhirst, Northumberland in 1913, the son of Thomas Norman and Kate Isabel Sample. Marriage announcement in *The Times*. He was educated at Aysgarth School and Lansing School, and he worked as the land agent for the Duke of Portland.

Smith, Lancelot Eustace (03/07/1933) Son of Clarence Dalrymple Smith OBE, JP of Lough Brow. Came from a family business called Smiths Dock Repairing Company and was Chairman of the Board of Directors.

Thompson, Montague Henry Brodrick (21/08/1937) Son of Alan Brodrick Thompson and Dorothy Margret Thompson of Newcastle upon Tyne. BA From Canterbury University. Killed in Action in Belgium on 13 May 1940.

Whitty, William Hubert Rigby (07/03/1938) Born in 1914 in Litherland, Lancashire and went to Liverpool College followed by Liverpool University from 1931-1935, where he was studying to become an electrical engineer.

608 (North Riding) Squadron

Ambler, Geoffrey Hill (07/02/1931) Marriage announcement in *The Times*. Son of Mr Frederick Ambler and Mrs Ambler of Chellow Grange, Bradford, Yorkshire. Nephew of Sir James Hill, who was the owner of James Hill & Sons Ltd, the largest private wool merchants in the country, and also Liberal MP for Bradford Central. Geoffrey's father, Frederick Ambler, owned Midland Mills in Bradford, his mother, Annie Hill, was the sister of Sir James Hill. Geoffrey was born at Baildon in 1904 and was educated at Shrewsbury and rowed for the school at Henley in 1922. He attended Clare College, Cambridge, where he obtained his BA degree and rowed in the winning university crews of 1924, 1925 and 1926. By 1930 he was Director of Fred Ambler Limited of Bradford, his father's woollen firm. A member of Yorkshire Aeroplane Club, he already had his pilots license and owned his own plane.

Appleby-Brown, William (07/02/1938) From Saltburn, his father was James Brown, who worked for the family firm J Brown and Co who were builder's merchants at Queens Square in Middlesbrough. The Brown family was a prominent Middlesbrough family that included Alderman John Wesley Brown who was MP for Middlesbrough in 1921. William attended Cambridge University where he learned to fly as a member of the University Air Squadron, he then joined the family firm. His family also had a shipping company called Lion Shipping that imported iron ore from Spain and Timber from the Baltic States. [10]

Baird, Dennis (11/09/1937) Came from West Hartlepool, family business, J.W. Baird and Company Ltd was importing various kinds of wood.

Burrell, Robert (15/12/1938) Marriage announcement in *The Times*. Son of Mr R Burrell and Mrs L Burrell of Glenwyne, Scorrier, Cornwall.

Clayton, John Lionel (07/02/1931) Harry Clayton's family owned a well-known retail business in Middlesbrough.[11]

Davis, William Howard (28/04/1930) Son of R.W. and J.P. Howard Davis of Elton House, Darlington. He lived in Saltburn and had also attended Cambridge University. He worked as Chief Accountant to Dorman Long.[12]

Johnson, Alan Strafford (17/02/1936) Son of Mr S.J. Johnson and Mrs Johnson of Birkdale. Marriage announcement in *The Times*.

Kennedy, P (14/08/1938) Came from Middlesbrough and had attended Oxford University. He was an accountant at ICI.[13]

APPENDIX 2

Lloyd-Graeme, Phillip (16/12/1934) Sir Philip Cunliffe Lister, a member of the Lloyd-Graeme family from Sewerby Hall and estate in the East Riding of Yorkshire. His father-in-law was Sir John Cunliffe-Lister, Baron of Masham and chief shareholder in Manningham Mills. Philip was educated at Winchester and University College Oxford. He was a barrister and a Conservative MP and he served in the squadron before the war, returning as Honorary Air Commodore under the name of the Rt Hon Viscount Swinton.

Newhouse, Henry Charles (05/01/1933) Came from one of the villages outside Middlesbrough, he attended Cambridge University and his family owned Newhouses Department Store in Middlesbrough.

Phillips, John Sherburn Priestly (Pip) (04/01/1937) Born in Dublin in November 1919; his father John Skelton Phillips was in the army and was then a civil engineer at ICI Billingham, whilst his mother, Rita, was related to J.B. Priestly. He attended St Olave's School in York before moving to the senior school, St Peter's School in York on 23 January 1933 where he was a full boarder. He left the school in July 1936 and moved to Crooksbarn Lane in Norton; Stockton on Tees. He was a successful rower for the school and he was a cadet in the OTC. He worked as an engineer in Darlington, employed by the London North Eastern Railway, joining 608 Squadron in 1937 at the age of eighteen.[14] He was awarded the DFC in 1940, and became a test pilot for Napier after the war.[15]

Pyman, Keith (07/02/1938) Member of Hurworth Hunt. Marriage announcement in *The Times*. Son of Frederick H Pyman JP and Mrs Pyman, Dunsley Hall, Sandsend near Whitby. He lived at Tall Trees, Far End, Yarm. He was a civilian pilot in the late 1920s and early 1930s; on 23 October 1930 DH60 Gipsy Moth G-ABFT was registered to him and the certificate of airworthiness issued a week later. The aircraft was used at Dunsley aerodrome near Whitby, North Yorkshire. He kept the aircraft until 31 July 1939 when it was registered to the Hartlepool and Teesside Flying Club at West Hartlepool. As Flt Lt Keith Pyman, he relinquished his commission on 2 March 1940, due to being medically unfit for service. The assumption that this was the result of being injured in a flying accident.

Robertson, James (17/03/1935) Lived in Saltburn with his family who were farmers.[16]

Shaw, Geoffrey (29/08/1930) Came from Nunthorpe and his family owned W.G. Shaw Engineering Co in North Ormesby. His father W.G. Shaw was the president of the Middlesbrough branch of the Institute of British Foundrymen. Geoffrey was educated in Scotland but then attended Cambridge University where he learned to fly as part of the University Air Squadron. He also owned his own aeroplane that he used for long business trips. He took part in the MacRobertson Air Race from England to Australia in 1934.[17]

Stead, Philip Kay (19/04/1937) Marriage announcement in *The Times*. Lived at Hillside, Glenhow, Leeds.

Thompson, Ivo Wilfred Home (29/08/1930) Son of Sir Wilfrid and Lady Thompson of Old Nunthorpe.[18]

Vaux, Peter Douglas Ord (20/07/1933) Marriage announcement in *The Times*. Younger son of Colonel Ernest Vaux CMG and DSO, Brettanby Manor, Barton, Yorkshire. Also wedding announcement in *The Times*. Court circular announcement 1980 in *The Times* announces service of thanksgiving for life of Wing Commander Peter Douglas Ord Vaux at St Cuthbert and St Mary Church, Richmond. Born in Grindon near Sunderland, he went to school at Harrow and then went on to Cambridge University where he joined the University Air Squadron and learned to fly. He was commissioned into the Auxiliary Air Force in July 1933 and he lived at Piercebridge in County Durham. He was an amateur jockey who rode in the Grand National and took part in various point to points. He rode with the Zetland and Bedale Hunts. He was also connected to the brewing side of the family. [19]

Williams, George (18/11/1938) Born in Shrewton near Salisbury in 1917. Attended St Probus Prep School in Salisbury, then moved to boarding school in Cornwall. Finally attended Cambridge University. Father was a gentleman farmer who was also a district and county councillor and JP.

Wilson, Anthony Neville (10/02/1931) Family were clothiers in the Tower House in Middlesbrough. [20]

Wright, Cosmo William (21/07/1931) Marriage announcement in *The Times*. Comes from West Lawn, Sunderland. Family were clothiers in the Tower House in Middlesbrough. [21]

609 (West Riding) Squadron

Ayre, George Desmonde (13/05/1938) A mining engineer in one of the Peake family collieries. Died at Dunkirk on 30 May 1940, aged 26. [22]

Barran, Philip Henry (20/04/1937) Son of Mr and Mrs P Austyn Barran of The Elms Chapel, Allerton, Leeds. Marriage announcement in *The Times*. A trainee mining engineer and manager of a brickworks at a colliery owned by his mother's family, he was also related to a Leeds Liberal MP. [23]

Beaumont, Stephen Gerald (20/04/1937) Son of Mr Gerald Beaumont of Wolley, Wakefield. Attended Uppingham School and then Christ Church, Oxford. An expert climber. A junior partner in a firm of solicitors.

Blayney, Adolf Jarvis (20/11/1936) A member of a textile family. [24]

Curchin, John (22/09/1938) Dearly loved son of the late H.W. Curchin, Naval Architect. Reported missing on 4 June 1941 and afterwards presumed killed in action.

Dawson, Joseph (08/07/1938) Son of Sir Benjamin Dawson, came from one of Yorkshires leading textile families. Arrived for training in a Lagonda. [25]

Drummond-Hay, Peter (28/08/1936) Married the niece of Lord Baden-Powell.

Dundas, John Charles (18/07/1938) Memorial service announcement in *The Times*. Son of Mr and Mrs F.J. Dundas of Dale Cottage, Crawthorne, Barnsley. An aristocrat, intellectual, athlete and journalist on the editorial staff of the *Yorkshire Post* who went to Oxford and was a specialist in foreign affairs. Related to the heads of two powerful Yorkshire families, the Marquess of Zetland and Viscount Halifax. Scholarship to Stowe at age twelve, scholarship to Christ Church, Oxford and the Sorbonne and Heidelberg University.

Edge, Alexander Rothwell (22/06/1937) A technical representative with I.G. Dyestuffs Ltd in Bradford. [26]

Humble, William (24/04/1936) Entry for the King's Cup Air Race on 6/7 September 1935. Marriage announcement in *The Times*. Son of Mr and Mrs William Humble of Skellow Grange, Doncaster.

Joynt, Dudley Persse (29/08/1938) Worked for an oil company. Rugby captain. [27]

Little, Bernard Williamson (12/07/1937) A solicitor in Wakefield. [28]

Nickols, Peter Richard (24/04/1936) Marriage announcement in *The Times*, only son of Richard Nickols of Spofforth Hall near Harrogate, Yorkshire.

Peake, Harold (10/02/1936) Member of Oxford University rowing team. Retired officer of the Yorkshire Dragoons Yeomanry. Late Master of the Rufford Hounds, a member of a Yorkshire colliery-owning family. Former member of the Territorial Army, he already flew an aeroplane, had rowed for Eton, Cambridge and England, and possessed a drive and ability that later would win him the chairmanship successively of the London Assurance, the Steel Company of Wales and Lloyds Bank Ltd. He lived at Bawtry Hall, which was located about fourteen miles from Doncaster, which had its own private airfield enabling him to commute to Yeadon each day by air.[29]

Richey, Paul (18/03/1937) Born in May 1916, he came from a notable fighting family. He was educated in Switzerland and at Downside before joining the AAF in 1937. He was awarded the DFC and Bar during 1942. He was the author of several books including *"Fighter Pilot"*. He rejoined the AAF when it was reformed after the war. He died on 23 February 1989, aged 72.

610 (County of Chester) Squadron

Bamberger, Cyril Stanley (17/06/1936) Born on 4 May 1919 in Hyde, Cheshire, he was educated locally and left school at fourteen to join Lever Brothers as an electrical apprentice in 1934. In 1936 he volunteered for the AAF and joined 610 Squadron as a photographer. He was accepted for pilot training in 1938. He was awarded a DSO and Bar in 1944. After the war he returned to Lever Brothers, before joining the management of a Guinness subsidiary. When 610 Squadron was reformed after the war he rejoined as a flight commander and became its CO in 1950. He went into business founding a packaging materials company, and then later, running an antiques business. He died on 3 February 2008, aged 88.

Chambers, Graham Lambert (01/03/1937) Studied at Cambridge University and gained an MA.

Davies-Cooke, Paul John (01/07/1937) Killed in Action, announcement in *The Times*. Son of P.T. Davies-Cooke of Gwysaney Mold.

Graham, Allan Delafield (23/04/1938) Killed in active service, announcement in *The Times*. Son of Allan J Graham of Brentwood, Hoylake.

Kerr, Gerald Malcolm Theodore (03/07/1937) Educated at Leeds Grammar School. Awarded an Eldon scholarship at Oxford for Natural Sciences in 1927. Announcement in *The Times*.

Leathart, James Anthony (15/06/1936) Born on 15 January 1915 in Upper Norwood, the son of a doctor. His grandfather had been an art loving industrialist, famous for Pre-Raphaelite art, who had created the Leathart Collection. James went to St Edward's School in Oxford, where he had his own car, and drove the headmaster around. He then went to Liverpool University to study Engineering. He joined the AAF and was a founder member of 610 Squadron. He was awarded the DSO. After the war he joined Mapleridge Enterprises, he then left to join Cleanacres, a crop spraying company. On retiring he followed his passions for bird watching and fishing. He married his wife, Dai, in 1939, she died in June 1998, and he never got over her loss. He died on 17 November 1998, aged 83.

Prichard, Charles Ross (10/05/1937) Marriage announcement in *The Times*. Son of Professor and Mrs H.A. Prichard of Oxford.

Smith, Andrew Thomas (09/04/1936) Killed in active service announcement in *The Times*. Husband of Dorothy Smith, New Pale Lodge, Manley near Frodsham, Cheshire and only son of Andrew Thomas Smith of Solna, Sefton Park. Liverpool.

Warner, William Henry Cromwell (07/05/1937) *The Times* announcement of Missing in Action. Son of Sir Lionel and Lady Warner, Yew Tree, Poplar Road, Birkenhead.

Wilson, Douglas Strachan (24/10/1936) Marriage announcement in *The Times*. Younger son of Mr James A Wilson of Albert Street, Aberdeen.

Wilson, John Kerr (14/06/1936) Killed in action announcement in *The Times*. Eldest son of Mr and Mrs H Kerr Wilson of Heswall, Wirral.

611 (West Lancashire) Squadron

Birley, Robert Neville (01/11/1936) Trinity College, Cambridge University Bar Examination results in *The Times*.

Blackwood, John Noel O'Reilly (12/07/1937) In Memoriam notice in *The Times*. Killed in Action on 25 January 1940 and buried with military honours in Dusseldorf. Worked for Pilkington Glass and his parents lived abroad.

Crompton, Ralph Kenyon (13/11/1937) Killed in action announcement in *The Times*. Eldest son of Mr and Mrs R Crompton of Betton Hall, Market Drayton. Educated at Charterhouse School and was a hunting man with the Cheshire hounds.

England, George Nicholas (08/07/1938) Trinity College Cambridge University, Bar Examination results in *The Times*.

Howroyd, David William Southam (18/08/1936) Worked as part of the family chemical business. Son of Mr and Mrs B.W. Howroyd, Merebank, Ullet Road, Liverpool.

Leather, William Johnson (14/05/1936) Marriage announcement in *The Times*. Son of George Leather of Stoneleigh, Woolton, Liverpool. Educated at Sedbergh and Kings College Cambridge University, he was a well-known rugby player.

Little, Thomas Donald (21/03/1938) Marriage announcement in *The Times*. Son of Mr and Mrs J.D. Little of Ethandune, Hoylake.

Pilkington, Geoffrey Langton (08/04/1936) Obituary in *The Times*. From 1932 until 1949 he was the Chairman of Pilkington Brothers Ltd, famous glass manufacturers. Educated at prep school, Stone House, Broadstairs, then Eton and Magdalen College, Oxford University. Joined the family firm in 1909 and became a sub-director in 1910 and a director in 1919. In 1911 he joined the Lancashire Hussars and served in England and in Egypt until 1916 when he transferred to the Royal Flying Corps. Living at Lower Lee, Woolton and Grayswood, he was a keen horticulturist.

Richards, Arthur Westley (10/08/1936) Attended Liverpool University and worked as a solicitor in Liverpool. Son of Mr and Mrs Westley Richards of West Kirby, Cheshire.

Scott-Malden, Francis David Stephen (03/10/1940) Born in 1917 at Portslade, East Sussex. Attended Winchester and King's College, Cambridge University. A member of Cambridge University Air Squadron. Holder of the DFC, DSO and Order of Orange Nassau with Swords.

Stoddart, Kenneth Maxwell (18/12/1936) Marriage announcement in *The Times*. Son of Wilfrid Bowring Stoddart of Beechwood House, Beechwood Road, Liverpool. Educated at Sedbergh School in Yorkshire and then on to Cambridge University, in civilian life he worked for the family business of ship suppliers. Lord Lieutenant of Merseyside.[30]

612 (County of Aberdeen) Squadron

Benzie, Douglas Gordon Emslie (11/10/1937) DFC awarded in 1941. Worked for Peat, Marwick, Mitchell and Co (Accountancy). Mr Douglas Gordon Emslie Benzie of Sunningdale, chartered accountant, left £571,011 net.

Berry, Herbert Oswald (02/07/1939) Fifth son of Lord Kemsley – died in hospital at Falmouth yesterday, age 33. Educated at Harrow and Pembroke College, Oxford. Served in AAF during the Second World War until he was invalided in 1944. He was until recently a director of Kemsley Newspapers Ltd. In 1940 he married Lady Mary Clementine Pratt, only daughter of Lord Camden. Funeral privately on 11 June at St Anne's, Dropmore. Son of James Gomer Berry, 1st Viscount Kemsley and Mary Lilian Holmes. Born 13 June 1918, he had a twin sister Mary, Marchioness of Huntly.

Davie, Norman Scott Ferguson (23/10/1937) Aviators Certificate for Norman Scott Ferguson Davie, No 612 Squadron, 9 December 1938.

Frain, George (10/10/1938) Flight Lieutenant Gorge Frain No 31 General Reconnaaissance School, Royal Canadian Air Force. Wing Commander George

Frain emigrated to New Zealand. Wing Commander George Frain MBE to be an Additional Officer in the military division of the said most excellent order. CBE awarded to Wing Commander George Frain OBE, RAF (retired), for services whilst on loan to the Royal Malaysian Air Force.

MacCulloch, Charles Chamberlain (18/12/1938) On 25 April 1941, at 1am, an Armstrong Whitworth Whittles V aircraft returning from operations, hit the hospital causing a huge fire and went on to crash in an adjoining field. Aircraft collided with the Wick Fever Hospital also claiming the lives of two domestic servants.

Middleton, Stewart Audjo (10/10/1932) Awarded the DFC in 1940.

Sadler, David Alexander (15/06/1939) Killed on active service, pilot officer under training David A Sadler. L6203 Botha Mk 2 Silloth on 28 August 1940, the aircraft crashed at Balladoyle Farm killing all of its crew.

Scott, Alan Milne (30/07/1937) Died aged 26 on 5 November 1940, son of James and Nellie Maitland Scott of Inchgarth, Pitfodels, B A County Cork. Award of AFC to Sqn Ldr A.M. Scott AAF (now deceased).

Stephen, Ian George Flaxington (30/06/1928) Births – on 24 January 1948 at Maidenhead Nursing Home to Daphne, wife of Ian G.F. Stephen – a daughter. Also marriage announcement - the engagement is announced between Anthea Mary, only daughter of Mr and Mrs I.G.F. Stephen of Crossleys, Bix, Henley on Thames.

Thomson, George Reid (24/05/1938) Engagement is announced between George Michael MacKinnon, son of Mr and Mrs G.R. Thomson, Kinellar House, Kinnellar, Aberdeenshire. Notification of marriage taking place.

Thomson, Ronald Bain (04/09/1937) A lecturer in Physical Education and Hygiene, he joined the newly formed 612 Squadron in 1937. He was Senior Lecturer at Pretoria Technical College in South Africa. He returned to Britain and rejoined 612 Squadron. Whilst with 172 Squadron he was awarded the DSO in 1943 and with 206 Squadron he received the DFC in 1943. He remained in the Royal Air Force until 1963, achieving the rank of Air Vice-Marshall.

613 (City of Manchester) Squadron

Anderson, A.F. (03/09/1939) DFC awarded. DSO awarded to Wing Commander A.F. Anderson. Bar to the DSO awarded to Group Captain A.F. Anderson.

Barthropp, Patrick Peter Colum (03/05/1939) Born in Dublin in 1920 and educated at St Augustine's Abbey School in Ramsgate; St Joseph's College near Market Drayton and Ampleforth College, North Yorkshire. He won colours in four sports and loved riding. After leaving he went to Rover's on an engineering apprenticeship, but, since he was able to fly, he volunteered for AAF and joined 613 Squadron in May 1939. Son of Mr and Mrs E.P. Barthropp of Maesbury House, Owestry, Shropshire.

Edy, Allen Laird (03/09/1939) DFC awarded. Born in 1916, the son of John Curtis Harrington Edy and Minnie Louise Edy of St Andrews, Manitoba, Canada.

Killed on 5 December 1941 when his Spitfire caught fire and spun into the ground near Ramsey, Isle of Man. He bailed out but was too close to the ground for his parachute to open.

614 (County of Glamorgan) Squadron

Cadman, Richard Edward Charles (15/10/1937) Born on 1 November 1894, son of James Cope Cadman and Betty Keeling. He married firstly Eileen Mary Johnson and they had a son Richard Edward Charles Cadman. Secondly he married Amy Howson and had a son Robert Andrew Cadman. He fought in the Royal Flying Corps in the First World War and is mentioned in despatches. He gained the rank of Squadron Leader in the service of 614 Squadron. He was invested as a Commander, CBE in 1951. He was appointed Honorary Air Commodore of 614 Squadron. Birth announced on 6 June 1952 at Vancouver General Hospital to Constance, wife of R.E.C. Cadman, 228, Mathers Avenue, West Vancouver BC, a fourth daughter.

Edwards, Martin Llewellyn (16/08/1937) Born on 21 May 1909, educated at Marlborough College and Lincoln College, Oxford. Worked as a solicitor and in 1934 he joined his uncle's practice in Merthyr Tydfil and later moved to Cardiff to his father's practice. His marriage was announced in 1935. Elected to the Law Society Council in 1957 and campaigned nationally for the improved education of solicitors. He was chairman of the Education and Training Committee, a member of the Lord Chancellor's Committee on Legal Education; he was also President of the Law Society in 1973/74. He was Knighted in 1974. He saw distinguished military service during the Second World War in both the Auxiliary Air Force and the RAF. He continued his association with the military by being closely involved with the Glamorgan Territorial and Auxiliary Forces Association. He died on Saturday, 20 June 1987, aged 78.

Farr, Peter (18/08/1937) Flying Officer Peter Farr relinquishes his commission on the grounds of ill health on 18 January 1940.

Haigh, John Guy Leonard (01/09/1939) Pilot Officer 91152 John Guy Leonard Haig, died 20 October 1939, aged 25. Memorial Pott Shrigley (St Christopher) Churchyard.

Lysaght, Philip Michael Vaughan (28/09/1937) Engagement announced between Flight Lieutenant P.M.V. Lysaght, son of Rev J.A.C. Lysaght and Mrs Lysaght of Caerleon. At Seabourne Nursing Home, Bournemouth, to Christine, wife of Sqn Ldr P.M.V. Lysaght – a daughter. Sqn Ldr Philip Michael Vaughn Lysaght previously reported missing now presumed killed in action. He was the son of Mr and Mrs J.A.C. Lysaght of Caerleon, Monmouth.

Merrett, Norman Stuart (17/08/1937) Played rugby for Clifton College Boarding School. He also played international hockey as the goalkeeper. Flying Officer Norman Stuart Merrett, only son of Mr and Mrs H.H. Merrett of Cwrt-Yr-Ala, near Cardiff.

Miles, Herbert Charles Wilson (01/07/1939) Killed on active service.

Pallot, Alexander Glen (04/05/1938) Chartered accountant of 128-129, Bute Street, Cardiff. Death announcement – Alexander Glen Pallot, FCA Wing Commander RAF (retired) on 6 February 2006, aged 91. Beloved husband of the late Marjorie, father of Ian and Hugh.

Rhys, Richard Owen (28/09/1937) Born 1915 in Aberystwyth, Pilot Officer 28/09/1937, Flying Officer 03/09/1940, Squadron Leader 01/06/1943, Wing Commander 11/01/1945. On 18 June 1946 at De Paul Hospital, St Louis, USA, to Jane, wife of Richard Owen Rhys – a daughter. Deputy Lieutenant Commissions, Group Captain Richard Owen Rhys of 3, Archer Road, Penarth, Glamorgan.

Rollinson, John Dudley (03/05/1938) Wing Commander John Dudley Rollinson DFC reported missing from air operations in January 1944 with number 630 Squadron, now officially presumed killed, the only son of Mr and Mrs T.D. Rollinson of Bexhill. Born in 1911 in Wolverhampton and educated at grammar school there. On 3 May 1938 he was commissioned in the AAF. Promoted to Wing Commander in September 1941 and awarded the DFC in January 1942 after making thirty operational sorties from Malta, he performed sterling work. Married in June 1943 to Jean Margaret Campbell WRAF.

Smyth, David (11/09/1937) Missing 18 November 1943, now presumed killed, Flight Lieutenant David Smyth, 614 Squadron. Whilst returning home after completing his tour of duty in North Africa, Sicily and Italy. Beloved second son of Mr and Mrs T Hugh Smyth, Edworth Manor, Biggleswade, aged 28. Born in 1915, educated at Haileybury and Queens College, Cambridge University.

Williams, William Griffith (14/06/1939) Bankruptcy Receiving orders, Williams W.G., 102, Newport Road, Cardiff Glamorgan. Medical Practitioner.

615 (County of Surrey) Squadron
Brady, Bernard John Richard (08/03/1938) Left school at fourteen and joined the Royal Navy as an able seaman. During the First World War he joined the Naval Air Wing and flew as an air-gunner/observer in the Middle East during the war. Towards the end of the First World War he trained as a naval pilot and transferred into the Royal Flying Corps. He served as a pilot for the remainder of the war. He then set up his own business as the manager of Aircraft Exchange and Mart that was located at Hanworth Air Park in Middlesex. [31]

Cazenove, Peter Frederick (16/05/1938) Marriage announcement in *The Times*. Son of Major and Mrs Percy Cazenove, New Hall, Thorpe-le-Soken, Essex.

Collard, Peter (04/02/1938) Killed in Action notice in *The Times*.

Eyre, Anthony (26/07/1938) Marriage announcement in *The Times*. Son of Mr G.W.B. Eyre of Purley. Obituary in *The Times*. Born at Lowestoft in 1918 and educated at Whitgift School, Croydon.

Gayner, John Richard Hensman (14/09/1937) Marriage announcement in *The Times*. Son of Dr Gayner and Mrs Francis Gayner of Old West Street House, Reigate.

Lloyd, John Richard (03/12/1938) Killed in action notice in *The Times*. Son of Lieutenant Colonel Sir John and Lady Lloyd of Dinas House, Brecon.

Murton-Neale, Peter Norman (12/09/1939) In ever loving memory of Flying Officer Peter Norman Murton-Neale of 615 Auxiliary Squadron, youngest son of A.F. Murton-Neale, Millway End, Reigate. Killed in action over Belgium on 14 May 1940.

Stern, Walter Otto (06/11/1937) Worked for the London Metal Exchange.

Truran, Anthony J (11/08/1937) In loving memory of Tony, Flying Officer A.J. Truran on this his birthday.

616 (South Yorkshire) Squadron
Casson, Lionel Harwood (Buck) (02/05/1938) Son of a steel buyer, born in Sheffield on 6 January 1915 and educated at Birkdale School and then the King's School, Ely, before embarking on a career in the steel industry. Although he was employed in a reserved occupation, he joined the Auxiliary Air Force and elected to remain with them on the outbreak of war when he had completed his pilot training. He fought with 616 Squadron throughout the war and was shot down over France and captured near St Omer. He was then sent to Stalag Luft III at Sagan. At the end of the war having been awarded the DFC, he returned to the steel industry in Sheffield.

Dundas, Hugh Spencer Lisle (07/04/1938) Born 22 July 1920. Educated at Stowe and then articled to a firm of solicitors in Barnsley. Commissioned into 616 Squadron AAF in 1939. Awarded DFC in August 1941, and DSO in 1944. After the war he was senior management at Rediffusion from 1961-1985, Chairman of Thames television between 1981 & 1987 and also Chairman of British Electric Traction between 1982 & 1987. He was also a member of the AAF when it was reformed after the war. He died on 10 July 1995, aged 74.

Holden, Kenneth (18/05/1938) Birth announcement – on 4 March 1940 at Lunfield Nursing Home, Altrincham, Cheshire, to Winkie, wife of Kenneth Holden, a daughter. Engagement announcement for Anne Marjorie, elder daughter of Mr and Mrs Kenneth Holden, of Downshutt, Alderley Edge, Cheshire. Engagement announcement for Jane Vivienne, daughter of Mr and Mrs Kenneth Holden of Downshutt, Alderley Edge, Cheshire.

Roberts, Ralph (12/02/1939) Attended Oxford University reading law. He was posted to the Fighter Pool at St. Athan on 26 November where he converted to Hurricanes. He then joined 2 Ferry Pilots Pool at Filton on 21 December, pending a squadron posting. In the meantime he ferried Hurricanes to front-line squadrons in France. In late December Roberts was posted to 615 Squadron in France and arrived at Vitry on 1 January 1940. He informed the CO that he had expected to go to 616 Squadron and was told that it would be arranged but that it would take time. Roberts flew Gladiators in France until operations ceased there and then he flew one back to Lympne. He did patrols over Dunkirk in Gladiators, operating from Manston. The squadron, which had lost its new Hurricanes in France, was re-equipped with replacements at Kenley in June and Roberts continued to fly with 615 until the end of July. He was then informed that his posting to 616 had finally come through, but pending ratification from Group he was asked to fly with 64 Squadron, also at Kenley, which was short of pilots. On 13 August Roberts claimed a Do17 destroyed. Two days later he was shot down over Calais-Marck in Spitfire K9964 SH*W and captured. He was sent to Stalag Luft III. Freed in May 1945, Roberts was released from the RAF on 9 March 1946 as a Flight Lieutenant. He died in 1994.

500 (County of Kent) Squadron

(Formed at RAF Manston on 16 March 1931 as a Special Reserve Squadron – Transferred into AAF on 25 May 1936.)

Anderson, Albany Peat (29/03/1935) Marriage announcement in *The Times*.

Balston, James Peter Henry (21/02/1939) Marriage announcement in *The Times*. Son of Mr and Mrs F.W. Balston of Toppesfield, Maidstone. Killed in action announcement in *The Times*.

Connors, Stanley Dudley Pierce (25/03/1936) Killed in action notice in *The Times*. Pilot and personal assistant to Air Commodore J.C. Quinnel.

Corry, William Heath (17/08/1937) Marriage announcement in *The Times*. From Dreelingstown, Kilkenny, son of Mr and Mrs H.W. Corry of Yaldham Manor, Kemsing, Kent.

Cousins, Arthur Robert (31/08/1939) Marriage announcement in *The Times*. Son of Lieutenant-Colonel and Mrs A.G. Cousins of Bix Manor, Henley-on-Thames.

Elgar, Charles Robinson (10/08/1937) Marriage announcement in *The Times*. Son of Walter Robinson Elgar JP and Mrs Elgar of Bobbing Place, Sittingbourne Kent.

Few, Leslie Maurice (24/07/1931) Flying Officer Leslie Maurice Few was killed at Brooklands on Saturday, 16 September 1933, in an accident while trying to land his twin engine Vickers Virginia bomber. He was buried under the wreckage and it took rescuers over an hour to get him out. Four other crew members escaped with slight injury. Age at the time of the crash was 29.

Green, Patrick (30/11/1935) Marriage announcement in *The Times*. DFC announcement in *The Times*.

Keppel, William Bertrand Arnold Joost (28/10/1935) Marriage announcement in *The Times*. From Umblanga Rocks, Durban, South Africa.

Le May, William Kent (28/10/1935) Marriage announcement in *The Times*. Son of Mr and Mrs Percy Kent Le May of St Leonards. Escaped from the crash which killed Flying Officer Lesley Maurice Few on Saturday, 16 September 1933.

Leatherdale, Thomas Ryan (25/07/1931) Born on 2 April 1910, his father was Thomas Leatherdale and his mother was Ethel Ann Wolden. Married Masie Prebble, died in 1970. Promoted to Flying Officer on 25 January 1933. Relinquishes his commission on account of ill health on 22 June 1938. Granted a commission as Pilot Officer for the duration of hostilities on 15 April 1941.

Mabey, Dennis Guy (07/04/1937) Killed in action announcement in *The Times*.

Paterson, Andrew MacDonald (18/12/1938) Announcement of death in *The Times*. Killed in action. Youngest son of Mr Henry S Paterson late of Birkenhead.

Reeves, Patrick (30/08/1939) Marriage announcement in *The Times*. Son of Mr and Mrs Francis Reeves, Court Lodge, Yabling, Kent.

Stockdale, George Geoffrey (19/09/1936) Marriage announcement in *The Times*. Son of Mr and Mrs G Holmes Stockdale of Little Trench, Tonbridge, Kent.

501 (County of Gloucester) Squadron
(Formed at Filton on 14 June 1929 as a Special Reserve Squadron – Initially known as (City of Bristol) Squadron. Renamed (County of Gloucester) Squadron on 1 May 1930. Transferred into AAF on 18 May 1936.)

Cridland, John Ryan (05/07/1938) Killed on active service notice in *The Times*. Son of Mrs Cridland of 119, Pembroke Road, Bristol.

Malfroy, Camille Enright (08/05/1935) Marriage announcement in *The Times*. Younger son of Mr and Mrs C.M. Malfroy of Wellington, New Zealand.

Miles, Allan Frederick William (04/05/1937) Six members of RAF presumed killed.

Rayner, Peter Herbert (21/07/1936) Killed in action.

Shaw, Cautley Nasmyth (24/02/1936) Son of Oliphant Shaw of Woorwyrite, Terang, Victoria, Australia.

Smith, Michael Fauconberge Clifford (22/01/1938) Killed in action.

Warren, John Anthony Crosby (29/05/1935) Death announcement in *The Times*. MA, AFRAcS, test pilot.

502 (Ulster) Squadron
(Formed at Aldergrove on 15 May 1925 as a Special Reserve Squadron – Transferred into AAF on 1 July 1937.)

Barclay, James Charles (13/05/1938) Previously reported prisoner of war, now reported missing believed killed in action, Squadron Leader J.C. Barclay.

Bell, Joseph Cecil Gosselin (01/07/1937) Engagement announced between Sqn Ldr J.C.G. Bell AAF, only son of the late Nicholas Gosselin Bell and Mrs Bell of Whitehouse, Co Antrim. Mr J.C.G. Bell elected to board of Rank Cintel as Managing Director.

Corry, Brian George (09/04/1933) Daughters marriage announcement in *The Times*. Educated at Campbell College public school, Belfast. Flying Accident – The Air Ministry regrets to announce that Leading Aircrewman Donal Martin lost his life as the result of an accident which occurred at Aldergrove on 14 November

1937 to an aircraft of No 502 Squadron. Leading Aircrewman Martin was a passenger in the aircraft. The pilot Flight Lieutenant Brian G Corry was dangerously injured.

Corry, Robin Terence (10/04/1933) Educated at Campbell College public school, Belfast. Mentioned in dispatches.

Harrison, Samuel John (01/01/1937) DFC awarded to Wing Commander S.J. Harrison, Auxiliary Air Force.

Henderson, Gordon (14/04/1938) 502 Squadron on 7 February 1941. Whitley T4223YG-G on escort duty. Engine cut on an escort to convoy SC20, and the Whitley was ditched in position 5530N 1055W 120 miles west of Malin Head Ireland. The crew were picked up by HMS *Harvester*. Flt Lt Gordon Henderson AAF was injured.

Holmes, Arthur Peter Buckley (05/05/1935) Died 23 January 1941, age 32. Son of Buckley Holmes and of Ethel Maud Holmes. Husband of Dorothy Margaret Probert Holmes. Buried Drumbeg (St Patrick) Church of Ireland Churchyard. Engagement announcement of Peter, only son of the late A.P.B. Holmes and of Mrs D.M.P. Holmes, Manor Farm, Hillhall, Lisburn, Co Down.

Kirkpatrick, Yvone Johnston (10/07/1937) Marriage took place on Friday, 7 September at St Ninian's Troon, Ayrshire of Mr Yvone Johnston Kirkpatrick of Newcastle, County Down.

May, William Morrisson (10/07/1937) Eldest son of William May, born on 8 April 1909 and educated at Methodist College Belfast. He became a chartered accountant in 1931 and four years later a partner in the firm of Quinn, Knox and Co. He was elected Unionist MP for Ards in 1949.

Newton, Robert Charles (12/02/1933) Flight Lieutenant R.C. Newton relinquishes his commission on account of ill health and is permitted to retain his rank. R.C. Newton becomes Managing Director of Cockburns, Glasgow.

Palmer, Thomas Mitchell (21/07/1937) Engagement is announced between Tom M Palmer, Kensington Close, London W8, son of the late Mr and Mrs Henry H Palmer of Belfast.

Sowell, John Swindale Nanson (01/03/1938) A marriage has been arranged between John Swindale Nanson, younger son of the Rev H and Mrs Sewell of Upton Grey Vicarage, Hampshire.

Stanley, Mervyn John Cameron (19/05/1935) Educated at Worchester Kings School. A Liberator aircraft, bound for Great Britain from Canada, with a crew of five, including two RAF officers, Wing Commander M.J.C. Stanley and Pilot Officer W.G.J. Woodmason has been reported missing. The three other missing airmen are Canadians.

503 (County of Lincoln) Squadron
(Formed at Waddington on 5 October 1926 as a Special Reserve Squadron – Transferred into AAF on 18 May 1936. Disbanded in January 1938, becoming 616 Squadron Auxiliary Air Force)

Bell, John Swift (20/07/1937) Killed on active service announcement in *The Times*. Of Weekites, Charterhouse and Christ's College Cambridge, son of Major and Mrs H.A. Bell of Lindum Close, Lincoln.

Forte, Michael Philip (30/05/1928) Pilot Officer Forte was killed on 6 February 1937 when on flying duty at Waddington. Dearly loved son of Philip and Molly Forte, 32, Barkston Gardens, SW5, aged 23. Death by misadventure was the verdict at the inquest held at Waddington on Pilot Officer Michael Philip Forte and Aircraftsman East, twenty, of Lincoln who were killed on Saturday when an aeroplane of No 503 Squadron crashed soon after taking off from the aerodrome.

Maw, Roger Hargreaves (30/05/1928) Born on 21 June 1906. Son of a Lincolnshire landowner. Educated at Westerleigh School, St Leonard's on Sea and Oundle Boarding School. He joined 503 Squadron in 1927 to learn to fly. He was shot down during the Second World War and is famous for designing the wooden vaulting horse used by his fellow prisoners of war, to escape. After the war he returned to Lincolnshire and farmed at Welton, near Lincoln, before retiring to the Wolds village of Walesby. He died on 19 August, age 86.

St. Aubyn, Edward Fitzroy (01/07/1937) Born in 1907 and educated at Eton. Married Miss Nancy Meyrick. Killed in action May 1943.

504 (County of Nottingham) Squadron

(Formed at Hucknell on 26 March 1928 as a Special Reserve Squadron – Transferred into AAF on 18 May 1936.)

Boyle, Richard (08/08/1938) Flying Officer Richard Boyle was killed on Saturday, 13 March 1948 when his Mosquito fighter crashed into a field at Moor Green, Nottinghamshire. He was aged 29. His colleague, Flight Lieutenant Michael Rook, age 34, was also killed.

Broadhead, Reginald Malcolm (18/07/1934) Property dealer. Ockwells Manor, Maidenhead Berkshire.

Browne, John Michael Godfree (25/07/1936) Killed in action. Eldest son of Mr Harold Browne.

Darwin, Gilbert William Lloyd (06/06/1937) Marriage announcement. Youngest son of Colonel Charles Waring Darwin, CB of Elston Hall, Newark.

Frisby, Edward Murray (31/10/1938) Engagement announcement in *The Times*. Son of J Rowley Frisby of 7, Grenfell Road, Leicester.

Grant-Dalton, Alan Cuyler (14/06/1933) Pilot Officer Grant-Dalton killed in an aeroplane accident on 3 November 1934. Son of A.T. Grant-Dalton of Johannesburg. His flight, DH60XMOTH, crashed when his wing failed in a loop and the aircraft crashed and burned at Chilwell Manor Golf Course, near Beeston, Notts.

Hutchinson, Marcus Mowbray (29/05/1933) Marriage announcement in *The Times*. Son of Mr and Mrs A.T. Hutchinson of Sothoron Lodge, Manor Road, Leicester.

Jackson, George William Lawies (Baron Allerton) (22/10/1938) Born 1903, the son of William Lawies Jackson.

Owen, John Samuel (22/02/1937) Killed in Action notice in *The Times*.

Parnall, James Boyd (11/07/1935) Killed in Action announcement in *The Times*.

Parsons, Philip Trevor (31/10/1938) Downing College, Cambridge University, BA announcement in *The Times*. Engagement announcement in *The Times*. Son of Flight Lieutenant W.W. Parsons. Obituary in *The Times*. Educated at Charterhouse and Cambridge. In 1938 he joined Messrs. Rolls-Royce Limited as a selected engineering pupil.

Phillips, David (10/01/1938) Marriage announcement in *The Times*. Son of Mr and Mrs C.W. Phillips of The Grange, Eastwood, Nottinghamshire.

Rook, Anthony Hartwell (23/06/1937) Son of Mr S.H. Rook of Nottingham.

Rook, Michael (08/08/1938) Born on 12 October 1915, he was educated at Oakham School and later at Uppingham School. He joined the family wine and grocery business – Skinner and Rook Ltd, as wine department manager in 1934. He loved motor racing and flying. He married at the age of twenty. In 1938 he joined 504 (County of Nottingham) Squadron. At the outbreak of war the squadron were sent to Lille in France, and later the squadron moved up to Wick as members of 12 Group, protecting northern cities and eastern approaches. The squadron moved south during 1939 and played an active role in the Battle of Britain. On 27 August 1941 he was posted to No 81 (F) Squadron and was sent to Northern Russia. Marriage announcement in *The Times*. Son of Colonel and Mrs W.R. Rook of Edwalton House, Nottingham. Killed Saturday, 13 March 1948 when his Mosquito fighter crashed in a field at Moor Green, Nottinghamshire, aged 34.

Seely, Sir Hugh Michael MP (10/06/1937) Son of Sir Charles Seely. MP for East Norfold. High Sheriff of Nottinghamshire. First Baron Sherwood of Calverton. Born on 2 October 1898. Guards.

Watson, Rupert Hartley (31/10/1935) Marriage announcement in *The Times*. Son of Lieutenant Colonel and Mrs G Hartley Watson of Powderham, near Exeter. Killed in active service announcement in *The Times*.

United Kingdom Officers of the Royal Air Force Volunteer Reserve

De l'Agazarian, Noel Le Chevalier (14/02/1939) Plays rugby for Dulwich College. Boxes for Wadham College, Oxford University. Engagement announcement for Noel Le Chevalier, eldest son of Mr and Mrs R de l'Agazarian of Kedington, Suffolk.

Agnew, Peter Graeme (22/12/1938) Plays rugby for Stowe School. Appears on Trinity College, Cambridge University economics tripos lists between June 1933 and June 1934. Degree awarded. Engagement announcement for Peter Graeme, only son of Mr and Mrs Alan Agnew of Lane Farm, Bovingdon, Herts. Births – on 19 August 1941, at Crabtrees, Berkhamstead, to Diana, wife of Flight Lieutenant P.G. Agnew RAFVR, of Thornhill, Moorark – a son.

Akroyd-Stuart, Anthony Charles Lettebleve (13/09/1938) Attended Lancing College.

Anderson, Albany Peat (07/06/1938) Marriage announcement – on 29 April 1939 at St Margaret's, Rottingdean, Sussex, Albany Peat Anderson to Pamela Alderton. Attended Eastbourne College.

Anderson, Keith Malcolm Graham (07/06/1938) Attended Harrow School. Swims for Harrow. Engagement announcement between K.M.G. Anderson, youngest son of Sir John Anderson and Lady Anderson of Eastcote Place, Eastcote. Attended Jesus College, Cambridge University,

Anderson, Malcolm Webster (28/12/1937) Attended Berkhamsted School and took part in running events. Plays rugby for Clifton College throughout 1933, 1934 and 1935. Attends Trinity College, Cambridge University and plays cricket for them. Engagement announced for Michael Herbert, younger son of J.S. Anderson of Scotsbridge House, Rickmansworth. Obituary in *The Times*.

Anderson, Michael Herbert (09/08/1938) Attended Clifton School. Attended Trinity College, Cambridge University. Engagement announcement for Michael Herbert, youngest son of the late Mr J.S. Anderson of Scotsbridge House, Rickmansworth. Marriage announcement for Michael Herbert, saying that the wedding will take place on 16 December at 12 o'clock at St Mary-the-Virgin, Hambledon, Henley-on-Thames. Obituary in *The Times*.

Andreae, Christopher John Drake (01/02/1938) Educated at Shrewsbury School and Caius College Cambridge University. Member of the University Air Squadron. On 11 August 1940 he returned to base in Spitfire N3293 with damage caused by cannon fire from an enemy fighter engaged off Dover. Four days later Andreae failed to return from a combat with Me109's over the Channel. He was 23-years-old.

Andrews, John Frank Hough (16/11/1937) Attended Hertford College, Oxford University. Engagement announced for John Frank Hough Andrews, second son of Mr and Mrs F.W. Andrews of Picket Post, Hants. The marriage arranged between Mr John Frank Hough Andrews and Miss Joan Needham took place quietly at Burley Church Hampshire on 9 September. Births – on 12 December 1942 to Joan, wife of Flight Lieutenant J.F.H. Andrews, a son (Michael). Announcement of death on active service.

Angas, Robert Howard (20/12/1938) Attended Geelong School in Australia and rows for Worcester College, Oxford University. DFC awarded for Flight Lieutenant R.H. Angas.

Bache, Leslie Longmore (16/11/1937) Born in Bootle, Cumberland in 1913, the son of Rev Joseph W.R. Bache and Ada B Bache. Flight Lieutenant Leslie Longmore Bache served with 41 Squadron from August to October 1941 when he was killed in action. He failed to return from a sweep over France, aged 28.

Baldwin, Philip Harold (16/11/1937) Attended St John's College, Cambridge University and awarded a degree in Archaeology. Attended University Air Squadron Dinner. Promoted to Group Captain. Son's engagement announced.

Ball, Cederic Edward (02/08/1938) Attended Newton College.

Balston, James Peter Henry (01/02/1938) The marriage of Flying Officer James Peter Henry Balston, second son of Mr and Mrs F.W. Balston took place quietly at St Luke's Church, Grayshott, on Saturday, 9 September. Flying Officer James Peter Henry Balston, reported missing, believed killed on active service was 26-years-old. He was the second son of Mr and Mrs Frank Balston of Toppesfield, Maidstone. In memoriam message.

Barber, Ernest Edward (04/07/1939) Awarded degree from Queen Mary College, Oxford University.

Barber, Francis Herbert Patrick (09/08/1938) Attended Bradfield College. Plays football for Bradfield College. Plays cricket for Bradfield College. Degree awarded from Clare College, Cambridge University. Engagement announcement for Patrick, eldest son of the late Mr R.N. Barber, The Whitehouse, Bidborough, Tunbridge Wells.

Barritt, Clifton Charles Joseph (01/02/1938) Air Force Cross to Squadron Leader C.C.J. Barritt.

Barry, Nathaniel John Merriman (15/11/1938) Son of Richard and Gladys Barry of Cape Province in South Africa. In 1938 he travelled to England to enrol at Pembroke College, Cambridge, to study Mechanical Engineering. He joined the University Air Squadron and with the outbreak of war in September 1939 was called up as a member of the RAF Volunteer Reserve. On 7 October 1940, Barry was forced to take to his parachute when his Hurricane V6800 was shot down above Wrotham by Me109's. Although he was able to leave the aircraft and deploy his parachute, he was found dead at Wilmington, to the south of Dartford. Less than two miles to the east, his Hurricane crashed in flames at Lane End in Darenth. Whether he was struck by a shell before baling out, or subsequently, is not known. He was twenty-two.

Beard, John Henry Cyril (01/02/1938) Engagement announcement, Flying Officer John Henry Cyril Beard of 54, Scarsdale Villas, Kensington, only surviving son of Mr and Mrs J Cyril Beard, Linton, Ferndown, Dorset. Birth announcement – on 20 February 1940 at Bryn Eglwys, Newton, Glamorgan. To Barbara, wife of Flying Officer J.H.C. Beard RAFVR, a son.

Beddow, W.P. (02/08/1938) Took part in Fencing for the Polytechnic team.

Bednell, Richard Davenport (01/02/1938) A member of Midland Aero Club.

Bisdee, John (21/05/1939) Born into an ordinary old Somerset family on 13 November 1915. Educated at Marlborough College and then Corpus Christi, Oxford University. Became a management trainee with Unilever and joined the RAFVR. After the war he became Chairman of Faberge-Gibbs and arranged the first advert ever to be shown on ITV for Gibbs SR toothpaste. Died on 21 October 2000, aged 84.

Bjelke-Peterson, Harald Ridley (23/05/1939) German radio has stated that Flight Lieutenant H Bjelke-Peterson from the School of Physical Education in Sydney, is a prisoner of war. He completed a physical training course in Berlin just before the outbreak of war. He had also trained with the RAFVR and had gone to England early in 1938 to continue his physical education studies. In addition to going to Germany, he had been in charge of a physical training camp for public schools in England and had won a physical education scholarship. Before the start of the war he did a special course with the RAFVR and was assigned to Bomber Command and had commanded a bomber with a crew of an Australian, a Canadian, a New Zealander and an Englishman. He is single and 28 years of age.

Blackstone, Maurice Edward (31/05/1938) Reported as being a promising scrum half for Oakham College. Takes part in RAF squash tournament. Kings commendation for valuable service in the air awarded to M.E. Blackstone DFC.

Body, John (11/06/1939) Pilot Officer John Body, who was 26-years-old, was the eldest son of Mr and Mrs T.M. Body of Middlesbrough. He was called to the Bar by the Inner Temple in November 1937, and practiced on the Western Circuit.

Bourne, James Hugh (16/11/1937) Attended Stowe School. Degree in Geography from Christchurch College, Oxford University. Marriage announcement on 3 April 1941 at Salisbury, South Rhodesia. On 22 March 1945 at The Acland Home, Oxford to Seymour, wife of Flight Lieutenant J.H. Bourne RAFVR – a son.

Bowes, Robert Lawrence (01/02/1938) Engagement announcement for Robert Lawrence Bowes, 5, Berkley Mews, W1.

Boyd, Archibald Douglas McNeill (18/10/1938) Engagement announcement for Pilot Officer Archibald Douglas McNeill Boyd RAFVR, elder son of Mr and Mrs A.J. Boyd of The Grange, Hook Heath, Woking.

Brackenridge, Gilbert Keith (01/02/1938) Cross country running for L Powell, Sons & Co.

Braham, David Frederick (18/10/1938) Rows and attends St Pauls School. Rows and attends Jesus College, Oxford University. Degree awarded from Oxford University.

Branson, John Peter Leslie (23/08/1938) Attended the third annual dinner of the University of London Air Squadron.

Brayne, Robert Cyril Lugard (07/02/1939) Attended Eton. Attended Oxford University. The engagement is announced for Robert Cyril Lugard Brayne, only son of Lieutenant Colonel W.F. Brayne (Indian Medical Service Retired) and Mrs Brayne, Kericho, Kenya.

Briginshaw, Oswald O'Neill (07/12/1937) Attended St Catherine's College, Cambridge University.

Britton, Allan Walter Naylor (23/11/1937) Attended Trinity College, Cambridge University. £100 entrance scholarship for classics awarded. Awarded second year scholarship.

Brock, Arthur Thomas (15/03/1938) Attended Queens College, Cambridge University. Squadron Leader A.T. Brock awarded DFC.

Brodie, A.R. (02/08/1938) Flying Officer A.R. Brodie RAFVR – DFC.

Browning, Neville Morgan (19/04/1938) Commanding Officer of 531 Squadron between October 1942 and January 1943. Attended New College, Oxford University. Swam for New College.

Bruce, Kenneth Douglas (29/03/1938) First class honours degree from Queen Mary College, London. Squadron Leader K.D. Bruce, pilot 48 Squadron was killed on 11 April 1942.

Burnett, Norman Whilmore (01/02/1938) Called up on 1 September 1939, he was with 266 Squadron at Wittering in June 1940. On 25 July he was posted to 46 Squadron at Digby. He crashed at Hollingbourne on 8 September following a combat over Sheppey. Admitted to hospital wounded having written off his plane. Following his recovery he re-joined 46 Squadron and sailed for the Middle East in the aircraft carrier HMS *Argus*. In Gibraltar the pilots and aircraft were transferred to the carriers HMS *Ark Royal* and *Furious*. On 6 June 1946 the squadron flew off to Halfar, Malta. Five days later he was flying Hurricane Z2480, when he was shot down by an MC200. A search to within sight of the coast of Sicily failed to find any trace of him. He is commemorated on the Malta Memorial.

Bury, Davis Stuart Harold (21/12/1937) Rowed for Eton. Studied Classics at Trinity College Cambridge University. Degree awarded. Killed in Action – Obituary.

Campbell, Kenneth (23/08/1938) Educated at Sedburgh School and then Clare College, Cambridge University. He was a member of the University Air Squadron. He was posthumously awarded the Victoria Cross as a flight lieutenant for an attack which damaged the German battlecruiser *Gneisenau* moored in Brest, France.

Carter, John Nemours (06/09/1938) Born 20 June 1920. Left Dulwich to go to the Royal College of Science with a view to taking a three year course in engineering for the BSc degree. He joined the University Air Squadron and subsequently the RAFVR. He was posted to the East Coast Command and stationed at Newmarket. Returning from a 'leaflet' flight with very bad weather with fog and no visibility his plane crashed in Suffolk and he and all the crew were killed on 3 March 1940.

Carter, Mark Medley (01/02/1938) Engagement announcement between Mr Mark Medley Carter, son of Mr and Mrs E.P. Carter of 6, Parkside Gardens, Wimbledon, SW19. Description and notice of marriage taking place. Flight Lieutenant M.M. Carter of No 3 Squadron was killed on 15 May 1940 when he was shot down in Hurricane N2534 near Vouzieries. He was 27-years-old.

Carter, Thomas Christopher (16/11/1937) Degree awarded from Corpus Christi College, Cambridge University.

Carver, John Champion (16/08/1938) Attended Christ Church College, Oxford University. Reported missing from operations, June 1942, Squadron Leader J.C. Carver RAFVR, third son of the late S.R.P. Carver.

Cazalet, Alexander Brise Travers (28/06/1938) Born in 1913, Flying Officer Alexander Brise Travers Cazalet was killed on 9 September 1940.

APPENDIX 2

Chase, Frederic John Alliston (26/04/1938) Rows for Sidney Sussex College, Oxford University. Rows for Sidney Sussex College in the Henley Royal Regatta. Engagement announcement for F.J.A. Chase, eldest son of Reverend F.A. and Mrs Chase of The Vicarage, North Walsham, Norfolk. DFC awarded. Announcement from Rugby School welcoming back five members of staff who have been on war service and who have returned to teach, F.J.A. Chase is one of them. Promoted to House Master of Stanley House, Rugby School.

Cheshire, Geoffrey Leonard (16/11/1937) School Scholarship from Stowe School. Permanent commission in RAF and relinquishes his commission in RAFVR. DSO awarded. VC awarded.

Chopping, Ralph Campbell (01/02/1938) Awarded £30 scholarship for Modern History at Charterhouse School. Attended Queens College, Oxford University. Squadron Leader Ralph C Chopping, age 29, missing from 7 Squadron operation over Brest.

Clark, H.A. (10/03/1939) Degree awarded Peterhouse College, Cambridge University. DSO awarded to Wing Commander H.A. Clark DFC.

Clarke, Thomas Hughes (15/08/1939) A marriage has been arranged for Squadron Leader Thomas Hughes Clarke RAFVR, second son of Mr and Mrs C.S. Clarke of Tracy Park, Wick, Gloustershire.

Clementi, Cresswell Montague (18/10/1938) Runs for Winchester College. Runs for Magdalen College, Oxford University.

Coates, John Arthur Gordon (15/08/1939) Born in 1920, he was educated at Wellington College and Trinity College, Cambridge University, where he read mechanical sciences and joined the University Air Squadron. Joined the RAFVR and awarded the DFC. In 1946 he began working as a manager at ICI, he was also the British delegate to the International Labour Organisation, one part of the United Nations. He was awarded the CBE in 1980 and died on 16 July 2009, aged 88.

Cobbe, Alexander William Locke (27/09/1938) Attended Winchester College and rowed for their team. Still in rowing team. Deaths – Cobbe – in steadfast love and proud memory, Bill (Flying Officer A.W.L. Cobbe RAFVR) missing, officially presumed killed in flying operations against the enemy on 8 September 1940. Same announcement in 1944.

Coleman, L.W. (03/01/1939) Named in Pembroke College, Cambridge University tripos June 1937 and June 1938. DFC awarded to Flight Lieutenant L.W. Coleman RAFVR. Bar to the DFC awarded to Flight Lieutenant L.W. Coleman RAFVR.

Coles, Denys Geoffrey Graeme (08/11/1938) Attended Clifton College and was a part of their rugby team. Played rugby for Trinity College, Oxford University. Obituary – Flying Officer D.G.G. Coles, missing now presumed killed. Eldest son of Major and Mrs D.F.P. Coles of Little Begbrook, Frenchay, Bristol. Educated at The Dragon School, Oxford and at Clifton College, which he represented them at rugby and boxing for two years. In 1936 he went to Trinity College, Oxford University, and played rugby there too. He was a member of the Oxford University Air Squadron.

Cooke, Kenneth Crossley (24/05/1938) Flying Officer, Kenneth Crossley, 62 Squadron RAFVR, killed in action on Royal Air Force Volunteer Reserve, 8 December 1941. Age 31. Son of Crossley and Muriel Cooke, husband of Veronica Mary Cooke, of Cobham, Surrey.

Corbett, Hugh Christopher (18/10/1938) Plays rugby for Stowe School. Obituary – Flying Officer Hugh Christopher Corbett killed on active service, was the elder son of the late Mr Adrian Corbett and Mrs Corbett of Tiddington House, Oxford. He was 22 years of age.

Cragg, Francis Talbot (18/11/1938) Attended Uppingham School, where he took part in athletic events. Also plays rugby for the school. Attended Cambridge University and runs for them. Marriage announcement in *The Times*.

Crompton, Philipp Richardson (05/04/1938) Attended Charterhouse School and took part in many different sporting activities including athletics, rugby, association football and cricket. Mentioned in several editions of *The Times* during 1933, 1934 1935 until October 1936. Received a scholarship for mathematics for Brasenose College, Oxford University, and again takes part in several different sporting events up until 1938. Marriage announcement for Flying Officer P.R. Crompton, son of Mr and Mrs Ralph Crompton of Betton Hall, Market Draydon. In September 1942 he was detailed to take part in an attack on Dussledorf. After crossing the Dutch coast he was attacked by a hostile aircraft which secured many hits. Despite his badly damaged bomber, Squadron Leader Crompton proceeded to the target, bombed it and flew safely back to base. Received Bar to DFC. Rode with Cheshire Forest Polo Team in Cheltenham Cup.

Crossman, Thomas Edward Stafford (28/12/1937) Plays rugby for Woodford School. Degree awarded from Christ Church College, Oxford University. Obituary – Flying Officer T.E.S. Crossman, youngest son of the Hon Mr Justice and Lady Crossman, lost his life last month on active service. He was 22 years of age.

Crowley-Milling, Denis (04/05/1937) Born in Rhyl, North Wales, on 22 March 1919, educated at Malvern College before leaving school and joining Rolls-Royce as an apprentice Aero-engineer. He learned to fly at weekends as a member of the RAFVR. He was awarded the DFC in 1941, and subsequently, the Bar to his DFC in 1942. He was also awarded the DSO in 1943. After the war he was the AOC Hong Kong in the 1960s, and from 1967-1970 he was the Principal Air Attaché in Washington. He had two group commands in the early 1970s, before taking up his final appointment in Turkey as the British Representative on the Permanent Military Deputies Committee of the Central Treaty Organisation. When he retired he was the Controller of the RAF Benevolent Fund. Appointed CBE in 1963 and KCB in 1973. He died on 1 December 1996, aged 77.

Cubitt, Eaton Geoffrey (27/09/1938) Plays rugby for Eton College. Degree awarded from New College, Oxford University. Memorial service held for those from New College, Oxford University who had lost their lives in the war.

D'Arcy-Irvine, Brian William Jesse (25/10/1938) Attended Stowe School. Attended Trinity College, Cambridge University.

Dacre, Kenneth Fraser (02/02/1941) Born 1 April 1922, the son of Air Commodore G.B. Dacre and Group Officer E.F. Dacre WAAF. He was educated in Chillon College Switzerland and Clare College, Cambridge University. Joined the University Air Squadron and the RAFVR in 1941. He was reported missing in September 1943 as a result of operations over north-west Germany. He was awarded the DFC in October 1943. He was presumed to have lost his life.

Davidson, John Peter Archibald (01/02/1938) Awarded a scholarship in law at St John's College Cambridge University. Elected for the McMahon Law Scholarship at Cambridge University. Bar examination Class II.

Davie, William Douglas Bow Symington (27/09/1938) Degree awarded from Trinity College, Cambridge University.

Davis, Peter Brian Newsom (01/02/1938) Degree awarded Trinity College, Cambridge University. Engagement announcement for Wing Commander P.B.N. Davis DSO, RAFVR, fourth and youngest son of the late Harold Newsom Davis of Bamville Wood, Harpenden Common. Obituary – Previously reported missing now known to be killed in action on 19 September 1944, whilst on a re-supply mission to the 1st Airborne Division, Arnhem, Wing Commander Peter Brian Newsom Davis DSO, fourth beloved son of the late H Newsom Davis and of Mrs Newsom Davis of Bamville Wood, Harpenden Common, Hertfordshire and dearly loved fiancé to Sheila Staveacre.

De Laszio, John Adolphus (21/09/1937) Born on 20 October 1912, he was the youngest son of Philip Alexius De Laszio. He was educated at Kings Mead Preparatory School, Seaford, Sussex, Lancing College and Balliol College, Oxford University. He served with the RAF during the Second World War, leading the French Section of the Air Ministry in Paris, from 1940 until 1943. Then he moved to the Special Operations Executive, co-ordinating support for the French Resistance, later being awarded the Croix de Guerre (with Palm) and the Légion d'Honneur. He also served with the S.O.E. in India and Ceylon, then moved to Norway to work with the Norwegian Air Force, receiving the Haakon Freedom Cross after Norway's liberation. After the war he went into business in South America and worked later as a stockbroker in London.

Debenham, Archibald Ian Scott (01/02/1938) DFC awarded to Squadron Leader A.I.S. Debenham RAFVR. "Making money work. Weekend courses for business men. Are you on the way up? You will benefit from one of these successful courses on basic financial practice. Make money work, one fee including hotel, 25 guineas. Vacancies 14-16 October and 4-6 November. Details from A.I.S. Debenham MA, MABIM, 6, Stratton Street, London W1." Marriage took place for Miss Marye Debenham, youngest daughter of Mr and The Hon Mrs A.I.S. Debenham of Lingfield, Surry. The reception was at Claridges.

Denby, Gordon Alfred (02/08/1938) Born in Chingford in 1915, he was the second son of Mrs Helen Denby of 41, Burbage Road, Herne Hill, SE24. He enlisted in the RAFVR in 1938 as a pilot under training. He was awarded the DFC in April 1941. He was reported missing in December 1942, and now presumed to have lost his life.

Born on 27 February 1915, he attended Dulwich College from 1928-1932, and then went on to work for the Imperial Tobacco Company and later Roneo Ltd. He was killed on 10 December 1942 when his plane suffered an engine fail and the aircraft came down in the sea 110 miles east of Peterhead.

Deville, Eric (26/07/1938) Rows for Christ's College, Cambridge University. Flying Officer E Deville reported missing.

DeWar, John Michael Firth (04/10/1938) Attended Rugby School. Attended Trinity College, Cambridge University.

Dey, Denis Herbert (01/02/1938) Flight Lieutenant Denis Herbert Dey, Royal Air Force Volunteer Reserve. He died on 6 October 1941, aged 27. He was the son of Dr Alexander Dey, M.B.E. and Eva Mary Dey and is buried in Kiltearn Parish Churchyard, Ross and Cromarty.

Disney, Hugh Anthony Shipley (08/03/1938) Attended Winchester College. Attended Brasenose College, Oxford University. Degree awarded. Engagement announcement for Acting Squadron Leader H.A.S. Disney RAFVR, second son of Wing Commander and Mrs H.A.P. Disney of Chorleywood. Births – on 25 February 1945 at Westminster Hospital, to Eira, wife of Wing Commander H.A.S. Disney RAFVR – a daughter (Sarah Wynn). Births – On 11 August 1947 at Westminster Hospital, to Eira, wife of Wing Commander H.A.S. Disney – a sister for Sarah (Anna Jane). Births – On 19 June 1950, to Eira, wife of Squadron Leader H.A.S. Disney of RAF Pembroke Dock, South Wales – a daughter. Births – On 21 September 1956 at Queen Charlottes Hospital, Goldhawk Road, W6, to Eira, wife of Wing Commander H.A.S. Disney of Stocking Corner, Naphill, High Wycombe – a son. Engagement announcement for Sarah Wynn, eldest daughter of Group Captain H.A.S. Disney, Cross Lane House, West Mersea, Essex. Engagement announcement for Anna, second daughter of Group Captain H.A.S. Disney of Greek House, West Mersea, Essex. Engagement announcement for Patrick, only son of Group Captain H.A.S. Disney of Cumnor, Oxfordshire.

Donaldson, David William (01/02/1938) Rows for Trinity College, Cambridge University at Henley Regatta. Cambridge University Law Tripos. Rows for Cambridge throughout 1935. Law degree conferred. Law Society exam results. Engagement announcement Flight Lieutenant D.W. Donaldson, second son of Mr and Mrs Thornycroft Donaldson of Southampton. Account of the wedding taking place. RAF Bomber Command with 149 Squadron (Sept 1940-Mar 1941), No 57 Squadron (Sept-Dec 1941), No 15 Squadron OUT (July 1942-Jan 1943), 156 Squadron (Jan-June 1943), 192 Squadron (June 1944-end of tour). Awarded DFC for his role in the raid on Merignac Aerodrome near Bordeux (Nov 1940). DSO announcement. Final law exam results. Taken into partnership with Messrs Parker, Garrett and Co. Appointed Secretary of National Employers Life Assurance. Appointed Secretary of National Employers Mutual General Insurance Association.

Douch, Alfred John (25/10/1938) Attended Jesus College, Oxford University. Births – On 26 October 1946, to Jean, wife of Wing Commander A.J. Douch RAFVR a daughter (Elizabeth Joan). Wing Commander A.J. Douch as Officer

APPENDIX 2

Commanding Oxford University Air Squadron. Engagement announcement for Elizabeth, youngest daughter of Wing Commander A.J. Douch.

Doughty, Neville Anthony Richard (13/09/1938) Squadron Leader Neville Anthony Richard Doughty was born in Raynes Park, London on the 5 April 1919, he lived at The Wick, Burton Road, Bournemouth with his parents until attending Douai Boarding School at Woolhampton, Berks, between 1930 and 1933, and Caterham School, Surrey, between 1934 until 1936 when he gained a place at University College, Gower Street, London. He became interested in flying and joined the University of London Air Squadron.

Douglas, Alfred Graham (01/02/1938) Mechanical Sciences Tripos, Trinity College, Cambridge University. Came second in the Stramongate Kendle 4 mile cross country race. Forthcoming marriage announcement for Mr A.G. Douglas, son of Mr and Mrs A Douglas of Ham House, South Nufield, Surrey. Previously reported missing, now presumed killed in action, Flying Officer A.G. Douglas.

Dyke, Norman Ball (04/07/1939) Member of University of London Air Squadron.

Falla, W.A.S. (09/11/1937) Awarded a diploma in psychological medicine by the Royal College of Surgeons. Dr W.A.S. Falla, medical superintendent at Bracebridge Heath Mental Hospital, Lincoln.

Fellowes, Michael Peregrine (14/12/1937) Marriage announcement – Squadron Leader Michael Peregrine Fellowes DSO, DFC, only son of Air Commodore Peregrine F.M. Fellowes, DSO, DFC.

Fisher, Basil Mark (26/07/1938) Born on 8 October 1916. Attended Eton College. Keeper of the Wall and Keeper of Fires at Eton. Attended Trinity College, Cambridge University, reading Modern Languages and History. Killed in action 15 August 1940. Funeral for Flying Officer B.M. Fisher RAFVR held in Eton College Chapel. In Memorium announcement – in proud memory of Flying Officer Basil Mark Fisher, from his brother Anthony. In *The Times* for 1942 also.

Formby, Myles Lonsdale (01/02/1938) Plays lacrosse for Magdalen College, Oxford University. Degree awarded at Oxford University. Engagement announcement for Myles Lonsdale, only son of the late Captain M.L. Formby of Goring-on-Thames. Marriage took place announcement. Wing Commander M.L. Formby posted to RAF Wittering.

Foster, William Bernard (4/01/1938) Played cricket for Winchester School. Moves to Christchurch College Oxford University.

Fox, Seth Allen (01/11/1938) Attended Lancing School and was part of their athletics team. Attended Worcester College, Oxford University. Part of Oxford University athletics team. Degree awarded. Engagement announcement for Seth Allen, only child of Mr and Mrs P.S. Fox of Prittlewell, Essex.

Franklin, John William (01/02/1938) Engagement announcement for Flight Lieutenant John William Franklin RAFVR, only son of Mr William E Franklin of 1, Great North Road, Stevenage, Hertfordshire.

Fraser, Joseph Frederick (01/02/1938) Played rugby for Malvern College. Plays rugby for Pembroke College, Cambridge University. First Tripos list Fraser J.F. Class II. Marriage announcement on 8 August 1940 at Maadi, Egypt, Flying Officer J.F. Frazer, son of Mr and Mrs F.H. Fraser of Millfield, East Grinstead, Sussex and Ceylon. Births – on 8 February 1945 at 11, Elms Road, Harrow Weald, to Anita, wife of Wing Commander J.F. Fraser, a brother for Patricia.

French, Frank John (29/03/1938) DFC awarded. Promoted from squadron leader to wing commander. Wing Commander F.J. French to RAF Colerne to command Administrative Wing.

Fry, Anthony Ellerton Ryan (19/04/1938) Born in South Africa, but when war was declared he was living in Denmark. He was recalled to join the RAFVR having learned to fly whilst attending London University as an Engineering student. DFC awarded 1941. Played rugby and association football for London University between 1936 and 1938.

Gardiner, Frederick Thomas (22/02/1938) Attended Trinity College, Cambridge University. Joined 610 Squadron in July 1940 and was wounded in the arm on 25 July 1940 over the Channel. Managed to safely land his aircraft. On 25 August 1940 he bailed out of his Spitfire over Dover and suffered slight wounds. He was awarded the DFC on 10 March 1944. Commanded 621 Squadron from December 1944 to November 1945. Wing Commander Frederick Thomas Gardiner DFC died on 2 November 2003.

Gardner, E.C. (03/01/1939) Attended St Edmunds School, Canterbury, and Jesus College, Cambridge University, being awarded a scholarship for maths. Degree awarded.

Gething, Philip Allistone (01/02/1938) Malvern student awarded a scholarship at Corpus Christi College, Cambridge University. Came second representing Corpus Christi College in intercollege athletics. Was awarded the Caldwell Scholarship. Engagement announcement for P.A. Gething, younger son of Mr and Mrs G.A. Gething of Wilmslow, Cheshire.

Gibbins, Ivor Dennis Harden (04/07/1939) Attended the funeral of Air Chief Marshall Sir James Robb, representing the AOC in C Coastal Command, Air Officer Commanding No 19 Group.

Giddins, John Gordon (11/07/1939) Attended Lancing public school. Attended Jesus College, Oxford University.

Goddard, Henry Gordon (01/02/1939) Engagement announcement between H.G. Goddard,, son of Mr and Mrs H.L. Goddard of Newton Harcourt Manor, Leicester. H.G. Goddard awarded degree at Oxford University. Report on marriage.

Goldsmith, Claude Waller (29/03/1938) Cheltenham school sports. Takes part in several sporting events for Cheltenham College, including rugby and athletics. Took part in Henley Royal Regatta as a member of the Imperial College boat club. Attends University of London Air Squadron dinner. Also takes part in Richmond Regatta. C.W. Goldsmith of South African origin, served in 603 and 54 Squadron, killed in action.

Gosling, Ernest Leslie (01/02/1939) Attended Leyton County High School and gained scholarship for Cambridge University in Engineering.

Graham, Derek Ian (16/11/1937) Obituary – Attended Eton and Oxford University.

Gray, Robert (04/01/1938) Death announcement – in October 1942, Squadron Leader Robert Gray, adored husband of Elizabeth Mary and darling elder son of Dr and Mrs Gray of Yew Tree, Malling, Kent.

Green, Jack Raymond (01/11/1938) Engagement announcement between Jack Raymond Green of St Johns College, Oxford University, third son of Mr and Mrs T Green of Hobart, Tasmania.

Greenhalgh, Geoffrey Taylor (01/02/1938) British European Flight Captain of BEA Viscount 800.

Griffiths, Joseph Walker (20/12/1938) Attended Westminster School.

Hancock, Ernest Lindsay (14/06/1938) Attended Lincoln College, Oxford University. Runs for Lincoln College. Runs in 440 yards race in 1937.

Hartley, Christopher Harold (02/09/1938) Attended Eton and was a member of the rowing team. Attends Balliol College, Oxford University. Degree awarded. DFC awarded to Group Captain C.H. Hartley AFC RAFVR.

Hayns, Geoffrey Uffindell (01/02/1938) Rowed in Clinker Fours at Cambridge University. Degree awarded from Queens College, Cambridge University.

Heath, Barry (26/07/1938) Barry Heath, DFC AE was born on 11 September 1916. He was a Spitfire pilot who flew in the Battle of Britain and was awarded the DFC. After the war he had a successful career in industry, rising to become chairman of the industrial conglomerate GKN. In 1978 he received a knighthood for services to export.

Hibberd, William Henry Alan (01/02/1938) Engagement announcement for Josephine Sandra, eldest daughter of Mr and Mrs W.H.A. Hibberd of Brookside, Kilmington, Devon.

Higgins, Charles Gauntlett (19/04/1938) On 21 July 1945, at Chakrata, India, Wing Commander Charles Gauntlett Higgins, beloved son of Beatrice and the late George Higgins of Upton Court, South Yarra.

Hill, James Jewill (16/11/1937) Deaths – on 11 April 1946, James Jewill Hill, Polwithen, Penzance, beloved husband of Laura, devoted father of Laura, Paull and Jim. Memorium – in loving and ever present memory of Flying Officer James Jewill Hill RAFVR BA Oxford, lost returning from Germany 29-30 October 1940. Marriage announcement for Paull Jewill Hill, elder son of the late James Jewill Hill of Polwithan, Penzance. Marriage took place notice.

Hill, Michael Rowland (18/10/1938) Squadron Leader M.R. Hill reported missing.

Hildyard, David Henry Thoroton (19/04/1938) Born on 4 May 1916, the son of a distinguished QC. Toby, as he was known, went to Eton, where he played cricket, and then to Christ Church College, Oxford University. He was also a member of the University Air Squadron. Engagement announcement for Wing Commander David Henry Thoroton Hildyard DFC, younger son of His Honour G.M.T. Hildyard KC and Mrs Hildyard of Flintham Hall, Newark, Nottinghamshire. He was invested as a Knight Commander, Order of St. Michael and St. George (K.C.M.G.). He was decorated with the award of the Distinguished Flying Cross (DFC) in 1943. He held the office of Ambassador to Chile between 1970 and 1973. He held the office of Ambassador to the United Nations, Geneva between 1973 and 1976.

Hillary, Richard Hope (18/10/1939) Born on 20 April 1919 in Sydney, Australia. His father was an Australian government official. Richard was educated in England at Shrewsbury School, and then Trinity College, Oxford University, where he was president of the rowing club and a member of the Oxford University Air Squadron. Having completed his training he moved, along with the rest of the squadron, to RAF Hornchurch on 27 August 1940. On 3 September 1940 he was shot down by a Messerschmitt Bf 109, and, unable to escape from his burning aircraft, he suffered extensive burns to his face and hands. Having eventually managed to escape the aircraft, he was eventually picked up by the Margate lifeboat from the North Sea. He endured three months of surgery in an attempt to repair the damage to his face and hands so that he was able to return to flying. He returned to service with No 54 Operational Training Unit at RAF Chartwell. He died on 8 January 1943 alongside his radio operator when he crashed his Bristol Blenheim during a night training flight. He was 23. He is remembered by his book *The Last Enemy*, in which he has written about his experiences as a Spitfire pilot. Obituary in *The Times*.

Hinnitt, Clifford Spencer (20/09/1938) Member of University of London Air Squadron.

Holden, John James (06/12/1938) Rows for Clare College, Cambridge University.

Holderness, John Browning (28/06/1938) John Browning Holderness was born in Rhodesia, the son of an English lawyer who emigrated from Yorkshire in 1902. Three years later Mr. Holderness became a partner in a law practice started by Sir Thomas Scanlen in Salisbury, Rhodesia in 1896. Although holding a law qualification, Holderness was commissioned in the Air Section of the Permanent Staff Corps of Southern Rhodesia. He transferred in May 1938 and went on attachment to the RAFVR. He joined 248 Squadron at Hendon when it was reformed there on 30 October 1939. In August 1940 Holderness was posted to 1 Squadron at Tangmere. He shared in the destruction of an Me110 on 7 September. He moved to 229 Squadron at Northolt on 17 October and was posted away in December 1940. After rejoining the Southern Rhodesian Forces on 26 August 1945, Holderness went back to Rhodesia and farmed until 1971. He then sold his farm and returned to the family law business. Holderness was killed in a road traffic accident near his home in South Africa on 15 April 2008, aged 96.

Hole, Kenneth William (01/02/1938) Took part in the Monte Carlo Rally and wrapped his Singer around a lamp post in Brussels. He then had to pawn the wreckage to enable him to get a train to Monte Carlo.

APPENDIX 2

Holland-Martin, Cyril George (01/02/1938) Born on 23 April 1902, he was educated at Eton and Christ Church Oxford. He was involved with ocean racing for over 50 years taking part in all the United Kingdom ocean races, including the Fastnet, as well as the Bermuda race. He learned to fly whilst at Oxford and owned his own plane. Engagement announcement for C.G. Holland-Martin, son of Mr and Mrs Robert M Holland-Martin of Overbury Court, Tewkesbury. Director of Overbury Estates Company Ltd. Director of British Tabulating Machine Company. Involved in the setting up of European Computer Manufacturers Association and became its first president. Retired from the board of International Computers and Tabulators.

Hopkinson, Richard Adrian (01/02/1938) Attended Oxford University. Engineering degree awarded. Obituary notes that he was reported missing in air operations over Norway in July 1940 and is now presumed dead. Youngest son of Mr and Mrs Martin Hopkinson of Bovingdon, Herts and grandson of the late Sir Alfred Hopkinson KC. Educated at Berkhamsted and University College, Oxford. He was a member of the Air Squadron having already obtained his Civil Pilots Certificate at the age of 19. On leaving Oxford he joined his uncles engineering works. He joined the RAFVR in 1938 and, at the start of the war he was working on aeronautics for the Rolls-Royce Company at Derby. He was 24-years-old.

Howell, Cecil Moreton (01/02/1938) Attended Trowbridge County High School and won a college award.

Hughes, Edward Gordon (04/07/1939) Attends Queens College, Cambridge University. Flying Officer E.G. Hughes RAFVR awarded DFC. Squadron Leader E.G. Hughes RAFVR awarded DSO. Engagement announcement for Wing Commander Gordon Hughes, DSO, DFC, youngest son of Mr A.J. Hughes, OBE, of Pages, Chigwell Row.

Hutchinson, Louis Gordon Oliphant (29/03/1938) Flying Officer Gordon Oliphant Hutchison was the son of Alexander Hutchinson. He married Edith Mary Ursula Maclure on 2 September 1939. He died on 4 January 1959.

Ingle, Alec (21/05/1937) Born on 15 February 1916 in Louth, Lincolnshire, he was educated at Pocklington School in Yorkshire. He then worked in the electricity industry in Yorkshire and Lancashire. Joined the RAFVR in 1937 to get flying experience. Very badly burned in September 1943, after his plane was shot down over Northern France and he was unable to get out. After he had recovered he was sent to a POW camp, Stalag Luft III, in Silesia. After the war he was a very keen yachtsman. He died on 5 June 1999, aged 83.

Inkster, James Fraser (01/02/1938) Commanding Officer of 515 Squadron from July 1943 to January 1944 in the rank of Wing Commander.

Ivey, Leslie William (01/02/1938) Attended the University of London Air Squadron service dinner. Passed Institute of Auctioneers and Estate Agents exams.

Jackson, Sidney Packwood (01/02/1938) Air Force Cross awarded to Squadron Leader S.P. Jackson.

James, Alfred William Douglas (03/05/1938) Attended Magdalen College, Oxford University. Engagement announcement for Squadron Leader A.W.D. James, only son of Rev T.W. Douglas and Mrs James of The Hollies, Bickley. Birth announcement – on 12 January 1940, at Woking Maternity Home, to Janet, wife of Wing Commander A.W.D. James DFC, British Military Administration, Malaya, twins (a son and a daughter). A.W.D. James writes a letter entitled, "The Right to Observe" to the Editor of *The Times*. Daughter's engagement announcement.

Jebb, Michael (20/09/1938) Studied and degree awarded from Trinity College, Cambridge University.

Jenkins, John Fraser Grant (06/12/1938) Attended Harrow. Attended Peterhouse College, Cambridge University.

Jewitt, George Percival (01/02/1938) Decree Absolute given by Mr Justice Henn Collins.

Johnston, George Herbert Arthur McGarel (04/01/1938) Born on 2 September 1916 in South Africa. He attended Cheltenham College and took part in a public schools expedition to Newfoundland. He went to Cambridge University and joined the University Air Squadron in 1937. In 1938 he was commissioned into the RAFVR. He was awarded a DFC in late 1942, and a DSO and Bar to his DFC in late 1944. After the war he left the United Kingdom to return to South Africa and lived there until his death in 1992.

Jones, Ben Everton (16/08/1938) Engagement announced for Pilot Officer Ben Everton Jones of 20, Margaretta Terrace, Chelsea. Births – on 1 November 1949 at Westminster Hospital, to Jean and Wing Commander Ben Everton Jones, 24, Woodcrest Road, Purley, a brother (Robin Michael) for Deborah.

Judd, Michael Thomas (16/11/1937) Born on 19 September 1917 at Scotney and was educated at Gresham's School, Holt, before going on to Wadham College, Oxford. He gained a good degree which led to the award of a Laming Travelling Fellowship at Queen's College. During his time at Oxford he had been commissioned into the RAFVR and trained as a pilot with the University Air Squadron. He was awarded a DFC in November 1942 and also was awarded the Air Efficiency Award. He left the RAF in 1945. After the war he set up home in Houston, Texas, where he established a partnership in oil exploration. He retired aged 82. He died in Houston on 22 August 2010. Birth – on 1 July 1944 at Winchester to Jean, wife of Wing Commander M.T. Judd DFC, AFC, a daughter.

Kay-Shuttleworth, Richard Ughtred Paul (24/01/1937) Attended Balliol College, Oxford University. Degree awarded.

Kempe, John William Rolfe (21/12/1937) Born in Nairobi, the son of an officer in the Colonial Service. He was brought up by his mother in Norfolk. Educated at Stowe School and Clare College Cambridge. Joined the University Air Squadron. In North Africa and Malta as well as with 602 Squadron. Demobilised in 1946 he was a teacher at Gordonstoun school before becoming a head teacher at a school in India. He also became head teacher at Gordonstoun. Marriage announcement for Squadron Leader J.W.R. Kempe.

Kershaw, John (25/10/1938) Death – in July 1940 during air operations Pilot Officer John Kershaw, the very dear second son of Harold and Pleasance Kershaw of Macclesfield, aged 22.

Kiralfy, Dennis Maurice Gerald (22/11/1938) Played water polo for Cambridge University. Flying Officer D.M.G. Kiralfy killed on active service.

Knight, Benjamin Edward (01/02/1938) Awarded degree at Cambridge University. Awarded MA at Cambridge University. On the night of 16 May 1944 a force of twenty-nine Mosquito's took off from RAF Oakington, Cambridgeshire to take part in an attack of Berlin. All aircraft returned safely, but on Mosquito M1988, the bomb doors opened in error as the plane tried to land. This resulted in a sudden loss of height and the aircraft crashed at 0254 into the trees at University Farm, Girton. Flying Officer Benjamin Edward Knight, son of Stephen Stoneham James and Amy Pricilla Knight, husband of Joyce Winifred Knight of Oxshott, Surrey, was killed in the crash, as were the full crew.

Knowles, Geoffrey Churton (09/11/1937) Engagement announcement for Squadron Leader Geoffrey Churton Knowles, eldest son of Mr and Mrs R Geoffrey Knowles of Limpsfield, Surrey.

Korndorffer, Jack (06/09/1938) Attended Kings College School in Wimbledon and played rugby for them. Attended Christ Church College, Oxford University and rows for them. Air Force Cross awarded to Squadron Leader J Korndorffer.

L'Estrange, Charles Henry Noel (01/02/1938) Attended the Royal Air Force Flying Club dinner. Honours degree awarded by Oxford University. Birth announcement on 26 May 1939 at Hampstead Nursing Home, to Theo, wife of C.H.N. L'Estrange, a son.

Landale, Peter Wellwood Fortune (04/07/1939) Attended Brasenose College, Oxford University.

Lang, William Laurie (10/05/1938) The marriage took place on Saturday at Christchurch Cathedral, Oxford, of Mr William Laurie Lang of Inglehome, Eccleston Park, Prescott, Lancashire, son of Mr and Mrs John Lang of Cleithaugh, Jedburgh, Roxburghshire.

Law, Robert Charles Ewan (21/02/1939) Attended Wrekin College and played rugby. Attended St Catherine's College, Cambridge University. Marriage announcement for Wing Commander R.C.E. Law DFC, RAFVR, younger son of Sir Charles and Lady Law of Bentworth Barnham, East Sussex. Births – on 12 August 1946 in Naples, to Norah, wife of Wing Commander R.C.E. Law DSO DFC, a son (Charles Ewan). Births – on 7 July 1949 to Norah, wife of Wing Commander R.C.E. Law DSO DFC, of Woodland Thatch, Bovingdon Green, Marlow – a son (Peter Ewan). Engagement announcement for Charles, elder son of Group Captain R.C.E. Law DSO DFC of Archery Fields, Bridge end, Warwick.

Engagement announcement for Peter Ewan, younger son of Group Captain R.C.E. Law DSO DFC, of Archery Fields, Bridge End, Warwick.

Lawrence, John Kempton (04/07/1939) Marriage announcement for John Kempton Lawrence of 12, St Charles Street, Mayfair. Births – on 13 June 1944 at Rubislaw Nursing Home, Aberdeen, to Eileen, wife of Squadron Leader J.K. Lawrence – a daughter.

Levy, G.S. (10/03/1939) Played lacrosse for Trinity College Cambridge University.

Lewis, David Curig (18/10/1938) Attended Shrewsbury School and Worchester College, Oxford University. Mr David Curig Lewis lost his life in an air collision near Sandwich, Kent between an aircraft of the Oxford University Air Squadron and one from the Bekesbourne Civil Flying School. He was the sole occupier of the RAF plane.

Liversidge, Harold (31/05/1938) Attended Trinity College, Cambridge University. Degree awarded from Trinity College.

Lofthouse, Charles Ward (01/02/1938) Charles Lofthouse was born on 26 September 1921 at Mountain Ash, Glamorgan. Lofthouse attended Kingsbury County School, London. After going on a scholarship to Harrow Art School, Lofthouse had difficulty finding a job in the aftermath of the depression, but eventually got work as an office boy with H.W. Dutton, the heating and ventilating engineers. He joined the RAFVR in 1940.

Longley, John Molony (05/07/1938) Attended Trinity College, Cambridge University. Engagement announcement for John Molony Longley, only surviving son of Major General Sir John R Longley KMCG CB and Lady Longley, Fouracre, Hartley, Witney. Birth announcement – on 3 September 1940 to Nancy, wife of Flight Lieutenant J.M. Longley RAFVR of Manor Cottage, Hanging Langford, Wiltshire – a daughter. Birth announcement – on 23 August 1944 at Old Sarum Nursing home, Salisbury, to Nancy, wife of Squadron Leader J.M. Longley RAFVR – a daughter. Birth Announcement – on 16 June 1946, at Fisherton de la Mere, Wiltshire to Nancy, wife of Squadron Leader J.M. Longley RAFVR – a son. Marriage announcement for Tessa, eldest daughter of Mr and Mrs J.M. Longley, The Old Rectory, West Knoyle, Wiltshire. Wedding report for Angela, youngest daughter of Mr and Mrs J.M. Longley, the Old Rectory, West Knoyle, Wiltshire. Engagement announcement for Matthew John Longley, only son of Mr and Mrs J.M. Longley of Ascot and Cap D'Agde, France.

Lowe, John Joseph (09/11/1938) Attended Gresham School and Queens College, Oxford University.

Lupton, Neville Lloyd (07/12/1937) Degree awarded from St John's College, Cambridge University.

MacAlister, John Edward, Seaton (01/02/1938) Attended St Pauls School, taking part in athletic events. Gained scholarship at Oxford to study modern history at Merton College. Took part in various swimming events throughout his time there. Death announcement – killed on 13 June 1940, aged 27.

APPENDIX 2

MacArthur, Malcolm Robert (25/10/1938) 25 April 1941. The King has been graciously pleased to approve the Distinguished Flying Cross to Flight Lieutenant Malcolm Robert MacArthur (70416), Royal Air Force Volunteer Reserve, 236 Squadron.

Mackie, Ian Neville William (9/08/1938) Engagement announced for Pilot Officer Ian Neville William Mackie RAFVR, only son of the late Captain and Mrs G.N. Mackie.

Magrath, Henry Morrison (19/07/1938) Attended Campbell College.

Marks, Michael John Colvile (29/11/1938) Plays football for Eton. Attended Christ Church College, Oxford University. Killed in action.

Marshall, Ronald Melville (28/06/1938) Attended Giggleswick School. Plays rugby for Trinity College Oxford University.

Martin, Cyril George Holland (01/02/1938) Attended Cranbrook School.

Martindale, Christopher Bernard (20/12/1938) Births – on 11 January 1946 at Chertsey Hill, Carlisle, to Kathleen, wife of C.B. Martindale, ARIBA Moor, Yeat, Wetheral, a sister for Christopher, Anne Catherine. Letter to *The Times* from Mr C.B. Martindale. His work was stated as J.H. Martindale and Son Architects, Bradwell House, Wolverhampton, Bucks. Further letter to *The Times*, same address.

Mason, Walter Ronald Price Knight (01/02/1938) Attended Exeter College, Oxford University. In memoriam – in proud and loving memory of Flying Officer, The Rev W.R.P.K. Mason RAFVR, missing 29 June 1940 and now presumed killed in action during bombing operations over Libya, younger son of Mrs Mason, Asgill lodge, Richmond and brother of Wing Commander N.W.F. Mason RAF. Message repeated in 1942.

Maw, Denys Mowbray (01/02/1938) Attended Queens College. Cambridge University. Awarded Air Force Cross.

McClure, Charles George Buchanan (01/02/1938) Rows for Trinity College, Oxford University at Henley Royal Regatta. Degree awarded from Oxford University. Engagement announcement, Squadron Leader C.G.B. McClure, only son of His Honour Judge McClure and Mrs G.B. McClure, The Garth, West Clandon, Surrey. Announcement of the wedding of Squadron Leader McClure. Air Force Cross awarded. Births – on 20 August 1946 at Woking Maternity Home, to Gay, wife of Wing Commander C.G.B. McClure AFC, a daughter. Engagement announcement for the daughter of Wing Commander C.G.B. McClure AFC, of The Shrubbery, Aspley Guise, Bletchley, Bucks. Wing Commander C.G.B. McClure MA, head of flight appointed to a personal chair in aeronautics, Cranfield Institute of technology.

McLannahan, George Goodhart (01/02/1938) Air Efficiency Award. 23 December 1940, posted to 93 Squadron for flying duties.

McNaught, George Wood (26/07/1938) University of London Law results for G.W. McNaught.

McNeill, Thomas Menzies (19/05/1939) Engagement announcement for Thomas Menzies McNeil OBE TD WS, son of the late Allan McNeil SSC and of Mrs McNeil, 26, Learmonth Terrace, Edinburgh. Flight Lieutenant T.M. McNeil attended the wedding of Lord Clysdale and Lady Elizabeth Percy.

Meads, Ernest Reginald (01/02/1939) DFC awarded to Squadron Leader E.R. Meads.

Miller, Charles Michael (23/08/1938) Death announcement – on 17 May 1992 at home, Eileen Deidre, beloved widow of Charles Michael Miller, DSO, DSC and Bars and adored mother of Joanna and Nigel. Reposted on 22 May.

Mitchell, Leicester John Cecil (01/02/1938) Was a member of London Aeroplane Club and took part in the 10 mile event – The Christchurch Sprint. Took part in the Hampshire Air Pageant in a Bristol Brownie. Came third in the London to Cardiff Air Race.

Moss, Brian Elwyn (16/11/1937) Played in the Oxford University Lacrosse team.

Newton, H.M. (01/02/1938) Attended Gresham School and Jesus College Cambridge University.

Nichols, Derek Alpin Douglas Lane (09/11/1937) Attended Magdalen College, Cambridge University. Engagement announcement for Miss J Nichols, only daughter of Mrs R.A. Nichols of East Horsley and of Mr D.A.D.L. Nichols of Woking. Marriage took place report. Engagement announcement for Gareth Lane, younger son of Mr D.A.D.L. Nichols of Woking.

Norris, Christopher Neil Foxley (24/01/1939) Attended Winchester College. Attended New College, Oxford University.

O'Malley, Derek Keppel Coleridge (01/11/1938) Rowed for Christ Church College, Oxford University. A member of the Inner Temple (Inns of court). Obituary – Flying Officer D.K.C. O'Malley attended Westminster School and Christ Church College, Oxford University, and at the Bar. An old member of the Oxford University Air Squadron. Engagement announcement for Stephen Keppel O'Malley, only son of the late D.K.C. O'Malley of 10, Royal Mansions, Henley on Thames.

Obolensky, Alexander (Prince) (24/05/1938) Played rugby for Trent College. Attended and played rugby for Brasenose College, Oxford University. Killed instantly in an aeroplane accident. He was a rugby international and a member of the English rugby team. Russian by birth, he became naturalised in 1936 and was given a commission in the RAFVR. He was a member of the Oxford University Air Squadron.

Ogilvie-Forbes, Malcolm Francis (01/02/1938) Births – on 30 June 1940 at College Farm, Upavon Wilts, to Fanchette, wife of M.F. Ogilvie-Forbes – a daughter. Christie's Auctioneers, Wednesday, 30 January, old English and foreign silver, the property of M.F. Ogilvie-Forbes.

Oldacres, Leonard John (01/02/1938) Born on 6 December 1916 in Chertsey, Surrey. Educated at Winchester College. Attended Christchurch College, Oxford University and took part in athletic events. He was a flying officer in the RAFVR and was based at Lille-Ronchin with No 4 Squadron when his plane was attacked and shot down at about 10 o'clock on 5 May 1940. He is buried at St Andre Communal Cemetery.

Ostlere, Edward (07/12/1937) Attended Glenalmond School. Deaths – in March 1941, killed on active service Flight Lieutenant Edward Ostlere RAFVR, dearly loved husband of Margaret Inkster of Kirkcaldy and only son of the late Mr Harold Ostlere and Mrs Ostlere, Marchmont, Kirkcaldy.

Parker, John Trevor Mauleverer (27/09/1938) Attended Eton and rowed for Trinity College, Cambridge University.

Parnell, Denis Geach (01/02/1938) Flight Lieutenant D.G. Parnell of 249 Squadron was killed on 18 September 1940. His Hurricane V6685 was shot down over Gravesend. He was 25-years-old and is buried at St Genny's in Cornwall.

Passy, Cyril Wolrich (16/11/1927) Awarded scholarship to Marlborough College. Awarded a scholarship to Cambridge University. Took part in the Cambridge University elections. Flying Officer C.W. Passy of 605 Squadron crash landed his Hurricane on 15 August 1940 after combat. Engagement announcement for Wing Commander C.W. Passy, OBE, DSO, son of Major and Mrs F.H.B. Passy, Blanchford, Cornwood, South Devon.

Pease, Arthur Peter (01/02/1938) Attended Eton College. Rows for Eton College. Attended Trinity College, Cambridge University. Funeral of Flying Officer Arthur Peter Pease, son of Sir Richard and Lady Pease of Prior House, Richmond, Yorkshire took place on Friday at Middleton-Tyas.

Pease, Ivor Edward (06/09/1938) Awarded degree from Magdalen College, Oxford University.

Percy, James Tate (01/02/1938) Flew civil aircraft for BOAC with the rank of Captain. Letter to *The Times* "towards Air Safety", written by J.T. Percy, Senior Pilot, British Overseas Airways Corporation. Letter to *The Times* "Safety in the Air" by J.T. Percy, Master, The Guild of Air Pilots and Navigators. Deaths – on 15 February, peacefully at Winscombe Nursing Home, Kingswood, Patricia Elizabeth, age 88, wife of the late James Tate Percy.

Phillips, Anthony Docray (09/08/1938) Attended Shrewsbury School. Played cricket at Shrewsbury School. Attended Magdalen College, Oxford University. Degree awarded at Magdalen College. Marriage announcement, son of Mr L.J. Phillips will take place in Singapore. DFC awarded to Flight Lieutenant A.D. Phillips. DSO awarded to Squadron Leader A.D. Phillips.

Phipps, Godfrey Fitzgerald (01/02/1938) Rowed for Brasenose College, Oxford University.

Pinckney, David John Colin (06/12/1938) Deaths – in 1942 reported missing believed killed during air operations in Burma, Flight Lieutenant D.J.C. (Colin) Pinkney RAFVR, aged 23.

Pollock, David Bertram (Viscount Hanworth) (16/11/1937) Born 1 August 1916 and educated at Wellington. Succeeded the title on 22 October 1936 on the death of his father. Graduated from Trinity College, Cambridge University.

Potter, Kenneth David (13/09/1938) Attended Forest School, London. Played rugby for Forest School. Attended Dover College and played rugby for them.

Powell, Geoffrey Frederic (01/02/1938) Degree awarded by Pembroke College, Oxford University. DFC awarded to Squadron Leader G.F. Powell. DSO awarded to Squadron Leader G.F. Powell.

Radbone, James Whaley (01/02/1938) Births, on 14 October 1939 at West End Nursing Home, Esher, to Betty, wife of Flying Officer J.W. Radbone – a son. Engagement announced between Mr Edward Barton Orr of Madras, India and Langland, Northwood, and Evelyn Betty, widow of Flight Lieutenant J.W. Radbone RAFVR.

Ratcliffe, George Brotherton (18/10/1938) Obituary in *The Times* – Born in Ealing on 2 January 1918, attended Harrow and then Balliol College, Oxford University. Active member of the Oxford University Air Squadron. Spent four years on the North West Frontier of India training Indian pilots to form the Indian Air Force. Went into business with his brother John. He was the chairman of the Brotherton Investment Trust and a founding director of Yorkshire Television. Chairman of Brotherton and Co a leading chemical manufacturer during the 1950s. Died on 13 May 1994 aged 76, leaving his wife, two sons and two daughters.

Rathbone, John Rankin (14/06/1938) Born in 1910, educated at Eton and Christchurch College, Oxford University. He rowed for Eton and Oxford University, and was also a member of the University Air Squadron. Married Miss Beatrice Frederika Clough and they had two children, a boy and a girl. Prospective Unionist MP for Cornwall. Became MP for Cornwall. Appointed by Colonel J.J. Llewellin, Civil Lord of the Admiralty as his Parliamentary Private Secretary. Obituary – Flying Officer J.R. Rathbone MP. We regret to state that Flying Officer J.R. Rathbone who was reported missing last month is now reported to have lost his life in operations against the enemy.

Rawlings, Colin Guy Champion (01/11/1938) Attended Charterhouse School and Queens College, Oxford University. Awarded DFC. Engagement announced for Colin Guy Champion Rawlings DFC of The Norman Chapel, Broad Camden, son of R.S.C. Rawlings of Gibraltar.

Rees, Patrick Elmore (01/02/1938) Air Navigator's Licence awarded by Air Ministry.

Reid, George Alfred (04/04/1939) Attended Uppingham School and University College, Oxford University.

APPENDIX 2

Rendle, Robert (19/04/1938) Engagement announcement for Mr Robert Rendle, eldest son of the late E.E. Rendle and Mrs Rendle of Bromley, Kent.

Rennie, Robert Stevenson (23/11/1937) Attended Worksop College and played rugby and cricket for them. Plays in Cambridge University cricket team. Passed exams for Chartered Insurance Institute. Marriage announcement.

Ricketts, H.H. (03/01/1939) Attended St John's College, Cambridge University.

Robins, Guy Herbert (01/02/1938) Played rugby in the match between Bromsgrove and Downside, as a half back.

Rogers, B.A. (01/02/1938) Attended Brentwood School. Attended Oxford University and in St Edmunds College. Rows for Oxford St Edmunds.

Ross, William Ronald (31/05/1938) On active service announcement – on 14 November 1939, killed as a result of a flying accident Pilot Officer William Ronald (Bill) Ross RAFVR, dearly loved only son of Lt Col and Mrs Harry Ross of 16, Grosvenor Place, SW1, age 27. Message repeated in 1941, 1943 and 1944.

Rylands, Joseph Edric (04/07/1939) Attended and played rugby for Bedford School. Marriage took place of Mr J Edric Rylands, nephew of Mr and Mrs W.B. Woodhouse.

Salusbury-Hughes, Kendrick Herbert (01/02/1938) In very proud memory of "Ken" – Squadron Leader K.H. Salusbury-Hughes RAFVR and his observer who did not return from night operations over Italy, 21 July 1943. Engagement announcement for the daughter of the late Squadron Leader K.H. Salusbury-Hughes.

Sandes, Terence Lindsay (27/09/1938) Engagement announced for Flight Lieutenant T.L. Sandes RAFVR, younger son of T Lindsay Sandes OBE, FRCS, MC and Mrs Sandes of South Africa. Awarded DFC. Engagement announcement for son, Neil also.

Sayer, Arthur John (1/02/1938) Engagement announced between Flying Officer Arthur John Sayer, younger son of Captain and Mrs J.A. Sayer of Sparham Hall, Norwich. Births – on 23 December 1940 at Claremont Nursing Home, Leeds, to Mabel, wife of Flight Lieutenant A.J. Sayer RAFVR – a daughter. In Memorial – sacred to the memory of Acting Squadron Leader Arthur John Sayer, beloved younger son of James and Margaret Sayer of Sparhum Hall, Norfolk – killed in action off the coast in Denmark on the night of 15 February 1944.

Sciortino, Bernard John (01/02/1938) Oxford University boat race crew 1936. Attended Oxford University. Took part in all rowing events for the university throughout 1935, 36, and 37. Obituary following death in an aeroplane accident in Kent.

Scott, William John Morr (01/02/1938) Played cricket for Clifton College. Attended the annual dinner of the Cambridge University Old Cliftonian Society.

Attended Corpus Christi College and awarded the Manners Scholarship. Cambridge University Golf Club competition and W.J.M. Scott came third. Killed 8 September 1940 in Spitfire R6756.

Seymour, A.H. (01/08/1938) Attended Worchester College, Oxford University. Degree awarded. External examination – Degree in Psychology at London University.

Sharp, Patrick Dualt (07/06/1938) Attended London University on BSC Engineering course.

Shelford, Douglas Frederic Ommanney (16/11/1937) Killed in action in the Western Desert in April 1942.

Shields, Iain Douglas (20/12/1938) Article in *The Times* "Four killed in air crash". Four men lost their lives in an air crash near Dalry, Kirkcudbrightshire. They formed the crew of RAF Bomber L9135 which was wrecked while on a training flight from Prestwick last night. The pilot was Flying Officer Iain Douglas Shields.

Shinne, Peter Lewis (28/02/1939) Attended Westminster School and Oxford University.

Simpson, Lindsay Athol (01/02/1938) Attended Oxford University.

Skeats, Herbert Arthur (09/11/1937) Flying Officer Herbert Arthur Skeats died 19 November 1940, aged 25, serving with 206 Squadron.

Smith, Clifford Parker Seymour (01/02/1938) Flying Officer Clifford Parker Seymour Smith was killed on active service.

Smith, Denis Bonham (01/02/1938) Attended St Paul's School and Corpus Christi College, Oxford University. Obituary – He read aeronautical engineering at Oxford University and learned to fly in the Oxford University Air Squadron. After the war he joined the English Electric Company who were working on the first jet bomber. From 1958 to 1970 he commanded the Hampshire wing of the Air Training Corps. He died aged 78.

Smith, Harold Souden (01/02/1938) Obituary – Killed on active service.

Smith, Kenneth Graeme Stewart (14/12/1937) Mr Kenneth Graeme Stewart Smith, Assistant Chief Secretary. And has been appointed Colonial Secretary, Gambia.

Smith, Maurice Armstrong (16/11/1937) Engagement announcement for Wing Commander Maurice Armstrong Smith DFC, eldest son of G Geoffrey Smith MBE, 70, Downage, Hendon. Death announcement – on 11 February 1987, Maurice Armstrong Smith, aged 71, of Beare Green.

Sollars, Reginald George (05/07/1938) Second Master at Wrekin College.

Spicer, Frederick (29/11/1938) French and German degree awarded at Queens College, Oxford University.

Statham, Ivan George (08/03/1938) Marriage announcement.

APPENDIX 2

Stephenson Ian Raitt (09/11/1937) Wing Commander Ian Raitt Stephenson, No 153 Squadron, RAFVR, a former Battle of Britain pilot, was killed in action on 26 November 1943. He was the son of the Revd. Herbert Stephenson, of St Paul's Manse, South Croydon, and was educated at King's College School, Wimbledon. He was a member of the London University Air Squadron in 1936-37, and was commissioned into the RAFVR in November 1937.

Stephenson, Arthur Kenneth Lennard (19/04/1938) Played cricket for Cranbrook School. High Jumps for Cranbrook School. Attends Sidney Sussex College, Cambridge University. Marriage announcement for A.K.L. Stephenson, son of the late Mr and Mrs A.S.H. Stephenson of Johannesburg, South Africa. DFC awarded.

Stewart, John William (05/07/1938) Attended Lancing College and then St John's College, Oxford University. Awarded English degree. Degree conferred at Oxford on 13 October 1938. Reported missing. Forthcoming marriage of Wing Commander J.W. Stewart DFC RAFVR, youngest son of Lieutenant Colonel W.M. Stewart CMG DSO and Mrs Stewart of Burnham, Somerset. Account of the wedding taking place.

Stranger, William Lloyd (12/07/1938) William Lloyd Stranger described as a civil air pilot of College House, London SW, was fined £2 and had his licence endorsed at Alton (Hants) Police Court yesterday for driving a motor car without due care and attention. It was stated that Stranger's car crashed into a telegraph pole and snapped it in two. His head went through the windscreen and the car was wrecked.

Strutt, Ivan Cornwallis (23/08/1938) Attended Peterhouse College, Cambridge University.

Sutherland, Ian Welsh (08/11/1938) Athletics for Merchant Taylors, Crosby. Deaths – on 4 August 1940, killed as a result of an accident, Ian Welch Sutherland, Pilot Officer, the dearly loved elder son of Captain D.W. Sutherland, Moness, St Andrews Road, Great Crosby. In November 1938 he obtained his commission in the RAFVR, He attended Magdalen College, Oxford University and he played in the back row of the Oxford scrum against Cambridge in the year before the war.

Swann, Graham Templer (26/07/1938) Plays football for St Peters College, Westminster. Played cricket for Westminster. Assistant Master at Harrow. British public school boys in Germany accompanied by Master G.T. Swann. Boys from Harrow Air Training Section of the OTC are attending RAF cadet camp, accompanied by Pilot Officer G.T. Swann. Obituary, killed on active service.

Taylor, William Thomson (01/02/1938) Plays rugby for Sedbergh public school throughout 1924, 25 and 26. Attends Brasenose College, Oxford University and plays rugby for them. Came second in "putting the weight" for Oxford University athletics.

Thevenard, George Holland (19/07/1938) Flying Officer, was killed along with his crew on 1 August 1940.

Thomas, William Kelman Burr (12/04/1938) Born April 1914 in Oban. Went to University in Scotland gaining a degree in modern languages. Spoke fluent French

227

and German. Attended the University of London Air Squadron dinner. Flying Officer W.K.B. Thomas was killed, aged 26, on 4 December 1941, flying as part of 106 Squadron over France.

Thompson, Walter Briggs (29/03/1938) Air Efficiency award. Air Force Cross Awarded in 1943.

Trouncer, Thomas Dowell (29/08/1939) Attended University College, Oxford University. Births – on 30 September 1935 at 27, Welbeck Street, W1, to Margaret, wife of T.D. Trouncer of 12, Harley Gardens, SW10 – a son (stillborn). Obituary – Flying Officer T.D. Trouncer attended Winchester School and University College, Oxford University, solicitor, member of Oxford University Air Squadron.

Truran, James William Jameson (01/02/1938) Awarded Air Force Cross in the Birthday Honours List. Order of St John of Jerusalem to Wing Commander J.W.J. Truran. The Bristol Aeroplane Company of Canada Ltd has appointed Mr J.W.J. Truran, a former principal scientific officer at the Ministry of Supply and Air Ministry Test Pilot, as a special project engineer.

Tucker, Aidan Boys (01/02/1938) Flying Officer A.B. Tucker of 151 Squadron was shot down by Bf109s on 12 August 1940 and crashed his Hurricane 1 (P3302) into the sea. He was then rescued and admitted to hospital with back wounds. Marriage announcement for Flying Officer Aidan Boys Tucker, youngest son of John Michael Tucker KCSG, JP and Mrs Tucker of Collett Hall, Ware, Hertfordshire. On 2 September 1943 at Moncton, Canada, to Bridget, wife of Flight Lieutenant A.B. Tucker – a son. Promotion from Flight Lieutenant to Squadron Leader.

Tucker, James Duncan (19/04/1938) Plays rugby for Bradfield College throughout 1929. Plays rugby for Old Bradfieldians. Plays cricket for Bradfield Waif's. Throughout 1934 and 1935.

Tull, Thomas Stuart (07/02/1939) Attended Rossall School. Attended Jesus College, Oxford University.

Verity, Hugh Beresford (08/11/1938) Awarded DSO to go with DFC, Squadron Leader H.B. Verity RAFVR. Births – Verity, on 1 June 1954 at the Royal Air Force Hospital, Wegberg, BAOR 34, to Audrey, wife of Wing Commander H.B. Verity, a daughter. Wing Commander H.B. Verity to Air Ministry for duty in the Department of Chief of Air Staff. Wing Commander H.B. Verity promoted to Group Captain.

Walbourne, Derrick Milner (09/11/1937) Flight Commander 156 Squadron, Wing Commander with 582 Squadron.

Walker, Wilford Hugh Maitland (01/02/1938) Air Efficiency Award to Wing Commander W.H.M. Walker.

Watson, Gerald (19/03/1938) Awarded DFC.

Weir, Archibald Nigel Charles (04/07/1939) Attended Winchester School and was a member of the fencing club. Attended Christ Church College, Oxford University and was a member of their fencing team. Deaths – Flying Officer Archibald Nigel Charles Weir DFC, 145 Squadron, was killed in action over the Channel on 7 November 1940.

Wells, Patrick Hardy Vesey (22/02/1938) Attended the University of London Air Squadron Dinner. Marriage announcement for P.H.V. Wells DSO. Patrick H.V. Wells of No 249 Squadron bailed out wounded on 7 September 1940. His Hurricane was shot down by return fire whilst attacking some Heinkel HE 111's near Faversham. Managing Director of Holmon Bros. (East Africa).

Wheeler, Harold Raymond (01/02/1938) Acting Flying Officer Harold Raymond Wheeler killed on active service.

Whittingham, Charles Derek (01/02/1938) Married Margaret E Gee in 1938, Married Hilda Roberts in 1947. Died on the 8 April 1958 at Valleyfields, Kirkcolm.

Whittome, Richard Wright (16/11/1937) Played in the Wellingborough School football team. Athletics for Wellingborough. Awarded the Fryer–Woolston Exhibition Award. Scholarship awarded for St Catherine's College, Cambridge University. Degree awarded in Mechanical Science. Obituary.

Wight-Boycott, Cathcart Michael (28/09/1937) Obituary – Educated at Marlborough College and Clare College, Cambridge University. He learned to fly with the University Air Squadron and when the RAFVR was formed, he was one of the first pilots to receive a commission.

Wilberforce, Reginald Garton (01/02/1939) Degree conferred at Cambridge University. Awarded Air Force Cross.

Wilkinson, Arthur Bernard (27/12/1938) Deaths – Treasured and ever loving memories of "Boy" Squadron Leader A.B. Wilkinson RAFVR, missing over Sicily, 13 July 1943.

Wood, Charles Alan (18/10/1938) Attended The Downs School, Colwall. Attended St John's College, Oxford University. Engagement announced for Pilot Officer C Alan Wood RAFVR, younger son of Mr and Mrs C.G. Wood, The Spinney, Harpenden.

Wood, James Douglas (01/02/1938) Attended Oxford University.

Woods, Trevor L McAlpine (27/11/1937) In ever loving memory, on this his birthday, of Trevor, our beloved only son, who lost his life returning from an intruder patrol inside Germany, on 11 May 1944.

Worthington, Alec Sillavan (28/12/1937) Attended Sedburgh School. Marriage announcement for Squadron Leader A.S. Worthington in Vienna.

Wright, Eric William (11/06/1939) Born on 21 September 1919 and educated at Cambridge County School. With war impending he joined the RAFVR to learn to fly. DFC awarded October 1946. Awarded the CBE in 1964 and also held the Air Efficiency Award. He died on 5 November 2007, aged 88. After the war he was granted a permanent commission in the RAF and was a member of the

RAF's official aerobatics team flying Vampires. In April 1948 he made the first Atlantic crossing by jet aircraft.

Yarrow, G.P. (03/01/1939) Attended Harrow and was in Elmfield House. Plays rugby for Harrow. Obituary – attended Harrow and Cambridge University and was a member of the Cambridge University Air Squadron.

Young, Edward Purcell (01/02/1938) Attended Westminster School and Christ Church College, Oxford University. Engagement announced for Edward Purcell Young, son of Mr E.A. Young OBE and Mrs Young of Rodway Hill House, Mangotsfield, Gloucestershire.

Young, Henry Melvin (13/09/1938) Rowed for Trinity College, Oxford University. Marriage announcement for Squadron Leader Henry Melvin Young. The marriage took place in Kent School Chapel, Kent, Connecticut, USA. DFC awarded. Memorial service for Squadron Leader H.M. Young RAFVR. Obituary – Born in London in 1915, he was educated at Amesbury Preparatory School, Hindhead and Kent School, Connecticut. Later he was at Westminster and from there to Trinity College, Oxford University. He joined the University Air Squadron in 1936. He lost his life in the raid on the Ruhr dams on 16 May 1943.

Appendix 3

Officers of the Re-formed Royal Auxiliary Air Force 1946-1957

600 (City of London) Squadron

Michael J Bridge (19/07/1949) After National Service he attended Oxford University reading Theoretical Physics and joined the University Air Squadron, then joined the RAuxAF. He was employed by de Havilland researching into missiles.[1] Death announcement – on 13 February 1954. In a flying accident, Flying Officer M.J. Bridge (Mick) 600 Squadron Auxiliary Air Force, aged 24, younger son of the late A.V. Bridge and Mrs Bridge of Bristol.

John Alan Chisholm-Will (12/07/1953) Solicitor of 3/4 Lincoln's Inn Fields, London. Chartered accountant of Nassau House, 122, Shaftesbury Avenue, London dealing with company liquidations.

Lindsay Hancock (05/08/1947) Solicitor.[2]

Keith N Haselwood (09/02/1952) City businessman.[3]

Thomas Norman Hayes (17/09/1946) Marriage announcement – Sqn Ldr Norman Hayes DFC, son of Mr and Mrs T.H. Hayes of Sunningdale, Chiselhurst. Birth announcement – on 18 April 1947 at 32, Hanover House, Regent's Park, NW8, to Anna, wife of Norman Hayes – a son.

Ralph Hiscox (30/01/1952) Birth announcement – on 31 July at The Woking Maternity Home, to Louie, Wife of Ralph Hiscox OBE – a daughter. Partner in Roberts & Hiscox and a Director of Ugdale Underwriting Limited and Lloyds Chairman. Death Announcement – on 6 May 1970. Suddenly, Ralph Hiscox, much loved husband of Louie, adored father of Frances, Robert and Lindsay, and grandfather of Philip, Charlotte and Renshaw. Obituary

Charles Mark Lambert (13/04/1951) Born on 15 June 1929, he lived a peripatetic childhood, since his mother lived from 1931-1937 in France, Italy, Austria, Yugoslavia and Latvia. This gave him a good grounding in languages which was helpful in his job as an international journalist. Coming to England after a spell at prep school, he was educated at Blundell's School, Tiverton. At 17, he joined his parents in France and studied at the French Lycee. He then went to Jesus College,

Oxford University, where he joined the University Air Squadron. He worked on the aviation magazine *"Flight"*. He died on 27 September 1994 from cancer, aged 65. Born in India and brought up in the UK.

Jack Meadows (17/09/1946) Joined the RAFVR in 1937. In 1946 he joined the RAuxAF. He was CO of 600 Squadron, but left when his civilian job at Unilever sent him to South Africa for eight years. He retired after thirty-five years with Unilever in 1981, and settled in Canada.

John (Jamie) Morrison (19/05/1951) The first black member of the RAuxAF.[4] Joined the RAFVR after the war and trained with several regular squadrons. Whenever he trained with a regular squadron they completed some forms and sent them to his unit. This went on for about two years, till after a pay parade the pay officer saw Jamie and said that he had never seen Jamie at a pay parade. Jamie answered that he never attended the pay parade as there was no money ever paid to him. The officer got a bit upset and said, "I have seen you work very hard over the last two years, why have you not been paid?" Morrison said that he didn't know. The officer shook his head and walked away. Sometime later Jamie was called to the Adjutant's office where he was told that a rather strange mistake had been made. There was no way that he could get a refund of the money that should have been paid, but Morrison should think about leaving the RAFVR and join the RAuxAF instead, so he filled the forms in and joined and started on 600 Squadron.

Colin Lee Irving Muntz (30/05/1950) Born 23 March 1929, killed in flying accident whilst on exercise, 25 April 1953, aged 24.

David Proudlove (26/10/1948) Marriage announcement – Marriage took place in London of Mr David Proudlove of 18, Cadogan Place, SW1. Birth announcement – on 27 October 1969 at The Lindo Wing, St Mary's Hospital, to Lena and David Proudlove, a daughter. Christening announcement - the infant daughter of Mr and Mrs David Proudlove was christened Lucy Margareta by the Rev A.F. Vickers in the Church of St Clement Danes yesterday. The godparents are Mr Jack Meadows, Mr John Westcott, Mrs Barbara Cantelo and Miss Eva Leander. Christening announcement – the infant son of Mr and Mrs David Proudlove was christened Christopher David by the Rev Dr N.E. Wallbank, in the Lady Chapel, the Priory Church of St Bartholomew the Great yesterday. The godparents are Senor Jorge Bareiro, Mr Ake Blombergson, Mrs Nicholas Delamain and Mrs Ian Garton. Member of the Guild of Air Pilots and Air Navigators. Mr David Proudlove has retired as managing director of Airclaims Group and has been made Deputy Chairman. Death announcement – Proudlove David, peacefully at home on 9 June, aged 86. Devoted husband to Lena, father to Lucy and Christopher and grandfather to baby Frederick. Much loved by all his family and friends. Private funeral at David's request.

Peter Graham Stewart (11/04/1950) Memorial service for Group Captain Peter Graham Stewart BE will be held at St Bartholomew The Great on Tuesday, 25 June at 6pm.

APPENDIX 3

601 (County of London) Squadron

John William Maxwell Aitken (17/09/1946) Born in Montreal on 15 February 1910. Educated at Westminster and Pembroke College, Cambridge. Son of Lord Beaverbrook and later general manager of the *Sunday Express*. Cambridge soccer blue and a scratch golfer as well as heir to the Beaverbrook newspaper title. Keen yachtsman. Won a DFC and a DSO between 1941 and 1943. Obituary in *The Times*.

Axford, Clive (27/11/1953) Death announcement – Clive passed away peacefully in his sleep in the early hours of 13 December. Beloved husband, father and grandfather.

Hugh Spencer Lisle Dundas (17/09/1946) Born 22 July 1920. Educated at Stowe and then articled to a firm of solicitors in Barnsley. Commissioned into 616 Squadron AAF in 1939. Awarded DFC in August 1941, and DSO in 1944. After the war he was senior management at Rediffusion from 1961-1985, Chairman of Thames television between 1981 & 1987 and also Chairman of British Electric Traction between 1982 & 1987. He was also a member of the AAF when it was reformed after the war. He died on 10 July 1995, aged 74.

Peter William Dunning-White (19/09/1946) Marriage announcement for Mr Peter William Dunning-White at the Savoy Chapel.

Emanuel (Prince) Gallitizine (19/07/1950) Prince Emanuel Gallitzine was born on the 28 May 1918 at Kislvodsk in Russia. Before The Revolution, his father had served as Aide-de-camp for Grand Duke Nikoli Nikolaevich, head of all the Russian armies until 1916. His mother was a daughter of Duke George Alexander of Mecklenburg-Strelitz. The family fled from Russia in 1919. They travelled on a Royal Navy ship in the Crimea which took them to Constantinople and then made their way by train to Paris. His father felt his son would get a better public school in England, so the family moved to London where his father opened a shop in Berkeley Square, and his son attended St Paul's and Lancing. He served in the RAFVR during the war, he joined the RAuxAF in 1950 as a pilot. In civilian life he was a pilot with British European Airlines before travelling the world as a salesman for the Avro aircraft company. He died on 23 December 2003, aged 84. Engagement announcement – Prince Emanuel Galitzine RAFVR, youngest son of Prince Vladimir Galitzine and of the late Catherine Galitzine.

Gordon E Hughes (15/02/1946) Marriage announcement – Wing Commander Gordon E Hughes DSO, DFC, younger son of Mr A.J. Hughes OBE and Mrs Hughes of Pages, Chigwell Row.

N Leyton (11/01/1952) Consultant at a London Hospital. Migraine and headache specialist.[5]

Christopher McCarthy-Jones (24/04/1947) Sales manager.[6]

Arden Merville-Crawley (17/09/1946) Kent cricketer, born in 1908 and attended Oxford University. Son of Arthur Stafford Crawley, Vicar of Benenden. Grandfather was an entrepreneur. Educated at Farnborough Prep School in 1917, then Harrow in 1920, then Oxford University. Worked as a reporter on *Daily Mail*. Joined Labour Party and stood as Labour Candidate for North Buckinghamshire. Documentary maker for the BBC. Editor in Chief of ITN. MP.

Thomas Moulson (16/11/1950) Born on 8 November 1930 in Manchester. He was the son of an ex-army sergeant. From 1949-1950 he trained as a National Service pilot at Feltwell, Norfolk and converted to jets at Middleton-St-George. He joined the RAuxAF and flew with 601 Squadron from 1950-1957. He was a sales and marketing executive with Nestle and Ford Motor Company before becoming a partner in a consulting company. He is now retired and lives in Newport Beach, California. He is 601 Squadrons official historian and has written two squadron histories.

Sir Mark Annesley Norman (07/07/1953) Born on 8 February 1927. Married Joanna Camilla Walker Kilgour on 30 May 1953. Educated at Winchester College. Succeeded to the title of 3rd Baronet Norman on 19 May 1943. Between 1948 and 1956 he worked with Airwork Ltd. Between 1953 and 1956 he was a member of the RAuxAF with 601 Squadron. He also was with Bristol Aircraft between 1956 and 1961. He was with British Executive and General Aviation, Annesley Maitland and Company Ltd, Britten-Norman and Gottas-Larsen Shipping Corps. Died 9 September 2013.

Nigel Desmond Norman (12/05/1953) Educated at Eton. Born on 13 August 1929. Second son of Sir Nigel Norman. Attended Twyford School before Eton. Excelled at rowing, boxing and rugby. Attended de Havilland Aeronautical Technical School between 1946 and 1950 where he qualified as an aeronautical engineer. In 1954 he set up Britten-Norman with his friend from Technical school. After designing the BN1, an ultra-light sporting aeroplane, they formed an air-spraying company, Crop Culture. Their fleet grew from three to more than seventy aircraft and it became the biggest company of its kind in the world. Appointed CBE in 1970. He was a Chartered Engineer and a Fellow of the Royal Aeronautical Society. He died of a heart attack on 13 November 2002.

Torquil Norman (12/05/1953) Educated at Eton. He got his pilot's licence when he was eighteen. He flew with the Fleet Air Arm during his National Service before joining 601 Squadron. He was the founder and chairman of Bluebird Toys, Britain's most successful toy company. Attended Cambridge University. Worked for some time as an investment banker.[7]

Paul H.M. Richey (15/01/1951) Born in Chelsea on 7 May 1916, the son of an Irish father and an Australian mother. Died in 1989, aged 72. Wrote the book *"Fighter Pilot."* After the war he joined the RAuxAF. During the Korean War in 1950, he was CO Of 601 Squadron. Worked as a Journalist.

Dennis Shrosbee (15/031952) Airline pilot for BOAC and BA.[8] Worked for HM Stationary Office in 1954.[9]

Peter Beckford Rutgers Vanneck (26/09/1950) Marriage announcement for Sub-Lieutenant the Hon Peter Beckford Rutgers Vanneck, Royal Navy, younger son

APPENDIX 3

of Lord Huntingfield and of the late Lady Huntingfield. Group Captain The Hon Peter Beckford Rutgers Vanneck has been appointed a Gentleman Usher to the Queen. Born on 7 January 1922 he spent time in Australia, where his father was the Governor of Victoria in the 1930s. He studied at Stowe School. He joined the navy during the Second World War. He left the navy in 1949 and studied at Trinity College Cambridge, joining the University Air Squadron. He was commissioned in the RAFVR in 1949, transferring into the RAuxAF in 1950. He studied engineering at Harvard University, and left the RAuxAF on 1 September 1973.He then went into business with Ransome's engineering company, followed by working as a stockbroker in London. He was the Sheriff of London in 1974 and Lord Mayor of London in 1977. Served as a Conservative MP in 1979 and he retired in 1989. He enjoyed yacht racing. He died on 2 August 1999 in London.

602 (City of Glasgow) Squadron

Robert Findlay Boyd (14/07/1947) Born in East Kilbride in 1915, joined 602 Squadron in 1935 and called up for full time service in 1939. Awarded DFC in September 1940 and the Bar to the DFC in October 1940. After the war he flew charter flights for Scottish Aviation, before trying pig farming, and then herring fishing, before moving to Skye where he kept the Ferry Inn at Uig.[10]

Pierre Clostermann (11/04/1952) Member of the House of Representatives in France, and author of three books.

James Johnston (06/05/1948) Born 15 August 1922 in Aberdeen, he attended Causewayend and Sunnybank Schools leaving at fourteen to work in woollen manufacture at Berryden Mills. In 1946 he worked for Ordnance Survey as Chief Surveyor of the West of Scotland. In 1948 he joined 602 Squadron. He retired in 1986. He met his wife Margaret in 1946, and she died in 2007. His remaining days were in a care home as he suffered from short term memory loss. He died on 11 May 2014, aged 91.

Andrew McDowall (17/08/1950) Worked for Rolls-Royce as a test pilot, before a contracts engineer for Brush Electrical Engineering.[11]

Hamish McWilliam (17/02/1946) Death announcement – on 3 April 1948, whilst flying on duty, Flying Officer Hamish McWilliam, aged 23, of 602 (City of Glasgow) Squadron AAF. Dearly loved elder son of Iain and Mary McWilliam of 3, Corsebar Drive, Paisley, and of Uigle, Campbeltown.

Robert Ivor Reid (22/03/1946) Killed on 31 July 1947 during the first annual camp at Woodvale. In Memorial – Reid, Robert Ivor, dearly loved and honoured eldest son of Mr and Mrs R.A.M. Reid and brother of Howard, Godfrey and Enid, 5, Cleveden Drive, Glasgow, W2. Born 13 August 1916. Killed while flying with 602 (City of Glasgow) Fighter Squadron AAF.

Marcus Robinson (17/09/1946) Rejoined on 1 August 1946 where he was given command of 602 Squadron. He relinquished his commission on 27 May 1956 and died in March 1988. Marriage arrangements between Squadron Leader

235

Marcus Robinson, only son of Mr and Mrs Wilson Robinson of Glasgow. Report of the marriage. Daughters engagement announced.

Stephen Mackay Harbourne (02/08/1949) Marriage announcement – Wing Commander Stephen Mackay Harbourne DSO DFC younger son of Mr and Mrs T.M. Stephen of Ravenswood, Ballater, Aberdeenshire. Managing Director of the *Daily Telegraph* and the *Sunday Telegraph*. Death announcement - at home on Monday, 20 August after a short illness, Stephen Mackay Harbourne CBE, DSO, DFC, AE. Beloved husband of Erica, and father of Layla and Virginia, grandfather of Hugh, Camilla, Frances, Sophie, Zsa Zsa, Elyse and Shona. Private cremation. Obituary – born the son of a banker in Elgin on 18 April 1916, he was educated at Shrewsbury School, which he left at fifteen to join the staff of the Allied Newspapers in London as a copy boy. In 1936 he went to the *Evening Standard*. Within ten years of war ending he was managing the Scottish *Daily Express* and the *Evening Citizen*. In 1958 he moved to London as general manager of the *Sunday Times*. Three years later he moved to the *Daily* and *Sunday Telegraph*. He died on 20 August 2001, aged 85. Thanksgiving service held on Thursday, 20 September at St Mary's, Shawcum Donnington, Newbury, Berkshire.

603 (City of Edinburgh) Squadron

Andrew Anderson (30/11/1950) School teacher in civilian life. Killed on 23 June 1951 on his first solo flight in a jet.

Brian Clapp (19/07/1949) Birth announcement – on 18 March 1967, at the City Hospital, Exeter, to Patricia and Brian Clapp, a son (William Henry), a brother for Elizabeth, Amanda and Lucy.

George L Denholm (17/09/1946) Birth announcement – on 24 November 1949 at Tidings Hill, Bo'ness to Betty, wife of George L Denholm – a son. Obituary – born on 20 December 1908, born and brought up in Bo'ness where his father ran a business importing wooden props for the local coalmines and exporting coal. He was educated at Fettes and St John's College Cambridge University. Died in Bo'ness on 16 June 1997, aged 88.

Timothy M.S. Ferguson (26/09/1950) Joined RAuxAF in 1950 as a pilot. In January 1955 he joined English Electric as a production test pilot, also flying the company's communication aircraft. He was involved in Jaguar and Tornado flight testing, and once landed a Jaguar on the M55 motorway as part of operating trials. He became Deputy Chief Test Pilot for BAC before retiring from the Test Flying in 1979 and transferring to product support. He was awarded the Derry and Richards Medal in 1977 for his high incidence and spinning experimental work.

George Kemp Gilroy (17/09/1946) Birth announcement – on 22 March 1948, at Kingdores, Tweedsmuir, to Evelyn, wife of George K Gilroy, RAuxAF – a son. Obituary – born in Edinburgh on 1 June 1915. Worked as a sheep farmer during the 1930s. Having served with 603 Squadron in the Second World War, he rejoined the RAuxAF in 1946. He also took up farming in Kirkbrightshire where he became a notable breeder of Galloway Cattle. He died on 25 March 1995, Aged 79.

APPENDIX 3

Donald Macmillan Knight (28/02/1952) Born in 1931, educated at Daniel Stewart's College, Edinburgh. He trained as a pilot during his National Service between 1949 and 1951. He qualified with distinction and completing operational conversion on the Meteor 4 and 7. Member of RAuxAF. He joined English Electric as a production test pilot in June 1953, transferring to experimental and development work in 1956. He became Deputy Chief Test Pilot in January 1964. He was forced to retire on health grounds in 1967. He changed jobs and went into sales and marketing becoming a Divisional Marketing Director. From 1986-1990 he was Resident Director for British Aerospace in Indonesia. Pilot rescued from crashed bomber – Mr Donald Macmillan Knight, aged 27, of Thorntrees Avenue, Preston, an experimental test pilot for English Electric, crashed his Canberra Mark 9 Into the sea, nine miles from Blackpool.

Duncan McIntosh (02/02/1956) Captain Duncan McIntosh is managing director and Pilot of Loganair which is a construction firm which flies construction gangs between sites and charters. Awarded OBE in birthday honours list. Marriage announcement – the marriage took place quietly in Edinburgh on Thursday, 22 September of Captain Duncan McIntosh of 6, Crawford Drive, Helensburgh, Dunbartonshire, and Lady Strathcona. Letter to *The Times* by the Chief Executives of several independent airlines expressing concern at the effects of the series of strikes by air traffic controllers.

Jack Meadows (23/09/1948) Born in India and brought up in the UK. Joined RAFVR prior to the start of the war. After the war he worked for Unilever from 1946, but joined the reformed RAuxAF. He retired in 1981 after thirty-five years with Unilever. He died on 20 July 2010.

John Morton Mears (09/05/1948) Death announcement – on 6 March 1949 as a result of a flying accident during air exercises, Flying Officer John Morton Mears, 603 Squadron Royal Auxiliary Air Force, youngest son of Sir Frank and Lady Mears, Whitehouse, Inveresk, Midlothian.

Hector Seymour Peter Monroe (Baron Monro of Langholm) (08/12/1947) Born in Edinburgh, he was educated at Upland House School in Sussex, Canford School in Dorset and King's College, Cambridge University. He was a member of Cambridge University Air Squadron. He joined the RAF in 1941. After he was demobbed in 1946 he became a farmer at Kirtlebridge near Lockerbie. He joined the RAuxAF between 1947 and 1954. Elected as a Dumfries County Councillor, and then MP for Dumfries in 1964. Died on 30 August 2006.

James Storrs Morton (17/09/1946) Mentioned in Dispatches. Engagement announced between Flt Lt James S Morton DFC, AAF, eldest son of Dr H.J.S. Morton of 28, Belsize Avenue, Hampstead. Marriage announcement 8 December 1941 at St Mary, Oatlands, Weybride. Bar to DFC. He became an instructor before retiring from the service with the rank of Wing Commander in 1946. He joined the RAuxAF from November 1946 to March 1951. He died in 1982 having had a heart attack on his driveway. He started a successful engineering business until he and his

237

family moved into Woodcote Manor with 100 acres of farmland and he gradually began the transition from engineering to farming.[12]

James Eric Storrar (07/11/1948) Born into a veterinary family in Chester on 26 June 1921. He was educated at Chester Grammar School. He joined the AAF when he was seventeen and flew throughout the war. In 1947 he went to Edinburgh University to train as a vet, and commanded the University Air Squadron, whilst re-joining the RAuxAF later on. He was a familiar figure driving his Jaguar with its registration letters JAS. He died on 29 March 1995, aged 73.

Archibald Little Winskill (02/08/1949) Born in January 1917 at Penrith, the son of an early motor car dealer. He was educated at Penrith and Carlisle Grammar School. He joined the RAFVR in 1937, after the war he joined the RAuxAF. Appointed CBE in 1960, CVO in 1973 and KCVO in 1980. Died on 9 August 2005.

604 (County of Middlesex) Squadron

Peter Bugge (19/03/1948) Test pilot for Comet.[13]

Brian Cross (29/02/1952) The pilot of a Meteor jet who baled out at 20,000 feet over the sea was rescued by an Albatross Amphibian of the United States Air Force. Pilot Officer B Cross, aged 21, was lucky to be alive as in baling out, he tore his parachute and made the drop on half of it. There was only a four-foot depth of water where he came down. Brian Cross is a post office engineer in civilian life. He was taken to North Weald where he was recovering from shock and a fractured ankle.

John Cunningham (17/09/1946) Born in 1917 and educated at Whitgift School, Croudon. Joined 604 Squadron as a pilot at age eighteen. He also joined the de Havilland Aeronautical Technical School and in 1938, having graduated in aeronautical engineering he was appointed a test pilot with De Havilland. After the war, he re-joined de Havilland as a test pilot. On 27 July 1949 he took to the air as captain of the world's first jet airliner, the Comet. He died on 21 July 2002, aged 84. Re-joined 604 Squadron after the war, driving a Triumph Roadster, and flying a silver Spitfire.

Lewin Edward Alton Healy (05/06/1950) Death announcement – on 17 July, peacefully after a long illness, borne with strength and humour Lewin Edward Alton Healy OBE, 604 Squadron AAF.

Jeremy Napier Howard-Williams (05/06/1950) Marriage announcement – Squadron Leader Jeremy Napier Howard-Williams DFC, younger son of Air Commodore E.L. Howard-Williams MC, and of Mrs T.C. Ratsey of Windrush, Cowes, Isle of Wight. Birth announcement – on 22 March 1954, to Gillian, wife of Sqn Ldr J.N. Howard-Williams, a brother – Christopher Jeremy, for Anthony. Involved in yachting competitions.

Keith Temple Lofts (27/05/1946) Squadron Leader Keith Temple Lofts of 604 Squadron RAuxAF was killed yesterday when his Vampire III jet aircraft crashed near Cranbrook, Kent, during the qualifying heat for the Cooper Trophy race, an annual contest between RAuxAF squadrons. He was thirty-three. Memorial Service for Squadron Leader Keith Temple Lofts will be held at St James Piccadilly on Wednesday, 6 June at 11.30am.

Ian Reginald Ponsford (02/08/1949) Born on 20 March 1922, he was educated at Abbotsholm School. Called up for the RAF in 1941. After the war he studied law, qualifying as a solicitor in 1949 and becoming senior partner in a London firm in 1975. He joined the RAuxAF in 1949 which enabled him to continue flying. Died on 29 December 2006, aged 84.

Derek Yates (11/08/1947) Derek Yates, a pilot from 604 Squadron was flying a Vampire Jet when he lost his bearings and ran short of fuel over Norfolk. He sighted a KB29 air tanker aircraft, and using his wing-tip lights, signalled an SOS. The American pilot of the tanker aircraft guided Yates through the clouds towards Sculthorpe (Norfolk) airfield where he landed with only enough fuel left for five minutes flying.

605 (County of Warwick) Squadron

William Bedford (03/10/1946) Chief Test Pilot for Hawker Siddeley.[14]

A.P. Belcher (02/08/1949) Injured when his plane crashed on take-off from Honiley, on 3 November 1951.

John Allan Cecil Cecil-Wright (19/10/1948) Born on 28 August 1886 and educated at Winchester School. Served in Royal Flying Corps and received the Air Force Cross. An industrialist who became Chairman of Warne, Wright and Rowlands Ltd who were screw, nut and bolt manufacturers. Conservative MP for Edrington. Chairman of the Kennel Club of Great Britain from 1948-1973.

Jerry Edgerton (27/02/1951) Civilian Pilot for Eagle Airways.[15]

G.O. Hauser (12/07/1953) A Vampire of 605 Squadron hit trees at Honiley on 27 November 1955. Pilot Officer G.O. Hauser died of his injuries the following day.

Patrick George Leeson (09/04/1946) Marriage announcement for Flight Lieutenant Patrick George Leeson, only son of Mr and Mrs G.W. Leeson of Brendan, Malvern.

G Hugh Louden (01/02/1947) MBE awarded.

M Mayne (11/01/1952) Meteor of 605 Squadron overshot the landing on 16 October 1955, Pilot Officer M Mayne and passenger were okay. Former bank worker who left to become a pilot for BOAC.[16]

Harry Pollitt (17/08/1956) Chief Test Pilot at Rolls-Royce.

R.L.M. Smalley (23/11/1955) Viking Airliner missing on a charter flight to Stavanger. On board was a party of thirty-four boys all aged fourteen, and two school masters. R.M.L. Smalley was the first officer on the flight. Vampire jet piloted by R.L.M. Smalley of 605 Squadron belly landed on the runway at Honiley following engine failure.

C.D. Tomalin (27/05/1946) Manager of the Great British diving team for the 1948 Olympics.[17]

J.D.P. Waite (22/03/1946) Controller – home sales for the steel company of Wales.

Barrington Allen Whitworth (10/07/1953) Marriage announcement - Barrington Allen Whitworth DFC, elder son of Mr and Mrs E.E.A. Whitworth of The School House, Tonbridge.

607 (County of Durham) Squadron

James Michael Bazin DSO, DFC (05/12/1946) Death announcement in *The Times*, 11 January 1985. Obituary in *The Times*, 24 January 1986. Died on 9 January 1985, aged 70. Distinguished Battle of Britain pilot. After the war he returned to the engineering industry. Left a will of £295,161 net. CO of 607 Squadron when it was reformed in 1946. Remained CO Until 1952.

William Francis Blackadder DSO, OBE (05/12/1946) Marriage announcement in *The Times*. Son of Mr and Mrs Robert Blackadder, Grange Road, Edinburgh. DSO awarded for shooting down three enemy aircraft. Edinburgh University. Cambridge and Scottish rugby player.[18]

George Dudley Craig (27/07/1946) Son of Mr and Mrs R.D. Craig, The Six Lords, Singleborough Bucks. George Dudley Craig OBE of Corbridge was born on 13 September 1913 in Bangkok, the son of R.D. Craig, a member of the Diplomatic Corp and Sarah Louise Craig. He was educated at Aysgarth Public School followed by Winchester School and then Pembroke College Cambridge where he gained a soccer blue and an MA in Law Studies. Prior to the Second World War he earned his living as a local solicitor. Marriage announcement in *The Times*.

Joseph Robert Kayll (17/09/1946) Born on 12 April 1914 and educated at Aysgarth and Stowe, he worked in the family timber business in Sunderland after leaving school. In 1934 he was commissioned into the AAF, and begun flying with 607 Squadron. He was awarded both the DFC and the DSO in 1940, before the Battle of Britain had begun. Taken prisoner in 1941, he was taken to Staleg Luft III, where he took up the role as escape officer. He famously organised the "Wooden Horse" outbreak in which three men escaped to Sweden and England. He organised other breakouts, but stopped after the Great Escape in 1944 when fifty escapees were shot on Hitler's orders. He was appointed OBE in 1945 for his escape work in the camps. He was demobbed in 1946, and immediately re-joined 607 Squadron Royal Auxiliary Air Force as its Commanding Officer. He also re-joined the family timber business. He died on 3 March 2000, aged 85.

Geoffrey Thomas Orde (04/05/1950) Born in May 1931 in Newcastle and moved to Penrith. Educated at the Royal Grammar School in Newcastle, which was grant aided. Father was an engineer with his own business. Left school at eighteen and went to university at Cambridge. Joined the RAuxAF in 1950 with 607 Squadron, as a pilot with the rank of squadron leader.

APPENDIX 3

608 (North Riding) Squadron

R.C. Alabaster (18/05/1951) Joined BOAC as a pilot. Later he became Flight Manager for Comets.[19]

William Hillary Appleby-Brown (01/08/1946) From Saltburn, his father was James Brown, who worked for the family firm J Brown and Co, builder's merchants at Queens Square in Middlesbrough. The Brown family was a prominent Middlesbrough family that included Alderman John Wesley Brown who was MP for Middlesbrough in 1921. William attended Cambridge University where he learned to fly as a member of the University Air Squadron, he then joined the family firm. His family also had a shipping company called Lion Shipping that imported iron ore from Spain and Timber from the Baltic States. In 1946 he became squadron commander until 1950. Later he became Chairman of J Wardman Brown & Co Ltd in Middlesbrough until 1972. Marriage announcement – youngest son of the late James Brown and of Mrs Brown, Marton Road, Middlesbrough.[20]

Allen Clough (30/05/1950) A draughtsman at Head Wrightson.

Hank Costain (08/11/1955) Born on 27 March 1922 in Porteynon, Gower, South Wales. Attended public school at Christ College, Brecon. His father was a refrigeration engineer. Left school at seventeen and became an apprentice metallurgical chemist. Joined RAF in 1940 as a pilot. Joined 608 Squadron in 1955 and became their commanding officer.

Arthur Gavan (17/09/1946) Born on 5 April 1920 in Hull. Trained as a pilot with the RAFVR, and flew Spitfires with 54 Squadron during the Battle of Britain. After the war he worked for Redcar Town Council, and joined the newly reformed 608 Squadron. In September 1955 he converted to helicopters and in December he joined 275 Squadron at Thornaby as a flight commander. On 22 June 1967. He was killed when his helicopter broke up and crashed into the sea after a main rotor blade detached.

William Goodrum (27/11/1953) A self-employed builder.

George Frederick Grant Goodwill (27/11/1953) Born on 4 October 1932 in Middlesbrough. Attended Hugh Bell School. Father was a test house manager at Head Wrightsons. Left school at fifteen and worked for ICI in the research department. Called up for national service in 1950 and trained as a pilot. At the end of national service he applied to join 608 Squadron as a pilot. Trained for a commercial pilots licence on leaving 608 Squadron when it was disbanded.[21]

Neil Hancock (27/11/1953) Worked for British Rail whilst he was at 608 Squadron between 1953 and 1957. When the squadron was disbanded, he went on to test fly for Scottish Aviation.[22]

Peter Hutchings (17/11/1947) Farmer and then became a civilian flying instructor.[23]

K.R. Jeffery (24/01/1947) Killed on 13 February when his Spitfire crashed at Commondale.

George Joyce (27/11/1953) Born on 22 March 1933 in Pelton Feld, County Durham. His father was a blast furnace fixer at Dorman Long. Attended Hugh Bell School. Worked in the labs at ICI as a laboratory assistant, and then at age eighteen, was called up for national service, where he was offered pilot training. When his national service was over, he went back to ICI and was trained as an analytical laboratory assistant. He then applied to join 608 Squadron as a pilot so he could continue flying. In 608 Squadron for three years from 1953-1957. When the squadron disbanded he applied to BOAC and Air Canada, and had to qualify for his commercial pilots licence. He then flew with BOAC as a commercial pilot for nearly twenty-five years.[24]

Peter Mackenzie (12/05/1953) Worked for Lloyds Bank in Stockton. Flew with 608 Squadron between 1953 and 1957. Once the squadron disbanded he got a job at Airworks in Anglesey flying Vampires.[25]

James Steedman (27/11/1953) Did national service with the RAF, then joined the RAuxAF as an engineering officer in 1953. In civilian life he was a draughtsman at ICI.

David Stewart (27/11/1953) Born in Airdrie, 12 miles east of Glasgow. Moved to Canada when he was four. Returned to the UK as a young man and joined the RAF in 1943. Whilst in India he requested a transfer to the Royal Canadian Air Force. Lived in Scarborough. With 608 Squadron between 1949 and 1952. Travelled every day by motorbike. Moved to Canada in 1952 and joined 424 Squadron flying Mustangs until 1957. Spent the next thirty-five years in sales and management with Ford Motor Co's Dealers.

William Swainston (27/11/1953) Draughtsman at Head Wrightson.

William Sykens (27/11/1953) An engineer at ICI.

Kenneth Temple (11/01/1952) An engineer.

Ernest Hector Watts (27/02/1951) Came from Scarborough. A flight lieutenant in 608 Squadron until 1957. A teacher in Scarborough. He died in 1990.

Thomas Allan Willis (02/08/1949) Born in 1923 in Middlesbrough, his father was a teamer at Dorman Longs. He went to Acklam Hall School. He went into the RAF and was a qualified pilot by the time he was twenty-one. He joined 608 Squadron after the war. Worked in the export department at ICI. The squadron were on their two week annual camp in Malta, when the camp was over one of the pilots was ill so Alan flew the plane back for him. He landed at Tunis to refuel, and when he took off again he crashed. He was 29-years-old. Press cutting stated 29-year-old Middlesbrough jet pilot was killed when his Vampire jet crashed at Elaouina Airport near Tunis. The plane stalled on take-off and dived into the ground. He was killed on Friday, 12 September 1952. His wife was pregnant at the time, and his son was born four months later. He was buried in Tunis, and a memorial service was held at St Barnabas Church in Middlesbrough on 17 September 1952.[26]

609 (West Riding) Squadron

Roland P Beaumont (17/09/1946) Born at Enfield, North London on 10 August 1920. Educated at Eastbourne College. Joined the RAF. Awarded DFC and DSO in 1939. In civilian life he joined Gloster Aircraft as an experimental test pilot. Test pilot for English Electric.

E Thomas Evans (09/04/1946) Mr E.T. Evans takes over the position of Company Secretary of BSR Ltd and will combine these duties with those of his present position as Chief Accountant.

S.H. Hanson (12/07/1953) Joined RAuxAF and 609 Squadron after completing two years national service. Pilot flying jets.

Malcolm Frederick Hargreaves (12/07/1953) Born on 9 March 1932 in Bradford, and attended Grange School. Completed two years national service and then applied to join the RAuxAF. He wanted to fly front line fighter jets. He flew with BOAC for twenty-five years. He was a keen yachtsman. Died from Alzheimer's disease on 16 March 2008.

James Heath (29/02/1952) Birth announcement – on 7 July 1957, at Newcastle General Hospital, to Marjorie and James Heath – a son (Robin John Swift). Joined RAuxAF and 609 Squadron after completing two years national service. Pilot flying jets.

Peter Hodgson (02/08/1949) Birth announcement – on 14 January to Cecilia and Peter Hodgson – a son (James).

Arthur Hudson (11/01/1952) Joined RAuxAF and 609 Squadron after completing two years national service. Pilot flying jets.

Francis Reacroft (27/11/1953) Joined RAuxAF and 609 Squadron after completing two years national Service. Pilot flying jets.

David R Shaw (11/01/1952) Joined RAuxAF and 609 Squadron after completing two years national Service. Pilot flying jets. Set up the 609 Squadron Association. Member of Leeds University Air Squadron.[27]

Malcolm Slingsby (27/02/1951) Joined RAuxAF and 609 Squadron after completing two years national service. Pilot flying jets. Set up the 609 Squadron Association.

Patrick H Womersley (17/09/1946) CO of 609 Squadron between 1947 & 1949. Marriage announcement in *The Times*, comes from Halifax.

610 (County of Chester) Squadron

Cyril Stanley Bamberger (02/08/1949) Born on 4 May 1919 in Hyde, Cheshire and educated locally, he left school at fourteen and joined Lever Brothers as an electrical apprentice. Joined the AAF in 1936 as an aerial photographer. Accepted for pilot training in 1938, after demob he returned to Lever before joining the management of a Guinness subsidiary. Re-joined RAuxAF, becoming CO in 1950. He founded a packaging materials company in civilian life. He died on 3 February 2008, age 88.

Hugh Dundas DSO, DFC, CBE (21/10/1947) Born on 22 July 1920 in Doncaster, and educated at Stowe. After leaving school he was articled to a firm of solicitors in Barnsley. Joined the AAF and served as a Spitfire pilot during the Second World War. Left the RAF in 1947 and joined RAuxAF later in that year. Worked for Beaverbrook newspapers until 1960 and then joined Rediffusion. Knighted in 1987, he died on 10 July 1995, aged 74.

James Anthony Leathart (03/03/1947) Born on 5 January 1915, the son of a doctor. Attended St Edward's School in Oxford, being one of the few students to own their own car. Went to Liverpool University to study engineering. re-joined the RAuxAF in 1947 he worked in civilian life for Mapelridge Enterprises, and later for Cleanacres, a crop spraying company. Retired to concentrate on fly fishing. He died on 17 November 1998, aged 83.

A.B. Mercer (17/09/1946) The weather cleared just in time for today's only event – a four lap race open to Royal Auxiliary Air Force pilots. Flying Officer A.B. Mercer came third with an average speed of 331 mph.

611 (West Lancashire) Squadron
Eric Ainsworth (02/08/1949) Pilot with 611 Squadron. Worked for Britax Weathershield as its financial director.

R.A. Bailey (01/05/1947) Killed on 3 July 1949 when he stalled and spun in on approach to Woodvale, returning from Exercise Foil at Coltishall in his Spitfire.

R.L.J. Barbour (01/01/1950) Took part in yachting regatta's. Took part in National Redwing Dinghy Championships in Paignton.

Robin Birley (01/01/1950) Marriage announcement in *The Times*.

Alec Finlay (26/10/1948) Appointed group planning director of British Airways.

Desmond Fopp (17/09/1946) Born on 13 March 1920, on a fruit farm at Cudlee Creek near Adelaide. Joined the RAFVR in 1938 and was trained as a pilot. After the war he joined the RAuxAF with 611 Squadron and trained on Vampire jets. He also trained as a helicopter pilot. Working as a civilian he was an air traffic controller for the Army Air Corps. He died on 8 August 2005, aged 85.

R.C. Gaskell (27/05/1946) Engagement announcement for Squadron Leader Reginald Charles Gaskell of Porthcawl, South Wales. Sons marriage also announced.

Peter Geldart (24/03/1947) Birth announcement – on Christmas Day, 1972, to Anne and Peter Geldart – a son (James George Bradley). Managing Director of Durie and Miller.

Robert Hugh Price Griffiths (09/04/1946) Killed when he crashed his Spitfire on Freckleton Marsh near Grange Farm after losing consciousness due to oxygen starvation at 21,000 feet. Died on 8 May 1948.

Colin Hodgkinson (17/09/1946) Born at Wells, Somerset on 11 February 1920, he was the son of a Royal Flying Corps pilot. Enjoyed country pursuits such as hunting, shooting and fishing. Educated at Pangbourne Nautical College. Began his flying career with the Fleet Air Arm in 1938. Having qualified as a pilot, he suffered following a mid-air collision which resulted in severe burns and the loss of both legs. Influenced by the success of Douglas Bader, he joined the RAF as a pilot. December 1943, he lost control of his aircraft over France. He was a prisoner of war for ten months. Joined the RAuxAF and 611 Squadron in 1946. In civilian life he had a career in public relations and advertising. He lived in France and died on 13 September 1996, aged 76.

Stanley H Lawrence (18/03/1947) Managing Director of New Day (Holdings). Becomes Vice Chairman of New Day Holdings, in addition to his role as group managing director.

William Johnson Leather (17/09/1946) Marriage announcement in *The Times*.

Peter C Lothian (23/09/1948) Killed when his Spitfire collided with another aircraft during a formation flight with 611 Squadron.

William James McCann (11/08/1951) Marriage announcement – elder son of Colonel W.F.J. McCann, DSO, OBE and of the late Mrs Mildred McCann of Tusmore, South Australia.

V.D. Page (05/12/1946) Awarded DFC. Awarded Bar To DFC.

Alan Pimblett (01/01/1946) Appointed to the board of fibre-glass, part of the Pilkington Group.

Francis David Stephen Scott-Malden (17/09/1946) Born on 26 December 1917 at Portslade, East Sussex and educated at Winchester and Kings College, Cambridge. He joined the University Air Squadron and in October 1939, was mobilised into the RAF. Joined RAuxAF in 1946 and served with 611 Squadron until disbandment in 1957. In civilian life he was a principal in the Department of Transport. In his retirement he enjoyed trout fishing and gardening. He died on 2 March 2000, aged 80.

Harry E Walmsley (17/09/1946) DFC awarded.

A.H. Warminger (19/09/1951) Lived in Norwich and in civilian life was a waste paper merchant. Main hobby was gliding and he set a new British record when he was able to take a glider up to 30,000 feet.

612 (County of Aberdeen) Squadron
Ramsey Roger Russell (17/12/1946) Grammar school student. Worked in his father's building contractor business.[28]

613 (City of Manchester) Squadron
Frederick Butterworth (02/08/1949) As a local Bournemouth Town Councillor he bought the Branksome Tower Hotel for £200,000 and sold it again three weeks later. Latest wills – Mr Frederick Butterworth of Bournemouth, Dorset left £603,422.

James Storrs Morton (17/09/1946) Marriage announcement in *The Times*.

Louis Ollier (23/09/1948) Killed age twenty-six when a Spitfire that he was piloting crashed in a field at Spalding, Lincolnshire. The squadron were near Norwich for their summer camp.

Gwyn Parry DFC (11/02/1947) Born near Wrexham in 1921. He studied Law at Oxford University, joining the University Air Squadron in 1931. He qualified as a solicitor, and eventually took up lecturing law at Manchester University. Joined the RAuxAF in early 1947. After three years with 613 Squadron he transferred to the RAuxAF Reserve. He died in September 2004, aged 83.

Jack B Wales OBE, DFC (17/09/1946) Killed in a flying accident on 7 December 1956. He was a production test pilot for A.V. Roe Aircraft Manufacturing Company. He was thirty-nine. Born January 1917. Joined the army in 1936. Seconded to the RAF and served as a fighter pilot. He joined 613 Squadron in 1946, and became CO in 1949.

614 (County of Glamorgan) Squadron
Nigel Palmer (03/05/1947) Killed when two Vampires belonging to 614 Squadron collided in the air over the Isle of Wight on 28 November 1954.

615 (County of Surrey) Squadron
Louis Charles Bazalgette (02/08/1949) Age twenty-nine, was fined £10 and ordered to pay £13 2s. 6d costs at Bromley Magistrates' Court on 20 August 1951 for driving a car in a dangerous manner at Farnborough on 22 July. He had been found not guilty of driving under the influence of alcohol.

Neville Frederick Duke (17/09/1946) Appointed Chief Test Pilot by Hawker Aircraft Ltd in 1951. Awarded the Seagrove Trophy by the Royal Automobile Club for breaking the world's air speed record in a Hawker Hunter. Born on 11 January 1922 and educated at the Judd School, Tonbridge. Fighter pilot during the war. He died on 7 April 2007, aged 85.

Denys Gillam (08/10/1946) Born on 18 November 1915 and was educated at Bramcote, Scarborough and at Wrekin College. Joined the RAF in 1935. After the war he joined the RAuxAF with 615 Squadron. He was Chairman of the Family carpet firm, Homfray and co. He died on 2 July 1991, age 75.

J.W. Charles Judge (19/02/1947) Test pilot for Vickers Armstrong Ltd in 1950. Moved to Rolls-Royce and then to Beagle as a test pilot. He joined Airmark in 1970, but was killed in a flying accident in 1970.

Ronald Gustave Kellett (17/09/1946) Marriage announcement in *The Times*. Born on 13 September 1909, and educated at Rossall School. Spent all of his civilian life working as a stockbroker. Served in the RAuxAF from 1946-1949, then enjoyed country pursuits such as hunting and shooting. He was also a keen sailor. He died on 12 November 1998, aged 89.

Hugh Merewether (04/04/1950) Pilot for Hawker Siddeley Group.[29]

Ian Smith (11/03/1951) Civilian pilot.

Trevor Wade (17/09/1946) Born 27 January 1920 and educated in Tonbridge, he joined the RAFVR aged eighteen and trained to become a pilot. He joined Hawker Aircraft as a test pilot in 1948, and was killed on 3 April 1951 when the prototype Hawker P1081 crashed near Lewes, Sussex.

616 (South Yorkshire) Squadron

Lionel Harwood Casson (27/02/1951) Son of a steel buyer, born in Sheffield on 6 January 1915 and educated at Birkdale School and then the King's School, Ely, before embarking on a career in the steel industry. Although he was employed in a reserved occupation, he joined the Auxiliary Air Force and elected to remain with them on the outbreak of war when he had completed his pilot training. He fought with 616 Squadron throughout the war and was shot down over France and captured near St Omer. He was then sent to Stalag Luft III at Sagan. At the end of the war having been awarded the DFC, he returned to the steel industry in Sheffield.

John W Harland (04/07/1947) In Memoriam – in devoted memory of John, Flt Lt of 616 Squadron RAuxAF. A dear son and brother who did not return from a night air exercise. 11 December 1952.

Kenneth Holden (18/03/1947) Marriage announcement. Birth announcement – on 4 March 1940 at Lynfield Nursing Home, Altringham, Cheshire, to Winkie, Wife of Kenneth Holden – a daughter. Business news – Mr Kenneth Holden has joined the board of Geigy (Holdings). Mr Kenneth Holden, Chairman of William Deacon's Bank Ltd has been appointed a director of G.N. Haden & Sons Ltd.

Roger Hargreaves Maw (17/09/1946) Born on 21 June 1906. Son of a Lincolnshire landowner. Educated at Westerleigh School, St Leonard's on Sea and Oundle Boarding School. He joined 503 Squadron in 1927 to learn to fly. He was shot down during the Second World War and is famous for designing the wooden vaulting horse used by his fellow prisoners of war, to escape. He re-joined the RAuxAF in 1946, whilst returning to Lincolnshire and farming at Welton, near Lincoln, before retiring to the Wolds village of Walesby. He died on 19 August, age 86.

500 (County of Kent) Squadron
Desmond De Villiers (17/09/1946) Test pilot for de Havilland.[30]

Charles Patrick Green (17/09/1946) Marriage announcement in *The Times*. Second son of Mr and Mrs Bay Green of Canterbury. DFC awarded. Wool merchant from Canterbury.

Hugh Charles Kennard (07/02/1952) Marriage announcement for Pilot Officer Hugh Charles Kennard only son of Mr and Mrs Charles Kennard of Linton, Kent.

501 (County of Gloucester) Squadron.
Richard Francis Wharton Cleaver (16/08/1946) Marriage announcement – Flight Lieutenant R.F.W. Cleaver, only son of Mr and Mrs R.L. Cleaver of Sevenoaks.

Birth announcement – on 9 November 1948, at Bristol Maternity Hospital, to Dorothy, wife of Flt Lt R.F.W. Cleaver – a daughter (Gillian Ruth). Birth announcement – on 16 March 1951, at Salisbury General Infirmary, to Dorothy, wife of Sqn Ldr R.F.W. Cleaver – a daughter (Elizabeth Jane).

Michael C Collings (15/02/1946) Architect.[31]

John G Crossley (13/11/1953) Killed aged twenty-eight, when his Vampire jet flew under the Clifton Suspension Bridge and hit the bank of the River Avon just prior to the final disbandment parade for the squadron. He was a single man who was employed by the flight test department of a subsidiary of the Bristol Aeroplane Company. He lived in Bristol but his home was in Blackburn. Electrical engineer for Bristol Aeroplane Company.[32]

Brian Dicks (13/11/1953) Navigator for BOAC.[33]

Robert Dunlop (26/10/1948) Flight Test Observer for Bristol Britannia.[34]

Alan Griffin (21/05/1949) Chartered Surveyor.[35]

A.C. Henderson (19/04/1947) Businessman.[36]

Geoffrey Higginbottom (09/02/1951) Pilot for Olympus-Canberra.[37]

Nigel Palmer (29/09/1953) Teacher.[38]

John Sharpe (23/11/1955) Architect.[39]

E Brien Smith (01/08/1946) The weather cleared just in time for today's only event – a four lap race open to Royal Auxiliary Air Force pilots. Flying Officer E.B. Smith came second in the race with an average speed of 446 mph. Worked as a test pilot for Gloster Aircraft Company. Killed in August 1956 in a mid-air collision.[40]

Robert Staton (12/05/1953) Made a director of Spearhead Chemicals.

Michael Webber (17/08/1953) Flight Test Observer for Bristol Britannia.

502 (Ulster) Squadron
W Bowden (27/07/1946) The weather cleared just in time for today's only event – a four lap race open to Royal Auxiliary Air Force pilots. The winner was Flying Officer W Bowden of No 502 (Ulster) Squadron, representing Northern Ireland, with an average speed of 325 mph, a civil engineer in civilian life.[41]

J Campbell (09/04/1946) Killed when his Mosquito aircraft flew into the southern slopes of Snowdon, 1000ft below the summit during a thunderstorm on Saturday, both occupants were killed.

William Hunter McGiffin (17/09/1946) Birthday Honours award of OBE.

504 (County of Nottingham) Squadron
Joseph Crescens Reynolds (02/08/1949) Death announcement – on 18 May 1971, peacefully at King Edward VII Hospital, Midhurst, Sussex, after suffering most bravely borne. Joseph Crescens Reynolds, Wing Commander Royal Auxiliary Air Force, 504 Squadron.

Michael Rook (11/12/1946) Marriage announcement in *The Times*. Son of Mr and Mrs W.R. Rook of Edwalton House, Nottingham. Born on 12 October 1915, he was educated at Oakham School and later at Uppingham School. He joined the family wine and grocery business – Skinner and Rook Ltd, as wine department manager in 1934. He loved motor racing and flying. He married at the age of twenty. In 1938 he joined 504 (County of Nottingham) Squadron. At the outbreak of war the squadron were sent to Lille in France, and later the squadron moved up to Wick as members of 12 Group, protecting northern cities and eastern approaches. The squadron moved south during 1939 and played an active role in the Battle of Britain. On 27 August 1941 he was posted to No 81 (F) Squadron and was sent to Northern Russia. Killed Saturday, 13 March 1948 when his Mosquito fighter crashed in a field at Moor Green, Nottinghamshire, aged 34.

Officers commissioned into the Royal Auxiliary Air Force with no squadron number given

Eric Ainsworth (08/03/1953) Financial Director of Britax.

T Appleton (19/04/1947) Business news – Mr T Appleton has been appointed director and general manager of Balfour Kilpatrick Installations. Mr T Appleton has been appointed a divisional director of the Super Tension Cables division of British Insulated Callander's Cables. Mr T Appleton has been appointed a director of Croydon Cable Television. He remains executive director of Balfour Kilpatrick and Balfour Beatty.

Anthony Barker (01/10/1948) Marriage announcement.

Arthur Barnes (14/04/1953) Birth announcement – on 20 July 1948, at the Howard Nursing Home, Maidstone, to Iris and Arthur Barnes of 4, Hayle Road, Maidstone, a girl.

James Michael Birkin (05/02/1956) Marriage announcement – Group Captain James Michael Birkin CB, DSO, OBE DFC, AFC, RAuxAF, second son of the late Major H.L. Birkin and of Mrs Birkin of Lincoln House, The Park, Nottingham. A memorial service for Air Commodore James Michael Birkin was held at St Clement Danes Church. Born on 23 April 1912. Aide-de-camp to Queen Elizabeth from 1957-963. High Sheriff of the Isle of Wight. Died on 17 November 1985.

Arthur Brearley (14/04/1953) Business appointments – made Director of post-experience Programmes at the management centre of the University of Bradford.

Dennis Curran (01/06/1950) Worked for the BBC, and supported a call for a change in TV control.

Walter Durward (19/05/1953) A BEA Viscount with four people on board was missing in a snow storm in the Scottish Highlands. The pilot was Walter Durward, aged 43, of Bridge of Weir, Renfrewshire.

William Gordon Evans (01/01/1953) 53, Craven Park Road, Stamford Hill, London, N15, trading as a Greengrocer at 16, Cleave Avenue, Farnborough, Kent, declared bankrupt.

David Charles Fairbanks (07/10/1953) David Charles Fairbanks Clothes, offering a prize of £100 for a wordsearch puzzle at Harrods.

H.B. Farnfield (19/04/1947) Elected to the council of the Airbrokers Association.

John Beresford Hardie (15/10/1947) Death announcement – Hardie, John Beresford, 4 September 1996, late of Sydney Australia.

John Cassford Jupe (23/11/1955) Death announcement – on 5 July in a road accident, John Cassford Jupe, aged 42, of 28, White Ledges, St Stephen's Road, Ealing, W3.

Charles Eagan Lamberton (26/10/1950) An airline captain who hid cigarettes and spirits on board a Viscount aircraft pleaded guilty at Southend Magistrate's Court to six summonses for evading duty on a total of 6000 cigarettes and concealing a further 4000 cigarettes and twelve half bottles of spirits on board the plane. Charles Eagan Lamberton, aged 43, the former personal pilot of King Faisal was fined a total of £300 with 25 guineas costs.

Leonard Younger Lee (14/01/1948) Marriage announcement.

Michael Taylor Moore (28/03/1950) Death announcement – Moore, Michael Taylor MA, MBB, RCS, LRCP, of Cirencester, formerly of Grittleton, Wiltshire, died peacefully on 7 June 2008.

Paul Richey (11/05/1953) Birth announcement – on 25 November 1946, at 36, Walton Street, London, SW3, to Teresa, wife of Wing Commander Paul Richey DFC, a son. Marriage announcement. The marriage took place quietly in Nice, on Friday, 5 October between Wing Commander Paul Richey, son of the late Lieutenant Colonel G.H.M. Richey and Mrs Adelaide Richey of 3, Orme Court, W2. Daughter's marriage announcement. Younger daughter's marriage announcement. Third marriage announcement for Wing Commander Paul Richey. Obituary - born in May 1916 and educated in Switzerland and Downside before joining the AAF in 1937. After war service he re-joined the RAuxAF.

Eric Spence (22/02/1953) Residing at 46, Brougham Street, Birkenhead, Chester, trading as E and J Spence, declared bankrupt.

Robert Forrester Stephen (17/01/1953) Marriage announcement – RAuxAF, son of the late H.B. Stephen MBE, of High Burnside.

Victor John Townsend (18/02/1952) An airline pilot, of Mayfield House, Lowfield, Surrey, pleaded not guilty at Surrey Assizes at Kingston upon Thames yesterday to wounding a Turkish waiter with intent to cause grievous bodily harm, by firing a pistol loaded with a blank cartridge in his face. He was found not guilty but was fined £100 for unlawful possession of a gas pistol, which was ordered to be confiscated. Death announcement – on 28 May, peacefully after a long illness bravely fought, Victor John Townsend, DFC.

John C Trigg (14/04/1947) Marriage announcement – John Trigg of Hinderwell, Surrey.

APPENDIX 3

United Kingdom Officers of the Royal Air Force Volunteer Reserve

Richard Bernard Pape (22/10/1946) The Military Medal has been awarded Richard Bernard Pape of the RAFVR who was shot down in 1941 close to the Dutch-German frontier. He managed to make his way to Amsterdam before being arrested and tortured. He escaped five months later, but was re-arrested and tortured. He spent a year in hospital before continuing his underground activities.

Albert James Smith (22/10/1946) Awarded the Military Medal. Born on 5 November 1924 in Cardiff, he was educated at the Central School, Newbridge. He joined the RAFVR in 1943, and was able to study for university entrance. He graduated from University College of Wales with first class honours. He married in 1950. He continued with his research at Aberystwyth and Oriel College Oxford which resulted in a Leverhulme Award to study in Florence. After three years teaching at Manchester Grammar School, he joined the Academic staff at University College, Swansea, before leaving to take up the Chair of English at the University of Keele in 1971. He wrote many books and held several teaching and research Fellowships abroad. He gave the British Academy's Warton Lecture in 1985. He died on 11 December 1991, aged 67. Memorial service announcement. Will announcement – Professor Albert James Smith of Whiteparish, Wiltshire, professor of English at Southampton University 1974-1990, left estate valued at £159,005 net.

John Hinchcliffe (22/10/1946) Awarded the Military Medal. Legal manager of News Group Newspapers. Born on 19 August 1910, educated at Colfe's Grammar School and King's College, London. Joined the *News Of The World* in 1931. Served in the RAFVR. Retired in 1975 and served as a local councillor, a school governor, and General Commissioner for Taxes. He died on 24 January 1993, aged 82.

Douglas George Parry (22/10/1946) Awarded the Military Medal. Born on 8 April 1915 and joined the RAFVR as soon as he left school. He flew throughout the war, being awarded the DFC and then the Bar. Demobbed in 1947, he became a structural engineer, remaining in the RAFVR until it was disbanded. He then became a Warning Officer in the UK Warning and Monitoring Organisation, retiring in 1991, having been appointed MBE. He died on 2 August 1999, aged 84.

Martin Andrew Nash (22/10/1946) Awarded the Military Medal. Wing Commander Martin Andrew Nash RAFVR awarded OBE in 2005.

Richard Alexander Gordon (05/02/1947) Marriage announcement – Flight Lieutenant Richard Alexander Gordon, youngest son of the late Mr A.R. Gordon and of Mrs Gordon, Farragon, Pitlochry. Death Announcement – Suddenly, on 24 December 1968 at Carriston Farm, Star of Markinch, Fife, Richard Alexander Gordon.

Robert Ian Robertson (05/02/1947) Death announcement – one week short of his eightieth birthday, peacefully at Princess Margaret Hospital, Windsor on 21 August 2002.

Michael John Philip Martin (24/02/1947) Marriage announcement for Squadron Leader Michael John Philip Martin DFC, AFC, RAFVR, younger son of Mr Philip A Martin of Charminster, Dorset. Engagement announcement for Michael John Philip Martin, DFC, AFC, of 14, Brook Green, Hammersmith, W6.

John Nicholas Emery (09/05/1947) Death announcement – very suddenly at his home Tigh Cull, Glenalmond, Perthshire, on Wednesday, 25 August 1982, John Nicholas Emery MA.

Leonard Rudkin (10/07/1947) Marriage announcement for daughter of Mr and Mrs Leonard Rudkin of Ladycroft, Marsh Lane, Mill Hill, NW7.

John Frederick Gulland (11/07/1947) Marriage announcement – Flight Lieutenant John Frederick Gulland, RAFVR, younger son of Mr and Mrs F.A. Gulland, Langley, Maidstone.

Ian Stewart Lloyd (12/04/1947) Born on 30 May 1921 in Durban, South Africa. Educated at Michaelhouse School and then Witwatersrand University. After demob from the South African Air Force he won a scholarship to Kings College, Cambridge University to read economics. Returned to South Africa for a while but so anti-apartheid that he returned to the UK and became a Conservative MP for Portsmouth Langstone which he held until 1992. He was knighted in 1986. He died on 26 September 2006, aged 85. He was a Spitfire pilot in the South African Air Force, and served with the RAFVR between 1947 and 1952. He sailed and skied for Cambridge University and graduated with an MSc in 1952.

John Hampton Hale (10/07/1947) Death announcement – Hale, John Hampton died peacefully in his sleep from cancer on 8 January, aged 77.

Michael Plaistowe Kilburn (14/07/1947) Born in London on 15 April 1922. Served with the RAFVR from 1940-1953, and was awarded the DFC and Croix de Guerre. Attended the Fairey Aviation Design School, training as an aeronautical engineer. Graduated in 1949 and worked as a test pilot for de Havilland. He retired in 1987.

Peter Frank Hall (25/07/1947) Death announcement – Hall on 29 March 1995, peacefully at his home in Shenton, Leicestershire, Peter Frank Hall, in his seventy-ninth year. Latest wills – Mr Peter Frank Hall of Shenton, Leicestershire - £1,253,150. Peter Frank Hall was a POW, in Stalag Luft Sagan from 2 May 1940 till 27 January 1945. His rank was flight lieutenant.

Edward Victor Campbell Smith (16/07/1947) Marriage announcement – Squadron Leader Edward Victor Campbell Smith, son of Mr and Mrs E Victor Smith of London, Ontario, Canada. Lived at 199, Sussex Gardens, London, W2, and worked as a manufacturing optician.

David Stewart Flett (13/08/1947) The pilot and owners of a freight plane which ran out of fuel and crashed into the Russian zone of Berlin were fined at Marylebone, London. The plane, which belonged to Silver City Airlines Ltd was on a flight from Berlin to Hamburg on 19 January 1953 when bad weather prevented it from landing. The pilot, David Stewart Flett decided to return to Berlin, but ran out of fuel and crashed on a railway line. The company was fined £300, and Captain Flett was fined £50 for failing to satisfy himself that he had enough fuel to complete the return journey.

Robert Christopher Hesketh Jones (13/08//1947) Marriage announcement – Flying Officer Robert Christopher Hesketh Jones, elder son of Mr A.E. Jones and Mrs Jones, Epping Place, Epping, Essex.

Donald Alfred James Draper (09/08/1947) By order of the High Court, dated 16 September 1985, Mr Donald Alfred James Draper of Pembroke House, 40, City Road, London, EC1, has been appointed Liquidator of the above named company. Donald Alfred James Draper, FCA, FIPA, of Fraser & Russell was appointed Liquidator. Listed as a Chartered Accountant.

Gordon Sim (25/08/1947) Director of Science and Engineering Lockheed-California Co. Born in Nottingham in 1911, he was educated in Nottingham and then at the Working Men's College in London. He became a journalist and was elected to London County Council. He joined the RAFVR and was commissioned as a pilot officer in April 1942. He remained in the RAFVR after the war, resigning his commission in 1952. He was elected to Parliament in 1945, and served until 1959, when he lost his seat. He was created Baron Beswick of Hucknall in 1964. He served as Parliamentary Under Secretary of State in 1965. He died on 17 August 1987.

Walter James Rosser (13/09/1947) Marriage announcement – on 3 November 1949 at Northampton, to Alys Mary Davison. Born in 1917 and educated at Northampton Grammar School, after which he studied architecture, he joined the RAFVR in October 1938. After the war he worked as an estate agent, whilst remaining in the RAFVR. Died on 13 October 2009, aged 92.

Douglas George Wiltshire (13/09/1947) Six different entries in *The Times* regarding a policeman who pulled Douglas George Wiltshire by his ears when he would not get out of his car. Mr Douglas George Wiltshire aged forty-eight of Brook House, Botley, Hampshire, is a farmer who runs three grocery shops in Southampton was claiming damages for assault and battery by PC Denis Stanley Barrett. He was eventually awarded £589 plus costs after a jury ruled that he had been illegally arrested. New trial before a new jury ordered.

Leslie Atkinson (31/10/1947) UK division director of Flexibox International. Daughter's marriage announcement. Sue, daughter of Mr and Mrs Leslie Atkinson of Manuden, Bishop's Stortford. Non-executive director of Foreign and Colonial Pacific Investment Trust.

Michael John Leeson (01/10/1947) Marriage announcement – Michael John Leeson, son of Mr and Mrs J.R. Leeson of Woodhouse Eaves, Leicestershire. Birth announcement – on 6 January to Lesley Marguerite and Michael John Leeson, of Hoby, Leicestershire – a daughter.

Douglas William Moore (06/11/1947) Death announcement – Moore, Douglas William, resident of Ferring for the last sixteen years, unexpectedly, but peacefully passed away at Worthing Hospital on 13 June 2010, aged 86.

Alfred Outram Pullman (06/11/1947) Posthumous award of the DFC to Alfred Outram Pullman, in recognition of Gallant and distinguished service in operations in Kenya. Flight Lieutenant Pullman, who was thirty-seven years of age, was killed in an accident in Kenya last February while flying a Harvard Aircraft. Father of Philip Pullman, British writer.

David Llewelyn Morgan (05/12/1947) Birth announcement – on 23 November 1967, to Elisabeth and David Llewelyn Morgan, of Stowe St Mary, Essex – a second son (Huw A.P. David Llewelyn) Chartered Accountant of Alfred Tooke and Co, 8, Upper Grosvenor Street, London. Letter to *The Times*, David Llewelyn Morgan, 25, Newbiggen Street, Thaxted, Great Dunmow, Essex. Son's marriage announcement.

Herbert Denham Parker (06/12/1947) Latest wills – Mr Herbert Denham Parker of Pinner, West London - £929,767.

George Herbert Chesterton (06/12/1947) Marriage announcement – George Herbert Chesterton, younger son of the Rev J.A. and Mrs Chesterton of Tenbury, Worcestershire.

Donald Alastair Stewart McKay (10/12/1947) Bar to DFM awarded to Donald Alastair Stewart McKay, RAFVR.

Ronald Henry Smith (02/12/1947) Marriage announcement – Robert Henry Smith, only son of Mr H.E. Smith CBE and Mrs Smith, of 8, Mostyn Road, SW19. Death announcement – Smith, Ronald Henry PHD, FRSE, died peacefully on 17 September 2009, aged 86.

Philip John Quarles Back (10/12/1947) The following have been appointed officers of the Dyers' Company for the Ensuing year – Renter Warden – Mr Philip John Quarles Back.

Thomas Henry Kerr (01/01/1948) Born in Nottingham on 18 June 1924. Educated at Magnus Grammar School, Newark. Joined the Air Training Corps whilst at school and the RAFVR in 1942. After the war he gained a first in physics at Durham University. Spent all of his working life researching aero-engineering. He retired in 1984, he was a freeman of the City of London, and a liveryman of the Guild of Air Pilots and Air Navigators. He died on 9 September 2004, aged 80.

Peter McAinsh (03/01/1948) Business appointments – Babcock Energy, Mr Peter McAinsh becomes Managing Director, Babcock Construction, article written for *The Times* by Peter McAinsh. He is an employer-member of the reconstituted Engineering Trading Board and newly appointed Chairman of ECIS, the Engineering and Construction Industry Sector.

Evelyn Herbert Webb (03/01/1948) Death announcement – Webb, Evelyn Herbert, on Saturday, 4 January 2002, aged 79.

APPENDIX 3

Andrew Graham Stewart McCallum (05/01/1948) Marriage announcement – elder son of Mr and Mrs H.G. McCallum, Endrick Bridge of Weir, Renfrewshire.

James Patrick Dix Rafferty (03/01/1948) Latest wills – Mr James Patrick Dix Rafferty of Cheam, Surrey - £529,817. J.P.D. Rafferty bequest helps art education at Epsom College.

Robert Andrew Routh (07/01/1948) Birth announcement – on 18 October at Westhaven Nursing Home, Lancaster, to Marrianne, wife of Robert Andrew Routh – a son (Robert Hugh).

David Knightly (26/01/1948) Marriage announcement – on 13 November 1953, at Caxton Hall, David Knightly to Betty Fahnestock. Christening announcement. Birth announcement. Death announcement for David Knightly – Died on 4 December 1981. Latest wills – David Knightly of Britford who created the container ship company, Concargo, left estate valued at £555,016 net.

John Lake (12/01/1948) Birth announcement – on 2 February 1947, at the Lansdowne Nursing Home, Tunbridge Wells, to Stephanie, wife of John Lake – a daughter.

George Buckley (16/04/1948) Birth announcement – on 3 May 1943, at 72, The Headlands, Kettering, to Beryl, wife of Flt Lt George Buckley – a son (Stephen George). Death announcement for son, Stephen George, suddenly of a heart attack, aged 55, son of the late George and Beryl.

Donal James Black (13/05/1948) Marriage announcement - on 14 February 1953, at St Joseph's Church, Highgate, London. Donal James Black, son of Mr and Mrs Stuart Black, of Edinburgh.

John Buist (07/05/1948) Born in Woodgaven, Fife in 1904 and educated at the Morgan Academy, Dundee and Glasgow University. Journalist who worked on the *Courier* and *Evening Telegraph* in Dundee, and *The Glasgow Herald*. Joined *The Times* in 1945. Left *The Times* in 1958 and went to the BBC. Retired to Scotland. Died on 27 June 1982, aged 77.

Peter Clifton Aspinall (14/06/1948) Death announcement – Peter Clifton Aspinall CBE, died on 18 May 2004.

Hugh Laughland (15/06/1948) Hugh Laughland appointed chief executive for Scottish and Universal Investments. Mr Laughland is former managing director of Scottish Aviation.

Thomas Cecil Clayton (19/07/1948) Roseneath, Cottram Lane, Ashton-on-Ribble, Lancashire. Director of Horsley Smith Group Ltd.

Gerald Arthur Mitchell (22/07/1948) Marriage announcement – Gerald Arthur Mitchell.

Norman James Crisp (17/08/1948) Born on 11 December 1923, he was a prolific author, television writer and dramatist, known for *Dixon of Dock Green*, *Dr Finlay's Case Book* and *Colditz*. Died on 14 June 2005, aged 81. Born in Southampton, he served in the RAF.

Leslie Alfred Davies (20/08/1948) Death announcement – Davies, Leslie Alfred on 14 November 1996, suddenly in hospital, aged 73 years. Donations for the Air Crew Association.

Michael Taylor Moore (14/08/1948) Death announcement – Moore, Michael Taylor of Cirencester, formerly of Grittleton. Died peacefully on 7 June 2008.

Harry Conrad Vaughan Hawker (06/09/1948) Aged thirty-eight, airline pilot of Nether Wallop, Hampshire, found not guilty of dangerous flying and low flying on 17 June at Seaview, Isle of Wight. Death announcement – Hawker, Harry Conrad Vaughan DFC, after a short illness at King Edward VII Hospital for Officers, on 23 May.

Hamish Rattray Selkirk (04/09/1948) Born in Rangoon where his father was a civil engineer, he was sent to Scotland to be brought up by his aunt. Educated at Harrow, he excelled at gymnastics and rugby. Served in the RAF during the war, he was turned down for a permanent commission in the RAF when war ended. He worked as a salesman for Dunlop. He died on 29 October 2004, aged 84.

Arthur William Cole (28/07/1948) Death announcement – Cole, Arthur William, on 17 September 1984, the result of a road traffic accident.

Gordon Wallis McCabe (08/09/1948) Marriage announcement – Gordon Wallis McCabe DSC, elder son of Mr and Mrs C McCabe, of Eversley, Boxley Road, Maidstone, Kent. Death announcement – McCabe, Gordon Wallis, aged 77, peacefully in hospital.

William Robert Miller (02/11/1948) Awarded OBE for services to British charitable interests.

Duncan Swale (18/11/1948) Son's marriage announcement – Robin, elder son of Mr Duncan Swale and Mrs Joan Swale of Chesterfield, Derbyshire.

Denis Winton (18/11/1948) Birth announcement – Winton – on 30 August 1947 to Loveday Alison, wife of Denis Winton – a daughter. Son's marriage announcement – Simon, youngest son of Mr Denis Winton of Newburgh, Fife.

Denis Richard Maguire (19/11/1948) Death announcement – Maguire, Denis Richard, 1 April 2004, died peacefully in hospital after a short illness, aged 81.

James Orr Barclay (28/10/1948) Death announcement – Barclay, James Orr, late RAF, formally of Ponteland, passed away with dignity on 27 December, aged 82.

Cyril James Palmer (30/09/1948) Marriage announcement – Christopher James Palmer of 29, Ashburn Place, South Kensington, eldest son of Mr and Mrs J.L. Palmer of Chetwode, Mannamead, Plymouth.

Arthur Patterson Walker (30/09/1948) Legal notices – Walker, Arthur Patterson, Bucketts Lund Farm, Well End, Borcham Wood, Hertfordshire. Air Traffic Controller. Died 17 October 1967.

John Peter Scott Taylor (03/11/1948) Birth announcement – on 10 December 1955 to Ruth Marion and John Peter Scott Taylor – a son, brother for Nigel. Deputy Principal Clerk to the House of Commons. Also Member of the Dulwich Leaseholder's Association.

APPENDIX 3

Roy Vine (12/11/1948) Former senior general manager at Barclay's Bank. Vice Chairman at Barclay's Bank and also a director of First National Finance Corporation.

Frank Burdekin (12/11/1948) Managing Director of J Burdekin, a family firm, established in 1891. Latest Wills – Frank Burdekin left an estate valued at £1,248,083 net.

Arthur Burdett (16/11/1948) Son's marriage announcement – David, youngest son of Mr Arthur Burdett and Mrs S.H. Oldham of 16, Sutherland House, W8.

Henry Fairfax Perrin (31/01/1949) Marriage announcement for Henry Fairfax Perrin, younger son of Canon Howard N and Mrs Perrin of The Pleasance, Grange Park, Westbury-on -Trym, Bristol.

Eric William Harbutt (03/12/1948) Company in liquidation – Eric William Harbutt of Bathampton, Bath, in the County of Somerset holding a general Power of Attourney from Harbutt's Plasticine Limited of the same address.

Terence Armstrong (06/12/1948) Birth announcement – on 6 April 1948, at Cambridge to Iris Decima and Terence Armstrong – a son (Kevin Patrick). Birth announcement – on 6 January 1950, to Iris and Terence Armstrong, 6, Melbourne Place, Cambridge – Benedict, a brother for Kevin.

John Edward Constantine (09/12/1948) John Edward Constantine, a public relations officer and his wife of Carshalton Park Road, Carshalton, were viciously assaulted by two men following a collision between their two cars early on New Years Day.

Stanley Davenport (10/12/1948) Marriage announcement – on Wednesday, 24 January 1945 in London. Stanley Davenport to Renee Page.

Eric Francis Burgess (13/12/1948) In Memoriam – Burgess, Eric Francis, DFC, killed flying, 29 September 1973.

Stephen Richard Coote Hales (15/12/1948) Death announcement – Hales, Stephen Richard Coote, slipped from us on the morning of 2 August.

Stuart Henry Dallas (30/12/1948) Marriage announcement – Mr Stuart Henry Dallas of Totnes, Devon.

Roy George Archer (31/12/1948) Mr Roy George Archer has won the Institute of Marketing's George Drexler Ofrex Travelling Award entitling him to a month's all-expenses paid study tour of Canada or America. He has chosen Canada.

Eric Victor Everett (17/01/1949) Death announcement – Everett, Eric Victor died 27 January, peacefully in hospital, aged 84.

Ayton Richardson Whitaker (17/01/1949) Marriage announcement - marriage arranged between Mr Ayton Richardson Whitaker and Miss Ann Viviennne Latimer will take place quietly at Christ Church, Mayfair.

Thomas Bruce Bickerton (19/11/1948) Marriage announcement – Mr Thomas Bruce Bickerton, younger son of Mr H.R. Bickerton of Pentre Coch Manor, near Ruthin, and the late Mrs Bickerton.

Henry Lawson-Tancred (19/11/1948) Marriage announcement – Henry, eldest surviving son of the late Sir Thomas Selby Lawson-Tancred, of Aldborough Manor, Boroughbridge, Yorkshire. Birth announcement – Lawson-Tancred, on 9 January 1959 at Stokeld Park, Wetherby, to Jean, wife of Sir Henry Lawson-Tancred – a daughter. Death announcement for Lady Lawson-Tancred, wife of Sir Henry Lawson-Tancred. Local inventor Sir Henry Lawson-Tancred has spent £15,000 of his own money on building a 30-kilowatt aerogenerator outside the village of Aldborough. Re-marriage announcement. Daughters marriage announcement. Sons marriage announcement. Obituary – Pioneering designer who built the first large wind turbines used in Britain in the 1970s. Born in 1924, he served in Bomber Command during the war. He inherited the baronetcy after his older brother Andrew was shot down and killed. He read engineering at Cambridge University before returning to the family estate. He died on 28 March 2010, aged 86.

John William Morrison (19/11/1948) Marriage announcement – Mr John William Morrison, eldest son of Mr W.S. Morrison, KC, MP, and Mrs Morrison of the Manor House, Withington, Gloucestershire.

David John Leslie (20/11/1948) Death announcement – Leslie, David John, on 25 September, with great courage and dignity at St Catherine's Hospice after a long illness.

Silvester Litton (20/11/1949) Marriage announcement – for son, Patrick, younger son of Mr and Mrs Silvester Litton of Worsley, Lancashire.

Michael Cawood Butler (01/12/1948) Death announcement – Butler - on 27 October 1985, Michael Cawood Butler, BSC, MRCVS, DTVM, of 5, South Road, Taunton, aged 62 years.

Alan Alfred Bath (12/12/1948) Silver wedding announcement for Alan Alfred Bath. Death announcement – Bath, Alan Alfred, aged 77, on 8 July 2001, peacefully after a long illness bravely born.

Alan James Wells (19/11/1948) Marriage announcement – Alan James Wells, eldest son of Dr and Mrs A.Q. Wells of Shipton Manor, Kidlington, Oxford.

Cornelius Turner (01/09/1948) Daughter's marriage announcement – Cornelia Jane Elizabeth, only daughter of Mr and Mrs Cornelius Turner of Yarm, Yorkshire, and Newton Ferrers.

Michael Franklyn Moore (08/12/1948) Death announcement – Moore, on 8 May 1994, suddenly and peacefully in hospital, Michael Franklyn Moore FCA.

John Patrick Ferard Reeve (15/12/1948) Marriage announcement – Mr John Patrick Ferard Reeve, elder son of Major and Mrs W Norman Reeve of 99, Cadogan Gardens, SW3. Obituary – born on 16 March 1923, served in RAF during the war, once demobbed he attended University College, Oxford to study. He became a stockbroker. His career was ended after a bad car crash and he took up writing, with a successful career as a children's religious author. His later life was blighted by a hip operation which infected him with MRSA, from which he never recovered. He died on 25 November 2008, aged 85.

Kenneth Wolstenholme (15/12/1948) Secretary of the Anglo-American Sporting Club. Born in Worsley, Lancashire, he attended Farnworth Grammar School. Started life as a journalist in Manchester. A member of the RAFVR, he was awarded the DFC in May 1944. He became a freelance journalist on radio before moving to the BBC in 1948. He was a famous commentator, remembered specifically for his commentary of the 1966 World Cup Final. He was also a presenter on Match of the Day. He died on 25 March 2002, aged 81.

John Martin Wheeler (20/12/1948) Marriage announcement – John Martin Wheeler of 17, Hasker Street, London. Son's marriage announcement.

Rupert Mawdesley Holmes (10/01/1949) Marriage announcement – Rupert Mawdesley Holmes, younger son of the late Colonel R.B.W. Holmes and Mrs Holmes of Aldeburgh, Suffolk.

Daniel James Hurley (10/01/1949) Daniel James Hurley of Field Road, Newport, climbed out of an Oxford twin-engined aircraft which crashed into the mist covered mountain between Blaina and Ebbw Vale, Monmouthshire yesterday and then walked down the mountainside. He was taken to Ebbw Vale Hospital suffering from shock.

Norman Shott (03/01/1949) Death announcement – Shott – Peacefully after a short illness on 17 April, aged 89 years, Norman Shott DFC, MA of Ponteland, Newcastle upon Tyne.

Richard Greville Earle (19/11/1948) Marriage announcement – Richard Greville Earle, of Merrylands Farm, Corscombe, Dorchester, youngest son of the late Mr J.G. Earle and of Mrs J.G. Earle, of Hingarston, Marnhull, Dorset.

Ronald Samuel Wolsey Kemp (11/12/1948) DFC, Southacre, 17, Downs Side, Cheam, Surrey. Joint Managing Director of Cresens Robinson & Company.

Alan George Winchester (13/01/1949) Death announcement – Winchester Alan George – (Edinburgh). Peacefully on Tuesday, 6 February 2007, at the Marie Cure Hospice, Edinburgh, aged 85.

Roger Hilary Davies (19/11/1948) Death announcement – Davies, Roger Hilary. On 29 August 2002 in hospital, aged 78, of Crewe Green, Shrewsbury.

Richard David Richardson (23/11/1948) Marriage announcement for Richard David Richardson of Flitwick, Bedfordshire.

David Murray Arthur Reid (24/11/1948) Latest wills – David Murray Arthur Reid of Tetbury, Gloucestershire, left estate valued at £3,440,437 net.

Joseph Andrew Christopher Hoare (08/12/1948) Latest wills – of Cranbrook, Kent, left estate valued at £2,775, 657 net.

Frederick Arthur Rotherham (25/01/1949) Marriage announcement – Flight Lieutenant Frederick Arthur Rotheram, only child of Mr and Mrs Bryan Rotherham of 42, Ashworth Mansions, Elgin. Venue, Maida Vale, W9.

John Sandford Balkwill (12/02/1949) Marriage announcement – on 29 December 1936, at St John's Church Notting Hill, John Sandford Balkwill, son of Henry Balkwill.

John William Scott (12/01/1949) Marriage announcement –John William Scott and Rhoda Janet Mayall.

Philip Macdonald Sheppard (05/02/1949) Professor P.M. Sheppard, FRS, Professor pf Genetics in the University of Liverpool since 1963, died on 17 October at the age of 55. Educated at Marlborough College and Worcester College, Oxford University, he served in the RAFVR. He was a keen shot and was captain of the Oxford University Rifle Club.

Charles Kenneth Ouin (25/01/1949) Marriage announcement – Flying Officer Charles Kenneth Ouin, son of Mr and Mrs C.L. Ouin of Sutton, Surrey. Death announcement – Ouin, Charles Kenneth. In his ninety-ninth year, peacefully at Beauchamp House on Monday, 11 October 2010.

John William Franklin (03/03/1949) Marriage announcement – Flight Lieutenant John William Franklin, RAFVR, only son of Mr William E Franklin, of 1, Great North Road, Stevenage, Hertfordshire.

James Richard Abe Bailey (01/03/1949) Born in 1919, the son of a white gold millionaire in South Africa. Educated at Winchester College he joined the RAF during the Second World War. Awarded DFC. After the war he attended Christ Church, Oxford University. Worked on a newspaper/magazine promoting the rights of Black South Africans. He died on 29 February, aged 80. Served in the Oxford University Air Squadron.

Cyril Frederick Lewis (29/01/1949) Death announcement – on 28 September Cyril Frederick Lewis CBE. Obituary – Solicitor, Chief Commoner, City of London in 1962 and a member of the Court of Common Council until 1977.

Ronald Henry Weeks (03/02/1949) Marriage announcement – Flight Lieutenant Ronald Henry Weeks, younger son of the late Mr And Mrs Hubert Weeks, of Woodborough, near Bath, Somerset.

Andrew Felix Waley (01/03/1949) Marriage announcement – only son of Mr and Mrs G.F. Waley of Cranleigh, Surrey. Andrew Felix Waley QC to be a circuit judge on the South Eastern Circuit. Obituary – born on 14 April 1926, he was Educated at Charterhouse and Worcester College, Oxford University. Member of Oxford UAS. Called to the Bar in 1953. Enjoyed sailing and owned his own barge. He died on 16 April 1995, aged 69.

Edward George Selwyn (17/02/1949) Marriage announcement – youngest son of the Rev S.J. and Mrs Selwyn of Matson House, Remenham, Henley-on-Thames.

Raymond Charles Rendall (03/03/1949) Marriage announcement – youngest son of Mr and Mrs Charles Burdett Rendall of 50, Hurlingham Court, London SW6.

John Richard Roberts (03/03/1949) Marriage announcement – John Richard Roberts of 28, Severn Street, Welshpool, and Mill Farm, Glyn Morlas, Chirk, only son of the late Mr R.S. Roberts of Welshpool. Death announcement – Roberts, John Richard, FRICS, Company Director. Died at home, aged 61, on 9 February.

Ian Cameron Black (21/03/1949) Aged 64. He worked at the Standard Charter Bank before retirement. Shot as he tried to stop two men robbing a bank in Southgate, North London.

Norman Alexander Blount (14/03/1949) Marriage announcement – on 20 July 1938, at Croydon, Surrey, Norman Alexander Blount of 16, Stafford Road, Croydon. Birth announcement – on 19 November 1941 at Pietermaritzburg, Natal, to Noel, wife of Norman Alexander Blount – a daughter.

Leslie John Fryer (03/03/1949) Awarded OBE for services to community in Buckland.

Ronald Sydney Matthews (04/04/1949) Death announcement – Matthews, Ronald Sydney, peacefully on 25 May, aged 72, after a short Illness. Obituary – Deputy Secretary and Principal Establishment Officer at the Department of Health and Social Security 1976-1981. Born on 26 July 1922, educated at Kingsbury County School, succeeded in Civil Service Entrance Exam and assigned to Ministry of Health. Volunteered for RAF. Successful career in Civil Service. Died on 25 May, aged 72.

David Bevil Morgan-Grenville (13/02/1949) Marriage announcement – only son of the Hon Harry and Mrs Morgan- Grenville of Temple Grange, Iver Heath, Buckinghamshire.

Honorio Bingham d'Assis-Fonseca (09/03/1949) Death announcement – on 17 November 1967, suddenly, in hospital, Honorio Bingham D'Assis Fonesca of 27, Wilton Crescent, Wimbledon, SW19.

Robert Alister Peel Bruce (31/03/1949) Marriage announcement – Pilot Officer Robert Alister Peel Bruce, son of Lieutenant Colonel and Mrs H.K. Bruce, Basil Street Hotel, Knightsbridge. Robert A.P. Bruce AFC, FCA, Abbots Leigh, Haywards Heath, Sussex, Director of Aquis Security Limited.

Cyril Hassall (08/04/1949) Frederick Samuel Foxall, fruiterer of Torina Road, Trent Vale, Stoke on rent, was remanded in custody charged with murdering Cyril Hassall, aged 31, of Church Lane, Hanford.

Laurie William John Leask (02/05/1949) Marriage announcement – Pilot Officer Laurie William John Leask, only son of Mr and Mrs W Leask, Sidmouth.

Michael Francis Phillips (21/05/1949) Marriage announcement – Michael Francis Phillips MA (Cantab) younger son of Mr and Mrs W.G. Phillips of Queenwood House, Bowood Park, Calne, Wiltshire.

Robert Plenderleith (27/05/1949) Marriage announcement – Flight Lieutenant Robert Plenderleith, DFC, son of Mr and Mrs A.M. Plenderleith, Drumore, Boxmoor, Hertfordshire. Worked as keeper of the technological department at the Royal Scottish Museum in Edinburgh.

Ivor Christopher Faulconer (25/05/1949) Marriage announcement – younger son of Mr and the Hon Mrs R.C. Faulconer of Nottlers House, Bricket Wood, St Albans. Marriage announcement – Mr Ivor Christopher Faulconer, widower.

Reginald Halton Cowin (02/06/1949) Killed when a twin-engine aircraft of Manx Airlines crashed in a wood near Dusseldorf. It had been chartered to fly home thirty-two British service men and members of their families.

John Joseph Parker (07/04/1949) Retired squadron leader awarded MBE.

Lewis Bernard Cannell (22/05/1949) England rugby player. Played nineteen times for England. Attended Oxford University. Born in Coventry and attended St Richard's College in Droitwich before moving to Northampton Grammar School. After his degree he studied medicine at St Mary's Hospital, qualifying as a doctor in 1958. He died of heart disease on 17 March 2003, aged 76.

Peter Frederick Woolland (20/06/1949) Marriage announcement – Flight Lieutenant Peter Frederick Woolland DFM, RAFVR, eldest son of Mr and Mrs A Woolland of Drewsteignton, Devon.

Maurice Stacey Steel (04/07/1949) Death announcement – Steel, on 12 May in Limassol, Cyprus, suddenly and peacefully, Maurice Stacey Steel DFC.

Cyril Noel Sworder (12/07/1949) Marriage announcement – on Saturday, 27 October 1973, at Tunbridge Wells, Cyril Noel Sworder to Mrs Eileen Vlasto.

Charles Richard Barnby (20/07/1949) Marriage announcement – Flight Lieutenant Charles Richard Barnby, only son of the late Colonel A.C. Barnby OBE, Royal Marines, and of Mrs Barnby, 2, Watts Avenue, Rochester.

Peter Francis Middleton (12/08/1949) Obituary – born in Leeds in 1920, educated at Clifton College, Bristol, and Oxford University to study English. Joined RAFVR. Flew with Lancashire Aircraft Corporation, before moving to BEA. Enjoyed sailing. Retired in 1974. His granddaughter is Kate Middleton, wife of Prince William.

Dan Michael Hayward (07/09/1949) Marriage announcement – on 16 August 1969, in Cambridge to Sheila Robina.

Hugh Morriss (25/08/1949) Captain Hugh Morriss of Bromborough, Cheshire, was piloting an Auster light aircraft, flying above Aber, Caernarvonshire, spotting men of The Cheshire Regiment who were on exercise, when his plane crashed. Soldiers from the regiment and mountain rescue found Mr Morriss who had sustained a broken ankle and a few minor Injuries.

Thomas Anthony Maclean Jack (14/10/1949) Marriage announcement – the marriage took place quietly in London of Mr Thomas Anthony Maclean Jack of Preston, Kent.

Redmond Charles Carroll (01/11/1949) Death announcement – Carroll, Redmond Charles, aged 89, in London, on his way out to spend his remaining years with his family in Hong Kong.

George Holmes Melville-Jackson (02/10/1949) Marriage announcement – Wing Commander George Holmes Melville-Jackson DFC, younger son of Mr and Mrs A Melville-Jackson of St Felix School, Felixstowe. Birth announcement – on 5 March 1951, at St Felix School, Felixstowe, to Elizabeth, wife of George Holmes Melville-Jackson – a daughter.

Oswald Philip Bradley (27/10/1949) Death announcement – Bradley, Oswald Philip. On Thursday, 25 June, 1998, peacefully in hospital in Jersey.

Neil Alvah Wylie (15/11/1949) Marriage announcement – son of Sir Francis and Lady Wylie of Boar's Hill. Oxford.

Richard Edgar Thomas (16/11/1949) Death announcement – Thomas, Richard Edgar, peacefully at Paxhill Nursing Home on 4 April 2005, aged 81.

Riley Anthony Winton Rudd (05/12/1949) Marriage announcement – 48, Kensington Court, W8. Only son of the late Mr Frederick Rudd and of Mrs Redford of Johannesburg. Business changes – appointed a Director of De Vere Holdings. Share Sale for Rowe, Rudd & Co. Named as a member of the Stock Exchange. Address given as 38, Trevor Square, London SW7.

John Gowen Collyear (13/11/1949) Knighted in the Queen's Birthday honours. Chairman of AE PLC.

Alan David Walder (26/12/1949) Marriage announcement – 10, Barkston Gardens, SW5, only son of the late James Walder and Mrs Walder of Wembley, Middlesex. Obituary – born on 13 November 1928, educated at Latymer School and Christ Church, Oxford University. Member of the Oxford University Air Squadron. Called to the Bar in 1956. Conservative MP for Clitheroe. Author of three historical books and some novels. Died on 26 October 1978, aged 49.

Norman Thomas Williams (26/12/1949) Death announcement – Williams, Norman Thomas MA (Oxon),aged 73. On 28 February after a long illness borne with great courage.

David Hamilton Darbishire (20/12/1949) Death announcement – Darbishire, David Hamilton died peacefully surrounded by his family in Guildford, Surrey, on Tuesday, 30 November 2010, aged 87.

The Hon David Bernard Montgomery (17/11/1949) (Viscount Montgomery of Alamein) Born on 18 August 1928, and educated at Winchester and Trinity College, Cambridge. Awarded CBE in 1975.

David Alfred Acland (26/12/1949) Marriage announcement – Eldest son of Mr and Mrs Arthur Acland of Standon Green End, Ware, Hertfordshire.

Arthur Brearley (02/01/1950) Death announcement – Brearley, Arthur of Bramhall Cheshire. Died suddenly on 23 February 2002 whilst on holiday in the Bay of Islands, New Zealand, aged 73.

Francis George Miles (07/01/1950) Sons marriage announcement – Frances Hugh Miles, younger son of Mr and Mrs Francis George Miles of Rableyheath, Hertfordshire.

Clive Compston Russell-Vick (13/01/1950) Marriage announcement – Pilot Officer Clive Compston Russell Vick, RAFVR, elder son of Mr Russell Vick. A solicitor, Clive Compston Russell Vick, of Seal, near Sevenoaks, Kent, was fined £50 with £10 10s costs at Aldershot for failing to maintain an aircraft and to keep maintenance records. Russell Vick said that he bought the machine, a monoplane fitted with a 40 hp engine, at the end of 1958 in Ireland. A three year certificate of air-worthiness had been given in December 1957.

Geoffrey Milner Barker (12/01/1950) Marriage announcement – only son of Major and Mrs A.T. Barker, of Northcote Lodge, Grange Road, Sutton, Surrey.

John Graham Parsons (21/02/1950) Marriage announcement – only son of the late Mr J.T. Parsons and of Mrs D.A. Parsons of Westbury, Wiltshire.

Christopher Hugh Threlfall (26/03/1950) Death announcement – Threlfall, Aix les Bains. 22 May 1960.

Thomas Maxwell-Hudson (06/04/1950) Marriage announcement – twin son of Dr Bernard Hudson MD, MCRP, and Mrs Enid Maxwell, formerly of Davos-Platz, Switzerland.

David Lester Hurford (17/05/1950) Death announcement – Hurford on 14 April, suddenly in the evening, David Lester Hurford, aged 62.

Edward John Posey (12/07/1950) Marriage announcement – younger son of Mr and Mrs M Posey of Hampstead.

David Cade Wigglesworth (19/07/1950) Appointed High Sheriff of Derbyshire.

Paul Broughton Cash (18/05/1950) Death announcement – early morning on Friday, 28 January 1972, Paul Broughton Cash of the Dog and Duck, Plucks Gutter, Canterbury.

Timothy Berthier Meek (09/06/1950) Death announcement – Meek, Timothy Berthier, died peacefully on Walheke Island, New Zealand on 5 October after a short illness.

Lawrence William Pilgrim (08/07/1950) Death notice – Pilgrim, Lawrence William of Sandstones, 18, Church Hill, Camberley, Surrey, GU15 2HA. Died on 26 September 1995, without a will. Latest Wills – Mr Lawrence William Pilgrim of Camberley, Surrey £940,465.

James William Simpson (10/07/1950) Daughters marriage announcement – Daughter of Dr and Mrs James William Simpson of High Trees, Julian Hill, Harrow-on-the-Hill.

George Derek Gordon Hall (26/08/1950) Obituary – born on 8 November 1924 and educated in South Shields, before winning a Scholarship to Queens College, Oxford University. Became President of Corpus Christie College Oxford. He died on Monday, 15 September, aged 50.

Edward James Wright (14/09/1950) An accountant, appointed liquidator for winding up of Eagle Merchandise Ltd.

APPENDIX 3

Colin Bruce Lyon (07/09/1950) First officer on a Viscount Airliner of Hunting Clan Air Transport which crashed on a test flight near Camberley, Surrey killing the crew of six.

John Robert Lowe (11/09/1950) Death announcement – Lowe, on 9 February, peacefully at his home, in his fifty-second year, after a long illness courageously borne, John Robert Lowe, consulting Engineer.

Alan Fordham (12/09/1950) Death announcement for wife.

Ewen Ranald Robertson (14/09/1950) Marriage announcement – DFC, youngest son of the late Mr J Robertson and of Mrs Robertson of Strathavon, Bournemouth.

John Terence Murphy (20/06/1950) Marriage announcement – marriage took place on Thursday, 10 September between Mr John Terence Murphy and Miss Jocelyn Wang. Memorial service for John Terence Murphy to be held on Friday, 12 November 1999.

Ronald Desmond Campbell (29/07/1950) A celebration of the life of Ronald Desmond Campbell DFC, AFC, will be held on Friday, 22 March 1996, at noon in St Clement Danes, Central Church of the Royal Air Force, Strand, London. WC2.

Royce William Watchorn (30/09/1950) Superintendent of the Leicestershire Constabulary.

Anthony Noel Savage (06/11/1950) Marriage announcement – eldest son of Mr G.V. Savage and Mrs Savage of Alverstoke, Hampshire.

Richard Brian Bensted-Smith (24/10/1950) Marriage announcement – younger son of Dr W.F. Bensted-Smith, of Newton Ferrers, Devon and the late Mrs K.E. Bensted-Smith.

John Geoffrey Cowap (24/10/1950) Marriage announcement – John Geoffrey Cowap, HM overseas Civil Service, only son of the late Mr John Chester Cowap and Mrs Cowap of Westway, Pennington, Hampshire,

Michael Hume Bell (07/02/1951) Marriage announcement – son of Mr and Mrs G.F. Bell of The School House, Highgate.

Richmond Davenport Buswell (23/09/1950) Public notices – late of Fulham, London, W14, died here on 29 June 2000 (Estate about £110,000).

David Moline Warner (05/01/1951) Daughters marriage announcement – Daughter of Mr David Moline Warner of Coulsdon, Surrey.

John Copinger Harvey (22/11/1950) Birth announcement – on 22 May 1954, at Watford Maternity Hospital, Hertfordshire, to Margaret, wife of John Copinger Harvey – a son (Edgar).

Philip Anfield Ouston (20/10/1950) Obituary – an undergraduate at Kings College, London. Held posts at Dundee, St Andrews, and at the British University of Columbia before holding the chair of French Language and Literature at Kings College. He died aged 64.

Donald William John Savage (27/01/1951) Marriage announcement – son of Mr and Mrs G.W. Savage of Carshalton Beeches, Surrey.

Leslie Clutton (17/03/1951) Death announcement – Clutton, Leslie, died peacefully 14 October 1996 at Derriford Hospital, Plymouth.

Herbert Edward Tappin (17/04/1951) Marriage announcement – on 19 November 1973, very quietly in Brighton, Herbert Edward Tappin of Bursledon, Hampshire.

Cecil Bertram White (21/05/1951) Death announcement – White, Cecil Bertram, on Monday, 20 September at Acland Hospital, Oxford, aged 81.

Frederick Henry Hatchard (23/05/1951) Latest appointments – to be a stipendiary magistrate for the West Midlands from 2 March.

Anthony Herbert Tomlin (31/05/1951) Obituary – Anthony Herbert Tomlin DFC died suddenly in Stamford on 18 July, aged 68. Born in Cricklewood and educated at Marlborough College and Lincoln College Oxford. Worked as a schoolmaster until retirement.

John Francis Phillips (07/05/1951) Thanksgiving service for the life of John Francis Phillips QC.

Archibald William Forster (24/09/1951) Awarded knighthood in Queens Birthday honours list. Chairman and Chief Executive of Esso UK.

John Michael Wragge (01/09/1951) Marriage announcement – John Michael Wraggen of Redwells, by Anstruther, Fife and Dalhousie School.

Nigel Desmond Norman (27/10/1951) Marriage announcement – second son of the late Air Commodore Sir Nigel Norman, and of Lady Perkins, of Rookwood Farm, On-The-Holy-Brook, Oakridge Gloucestershire. Death announcement – Norman, Nigel Desmond, CBE, FRAeS, suddenly on 13 November. Obituary – born in London in 1929, he was educated at Eton, and then the de Haviland Aeronautical Technical School. He qualified as an aeronautical engineer. In 1954 he set up Britten-Norman Designing aircraft. They then formed a crop spraying company. Appointed CBE in 1970, he died of a heart attack on 13 November 2002, aged 73.

John Everard Digby (27/08/1951) Death announcement – Digby, John Everard, on 19 April 2003, aged 78, at Royal Surrey Hospital, Guildford.

Donald Roger Jones (17/09/1951) Death announcement – Jones, Donald Roger aged 72, suddenly on Friday, 12 October.

Alec Anthony Kinch (17/09/1951) Death announcement – Kinch, Alec Anthony, CBE, very peacefully at St Christopher's Hospice on 25 October, aged 72. Obituary – educated at Ampleforth and Christ Church, Oxford. Called to the Bar in 1951. In 1973 he was approached to join the European Commission. He took early retirement in 1986, and was awarded the CBE in 1987.

Hector Seymour Peter Monro (04/01/1952) The life barony conferred on Sir Hector Seymour Peter Monro has been gazetted by the name, style and title of Baron Monro of Langholm, of Westkirk in Dumfries and Galloway. Obituary – born on 4 October 1922, he was educated at Canford School, and King's College Cambridge, he joined the University Air Squadron. He farmed in Craigcleuch, and in 1952 he took up politics and became a Conservative MP. Keen on all country sports, including shooting. He was knighted in 1981 and was sworn of the Privy Council in 1995. He died on 30 August 2006, aged 83.

John Willis Rogers (07/11/1951) Scholarship awarded by Lincoln's Inn for John Willis Rogers of Fitzwilliam House, Cambridge University. A QC, appointed an Ordinary Bencher by Lincoln's Inn. Appointed as a circuit judge. Death announcement – Rogers, John Willis QC, on 12 May 2004, peacefully after an illness bravely borne. Latest wills – left estate of £987,166 net.

Basil Ziani de Ferranti (07/11/1951) Marriage announcement – younger son of Sir Vincent and Lady de Ferranti, of Rose Hill, Alderley Edge, Cheshire. Son's marriage announcement. A service of thanksgiving for the life and work of Mr Basil Ziani De Ferranti will be held on Wednesday, 9 November 1988.

Ernest Gladstone Ross (20/02/1952) Marriage announcement – Flying Officer Ernest Gladstone Ross, eldest son of Mr and Mrs E.G. Ross, Ellonville, Hawkhead Road, Paisley. Birth announcement – Ross – on 20 April 1948, at the Park Nursing Home, 12, Claremont Terrace, Glasgow, to Marian, wife of Ernest Gladstone Ross, of Noddsdale Cottage, Brisbane Glen, Largs, Scotland – a daughter.

Kenneth William Wright (15/01/1952) Awarded OBE in the Queen's Birthday honours.

Arthur David Morse (10/06/1952) Marriage announcement – eldest son of Mr and Mrs Sydney Morse of Chedgrave Manor, Loddon, Norfolk.

Charles Mark Lambert (10/06/1952) Obituary – born on 15 June 1929, educated at Blundell's School, Tiverton and then the French Lycee. He went to Jesus College, Oxford University and was a member of the UAS. From 1953-1965 he worked on "*Flight*" Magazine. Rejoining it in 1973. He died on 27 September 1994, aged 65.

William James Todd (28/04/1952) The crew of four and eleven technicians were killed when a Bristol Britannia aircraft crashed at Downend near Bristol. It was a prototype test flight. He was the Radio Officer.

John Denham Pinnock (15/06/1952) Marriage announcement – younger son of D Denham Pinnock of Shrewsbury House, Cheyne Walk, SW3, and the late Mrs C.E. Pinnock. Death announcement – Pinnock, John Denham, suddenly in Yeovil District Hospital on 17 August.

Richard Thomas Addis (16/06/1952) Marriage announcement – son of Mr and Mrs William Addis, of Government House, Seychelles, and of Woodside, Frant, Sussex.

Alexander William Percy (30/11/1952) In Memoriam – Alexander William Percy who died on 6 October 1954.

The Earl of Bective (07/11/1952) Marriage announcement – son of the Marquess and Marchioness of Headfort, of Headfort House, Kells, Co Meath, Ireland. Son's marriage announcement. Birth announcement for his son's wife.

Edward William Tandy (27/09/1952) Son's marriage announcement.

Michael John Marshall (22/10/1952) OBE awarded in Queen's Birthday Honours for services to the Engineering industry and to the community in Cambridgeshire,

John David Payne (24/01/1953) Death announcement – Payne, John David on 21 December 2004 at home after long illness courageously borne.

John Anthony Ince (05/11/1952) Golf professional who was ordered by a High Court Judge to return his two infant children to his wife's custody, is in Sweden with one of his children. The other is in King's Lynn. His son was handed back to the mother in Glasgow.

Donald Frederick Leach (14/09/1953) Adopted as prospective Labour candidate for Kinross and West Perthshire. Awarded CBE in the Queen's birthday Honours.

Donald Keith Jones (19/07/1953) Death announcement – Jones, Donald Keith, died peacefully on 25 February, aged 68.

Kenneth Christopher Kime (20/09/1953) OBE awarded, Squadron Leader Kenneth Christopher Kime, for services to the Soldiers, Sailors and Airmen's Families Association – forces help in Cleveland.

John Malcolm Wardle (09/10/1953) Death announcement - Wardle, John Malcolm, LLB, died peacefully at home on 12 December 1994. Latest wills – Mr John Malcolm Wardle of Knowle, Sollihull, West Midlands, left estate valued at £3,183,295 net.

Cedric Neale Thomas (05/10/1953) Disciplinary Committee of the Law Society, sitting in public in London ordered Cedric Neale Thomas to be struck off, formerly of North Ferriby, East Yorkshire and now of Parkstone, Dorset.

John Michael Vereker Horsman (29/08/1953) Marriage announcement – on 20 July, John Michael Vereker Horsman of Linstead Farm, Cralfield, Suffolk.

Roger Henry Herbert (04/01/1954) Death announcement – Herbert, Roger Henry, on 3 January 2007, aged 73.

Stuart David Hollander (09/06/1954) Death announcement – Hollander, Stuart David, on 28 July, peacefully at home in Moor Park.

Peter John Reyner (09/06/1954) Death announcement – Reyner, Peter John, aged 76, died suddenly on 12 June 2009.

Richard Malvern Allen (17/03/1955) Death announcement – Allen, Richard Malvern, died peacefully at home on 3 July 2009, aged 76.

John Williams Norton (11/10/1955) Marriage announcement – younger son of Mr and Mrs F.J. Norton, Oakhurst, Pine Road, Chandler's Ford, Hampshire.

APPENDIX 3

David Beverley Newell (19/10/1955) Death announcement – Newell, David Beverley, died on Monday, 29 March 2010, at Freeland Nursing Home, in his eightieth year.

John Cocke (12/09/1955) Appointed to the board of Bemrose and Son.

David Humphrey Woolley (17/11/1955) Marriage announcement – son of Sir Charles and Lady Woolley, Orchard Hill, Liss, Hampshire.

Christopher Murray Jackson (21/01/1957) Marriage announcement - son of the late Reverend Howard Jack of Boxmoor, Hertfordshire.

Bibliography

The National Archives

Air 1 Air Ministry, Air Historical Branch: Papers, Series 1, discovery. nationalarchives.gov.uk

Air 2/253 Associations of the Auxiliary Air Force, 25 July 1924.

Air 2/263 Air Ministry and Successors: Operational Record Book, 608 (North Riding) Squadron Auxiliary Air Force 1930 - 1957.

Air 2/273 Formation of Territorial Air Force, 20 May 1919.

Air 2/273 Formation of Auxiliary Air Force, 24 January 1925.

Air 2/696 Re-organisation of Special Reserve Squadrons as Auxiliary Air Force Squadrons.

Air 2/13172 Future of the Royal Auxiliary Air Force.

Air 19/725 Royal Auxiliary Air Force.

Air 19/743 Royal Auxiliary Air Force.

Air 20/932 Auxiliary Air Force Reconstitution.

Air 27, Air Ministry, Series details: Air Ministry and Successors; Operations Record Books, Squadrons 1911-1972.

Air 27 Air Ministry and Successors: Operational Record Book, RAF Thornaby Station 1930 – 1957.

Air 27/2097. 608 Squadron: Operations Record Book March 1930 – December 1940.

Air 27/2676. 608 Squadron January 1947 – December 1954.

Air 27/2712. 608 Squadron February 1955 – March 1957.

Air 28/1132. Operational Record Book, RAF Thornaby January 1946 – June 1946 and July 1950 – December 1950.

Air 28/1276. Operational Record Book, RAF Thornaby January 1951 – December 1955.

Air 28/1428. Operational Record Book, RAF Thornaby January 1956 – October 1958.

BIBLIOGRAPHY

Air 41/4 RAF Monograph, Flying Training 1934-1942, Air Historical Branch.

Air 41/23/30 Conclusions of a meeting of the Cabinet held at 10 Downing Street, S W 1 on Tuesday, 11 July 1922.

Air 41/24/138 Formation of an Auxiliary Air Force, 13 September 1922.

Air 41/24/164 Letter from Secretary of State for Air to the Secretary, Cabinet, 5 February 1924.

Air 41/24/165 Auxiliary Air Force and Air Force Reserve Bill, 3 March 1924.

Air 41/24/267 Plan for Further Expansion of First Line Strength of the Royal Air Force January 1937.

Air 41/65 Royal Air Force Manning Plans and Policy.

Air 41/129/19 Needs of the Armed Forces and the Ministry of Supply for Land for Training and Other Purposes, June 1947.

Air 41/129/44 Defence Programmes 1951-54, January 1951.

WO 296/21 Territorial and Reserve Forces Act 1907.

Interviews

Mr P Alexander, Birmingham, telephone conversation, Saturday, 6 August 2005.

Mrs E Appleby-Brown, Saltburn by Sea, Saturday, 16 March 2002.

Mrs V Bracknell, Guisborough, Sunday, 12 March 2006.

Mr Ted Brown, Boosebeck, Wednesday, 12 November 2003.

Mr Sydney Buckle, Stockton on Tees, Saturday, 15 November 2003.

Mr Harold Coppick, Billingham, Monday, 20 October 2003.

Mr Ernie Crombie, Former Member of Queens University Air Squadron, ernie_airni@gmail.com

Mr G Crow, Belmont, Saturday, 27 March 2004.

Mr Walter Hilary Davies, Great Ayton, Tuesday, 23 November 2004.

Mr Vic Fleming, Redcar, Tuesday, 18 November 2003.

Mrs J Gilbert, Stockton on Tees, Friday, 19 April 2002.

Mr Grant Goodwill, Middlesbrough, Thursday, 11 November 2004.

Mr. Albert Guy, Newton Aycliffe, Saturday, 6 March 2004.

Mr T Harbron, Stockton on Tees, Tuesday, 11 November 2003.

Mr S.J. Hawksfield, Billingham, Friday, 9 May 2003.

Mr A Huitson, Stockton on Tees, Thursday, 13 November 2003.

Mrs Valerie Kayll, Witton Gilbert, Durham, Monday, 25 July 2005.

Mr G Joyce, Billingham, Friday, 12 November 2004.

Mr D Lambert, Abingdon, Saturday, 25 October 2003.

Mr D Landing, Stockton on Tees, Tuesday, 5 July 2005.

Mr C Matthews, Chilton Moor, Thursday, 22 November 2001.

Mr P Meston, Bearsden, Glasgow, Thursday, 6 January 2005.

Mr G Milburn, Ilderton, Friday, 21 November 2003.

Mr Noel Mitchell, Former Member of Queens University Air Squadron, noel.mitchel@btinternet.com

Mr John Pollock, Stockton on Tees, Monday, 3 December 2001.

Mr M Ruecroft, Trimdon Grange, Friday, 2 April 2004.

Mr C Quinn, Middlesbrough, Tuesday, 21 March 2006.

Mr Jim Steedman, Stockton on Tees, Saturday, 18 October 2003.

David Stewart, Friday, 19 March 2004. Internet interview. dkstewart@mountaincable.net,

David Stewart, Monday, 22 March 2004, dkstewart@mountaincable.net

Wing Commander Ken Stoddart, Monday, 25 July 2005.

Mrs V Sykes, Middlesbrough, Saturday, 1 November 2003.

Mr Alan Taylor, Former Member of Queens University Air Squadron athtaylor@btinternet.com

Mrs H Thrower, Stockton on Tees, Monday, 7 January 2002.

Mr Peter Vaux's son, Darlington, Friday, 18 November 2005.

Mr Ronnie Waterson, Billingham, Monday, 15 November 2004.

Mr George Williams, Sunningdale, Ascot, Monday, 3 January 2005.

Mrs A Willis, Eaglescliffe, Thursday, 4 November 2004.

Mr N Winstanley, Stockton on Tees, Thursday, 30 October 2003.

Mr C Wright, Monday, 13 December 2004, colin_wright_nz@yahoo.co.uk

Newspapers

Daily Telegraph, 1937.

Eastern Weekly News, 1948.

The Gazette, 1937 – 1941.

The Guardian Digital Archive 1821-2000.

The London Gazette, 1926 – 1957.

North Eastern Daily Gazette, 1930 – 1958.

North Eastern Weekly News, 1947.

Northern Daily Mail, 1947.

Northern Echo, 1946 - 1947.

BIBLIOGRAPHY

The Times Digital Archives, 1925 – 1985.
Flight Magazine Digital Archive.
RAF Quarterly.

Books

Addison, Paul & Crang, Jeremy A (eds)	*The burning Blue. A New History of the Battle of Britain*, (London, 2000)
Alvarez, Al	*When Did It All Go Right?* (London, 1999)
Andreski, Stanislav	*Military Organization and Society* (London, 1954, Second Edition 1968)
Armitage, Michael	*The Royal Air Force – An Illustrated History* (London, 1993).
Avner, Otter	*Property and Politics 1870 – 1914. Landownership, Law, Ideology and Urban Development in England* (Aldershot, 1992).
Bainbridge, Beryl	*Forever England. North and South* (London, 1987).
Baker, Alan R.H. & Billings, Mark (eds)	*Geographies of England. The North South Divide, Imagined and Material*, (Cambridge, 2004).
Baradat, Leon P.	*Political Ideologies. Their Origins and Impact* (London, 1997).
Baum, Willa K.	*Transcribing and Editing Oral History* (Tennessee, 1977).
Beauman, Katherine Bentley	*Partners in Blue. The Story of Women's Service with the Royal Air Force* (London, 1971).
Beaven, Brad	*Leisure, Citizenship and Working-Class Men in Britain, 1850-1945* (Manchester, 2005).
Beckett, Ian F.W. & Simpson, Keith (eds)	*A Nation in Arms. A Social Study of the British Army in the First World War*, (Manchester, 1985)
Bell, D	*The Coming of Post-Industrial Society* (New York, 1973).
Bell, Lady	*At the Works* (Middlesbrough, 1997).

Benson, John   *The Working Class in Britain 1850-1939*
                        (London, 1989 & 2003).

Benwell Community   *The Making of a Ruling Class, Final Report*
Project   *Series No. 6* (Benwell, 1978).

Bialer, Uri   *The Fear of Air Attack and British Politics*
                        1932-1939 (London, 1980)

Bingham, Adrian   *Gender, Modernity and the Popular Press in*
                        Inter War Britain (Oxford, 2004).

Birch, A.H.   *Small Town Politics – A Study of Political Life*
                        in Glossop (London, 1959).

Bishop, Patrick   *Fighter Boys Saving Britain 1940* (London,
                        2004).

Black, Jeremy   *Maps and History – Constructing Images of the*
                        Past (London, 1997).

Blunt, Barry   *608 Mosquito Bomber Squadron*
                        (Stockport, 1998).

Bond, Brian   *British Military Policy Between the Two World*
                        Wars (Oxford, 1980).

Boog, Horst (Ed)   *Conduct of the Air War in the Second*
                        World War. An International Comparison
                        (London, 1992)

Borsay, Peter   *A History of Leisure* (Basingstoke, 2006).

Bourne, J.M.   *Britain and the Great War 1914 – 1918* (New
                        York, 1989).

Bowman, Timothy &   *The Edwardian Army: Recruiting, Training*
Connelly, Mark L   *and Deploying the British Army, 1902-1914*
                        (Oxford, 2012)

Bowyer, Chaz   *The History of the RAF* (London, 1977).

Bowyer, Chaz   *The Royal Air Force 1939 – 1945*
                        (Barnsley, 1996).

Bowyer, Michael J.F.   *Aircraft for the Few. The RAF's Fighters and*
                        Bombers in 1940 (Yeovil Somerset, 1991).

Boyle, Andrew   *Trenchard* (London, 1962).

Branson, Noreen &   *The History of British Society. Britain in the*
Heinemann, Margot   *Nineteen Thirties* (London, 1971).

BIBLIOGRAPHY

Brooks, Robin J.   *Kent's Own. The History of 500 (County of Kent) Squadron Royal Auxiliary Air Force* (Gillingham Kent, 1982).

Brown, David   *Thornaby Aerodrome and Wartime Memories* (Stockton, 1992).

Brown, David   *Bombs by the Hundred on Stockton on Tees* (Stockton, 1990).

Brown, E.   *Wings on My Sleeve* (London, 2006).

Buckley, John   *Air Power in the Age of Total War* (London, 1999)

Buckley, John   *RAF and Trade Defence 1919-1945 Constant Endeavour* (Staffs, 1995)

Burns, M.G.   *Bader, the Man and his Men* (London, 1990).

Bush, M.L.   *Social Orders and Social Classes. Europe Since 1500* (Harlow, 1992).

Butler, Tim & Savage, Mike (eds)   *Social Change and the Middle Classes* (London, 1995).

Calder, Angus   *The Myth of the Blitz* (London, 1992).

Cannadine, David   *Aspects of Aristocracy. Grandeur and Decline in Modern Britain* (New Haven, 1994).

Cannadine, David   *Class in Britain* (London, 1998).

Cannadine, David   *The Decline and Fall of the British Aristocracy* (New Haven, 1990).

Cannadine, David   *Lords and Landlords: The Aristocracy and the Towns 1774 – 1967* (Leicester, 1980).

Carr, E.H.   *What is History* (London, 1990).

Catterall, Peter   *British History 1945 – 1987: An Annotated Biography* (Oxford, 1990).

Caunce, Stephen   *Oral History and the Local Historian* (London, 1994).

Chamier, John Adrian   *The Birth of the Royal Air Force* (London, 1943).

Chorlton, Martyn   *Airfields of North-East England in the Second World War* (Newbury, 2005).

Chun, Lin   *The British New Left* (Edinburgh, 1993).

Clark, Alan   *Aces High. The War in the Air over the Western Front 1914 – 1918* (London, 1973).

Clarke, Graham	*The Photograph* (Oxford, 1997).
Clayton, P.B. (MC, FSA)	*Tales of Talbot House: Everyman's Club in Poperinghe & Ypres 1915-1918* (London, 1919).
Clayton, T & Craig, P	*Finest Hour* (London, 1999).
Coombs, L.F.E.	*The Lion has Wings. The Race to Prepare the RAF for World War II: 1935 - 1940* (Shrewsbury, 1997).
Crang, Jeremy A	*The British Army and the People's War* (Manchester, 2000)
Crockett, Richard	*Twilight of Truth. Chamberlain, Appeasement and the Manipulation of the Press* (London, 1989).
Crompton, Rosemary	*Class and Stratification. An Introduction to Current Debates* (Cambridge, 1998).
Cronin, James E	*The Politics of State Expansion – War, State and Society in Twentieth Century Britain* (London, 1991).
Cross, J.A.	*Lord Swinton* (Oxford, 1982).
Crossick, Geoffrey (ed)	*The Lower Middle Class in Britain 1870 – 1914* (London, 1977).
Cunningham, Hugh	*The Volunteer Force: A Social and Political History 1895 -1908* (London, 1975).
Davidson, M & Taylor J	*Spitfire Ace. Flying the Battle of Britain* (London, 1988).
Dean, Sir Maurice	*The Royal Air Force and Two World Wars* (London, 1979).
De Groot, Gerard J	*"Blighty. British Society in the Era of the Great War"* (Harlow Essex,1996).
De Groot, Gerard J	*The First World War* (Basingstoke, 2001).
Deighton, L	*Fighter. The True Story of the Battle of Britain* (London, 1977).
Delve, Ken & Pitchfork, Graham	*South Yorkshire's Own. The Story of 616 Squadron* (Exeter, 1990).
Dennis, Peter	*The Territorial Army 1906-1940* (Suffolk, 1987).
des Honey, J.R.	*Tom Brown's Universe. The Development of the Victorian Public School* (London, 1977).

Devine, David — *The Broken Wing – A Study in the British Exercise of Air Power* (London, 1966).

Dickson, Wing Commander Alex (ed) — *The Royal Air Force Volunteer Reserve – Memories* (RAF Innsworth Gloucester, 1997).

Donnison, David & Soto, Paul — *The Good City – A Study of Urban Development and Policy in Britain* (London, 1980).

Dundas, H — *Flying Start. A Fighter Pilots War Years* (London, 1988).

Dyhouse, Carol — *Students: A Gendered History (London, 2006).*

Edgerton, David — *Warfare State: Britain, 1920-1970* (Cambridge, 2006).

Edgerton, David — *Britain's War Machine* (London, 2012).

Edgerton, David — *England and the Aeroplane: Militarism, Modernity and Machines* (London, 2013).

Elias, Norbert — *The Civilizing Process* (Oxford, 1994).

Evening Gazette, — *Teesside at War – A Pictorial Account 1939 – 1945* (Manchester, 1989).

Eyre, Richard — *National Service Diary: Diary of a Decade* (London, 2003).

Ferguson, Aldon P — *Beware Beware! The History of 611 (West Lancashire) Squadron Royal Auxiliary Air Force* (Reading, 2004).

Finlayson, Geoffrey — *Citizen, State and Social Welfare in Britain 1830 – 1990* (Oxford, 1994).

Fisher, Nigel — *Harold MacMillan. A Biography* (London, 1982).

Floud, J.E. (ed), Halsey, A.H., Martin, F.M. — *Social Class and Educational Opportunity* (London, 1956).

Francis, Martin — *The Flyer. British Culture and the Royal Air Force* (Oxford, 2008).

Fredette, Raymond H — *The First Battle of Britain 1917/1918 and the Birth of the Royal Air Force* (London, 1966).

French, David — *Raising Churchill's Army* (Oxford, 2000).

Fuchser, Larry William — *Neville Chamberlain and Appeasement. A Study in the Politics of History* (London, 1982).

Gathorne-Hardy, Jonathan	*The Public School Phenomenon* (Sevenoaks Kent, 1977).
Giddens, Anthony	*Classes, Power and Conflict* (London, 1981).
Giddens, Anthony	*The Class Structure of the Advanced Society* (London, 1973).
Goldthorpe, John H	*Social Mobility and Class Structure in Modern Britain* (Oxford, 1987).
Goodson, James	*Tumult in the Clouds. The Classic Story of War in the Air* (London, 2003).
Grainger, J.H.	*Patriotisms. Britain 1900-1939* (London, 1986).
Grant, R.G.	*Flight. 100 Years of Aviation* (London, 2004).
Grayson, Richard S	*Austen Chamberlain and the Commitment to Europe. British Foreign Policy 1924 – 1929* (London, 1997).
Gunn, Simon	*History and Cultural Theory* (Harlow, 2006).
Gunn, Simon & Rachel Bell	*Middle Classes: Their Rise and Sprawl* (London, 2011).
Gunn, Simon	*The Public Culture of the Victorian Middle Class. Ritual and Authority in the English Industrial City 1840 – 1914* (Manchester, 2000).
Hall, Jeffrey	*Sport, Leisure and Culture in Twentieth Century Britain* (London, 2002).
Hall, Roger, DFC	*Clouds of Fear* (London, 1977).
Halpenny, Bruce Barrymore	*Action Stations: 4, Military Airfields of Yorkshire* (Cambridge, 1982).
Halsey, A.H.	*Change in British Society from 1900 to the Present Day* (Oxford, 1995).
Halsey, A.H. (ed) Webb, Josephine	*Twentieth Century British Social with Trends* (Basingstoke, 2000).
Hannah, Leslie	*The Rise of the Corporate Economy* (London, 1976).
Harley, J.B.	*Maps for the Local Historian – A Guide to the British Sources* (London, 1972).
Harris, Paul P	*This Rotarian Age* (Chicago, 1935).

BIBLIOGRAPHY

Hering, Sqn Ldr P.G.　　*Customs and Traditions of the Royal Air Force*
　　　　　　　　　　　(Aldershot, 1961).

Heywood, Andrew　　　*Political Ideologies. An Introduction*
　　　　　　　　　　　(Basingstoke, 1998).

Hickman, Tom　　　　*The Call-Up. A History of National Service*
　　　　　　　　　　　(London, 2004).

Hill, Jeffrey　　　　　*Sport, Leisure and Culture in Twentieth
　　　　　　　　　　　Century Britain* (Basingstoke, 2002).

Hillary, Richard Hope　*The Last Enemy* (London, 1942).

Hindle, Brian Paul　　*Maps for Local History* (London, 1988).

Hinton, James　　　　*Women, Social Leadership and the Second World
　　　　　　　　　　　War. Continuities of Class* (Oxford, 2002).

H.M.S.O.　　　　　　*Coastal Command. The Air Ministry Account
　　　　　　　　　　　of the Part Played by Coastal Command in the
　　　　　　　　　　　Battle of the Seas 1939 – 1942* (London, 1942).

Hoare, Samuel　　　　*Empire of the Air. The Advent of the Air Age
(Viscount Templewood)　1922-1929* (London, 1957).

Hobsbawm, Eric　　　*The Forward March of Labour Halted?
　　　　　　　　　　　Marxism Today* (London, 1978).

Horrall, Andrew　　　*Popular Culture in London c. 1890-1918.
　　　　　　　　　　　The Transformation of Entertainment
　　　　　　　　　　　(Manchester, 2001).*

Howarth, Ken　　　　*Oral History* (Stroud, 1999).

Howarth, Stephen　　*The Royal Navy Reserves in War And Peace
　　　　　　　　　　　1900-2003* (Barnsley, 2003)

Howes, S.D.　　　　*Goosepool. The History of RAF and RCAF
　　　　　　　　　　　Middleton St. George and Teesside Airport
　　　　　　　　　　　(Darlington, 2003).*

Humphries, S　　　　*Hooligans or Rebels? An Oral History
　　　　　　　　　　　of Working-Class Childhood 1889-1939
　　　　　　　　　　　(London, 1981).*

Hunt, Leslie　　　　　*Twenty-one Squadrons. The History of The Royal
　　　　　　　　　　　Auxiliary Air Force 1925-1957* (London, 1972).

Hyde, H Montgomery　*British Air Policy Between the Wars 1918-1939*
　　　　　　　　　　　(London, 1976).

Jackson, Alan A   *The Middle Classes 1900 – 1950* (Nairn Scotland, 1991).

James, John   *The Paladins. A Social History of the Outbreak of World War II* (London, 1990).

James, Lawrence   *The Middle Class. A History* (London, 2006.).

Janowitz, Morris   *The Professional Soldier. A Social and Political Portrait* (USA, 1960).

Jewell, Helen M   *The North-South Divide. The Origins of Northern Consciousness in England* (Manchester, 1994).

Johnstone, Sandy   *Enemy in the Sky* (London, 1976).

Johnstone, Sandy   *Diary of an Aviator* (Shrewsbury, 1993).

Jones, Neville   *The Beginnings of Strategic Air Power. A History of the British Bomber Force 1923-1939* (Abingdon, 1987).

Joyce, Patrick (ed),   *Class* (Oxford, 1995).

Kaye, Harvey J   *The British Historians. An Introductory Analysis* (Cambridge, 1984).

Kennedy, Paul   *The Realities Behind Diplomacy. Background Influences on British External Policy 1865 – 1980* (London, 1981).

Kennedy, Paul   *The Rise and Fall of British Naval Mastery* (London, 1983 & 2004).

Kenny, Michael   *The First New Left. British Intellectuals After Stalin* (London, 1995).

Kerr, J Lennox & Granville, Wilfred   *The RNVR. A Record of Achievement* (London, 1957)

Kidd, Alan & Nicholls, David (eds)   *Gender, Civic Culture and Consumerism. Middle Class Identity in Britain 1800 – 1940* (Manchester, 1999).

Kidd, Alan & Nicholls, David (eds)   *The Making of the British Middle Class. Studies of Regional and Cultural Diversity Since the Eighteenth Century* (Stroud, 1998).

Koss, Stephen E   *Lord Haldane: Scapegoat for Liberalism* (USA, 1969).

BIBLIOGRAPHY

Lavery, Brian   *Hostilities Only. Training in The War-Time Royal Navy* (London, 2004)

Lawton, Richard (ed)   *The Census and Social Structure. An Interpretative Guide to 19th Century Censuses for England and Wales* (London, 1978)

Leahy, William H, McKee, David L, & Dean, Robert D   *Urban Economics* (New York, 1992).

Leonard, J.W.   *Constantine College* (Middlesbrough, 1981).

Louis, W.M. Roger & Owen, Roger (eds)   *Suez 1956. The Crisis and its Consequences* (Oxford, 1991).

Lucas, Laddie (ed)   *Voices in the Air 1939-1945. Incredible stories of the World War II Airmen in Their Own Words* (London, 2003).

Lummis, Trevor   *Listening to History* (London, 1987).

Mackay, James   *Collecting Local History* (London, 1984).

Mackay, Robert   *Half the battle. Civilian Morale in Britain during the Second World War* (Manchester, 2002).

McKenzie, John M   *Imperialism and Popular Culture* (Manchester, 1986).

MacKenzie, S.P.   *The Home Guard – A Military and Political History* (Oxford, 1996).

McKibbin, Ross   *Classes and Cultures. England 1918-1950* (Oxford, 1998).

McKibbin, Ross   *The Ideologies of Class. Social Relations in Britain 1880-1950* (Oxford, 1990).

Marwick, Arthur   *Britain in the Century of Total War. War, Peace and Social Change 1900-1967* (Harmondsworth, 1968).

Marwick, Arthur (ed)   *Total War and Social Change* (London, 1988).

Millin, Sarah Gertrude   *General Smuts* (London, 1976).

Morris, R.J.   *Class, Sect and Party. The Making of the British Middle Class. Leeds 1820 – 1850* (Manchester, 1990).

Morris, Robert J & Trainer, Richard H (eds)   *Urban Governance. Britain and Beyond Since 1750* (Aldershot, 1998).

Moulson, Tom   *The Flying Sword. The Story of 601 Squadron* (London, 1964).

Moulson, Tom   *The Millionaires' Squadron. The Remarkable Story of 601 Squadron And The Flying Sword* (Barnsley, 2014)

Mowat, Charles Loch   *Britain Between the Wars 1918 – 1940* (London, 1955).

Murray, W   *War in the Air 1914 – 1945* (London, 1999).

Nesbitt, Roy Conyers   *Coastal Command in Action 1939 – 1945* (Gloucestershire, 1997).

Nesbitt, Roy Conyers   *An Illustrated History of the RAF* (Surrey, 1990).

Newton, Tony   *Pins and Needles and Paperclips: Treasures from the Royal Aero Club Archives* (London, 2006).

Nicholas, Katherine   *The Social Effects of Unemployment in Teesside* (Manchester, 1986).

Norman, B   *Wartime Teesside* (Lancaster, 1989).

Norris, Andrew   *Reminiscence with Elderly People* (Bicester Oxon, 1986).

North, G.A.   *Teesside's Economic Heritage* (Cleveland, 1975).

Obelkevich, James & Catterall, Peter (eds)   *Understanding Post-War British Society* (London, 1994).

O'Connell, Sean   *The Car in British Society. Class, Gender and Motoring 1896 – 1939* (Manchester, 1998).

Omissi, David E   *Air Power and Colonial Control. The Royal Air Force 1919 – 1939* (Manchester, 1960).

Onderwater, Hans   *"Gentlemen in Blue". 600 Squadron* (Barnsley, 1997).

Ottler, Patrick   *Yorkshire Airfields in the Second World War* (Newbury 1998).

Owens, Francis Gerard   *Winds of Change – Stockton on Tees 1800-1939* (Stockton on Tees, 1990).

Panichas, George A (ed)   *Promise of Greatness. The War of 1914 – 1918* (London, 1968).

BIBLIOGRAPHY

Parker, M   *The Battle of Britain July – October 1940.*
                            An Oral History of Britain's 'Finest Hour'
                            (London, 2000).

Parker, R.A.C.   *Chamberlain and Appeasement. British Policy*
                            and the Coming of the Second World War
                            (London, 1993).

Pearce, I   *Lost on Easby Moor. The Last Flight of Hudson*
                            NR -E (Wolviston, 2003).

Peden, G.C.   *British Rearmament and the Treasury*
                            1932 – 1939 (Edinburgh, 1979).

Peden, G.C.   *Arms, Economics and British Strategy.*
                            From Dreadnoughts to Hydrogen Bombs
                            (Cambridge, 2007).

Perkin, Harold   *The Rise of Professional Society. England since*
                            1880 (London, 1989).

Piper, Ian   *We Never Slept. The History of 605 (County of*
                            Warwick) Squadron Royal Auxiliary Air Force
                            1926 – 1957 (Tamworth, 1996).

Pollard, A.J. (ed)   *Middlesbrough – Town and County*
                            1830 – 1950 (Stroud, 1996).

Powell, W.W. (ed)   *The Non-Profit Sector, A Research Handbook*
                            (New Haven 1987).

Powers, Barry D   *Strategy without Slide Rule. British Air Strategy*
                            1914-1939 (London, 1976).

Price, Mary   *The Photograph: A Strange Confined Space*
                            (Stanford University, 1994).

Price, R   *An Imperial War and the British Working Class.*
                            Attitudes and Reactions to the Boer War 1899 –
                            1902 (Toronto, 1972).

Prysor Glyn   *Citizen Sailors. The Royal Navy in The Second*
                            World War (London, 2002).

Rawlings, John D.R.   *The History of the Royal Air Force*
                            (Feltham, 1984).

Reader, W.J.   *At Duty's Call – A Study in Obsolete Patriotism*
                            (Manchester, 1988).

Reader, W.J.   *Imperial Chemical Industries. A History,*
                      Volume 2. The First Quarter Century
                      1926 - 1952 (London, 1975).

Reader, W.J.   *Professional Men. The Rise of the Professional*
                      Classes in Nineteenth Century England
                      (London, 1966).

Reid, Alastair J   *Social Classes and Social Relations in Britain*
                      1850 – 1914 (Basingstoke, 1992).

Richards, Denis   *Royal Air Force 1939 – 1945, Volume 1 – The*
                      Fight at Odds (London, 1974).

Richardson, Dick   *The Evolution of British Disarmament Policy in*
                      the 1920s (London, 1989).

Richardson, Joy   *Looking at Local Records* (London, 1983).

Rider, Philip   *Local History – A Handbook for Beginners*
                      (London, 1983).

Rock, William R   *British Appeasement in the 1930s* (London,
                      1977).

Roskill, S.W.   *The War at Sea Volume 2, The Period of*
                      Balance (London, 2004).

Ross, David; Blanche, *"The Greatest Squadron of Them All"*
Bruce & Simpson,   *The Definitive History of 603 (City of*
William   *Edinburgh) Squadron, RAUXAF Volume I,*
                      Formation to the end of 1940 (Grub Street,
                      London, 2003).

Ross, David; Blanche, *"The Greatest Squadron of Them All"*
Bruce & Simpson,   *The Definitive History of 603 (City of*
William   *Edinburgh) Squadron, RAUXAF Volume II,*
                      1941 to Date (Grub Street, London, 2003).

Ross, Tony   *75 Eventful Years. A Tribute to the Royal Air*
                      Force 1918 – 1993 (London, 1993).

Royal Air Force   *Royal Air Force Reserve and Auxiliary Forces*
Historical Society   (Oxford, 2003).

Royal Air Force   *"Defending Northern Skies 1915-1995"*
Historical Society   (Oxford, 1996).

Royal Air Force   *Memories* (Gloucester, 1997).
Volunteer Reserve

BIBLIOGRAPHY

Royle, Edward — *Modern Britain. A Social History 1750-1997* (London, 1987).

Royle, Trevor — *National Service. The Best Years of Their Lives* (London, 2008).

Rubinstein, W.D. — *Capitalism, Culture and Decline in Britain 1750 – 1990* (London, 1994).

Samuel, Raphael (ed) — *Patriotism. The Making and Unmaking of British National Identity. Volume 1 History and Politics* (London, 1989).

Samuel, Raphael (ed) — *Patriotism. The Making and Unmaking of British National Identity, Volume 2 Minorities and Outsiders* (London, 1989).

Samuel, Raphael (ed) — *Patriotism. The Making and Unmaking of British National Identity, Volume 3 National Fictions* (London, 1989).

Saward, Dudley — *'Bomber' Harris,* (London, 1984).

Schindler, Colin — *National Service. From Aldershot To Aden. Tales From the Conscripts1946-1962* (London, 2012).

Schmidt, Gustav — *The Politics and Economics of Appeasement. British Foreign Policy in the 1930s* (Leamington Spa, 1986).

Scott, W.H., Banks, J.A., Halsey, A.H. & Lupton, T — *Technical Change and Industrial Relations. A Study of the Relations between Technical Change and the Social Structuring of a Large Steelworks* (Liverpool, 1956).

Seldon, Anthony & Pappworth, Joanna — *By Word of Mouth. Elite Oral History* (London,1983)

Sharp, Thomas — *Town and Countryside. Some Aspects Of Urban and Rural Development* (London, 1932).

Sharpe, M — *History of the Royal Air Force* (London, 1999).

Smith, David J — *Britain's Military Airfields 1939 – 1945* (Yeovil Somerset, 1989).

Smith, H.L. (Ed) — *War and Social change. British Society in the Second World War* (Manchester, 1986).

Smith, Harold — *Britain in the Second World War. A Social History* (Manchester, 1996).

285

Smith, Malcolm — *British Air Strategy Between the Wars* (Oxford, 1984).

Smithies, Edward — *Aces, Erks and Backroom Boys, Aircrew, Ground Staff and Warplane Builders Remember the Second World War* (London, 2002).

Smuts, J.C. — *Jan Christian Smuts* (London, 1952).

Sockett, E.W. — *608 Squadron and RAF Thornaby* (Middlesbrough, 1975).

Steel, Nigel & Hart, Peter — *Tumult in the Clouds. The British Experience of the War in the Air 1914 – 1918* (London, 1997).

Stevens, J.R. — *Searching for the Hudson Bombers. Lads, Love and Death in World War II* (Victoria, 2004).

Stevenson, John — *British Society 1914 – 1945* (London, 1984).

Stevenson, John — *The Pelican Social History of Britain. British Society 1914 – 1945* (London, 1984).

Taylor, A.J.P. — *English History 1914 – 1945* (Oxford 1965).

Taylor, Gordon — *London's Navy. A Story of the Royal Naval Volunteer Reserve* (London, 1983).

Taylor, Roy — *RAF National Service in Six Movements. A Conscript's Experiences in the RAF in the 1950s* (London, 2006).

Tedder, The Lord G.C.B. — *Air Power in War – The Lees Knowles Lectures by Marshal of the Royal Air Force* (London, 1947).

Terraine, John — *The Right of the Line: The Royal Air Force in the European War 1939-1945* (London, 1985).

Terraine, John — *Business in Great Waters. The U-Boat Wars, 1916-1945* (London, 1989).

Thomas, Hugh — *The Suez Affair* (Harmondsworth Middlesex, 1967).

Thompson, E.P. — *The Making of the English Working Class* (London, 1963).

Thompson, F.M.L. (ed) — *The Cambridge Social History of Britain 1750-195, Volume 2, People and their Environment* (Cambridge, 1990).

Thompson, F.M.L. (ed) The Cambridge Social History of Britain 1750-1950, Volume 3 Social Agencies and Institutions (Cambridge, 1990).

Thompson, Neville *The Anti-Appeasers. Conservative Opposition to Appeasement in the 1930s* (London, 1971).

Thompson, Paul *The Voice of the Past. Oral History* (Oxford, 2000).

Tiratsoo, Nick (ed) *From Blitz to Blair. New Labour and its Past* (London, 1997).

Titmuss, Richard *Problems of Social Policy* (London,1950).

Tosh, John *The Pursuit of History* (London, 2000).

Turner, John *MacMillan* (London, 1994).

Turner, John *Britain and the First World War* (London, 1988).

Vinen, Richard *National Service. A Generation in Uniform 1945-1963* (London, 2015).

Waites, Bernard *A Class Society at War. England 1914 –1918* (Leamington Spa, 1987).

Watkins, David *Fear Nothing. The History of No. 501 (County of Gloucester) Fighter*

Weight, Richard & Beach, Abigail (eds) *The Right to Belong Citizenship and National Identity in Britain 1930 – 1960* (London, 1998).

Weight, Richard *Patriots. National Identity in Britain 1940-2000* (London, 2002).

Weisbrod, B.A. *The Non Profit Economy* (Cambridge Massachusetts, 1988).

Wellum, G *First Light* (London, 2003).

White, Ian *If you want Peace, Prepare for War. A History of No 604 (County of Middlesex) Squadron, RAuxAF, in Peace and in War*

Wiener, Martin J *English Culture and the Decline of the Industrial Spirit 1850 – 1980* (Cambridge, 2004).

Williams, Raymond *Keywords – A Vocabulary of Culture and Society* (London, 1976).

Willmott, P & Young, M   *Family and Class in a London Suburb* (London, 1960).

Wilson, Keith M   *Empire and Continent – Studies in British Foreign Policy from the 1880s to the First World War* (London, 1987).

Wright, Richard   *Patriots. National Identity in Britain 1940 – 2000* (London, 2002).

Young, Michael   *The Rise of the Meritocracy* (London, 1994).

Yow, Valerie Raleigh   *Recording Oral History. A Practical Guide for Social Scientists* (London, 1994).

Ziegler, F.H.   *The Story of 609 Squadron. Under the White Rose* (London, 1971).

Journals

Blanche, B   'Weekend Fliers', *Aeroplane* 27, 8 (1999).

Boswell, Jonathan   'The Informal Social Control of Business In Britain 1980 – 1939', *Business History Review* 57, 2 (1983).

Bowyer, M.J.F.   'Royal Auxiliary Air Force'. *Scale Aircraft Modelling* 7, 1 (1984).

Crowson, N.J.   'Contemporary Record', *The Conservative Party and the Call for National Service, 1937 – 1939: Compulsion Versus Voluntarism* 9, 1 (1995).

Dewey, P.E.   'Military Recruiting and the British Labour Force during the First World War', *The History Journal,* 27, 1 (1984).

Douglas, R   'Voluntary Enlistment in the First World War and the Work of the Parliamentary Recruiting Committee' *Journal of Modern History* 4, (1970).

Farr, Martin   'A Compelling Case for Voluntarism: Britain's Alternative Strategy 1915 – 1916', *War in History* 9, 2 (2002).

Finlayson, G   'A Moving Frontier – Voluntarism and the State in British Social Welfare', *Twentieth Century British History* 1, 2 (1990).

BIBLIOGRAPHY

Gunn, Simon 'Class Identity and the Urban: the Middle Class in England c. 1790 – 1950', *Urban History* 31, 1 (2004).

Harris, Jose 'Political Thought and the Welfare State 1870-1914: An Intellectual Framework for British Social Policy', *Past and present* 135 (1992).

Hartigan, J 'Volunteering for the Army in England. August 1914 – May 1915' *Midland History* 24 (1999).

Hinton, James 'Middle-class Socialism: Selfhood, Democracy and Distinction in Wartime County Durham', *History Workshop Journal* 62.

Mansell, Dr A 'Professionals, Amateurs and Private Armies. Pilot Entry Portals in the RAF Expansion of 1934 to 1939', *Proceedings of the RAF Historical Society* 11 (1993).

Mansell, Tony 'Flying Start: Educational and Social Factors in the Recruitment of Pilots of the Royal Air Force in the Inter-War Years' *History of Education* 26, No. 1 (1997).

Paris, M 'The Rise of the Airmen: The Origins of Airforce Elitism c. 1890 – 1918', *Journal of Contemporary History* 28 (1993).

Petler, Martin '"Temporary Gentlemen" in the aftermath of the Great War: Rank, Status and the Ex-officer Problem', *The Historical Journal* 37, 1 (1994).

Rieger, B 'Fast Couples: Technology and Modernity in Britain and Germany during the Nineteen-Thirties', *Historical Research* 76, 193 (2003).

Russell, Dave 'The Heaton Review 1927 – 1934: Culture, Class and a Sense of Place in Interwar Yorkshire', *Twentieth Century British History* 17, 3 (2006).

Saler, Michael 'Making it New: Modernism and the Myth of the North in Interwar England', *Journal of British Studies* 37 (1998).

Samuel, Raphael 'Middle Class Between the Wars (Parts 1 and 2)', *New Socialist* (1983).

Samuel, Raphael — 'Suburbs Under Siege. The Middle Class Between the Wars (Part 3)', *New Socialist* (1983).

Smith, J — 'Urban Elites c. 1830 – 1930 and Urban History', *Urban History* 27, 2 (2000).

Smith, Malcolm — The Royal Air Force, Air Power and British Foreign Policy 1932-1937. *Journal of Contemporary History*, 12, No. 1 (1977).

Whitmarsh, Andrew — British Army Manoeuvres and the Development of Military Aviation, *War in History*, Vol 14, Issue 3 July 2007.

Theses

Mahoney, Ross Wayne — The Forgotten Career of Air Chief Marshal Sir Trafford Leigh-Mallory 1892-1937: A Social and Cultural History of Leadership Development In the Inter-War Royal Air Force.

Collections

Banks, J.A. — 'The Social Structure of Nineteenth Century England as seen through the Census, Chapter 6, P 179 – 224' in Richard Lawton (ed) *The Census and Social Structure. An Interpretative Guide to 19th Century Censuses for England and Wales* (London, 1978).

Briggs, Asa — 'Middlesbrough:The Growth of a New Community, Chapter 1, p. 2-7' in A. J Pollard (ed), *Middlesbrough Town And Community 1830-1950*, (Stroud, 1996).

Cunningham, H — 'Leisure and Culture, Chapter 6, p279-341' in F.M.L. Thompson *Cambridge Social History*, 2 (Cambridge, 1990).

BIBLIOGRAPHY

Fielding, Steven	'The Good War', in Nick Tiratsoo (ed) *From Blitz to Blair. New Labour and its Past* (London, 1997).
Freeman, Squadron Leader A.F.	'The Post-War Royal Auxiliary Air Force' in Royal Air Force Historical Society *Royal Air Force Reserve and Auxiliary Forces* (Oxford, 2003).
Hansmann, H	'Economic Theories of Non-Profit Organisations' in *W.W. Powell (Ed) The Non Profit Sector, A Research Handbook* (1987).
Harris, Jose	'Society and the State in 20th Century Britain, Chapter 3, p. 63 – 117 in F.M.L. Thompson *The Cambridge Social History of Britain 1750 – 1900, Vol 3, Social Agencies and Institutions* (Cambridge, 1990).
Jefford, Jeff	'Post-War Reserves to 1960' in Royal Air Force Historical Society *Royal Air Force Reserve and Auxiliary Forces* (Oxford, 2003).
Law, Christopher M	'Employment and Industrial Structure' in James Obelkevich and Peter Catterall *Understanding Post-War British Society* (London, 1994).
Lewis, Jane	'The Voluntary Sector in The Mixed Economy of Welfare, Introduction Page 4.' in David Gladstone (Ed) *Before Beveridge, Welfare before the Welfare State, Civitas Choice in Welfare* 47 (London, 1999).
Mansell, Dr Tony	'Royal Air Force Volunteer Reserve 1936 – 1939' in Royal Air Force Historical Society *Royal Air Force Reserve and Auxiliary Forces* (Oxford, 2003).
Morris, R.J.	'Clubs, Societies and Associations, Chapter 8, p.395 – 443' in F.M.L. Thompson *Cambridge Social History* 3, (Cambridge, 1990).
Salamon, L.M.	'In Public Service. The Scope and Theory of Government; Non Profit Relations' in W.W. Powell (ed*) The Non Profit Sector. A Research Handbook*

Seed, John	'"Middling Sort" in Late 18th Century and Early 19th Century England' in M.L. Bush (ed) *Social Orders and Social Classes in Europe Since 1500* (Harlow, 1992).
Shores, Christopher	'The Auxiliary Air Force in W W II' in Royal Air Force Historical Society *Royal Air Force Reserve and Auxiliary Forces* (Oxford 2003).
Summerfield, P.	'The Levelling of Class' in H. L. Smith (ed) *War and Social Change. British Society in the Second World War* (Manchester, 1986).
Terraine, John	'Theory and Practice of Air War: The Royal Air Force' in Horst Boog (Ed) *The Conduct of the Air War in the Second World War: An International Comparison.* (Oxford, 1992).
Thane, P	'Government and Society in England and Wales 1750-1914' in F.M.L. Thompson (ed), *The Cambridge Social History of Britain,* Page 1 (Cambridge 1919).

Web Addresses

Morris, Suzannah	'Social Policy from the Victorians to the Present day, Voluntary Provision in a Mixed Economy.' (The London School of Economics and Political Science.) www.fathom.com/course/21701744 18 May 2011.
National Archives	Air Ministry Series Details: Air Ministry and Successors: Operations Record Books, Squadrons, 1911 – 1972. www.nationalarchives.gov.uk
Round Table	'About Roundtable' Origins www.roundtable.co.uk/about/phb 4 June 2011.
Charles Gambier Jenyns	www.rogerco.freeserve.co.uk/ 5 August 2011.
Jack Elkan David Benham	www.roll-of-honour.com/ www.uk-cigars.co.uk 5 August 2011.

BIBLIOGRAPHY

William Henry Rhodes-Moorhouse	www.carpages.co.uk/news 7 August 2011.
Arthur Hammond Dalton	www.cwgc.org/search 6 August 2011.
Edward Lawrence Colbeck-Welch	www.kcl.ac.uk 6 August 2011.
Peter Kenneth Devitt	www.hyderabad.co.uk 6 August 2011.
Anthony Henry Hamilton Tollemache	www.ww2awards.com 6 August 2011.
Paul Richey	www.tangmerepilots.co.uk 6 August 2011.
Geoffrey Ambler	www.rafweb.org//biographies 6 August 2011.
Kenneth Maxwell Stoddart	www.bowringpark.co.uk 6 August 2011.
Various AAF officers	www.thepeerage.com 5 August 2011.
Walter Leslie Runciman & Lancelot Eustace Smith	www.norav.50megs.com 8 August 2011.
Cecil Leonard Knox	www.remuseum.org 3 August 2011.
Various AAF officers	http://en.wikipedia.org 6 August 2011.
RAF Air Bases in England	www.anti-aircraft.co.uk 2 February 2011.
Flight Magazine Digital Archive	www.flightglobal.com 2 February 2011.
RAF Quarterly Archive	www.flightglobal.com 2 February 2011.

Endnotes

Introduction
1. Laddie Lucas (ed), *Voices in the Air 1939-1945. Incredible stories of the World War II Airmen in Their Own Words,* (London, 2003) p 36.
2. Dr A. Mansell, 'Professionals, Amateurs and Private Armies. Pilot Entry Portals in the RAF Expansion of 1934 to 1939' *Proceedings of the RAF Historical Society Number 11,* (1993) pp 55-62.
3. Ibid, p 57.
4. Interview with Mr Albert Guy, Newton Aycliffe, 6 March 2004.
5. Interview with Mr Ted Brown, Boosebeck, 12 November 2003.
6. *The Times,* 13 March 1937, p 9.
7. TNA, AIR1, Air Ministry, Air Historical Branch: Papers, Series1, discovery. nationalarchives.gov.uk/ Viewed 23 October 2016.
8. TNA, AIR27, Air Ministry, Series details: Air Ministry and Successors: Operations Record Books, Squadrons, 1911-1972 www.nationalarchives.gov.uk
9. Carol Dyhouse, *Students: A Gendered History,* (London, 2006) p 5.
10. Ibid, p 5.

Chapter 1. The Creation of the Reserve Forces
1. Paul Kennedy, *The Realities Behind Diplomacy. Background influences on British External Policy 1865-1980,* (London, 1981) p 274.
2. Sir Maurice Dean, *The Royal Air Force and Two World Wars,* (London, 1979) p 11.
3. J.A. Chamier, *The Birth of the Royal Air Force,* (London, 1943) p 92.
4. Ibid, p 93.
5. Michael Armitage, *The Royal Air Force – An Illustrated History,* (London, 1993) p 37.
6. Maurice Dean, *The Royal Air Force and Two World Wars,* (London, 1979) p 7.
7. Michael Armitage, *The Royal Air Force – An Illustrated History,* (London, 1993) p 37.

ENDNOTES

8. Stephen E Koss, *Lord Haldane: Scapegoat for Liberalism*, (New York, 1969) p 103.

9. Chaz Bowyer, *History of the RAF*, (London, 1977) p 21.

10. Tony Newton, *Pins and Needles and Paperclips: Treasures from the Royal Aero Club Archives*, (London, 2006) p 17.

11. Gerald J De Groot, *The First World War*, (Basingstoke, 2001) p 98.

12. Andrew Whitmarsh, 'British Army Manoeuvres and the Development of Military Aviation 1910-1913', in *War in History*, Volume 14 Issue 3, July 2007, p 326.

13. Jan Christian Smuts, *J.C. Smuts*, (London, 1952) p 107.

14. John D.R. Rawlings, *The History of the Royal Air Force*, (Feltham, 1984) p 52.

15. G.C. Peden, *British Rearmament and the Treasury 1932-1939*, (Edinburgh, 1979) p 38.

16. The National Archives (TNA), Chief of the Air Staff, *Permanent Organization of the Royal Air Force and Note by the Secretary of State for Air*, (London, 1919).

17. Armitage, *The Royal Air Force*, p 33. Also in Paul Kennedy, *Realities Behind Diplomacy. Background Influences on British External Policy 1865 –1980* (London, 1981), p 274.

18. Peter Dennis, *The Territorial Army 1906-1940*, (Suffolk, 1987) p 3.

19. Hugh Cunningham, *The Volunteer Force*, (London, 1975) pp 104-109.

20. Richard Price, *An Imperial War and the British Working Class. Attitudes and Reactions to the Boer War 1899-1902* (Toronto, 1972). p 103.

21. Cunningham, *Volunteer Force*, pp 103-109.

22. Peter Dennis, *The Territorial Army 1906-1940*, (Suffolk, 1987) p 3.

23. Koss, *Lord Haldane*, p 104.

24. TNA, Air 2/253, Associations of the Auxiliary Air Force, "Territorial Army and Auxiliary Air Force Joint Association for the City of Glasgow," 25 July 1924, pp 1-6, Sections 1-25

25. TNA, AIR 2/273, Formation of the Territorial Air Force, "Territorial Air Force", Chief of Air Staff, 18 May 1920.

26. Andrew Boyle, *Trenchard*, (London, 1962) p 203.

27. Winston Churchill, Speech to the House of Commons, 1 March 1921. Available at: http://hansard.millbanksystems.com/commons/1921/mar/01/mr-churchills-statement 1 March 1921 Viewed 11 June 2013.

28. TNA, AIR 2/273, Formation of the Territorial Air Force, "Territorial Air Force", Chief of Air Staff, 18 May 1920.

29. Viscount Templewood, *Empire of the Air. The Advent of the Air Age 1922-29*, (London, 1957), pp 190-191.

30. Armitage, *The Royal Air Force,* p 58.
31. TNA, AIR2/696, Re-organisation of Special Reserve Squadrons as Auxiliary Air Force Squadrons, "Notes regarding the formation of Special Reserve and Auxiliary Air Force squadrons, Necessity for two separate organisations, 6 September 1923
32. TNA, Cabinet Papers Number 47 (25) Sir Samuel Hoare's statement on Air Estimates, 7 October 1925.
33. TNA, AIR2/696, Re-organisation of Special Reserve Squadrons as Auxiliary Air Force Squadrons, "Notes regarding the formation of Special Reserve and Auxiliary Air Force squadrons. Necessity for two separate organisations, 6 September 1931.
34. Ibid, 6 September 1931.
35. John James, *The Paladins. A Social History of the RAF up to the Outbreak of World War II,* (London, 1990) p 98.
36. Armitage, *The Royal Air Force,* p 58.
37. TNA, AIR2/696, Re-organisation of Special Reserve Squadrons as Auxiliary Air Force Squadrons, "Notes regarding the formation of Special Reserve and Auxiliary Air Force squadrons, Necessity for two separate organisations, 6 September 1931.
38. Ibid 6 September 1931.
39. Leslie Hunt, *Twenty-One Squadrons. The History of the Royal Auxiliary Air Force 1925-1957,* (London, 1972), p 10.
40. TNA, AIR2/696, Re-organisation of Special Reserve Squadrons as Auxiliary Air Force Squadrons, "Notes regarding the formation of Special Reserve and Auxiliary Air Force squadrons, Necessity for two separate organisations, 6 September 1931.
41. James, *The Paladins,* p 98.
42. Viscount Templewood, *Empire of the Air*, p 190.
43. TNA, AIR2/696, Re-organisation of Special Reserve Squadrons as Auxiliary Air Force Squadrons, "Notes regarding the formation of Special Reserve and Auxiliary Air Force squadrons", Air Council, "The future of the Special Reserve Squadrons," 5 April 1935.
44. TNA, AIR2/696, Re-organisation of Special Reserve Squadrons as Auxiliary Air Force Squadrons, "Notes regarding the formation of Special Reserve and Auxiliary Air Force squadrons", Air Council, "The future of the Special Reserve Squadrons," 5 April 1935.
45. Tom Moulson, *The Flying Sword, the Story of 601 Squadron,* (London, 1964), p 93.
46. TNA, Cabinet Papers, Number 71 (34) 21 May 1934.

47. Royal Air Force, *Short History of the Royal Air Force*, Chapter 2, The inter-War Years, p 88. Available at: http://www.raf.mod.uk/history/ shorthistoryoftheroyalairforce.cfm Viewed on 6 November 2016.

48. Neville Jones, *The Beginnings of Strategic Air Power. A History of the British Bomber Force 1923-1939*, (Abingdon, 1987), p 102.

49. Jones, *The Beginnings of Strategic Air Power.* p 102.

50. J.A. Cross, *Lord Swinton*, (Oxford, 1982) p 144.

51. Jones, *The Beginnings of Strategic Air Power*, p 103.

52. TNA, AIR 41/4, RAF Monograph (Second Draft) "Flying Training 1934-1942, Air Historical Branch, p 44.

53. Dean, *The Royal Air Force,* p 78.

54. Tony Mansell, 'The Royal Air Force Volunteer Reserve 1936-1939' in *RAF Reserve and Auxiliary Forces*, (Oxford, 2003) p 30.

55. TNA, AIR41/65, The Second World War 1939-1945. Royal Air Force Manning. Plans and Policy, 'The formation of the Royal Air Force Volunteer Reserve' p 15.

56. TNA, AIR 41/4, RAF Monograph, Flying Training 1934-1942, Air Historical Branch, 'Reserves', p 113.

57. Mansell, 'The Royal Air Force Volunteer Reserve,' p 32.

58. TNA, AIR41/65, The Second World War 1939-1945. Royal Air Force Manning. Plans and Policy, 'The formation of the Royal Air Force Volunteer reserve' p 15.

59. Ibid.

60. Wing Commander Alex Dickson, *The Royal Air Force Volunteer Reserve - Memories, RAF* Innsworth (Gloucester, 1997) p 24.

61. Barry D Powers, *Strategy without Slide Rule. British Air Strategy 1914-1939*, (London, 1976) p 243.

62. Rawlings, *The History of the Royal Air Force,* p 87.

63. Christopher Shores, The Auxiliary Air Force in WWII, in *Royal Air Force Reserve and Auxiliary Forces,* (Oxford, 2003) p 40.

64. Shores, The Auxiliary Air Force in WWII, p 54.

65. Peter Dennis, *The Territorial Army 1906-1940,* (Suffolk, 1987) p 3.

Chapter 2. The Recruitment Process of the Territorial Air Force 1925-1939

1. Christopher Shores, 'The Auxiliary Air Force in WWII,' in *Royal Air Force Reserve and Auxiliary Forces,* (Oxford, 2003) pp 40-41.

2. Wing Commander Gerry Margiotta, 'University Air Squadrons in WWII', in *Royal Air Force Reserve and Auxiliary Forces,* (Oxford, 2003) p 67.

3. The National Archives (TNA), AIR 2/273, Formation of Auxiliary Air Force, 'Summary of Scheme for Auxiliary Air Force', Appendix II, 24 January 1925.

4. *The Times*, 18 October 1923, p 13.

5. *The Times*, 18 October 1923, p 13.

6. *The Times*, 14 November 1923, p 19.

7. TNA, AIR 2/273, Formation of Auxiliary Air Force, "Summing up of scheme for Auxiliary Air Force", Appendix II, 24 January 1925.

8. *The Times*, 15 October 1925, p 15.

9. *The Times*, 5 January 1924, p 7.

10. Ibid, p 7.

11. Leslie Hunt, *Twenty-One Squadrons: The History of the Royal Auxiliary Air Force 1925-1957,* (London, 1972) pp 10-11.

12. David Watkins, *Fear Nothing. The History of No 501 (County of Gloucester) Fighter Squadron,* (Cowden, 1990), pp 1-2.

13. Ibid, p 2.

14. Watkins, *Fear Nothing,* p 6.

15. Ibid, p 6.

16. Ernie Crombie, Personal Communication, 3 October 2014 (Former member of Queens University Air Squadron).

17. Tom Moulson, *The Flying Sword. The Story of 601 Squadron*, (London, 1964).

18. Tony Ross, *75 Eventful Years – A Tribute to the Royal Air Force 1918-1993,* (London 1993) p 231.

19. Shores, *The Auxiliary Air Force in WWII,* p 41.

20. Moulson, *The Flying Sword,* p 15.

21. Len Deighton, *Fighter. The true Story of the Battle of Britain,* (London, 1977) p 44-45.

22. Ian White, *If You Want Peace, Prepare For War. A History of No 604 (County of Middlesex) Squadron RAuxAF, in Peace and in War.* (London, 2005) p 8-9.

23. Wing Commander Jeff Jefford, 'Air Force Reserves 1912 to Munich', in *Royal Air Force Reserve and Auxiliary Forces,* (Oxford, 2003) p 21-22.

24. TNA, AIR2/696, Reorganisation of Special Reserve squadrons as Auxiliary Air Force squadrons, "the future of the Special Reserve Squadrons", 5 April 1935.

25. Ibid, p 5.

26. TNA, AIR2/696, Reorganisation of Special Reserve squadrons as Auxiliary Air Force squadrons, "the future of the Special Reserve Squadrons", 5 April 1935

27. Jefford, '*Air Force Reserves 1912 to Munich,*' p 22-23.

28. Margiotta, '*University Air Squadrons in WWII,*' p 67.

29. Margiotta, '*University Air Squadrons in WWII,*' p 67-68.

30. *The Times*, 6 March 1926, p 16.

31. https://www.rafmuseum.org.uk/images/online_exhibitions/LUAS-PosterLG.jpg

32. Sir Maurice Dean, *The Royal Air Force and Two World Wars,* (London, 1979) p 78.
33. Dean, *The Royal Air Force,* p 31.
34. Wing Commander Alex Dickson, *The Royal Air Force Volunteer Reserve - Memories, RAF Innsworth* (*Gloucester*, 1997) p 24.
35. John D R Rawlings, *The History of the Royal Air Force*, (Feltham, 1984) p 87.
36. Tony Mansell, 'Flying Start: Educational and Social Factors in the Recruitment of Pilots of the Royal Air Force in the inter-war years,' *History of Education*, Volume 26, No 1, 1997, pp 71-90.
37. P.B. Clayton, MC, FSA, *Tales of Talbot House: Everyman's Club in Poperinghe & Ypres 1915-1918*, (London, 1919) p vii.
38. The Round Table, *About us*, p 1. Available at: www.roundtable.co.uk/about. php. Viewed on 11 April 2016.
39. A.J. Reid, *Social Classes and Social Relations in Britain 1850-1914* (Basingstoke, 1992) p 173.

Chapter 3. The Social Composition of the Territorial Air Force Prior to 1939

1. White, *"If you want peace, prepare for war",* p 97.
2. Dr A Mansell, 'Professionals, Amateurs and Private Armies. Pilot Entry Portals in the RAF Expansion of 1934 to1939' *Proceedings of the RAF Historical Society Number 11,* (1993) pp 60-61.
3. Ibid, pp 60-61.
4. Hans Onderwater, *Gentlemen in Blue. 600 Squadron*, (Barnsley, 1997), p 43.
5. *The Times*, 9 August 1929, p 6.
6. Onderwater, *Gentlemen in Blue,* p 42.
7. Ibid, p 44.
8. Tom Moulson, *The Flying Sword. The Story of 601 Squadron*, (London, 1964) p 11.
9. Ibid, p 22.
10. Moulson, *The Flying Sword,* p 67.
11. Ibid, p 67.
12. White, *If you want Peace, Prepare for War,* p 6.
13. Moulson, *The Flying Sword,* p 68.
14. Len Deighton, *Fighter The True Story of the Battle of Britain,* (London, 1977), p 44.
15. White, *A History of No 604 (County of Middlesex) Squadron RAuxAF.* p 6.
16. Ibid, p 8.
17. White, *A History of No 604 (County of Middlesex) Squadron RAuxAF,* p 18.
18. *The Times*, 18 September 1926, p 5.

19. Deighton, *Fighter,* p 40.
20. David Ross, *The Greatest Squadron of them all. The Definitive History of 603 (City of Edinburgh) Squadron RAuxAF, Volume 1, Formation to the end of 1940.* (London, 2003) p 2.
21. David Ross, 'Saluting the few: the remarkable story of Edinburgh's 603 Squadron,' Available at www.scotsman.com. Viewed on 26 January 2016.
22. Ross, *The Greatest Squadron of them all, Volume 1,* p 6.
23. Ibid, p 7.
24. Ibid, p 8.
25. *The Times,* 24 December 1934, p 8.
26. Interview with Mrs E Appleby-Brown, Saltburn by Sea, 16 March 2002.
27. Lady Bell, *At The Works,* (Middlesbrough, 1997), p 79.
28. Interview with Mrs E Appleby-Brown, Saltburn by Sea, 16 March 2002
29. Ibid, 16 March 2002.
30. Ibid, 16 March 2002.
31. Interview with Mr P Vaux's son, Darlington, 18 November 2005.
32. Interview with Mrs E Appleby-Brown, Saltburn by Sea, 16 March 2002.
33. Interview with Mrs E Appleby-Brown, Saltburn by Sea, 16 March 2002.
34. F.H. Ziegler, *The Story of 609 Squadron. Under the White Rose,* (London, 1971), p 39.
35. Ziegler, *The Story of 609,* p 52.
36. Leslie Hunt, *Twenty-One Squadrons. The History of the Royal Auxiliary Air Force 1925-1957,* (London, 1972) p 181 & p 195.
37. Ziegler, *The Story of 609,* p 60.
38. Aldon P Ferguson, *Beware! Beware! The History of 611 (West Lancashire) Squadron Royal Auxiliary Air Force* (Reading, 2004) p 9.
39. Neville Jones, *The Beginnings of Strategic Air Power. A History of the British Bomber Force 1923-1939,* (Abingdon, 1987), p 29.
40. Wing Commander Alex Dickson, *The Royal Air Force Volunteer Reserve, Memories,* (London, 1997) pp 24-25.
41. Dickson, *The Royal Air Force Volunteer Reserve,* p 33.
42. Ibid, p 34.

Chapter 4. The War Years

1. Shores, p 40.
2. Shores, p 54.
3. Times, 14 November 1942
4. http://www.vconline.org.uk/anthony-h-h-tollemache-egm/4589798722
5. http://bbm.org.uk/airmen/Pritchard.htm

ENDNOTES

6. http://www.bbm.org.uk/airmen/HayesTN.htm
7. https://www.independent.co.uk/news/people/obituary-marshal-of-the-raf-lord-elworthy-1453675.html
8. http://www.bbm.org.uk/airmen/AitkenJWM.htm
9. http://601squadron.com/men-of-601-squadron/a-through-e/cleaver-gordon-mouse/
10. The London Gazette, 24 September 1940, page 5654
11. https://www.tracesofwar.com/awards/9/Distinguished-Service-Order-DSO.htm
12. https://www.tracesofwar.com/awards/9/Distinguished-Service-Order-DSO.htm
13. https://www.tracesofwar.com/awards/9/Distinguished-Service-Order-DSO.htm
14. https://www.telegraph.co.uk/news/obituaries/1513432/Wing-Commander-Bunny-Currant.html
15. Ibid
16. Hunt, p 182.
17. National Archives, 608 Squadron Operational Record Book, April 1940.
18. National Archives, 608 Squadron Operational Record Book, November 1939.
19. National Archives, 608 Squadron Operational Record Book, November 1939.
20. National Archives, 608 Squadron Operational Record Book, January 1940.
21. National Archives, 608 Squadron Operational Record Book, May 1940.
22. *North Eastern Daily Gazette*, 28 March 1941.
23. *North Eastern Daily Gazette*, 28 March 1941.
24. National Archives, 608 Squadron Operational Record Book, 1941.
25. National Archives, 608 Squadron Operational Record Book, 1941.
26. National Archives, 608 Squadron Operational Record Book, August 1942.
27. National Archives, 608 Squadron Operational Record Book, August 1942.
28. National Archives, 608 Squadron Operational Record Book, August 1942.
29. National Archives, 608 Squadron Operational Record Book, November 1943.
30. National Archives, 608 Squadron Operational Record Book, December 1942.
31. National Archives, 608 Squadron Operational Record Book, February 1943.
32. National Archives, 608 Squadron Operational Record Book, August 1943.
33. National Archives, 608 Squadron Operational Record Book, July 1944.
34. www.bbm.org.uk/Burrnett.htm Viewed on 08/08/2013
35. *The Times*, Tuesday, 5 July 1938, p 10
36. *The Times*, Wednesday, 19 August 1942, p 1
37. https://www.independent.co.uk/news/people/obituary-lord-cheshire-vc-1537228.html
38. *The Times*, Wednesday, 5 April 1944, p 7

Chapter 5. The reconstitution of the Territorial Air Force 1946-1957

1. The National Archives (TNA), AIR20/932, Auxiliary Air Force Reconstitution, 'Auxiliary and Reserve Air Forces', Note from Secretary of State for Air, 14 April 1946.

2. TNA, AIR20/932, Auxiliary Air Force Reconstitution, "Memo from W G Clements F8 12," 12 September 1946.

3. TNA, AIR20/932, Auxiliary Air Force Reconstitution, "Air Ministry Minute Sheet" Note from E L Colbeck-Welch, DDFT Ops, 3 May 1946.

4. TNA, AIR20/932, Auxiliary Air Force Reconstitution, "Auxiliary Air Force Post-War", D D Pol (G) 2, 2 October 1945.

5. Ibid, 2 October 1945.

6. Squadron Leader A.F. Freeman, "The Post-War Royal Auxiliary Air Force," *Royal Air Force Reserve and Auxiliary Forces*, (Oxford, 2003), p 99.

7. Ibid, p 100.

8. TNA, AIR20/932, Auxiliary Air Force Reconstitution, "Reconstitution of the Auxiliary Air Force," Memo from the Assistant Chief of Air Staff, 10 September 1945.

9. TNA, AIR 20/932, Auxiliary Air Force Reconstitution, Auxiliary Air Force Post-War, D D Pol (G) 2, 2 October 1945.

10. TNA, AIR20/932, Auxiliary Air Force Reconstitution, "Reconstitution of the Auxiliary Air Force", Letter from the Air Officer Commanding-in-Chief, Headquarters Fighter Command, 25 April 1946.

11. Wing Commander Jeff Jefford, 'Post-War Reserves to 1960,' *Royal Air Force Reserve and Auxiliary Forces*, (Oxford, 2003) p 79.

12. Ibid, p 82.

13. TNA, AIR20/932, Auxiliary Air Force Reconstitution, "Note by the Secretary of State for Air", 12 October 1945.

14. TNA, AIR20/932, Auxiliary Air Force Reconstitution, "Note by the Secretary of State for Air", 12 October 1945.

15. *Yorkshire Post*, 7 November 1946.

16. *Flying Review,* 17 August 1948.

17. Freeman, '*The Post-War Royal Auxiliary Air Force,'* p 100.

18. *North Eastern Daily Gazette,* 15 March 1948.

19. Jefford, '*Post-War Reserves to 1960,'* p 89.

20. TNA, AIR20/932, Auxiliary Air Force Reconstitution, "Minute Sheet – Reserve Air Forces," D D B Ops, 23 January 1946.

21. TNA, AIR2/13172, "Memo from Air Ministry", 19 January 1948.

22. Freeman, '*The Post-War Royal Auxiliary Air Force,'* p 98.

23. Ibid, p 99.

24. Freeman, '*The Post-War Royal Auxiliary Air Force*', p 100.

25. *The Times*, 24 September 1948, p 4.

26. *The Times*, 29 October 1948, p 6.

27. *The Times*, 3 February 1949, p 3.

28. *The Times*, 24 May 1949, p 2.

29. *The Times*, 31 October 1949, p 4.

30. *The Times*, 13 March 1950, p 2.

31. *The Times*, 4 September 1953, p 3.

32. Tom Hickman, *The Call-Up. A History of National Service,* (London, 2004) p 3.

33. Hickman, *The Call-Up*, pp 4-5.

34. Ibid, p 3.

35. Hickman, *The Call-Up*, p 3.

36. Ibid, p 42.

37. TNA, Air 19/743, Royal Auxiliary Air Force, "Notes relating to the Auxiliary, Reserve and Cadet Forces," undated, p 2.

38. Hickman, *The Call-Up,* p 44.

39. Ibid, p 58.

40. TNA, Air 19/743, Royal Auxiliary Air Force, Notes relating to the Auxiliary, Reserve and Cadet Forces, undated, p 2.

41. TNA, AIR2/13172, "Memo from Air Ministry", 19 January 1948.

42. Jefford, '*Post-War RAF Reserves To 1960*' pp 80-81.

43. Ibid, p 81.

44. TNA, Air 19/743, Royal Auxiliary Air Force, Notes relating to the Auxiliary, Reserve and Cadet Forces, undated, p 5.

45. *The Times*, 21 October 1947, p 3.

46. *The Times*, 15 September 1948, p 5.

47. *The Times*, 24 February 1949, p 4.

48. *The Times*, 13 May 1950, p 6.

49. *The Times*, 13 May 1950, p 6.

50. *The Times*, 26 February 1952, p 3.

51. *Flight*, 15 July 1948.

52. *Flying Review,* 17 August 1948.

53. *The Times*, 19 January 1949, p 6.

54. Ibid, p 6.

55. *Flight*, 27 January 1950, p 23.

56. *The Times*, 4 March 1950, p 4.

57. Ibid, p 4.

58. *Flight,* 11 May 1950, p 25.

59. *The Times*, 23 June 1950, p 3.

60. Ibid, p 3.
61. *Flight*, 22 December 1950, p 11.
62. Ibid, p 11.
63. *Flight*, 4 January 1951, p 17.
64. *Flight*, 4 January 1951, p 17.
65. *Flight* 23 March 1951, p 28.
66. Ibid, p 28.
67. *Flight*, 27 June 1952, p 9.
68. *Flight*, 19 September 1952, p 2.
69. *Flight* 27 March 1953, p 11.
70. *Flight*, 27 March 1953, p 11.
71. Freeman, *'The Post-War Royal Auxiliary Air Force'*, p 99.
72. Wing Commander Gerry Margiotta, 'University Air Squadrons In WWII' *Royal Air Force Reserve and Auxiliary Forces*, (Oxford, 2003) p 77.
73. Ibid, p 77.
74. Margiotta, *'University Air Squadrons in WWII,'* p 77.
75. Royal Air Force, History of the University Air Squadrons. Available at: http://www.raf.mod.uk/universityairsquadrons/history/ Viewed 20 October 2014.
76. Margiotta, *'University Air Squadrons in WWII'* p 77.
77. Interview with Mr Alan Taylor, (Former member of Queens University Air Squadron), 2 November 2014.
78. Interview with Mr Noel Mitchel, (Former member of Queens University Air Squadron), 31 October 2014.
79. Jefford, *'Post-War Reserves to 1960'* p 93.
80. Jefford, *'Post-War Reserves to 1960'* p 95.
81. Jefford, *'Post-War Reserves to 1960'* p 96.
82. David Brown, *Thornaby Aerodrome and Wartime Memories*, (Stockton on Tees, 1992) p 59.
83. Hans Onderwater, *Gentlemen in Blue. 600 Squadron*, (Barnsley, 1997), p 365.
84. Tom Moulson, *The Flying Sword, the Story of 601 Squadron*, (London, 1964), p 178.
85. David Watkins, *Fear Nothing. The History of No 501 (County of Gloucester) Fighter Squadron, Royal Auxiliary Air Force,* (Cowden, 1990), p 93.
86. Tom Moulson, *The Millionaires Squadron. The Remarkable Story of 601 Squadron and the Flying Sword,* (Barnsley, 2014) p 206.
87. Ibid, p 206
88. TNA, Air Ministry Notice No.23, 15 January 1957.
89. Moulson, *The Millionaires Squadron,* p 205.
90. Leslie Hunt, *Twenty-One Squadrons – The History of the Royal Auxiliary Air Force 1929-1957,* (London,1972), p 429.

91. Ian Piper, *We never slept. The story of 605 Squadron*, (Trowbridge, 1996), p 229.

92. Moulson, *The Millionaires Squadron*, pp 209-10.

93. Group Captain Peter Harris, '*Forty Years of Volunteer Service*,' Royal Air Force Reserve and Auxiliary Forces, (Oxford, 2003) p 164.

Chapter 6. The social composition of the Territorial Air Force after 1945

1. James Obelkevich and Peter Catterall (eds), *Understanding Post-War British Society*, (London,1994) p 5.

2. Richard Vinen, *National Service. A Generation in Uniform 1945-1963*, (London, 2015) p 80.

3. Christopher Law, 'Employment and Industrial Structure,' in James Obelkevich and Peter Catteral (eds), *Understanding Post-War British Society*, (London, 1994) p 91.

4. Edward Royle, *Modern Britain: A Social History 1750-1997*, (London, 1987) p 12.

5. Ibid, p 12.

6. Angus Calder, *The Myth of the Blitz*, (London, 1992) p 3.

7. Robert Mackay, *Half the Battle. Civilian Morale in Britain during the Second World War*, (Manchester, 2002) p 19.

8. Mackay, *Half the Battle*, p 19.

9. Brad Beaven, *Leisure, Citizenship and Working-Class Men in Britain 1850-1945*, (Manchester, 2005) p 9.

10. Vinen, *National Service. A Generation in Uniform*, p 9.

11. Sqn Ldr A.F. Freeman, '*The Post-War Royal Auxiliary Air Force*,' Royal Air Force Reserve and Auxiliary Forces, (Oxford, 2003) pp 96-109.

12. David Ross et al, *The greatest Squadron of Them All. The Definitive History of 603 (City of Edinburgh) Squadron RAuxAF. Volume II. 1941 to date*, (London, 2003) p 292.

13. Ibid, p 292.

14. Hans Onderwater, *"Gentlemen in Blue. 600 Squadron*, (Barnsley, 1997) p 327.

15. Tom Moulson, *The Millionaires Squadron. The Remarkable Story of 601 Squadron and the Flying Sword*, (Barnsley, 2014) p 192.

16. Ibid, p 171.

17. Ibid, p 168.

18. Ibid, p 170.

19. Moulson, *The Millionaires Squadron*, p 170.

20. Ian White, *If you want peace, prepare for war. A History of No 604 (County of Middlesex) Squadron RAuxAF in Peace and War*, (London, 2005) pp 109-110.

21. Ian Piper, *We never slept. The Story of 605 Squadron*, (Tamworth, 1996) p 210.

22. Leslie Hunt, *Twenty-One Squadrons. The History of the Royal Auxiliary Air Force 1925-1957,* (London, 1972) p 242.

23. *The Times*, 2 August 1946, p 6.

24. Robin J Brooks, *Kent's Own. The History of 500 (County of Kent) Squadron Royal Auxiliary Air Force,* (Gillingham, 1982) p 145.

25. Ross, T*he Greatest Squadron of them all,* p 296.

26. *The Times*, 29 August 1946, p 4.

27. *Northern Echo*, 11 July 1947, p 11.

28. TNA, AIR27/2676, 608 Squadron Operational Record Book, January 1947-December 1954.

29. *Northern Echo*, 8 August 1947.

30. *North Eastern Weekly News*, 22 August 1947.

31. David Brown, *Thornaby Aerodrome and Wartime Memories,* (Teesside,1992) p 59.

32. TNA, AIR27/2712, 608 Squadron Operational Record Book, February 1955-March 1957.

33. *North Eastern Daily Gazette*, Monday, 2 November 1958.

34. *North Eastern Daily Gazette*, 15 March 1948.

35. TNA, AIR27/2676, 608 Squadron Operational Record Book, January 1947-December 1954.

36. Wing Commander Jeff Jefford, 'Post-War RAF Reserves To 1960,' *Royal Air Force Reserve and Auxiliary Forces,* (Oxford, 2003) p 89.

37. Interview with Mr M. Ruecroft, Trimdon Grange, Friday, 2 April 2004.

38. Jefford, 'Post-War RAF Reserves To 1960' *Royal Air Force Reserve and Auxiliary Forces*, (Oxford, 2003) p 89.

39. F.H. Ziegler, *The Story of 609 Squadron. Under the White Rose,* (London, 1971) p 318.

40. Ibid, p 320.

41. Ibid, p 321.

42. Aldon P Ferguson, *Beware Beware, The History of 611 (West Lancashire) Squadron Royal Auxiliary Air Force,* (Reading, 2004) p 148.

43. Hunt, *Twenty-One Squadrons,* p 339.

44. *The Times*, 2 August 1946, p 6.

45. Hunt, *Twenty-one Squadrons,* p 411.

46. Delve, Ken & Pitchfork, Graham, *South Yorkshire's Own. The Story of 616 Squadron,* (Exeter, 1992), p 42.

47. Ibid, p 42.

48. *The Times*, 15 September 1948, p 5.

49. *The Times*, 13 May 1950, p 6.

ENDNOTES

50. Group Captain Peter Harris, 'Forty Years of Volunteer Service' *Royal Air Force Reserve and Auxiliary Forces,* (Oxford, 2003) p 164.

Conclusion

1. Edward Royle, *Modern Britain. A Social History 1750-1997,* (London, 1987) p 12.
2. Jeffrey Hill, *Sport, Leisure and Culture in Twentieth Century Britain*, (London, 2002), p 131.
3. Ross McKibbin, *Classes and Cultures. England 1918-1951*, (Oxford, 1998) p 380.
4. Frank H Ziegler, *The Story of 609 Squadron Under the White Rose*, (London, 1971).
5. Aldon P Ferguson, *Beware Beware, The History of 611 (West Lancashire) Squadron,* (Reading, 2004).
6. Ken Delve and Graham Pitchfork, *South Yorkshire's Own, The Story of 616 Squadron,* (Doncaster, 1990).
7. G Finlayson, '*A Moving Frontier – Voluntarism and the State in British Social Welfare,*' *Twentieth Century British History*, Volume 1, Number 2 (1990), pp 183-206. Tom Moulson, *The Flying Sword. The Story of 601 Squadron.* (London, 1964) Wing Commander Alex Dickson, RAFVR, *The Royal Air Force Volunteer Reserve Memories,* (Innsworth, 1997).

Appendix 2

1. *The Millionaires Squadron*, Tom Moulson, (Barnsley, 2014) Chapter 1, pp 12-13.
2. David Ross et al, "*The Greatest Squadron of them all" The Definitive History of 603 (City of Edinburgh) Squadron, RAUXAF*, Volume I Formation to the end of 1940, (London, 2003) p 5/6..
3. "*The Greatest Squadron of them all*", p 327.
4. Ibid, p 10
5. Ibid p 347-350
6. "*The Greatest Squadron of them all*", p 10, 29, 339-341
7. Ibid, p 354-355
8. Ibid, p 116
9. Ian Piper, *We Never Slept. The Story of No 605 (County of Warwick) Squadron Royal Auxiliary Air Force 1926-1957*, (Tamworth, 1996) p 53
10. Interview with Mrs Elizabeth Appleby Brown, Saltburn by the Sea, Saturday, 16 March 2002.
11. Ibid

12. Ibid
13. Ibid
14. Avril Pedley, Archivist and Alumni Officer, St Peters School, Clifton, York YO3 6AB
15. Letter from Mr D Gilling-Smith, Surrey, 16 May 2009
16. Interview with Mrs Elizabeth Appleby Brown
17. Ibid
18. Ibid
19. Interview with Mr Peter Vaux's son, Barton, Friday, 18 November 2005
20. Interview with Mrs Elizabeth Appleby Brown
21. Interview with Mr George Williams, Ascot, Monday, 3 January 2005
22. Ziegler, F.H., *The Story of 609 Squadron, Under The White Rose*, (London, 1971) p 49
23. Ibid, p 49
24. Ibid, p 52
25. Ibid, p 52
26. Ibid, p 49
27. Ibid, p 49
28. Ibid, p 48
29. Ziegler, p 39
30. Interview with Wing Commander Ken Stoddart, Monday, 25 July 2005
31. Leslie Hunt, *Twenty-One Squadrons. The History of the Royal Auxiliary Air Force 1925-1957*, (London, 1972) p 259

Appendix 3

1. Hans Onderwater, *Gentlemen in Blue, 600 Squadron*, (Barnsley, 1997) p 311
2. Ibid, p 349
3. Ibid, p 342
4. Ibid, p 313
5. Leslie Hunt, *Twenty One Squadrons*, p 93
6. Tom Moulson, *The Millionaires Squadron. The Remarkable Story of 601 Squadron and the Flying Sword*, (Barnsley, 2014) p 192
7. Ibid, p 168
8. Leslie Hunt, *Twenty-One Squadrons,* p 93
9. Moulson, *The Millionaires Squadron*, p 201
10. Leslie Hunt, *Twenty One Squadrons*, p 39
11. Ibid, p 39
12. *The Greatest Squadron of them all*, p 347-350
13. Leslie Hunt, *Twenty One Squadrons*, p 160

ENDNOTES

14. Ibid, p 135
15. Piper, *We Never Slept*, p 229
16. Ibid, p 229
17. Hunt, *Twenty One Squadrons*, p 135
18. Ibid, p 135
19. Leslie Hunt, *Twenty One Squadrons*, p 192
20. Elizabeth Appleby Brown, 2002
21. Interview with Mr Grant Goodwill, Thursday, 11 November 2004
22. Interview with Mr George Joyce, Friday, 12 November 2004
23. Hunt, *Twenty One Squadrons*, p 192
24. George Joyce, 2004
25. Ibid, 2004
26. Interview with Mrs Lesley Willis, 4 November 2004
27. Hunt, *Twenty One Squadrons*, p 220
28. Hunt, *Twenty One Squadrons*, p 339
29. Hunt, *Twenty One Squadrons*, p 375
30. Hunt, *Twenty One Squadrons*, p 375
31. David Watkins, *Fear Nothing. The History of No 501 (County of Gloucester) Squadron Royal Auxiliary Air Force* (Cowden, 1990), p 92
32. Watkins, *Fear Nothing*, p 94
33. Ibid, p 92
34. Ibid, p 92
35. Ibid, p 92
36. Ibid, p 87
37. Ibid, p 92
38. Ibid, p 92
39. Ibid, p 87
40. Ibid, p 87
41. Ibid, p 92

Index

INDEX